The Art of the Network

D1570773

POLITICS, HISTORY, AND CULTURE
A series from the International Institute at the University of Michigan

SERIES EDITORS
George Steinmetz and Julia Adams

SERIES EDITORIAL ADVISORY BOARD
Fernando Coronil
Mamadou Diouf
Michael Dutton
Geoff Eley
Fatma Müge Göcek
Nancy Rose Hunt
Andreas Kalyvas
Webb Keane
David Laitin
Lydia Liu
Julie Skurski
Margaret Somers
Ann Laura Stoler
Katherine Verdery
Elizabeth Wingrove

Sponsored by the International Institute at the University of Michigan
and published by Duke University Press, this series is centered around
cultural and historical studies of power, politics, and the state—a field that
cuts across the disciplines of history, sociology, anthropology, political
science, and cultural studies. The focus on the relationship between state
and culture refers both to a methodological approach—the study of
politics and the state using culturalist methods—and a substantive one
that treats signifying practices as an essential dimension of politics. The
dialectic of politics, culture, and history figures prominently in all the
books selected for the series.

The Art of the Network

Strategic Interaction and Patronage
in Renaissance Florence

Paul D. McLean

Duke University Press
Durham and London 2007

© 2007 Duke University Press
All rights reserved
Printed in the United States of America on acid-free paper ∞

Typeset in Bembo by Tseng Information Systems, Inc.

Library of Congress Cataloging-in-Publication Data
McLean, Paul, 1962–
The art of the network: strategic interaction and patronage in Renaissance Florence /
Paul McLean.
p. cm. — (Politics, history, and culture)
Includes bibliographical references and index.
ISBN-13: 978-0-8223-4100-0 (cloth: alk. paper)
ISBN-13: 978-0-8223-4117-8 (pbk.: alk. paper)
1. Florence (Italy)—Social life and customs. 2. Social networks—Italy—Florence—
History. 3. Patronage, Political—Italy—Florence—History. 4. Patron and client—
Italy—Florence—History. 5. Letter writing, Italian—History. 6. Renaissance—Italy—
Florence. I. Title.
DG735.6.M39 2007
945.51—dc22   2007017993

For Susan

Contents

Tables and Figures

Preface

Respected Reader, dearest to me as much as a brother or sister (*carissimo quanto fratello o sorella*): I have not written a book to you in the past, there not having been any need for one (*non essere suto di bisogno*). But the reason for writing this one (*Ma la cagione di questa*) is to remind you (*per ricordarvi*), as much as I know and am able (*quanto so e posso*), that the social network ties we have with each other are not merely given, nor do they have a simple fixed meaning. They are constructed, managed, and maintained by means of the cultural work involved in discursive practice. Discursive practices are in part routine and in part improvised from the recombination of elements in our culture's toolkit of practices. Through them we craft a presentation of ourselves as worthy of being tied to others, and we commit ourselves to interactionally constructed identities. I pray of you and entreat you (*vi priego e supplico*) that you lend me your attention as I try to make this argument clear, and that you not consign me or my efforts to oblivion (*non mi mette nel dimenticario*). I pray of you (*vi priego*) that it may be pleasing to you (*vi piaccia*) to look upon this book with favor, that you contrive to read it in a spirit of kindness (*benignità*) and attentiveness (*sollecitudine*), and that you exert a little bit of effort (*affaticarvi*) to make the connections between sociological theory and historical data where I do not establish them clearly myself. Were you to do this, I would regard it as a most singular pleasure (*un piacere singularissimo*), greater than the contentment I would have from your reading any of my other works. For certain, if this book is thoughtfully considered, I have a firm hope (*ho ferma speranza*) that it will bring me both honor and advantage (*onore et utile*), and, by means of your sublime intellect and innumerable virtues (*mediante le vostre virtù innumerabili*), in every possible way (*in ogni modo*) provide both advantage and honor (*utile et onore*) to you as well.

I really don't always write this way. But the patronage letters that form the basis for this book *are* written this way, and so this style has floated around in my head for a long time. In different spurts over the last fifteen years, I have looked at thousands of these letters, and I have collected, transcribed, and coded over eleven hundred of them from the Florentine State Archives, most containing many of the elements interspersed above (and dozens more). My sample is a relatively small one, considering that hundreds of thousands of Florentine letters from the late fourteenth century through the early sixteenth survive. By patronage letters, I mean letters written to influential people whereby one sought to be given help or granted a favor of some kind—a tax break, a chance at office holding, help with a legal problem, matchmaking, the list goes on—or one sought help and favor (*aiuto e favore*) for one's friends. Patronage letter writing was an institution in Florentine society: regular sequences of activity that supported and reproduced a set of shared expectations about the world and how it operates. It was an important tool for trying to achieve social mobility, security, and the recognition of others. It was, in short, a critical part of Florentine culture.

To examine the culture of patronage letter writing brings one face to face with some foundational sociological ideas. One is that culture is fundamentally interactional. It is a means for relating to others. We are who we are because of our culture, but we also work to become who we can be by means of cultural techniques. Culture is both a world we live in, and a tool we use, a duality best examined when we focus on the interactional setting in which culture operates. Its interactional quality, combined with the fact that patronage letters were manifestly opportunities for *both* strategic action *and* the achievement of constitutive identities, makes Florentine patronage letter writing an apt case for sociologists of culture to study.

Chapter 1 lays out the theoretical framework, building on different strands of sociological theory. Chapter 2 focuses on the formal principles of Florentine letter writing and their provenance. Chapter 3 recounts the changing meaning of the elusive but powerful idea of honor that played such an important role in Florentine sensibilities for over two hundred years. Together, chapters 2 and 3 treat the counterpoint between form and content, between routine cultural practices and the meanings they conjure. Chapter 4 is a quantitative study of actual practices in Florentine patronage letter writing, comparing different sorts of requests, and comparing the content of letters during different periods of the fifteenth century. Chapter 5, in part based on my article in the *American Journal of Sociology* in July 1998, offers a more detailed analysis of office-seeking letters. Chapter 6 examines patterns appearing specifically in recommendation letters. In chapters 5 and 6, I offer more detailed analyses of particular letters, wherein one can see some of the artfulness involved in tweaking institutionalized practices with an eye toward offering convincing and compelling presentations of self. Not through simple repetition, but through improvisational recombination and commentary on the institutionalized forms, is such a believable, and therefore seemingly authentic, self represented.

From a sociological standpoint, the Florentine culture of patronage is largely a case for illustrating a theory of culture in general. But Renaissance Florence is never really "just a case." It's a very special case. It was, to put it somewhat simplistically, a crucible producing modernity. This book is also, therefore, necessarily a book in history and in historical sociology. This is true throughout, but especially in chapters 3, 4, 7, and 8. Chapter 3 provides the social history of the concept of honor and links changes in its meaning to underlying social structural changes, in the spirit of Georges Duby, Norbert Elias, and Eiko Ikegami. Chapter 4 may interest historians by documenting trends in the language that flowed in and out of Florentine patronage correspondence over the course of the fifteenth century. Chapter 7, built from my article in *Comparative Studies in Society and History* in July 2005, links micro-level practices to macro-level institutional developments, particularly the structure and organization of the state, and shows their coevolution. Chapter 8 tries to establish the *kind* of self that was being constructed in these letters where presentation of self figures so prominently. Was it the modern self, an object of concern to philosophers, psychologists, historians, sociologists, cultural anthropologists, and literary critics? It appears not to have been quite that. Instead it resembled the contextually variable, relational self that modern-day psychologists and cultural anthropologists observe in certain contemporary East Asian cultures. Nevertheless, we can see the beginning traces of ourselves in the techniques the letter writers employed to obtain advancement and recognition through their cultural agency in the domain of patronage seeking.

Florentines used their friends and followers to advantage, but they also understood themselves to be made by their friends and followers. I have used many friends in writing this book; equally I have been made by them. I have worked diligently for many years on this project, but I would have failed miserably without their help. First, Ann Mische and Vilna Bashi have been the best colleagues and friends to me, reading many pages of this book and offering both astute intellectual criticism and compassionate moral support. I especially thank them for their input in the face of my near-comedic level of self-deprecation. I say without lying (*sanza mentire*) that John Levi Martin likewise has been in every way a valued friend to me (*a me amicis-simo*) and, alas, erstwhile colleague. The Department of Sociology at Rutgers University has been a great academic home. In addition to those mentioned above, I specifically thank my colleagues József Böröcz, Ethel Brooks, Karen Cerulo, Chip Clarke, Judy Gerson, Ellen Idler, Julie Phillips, Pat Roos, Tom Rudel, Randy Smith, Arlene Stein, and Eviatar Zerubavel, for their input at various stages of this project. For their questions, conversation, and liveli-ness, I thank my students, especially Eric Kaldor, Dmitry Khodyakov, Julie Kim, Vanina Leschziner, Janet Lorenzen, Sourabh Singh, Ian Watson, and King-to Yeung. I also deeply appreciate the support and assistance of two fine scholars of Renaissance Florence — Bill Connell of Seton Hall Univer-sity, and David Marsh of the Italian Department at Rutgers — who gently corrected a few of my most egregious errors. Had I sought more of their advice and assistance, no doubt this book would be much better than it is. To be honest, I have found it profoundly humbling to try to do this research knowing that I am not a master philologist or cultural historian.

I am grateful to the University of Chicago for providing funding that got this project started many years ago, and to the Casa di Ospitalità Sette Santi in Florence, which put me up mercifully cheaply during one of my extended stays in Florence many years ago. The digitalization of the *Mediceo Avanti il Principato* archive in recent years is a phenomenal gift to present and future generations of scholars. I have used it repeatedly and am deeply grate-ful to those responsible for accomplishing it. I cherish the time I spent at Chicago in the Organizations and State-Building Workshop and at Wilder House learning from the likes of Andy Abbott, Chris Ansell, Dan Carpen-ter, Bruce Carruthers, Kevin Esterling, Roger Gould, Gary Herrigel, Carla Hess, Steve Laymon, David Mandell, Dan McFarland, Dwight Semler, Bat Sparrow, and Guy Stuart. I also would like to thank the Santa Fe Institute for providing space and interactions that stimulated my thinking about this project, and the Center for the Critical Analysis of Contemporary Culture at Rutgers University for a fantastic year-long seminar under the direction of Jackson Lears on the themes of chance, fatefulness, power, and selfhood. I thank Julia Adams of Yale University for her enthusiastic support of this project. My old friend and *maestro della bottega* John Padgett has been a source of support and a source of astonishment to me for more than twenty years. I absolutely could not have conceived and executed this project without his inspiration and guidance. He has done more than any other to make me the scholar I have become. I owe a lifelong debt to my brother Don McLean at McGill University for being such a shining example of the *uomo da bene*. I thank my children, Eli, Adam, and Julia, for their exuberance, intelligence, and love. Most of all, I wish to thank Susan Liebell, and I dedicate this book to her—as Renaissance Florentines might have said, thanking her and reminding you again and again of the love she has always demonstrated toward me. She has been more than intellectual companion, more than friend, more than fellow parent, more than spouse. I say to her, as warmly as possible, now more than ever (*più che mai*): this author is *tuo più che suo*, more yours than his own.

I write no more here so as not to weary you (*per non tediarvi*), except that if you see one way or another whereby my book may help you, advise me of it (*avisatemi*) and I will do whatever I can (*quanto posso*) most willingly (*molto volentieri*) to make it ever more useful. I recommend myself to you.

1

The Principles of Networking
as a Social Process

Honored like a most singular father, in the past few days, having confidence in your fatherly assistance, as I know I can, I wrote to you that it be pleasing to you to be with Cosimo, that he condescend to write to Rome, that I should have a reappointment to this office, and from you I have had no reply, such that I think my letter will have suffered from a bad service in the mail. Thus, again I pray and beg of you, my Averardo, that you would want to be the means (*operatore*) by which I had this reappointment, or some other office, so that I were able to return here. It would give me the heart to be a man like the others (*darebbemi il cuore dessere uno huomo come gli altri*). You understand my meaning.

Francesco Nardi to Averardo de' Medici, September 20, 1429

From an economic standpoint, we typically imagine that careers are constructed out of a series of jobs, or even more restrictively out of a durable association with some particular organization. On the face of it, that is what is being constructed in the letter of Francesco Nardi, written to Averardo de' Medici, that begins this chapter (see figure 1 for a photograph of the document). Indeed this material benefit is a key part of what *is* being requested here. But something deeper and more lasting than an appointment to office is being sought after and constructed here as well: a relationship with another person that is deeply constitutive of oneself. Nardi is undoubtedly self-interested in his pursuit of office, but he rhetorically acknowledges, and in effect promises to enact, the transformative power of connections to powerful others ("give me the heart to be a man like the others"). He projects himself into an identity. Thus "career," from a sociological standpoint, can be construed more broadly than as activity: each of us constructs a career in the course of our lives constituted by the portfolio of ties to others with whom we are associated. Our careers are made—and we are made—through our interactions with others, as well as through the performance of those tasks to which we have access by virtue of our

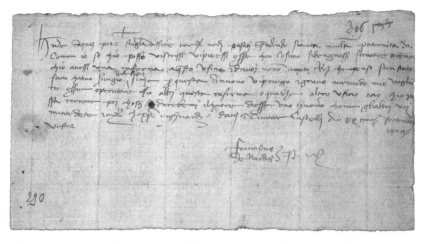

Fig. 1. Francesco Nardi to Averardo de' Medici, September 20, 1429 (A.S.F., *MAP* II, 292r). Used by permission of the Ministero per i Beni e le Attività Culturali, Italy.

connections to others. We become more fully the persons we are through interaction, our personhood being constructed out of a number of different identities we adopt, singly or in combination, in different interactional settings (Simmel 1955; Emirbayer and Mische 1998, 1007). We may achieve autonomy, and achieve a private conception of self independent of attributions of identity put upon us by others, through the accumulation of multiple network ties and participation in social interaction coursing across multiple networks and diverse cultural domains.

Implicitly, this is what the fashionable idea of "networking" for success is all about. But networking is paradoxical. We want autonomy, but the only way to get it is by becoming connected. Freedom must be relationally achieved; autonomy without connection is isolation. Compounding the paradox is the fact that during the early stages of the networking game, we are in danger of being channeled into the same narrow identities and associations over and over again. We get "typecast" (Faulkner 1983). Networking is not only about getting in, but also branching out, moving up, and attaining control. This is no easy task.

Completely of a piece with the paradox of networking is our modern self-conception. We imagine ourselves disconnected from others, genuinely thinking, feeling, and speaking as if we had an "inner" self divided by an invisible wall from the outside (Elias 1978, 213). Yet this vision of self is relationally constructed and expressed through interaction. Or seen from the other direction, we might well understand that networking is a relational process. Nonetheless, we embark upon it with a genuine private sense of our aims and objectives, and we pause repeatedly to think about and articulate what these particular connections mean for us. Again, Nardi asks for an appointment in order "to be a man like the others." This claim is more complex than it appears. To be "like the others" undoubtedly alludes to other Medici partisans; consequently he is projecting himself into the particular *role* of partisan. Simultaneously, "to be a man" conjures up an image of responsibility and autonomy. One could even argue that his promise of partisan loyalty is enhanced because it comes from someone who makes an implicit claim to autonomy.

The importance of networks and the value of networking seem never to have been so widely appreciated as they are today, both outside (Gladwell 2000) and inside (Barabási 2002, Watts 2003) the academy, and sometimes at the intersection of the two.[1] But lay appreciation of networking, and enthusiasm for it in much of mainstream sociology, remains weak in two fundamental ways. First, the historical antecedents of contemporary networking and the concept of self that accompanies it remain largely unexamined. This book provides a detailed examination of the constitutive importance of social networks and the rhetorical techniques individuals used interactionally to forge ties with each other in fifteenth-century Florence. Florence represents a case in a multitude of ways—political, economic, artistic, psychological—at the dawn of modernity. The city was an exemplar of civic republicanism, a kind of participatory self-government that we admire to this day. It was arguably the most important commercial engine of late medieval Europe, the home of energetic merchant-bankers and cloth manufacturers who together crafted organizational forms and credit devices essential for the spread of capitalism (Padgett and McLean, 2006). It was the cradle of the Renaissance, the birthplace of perspective painting, home to Donatello, Brunelleschi, Masaccio, Michelangelo, and a host of others. And, as I will argue, Florentine social networks provided a generative ecology for the emergence of a quasi-modern, relational conception of the self—a place in which personal connections mattered intensely, and individuals reflected upon the consequences of networking for themselves.

The second weakness I see in thinking about networking is that the relationship between social networks and individual action is little theorized and relatively unexplored. *How* do individuals network? What techniques do they use? What makes it possible for people to find each other and connect with each other across large distances? To address these questions requires systematic and up-to-date attention to the enormous question of culture (cf. Emirbayer and Goodwin 1994), as I will argue in detail throughout much of the rest of this chapter.

The Renaissance Art of Networking

Scholars have imagined the Italian Renaissance as an epochal time when making social connections became something of an art (Castiglione 1959, Greenblatt 1980, Biagioli 1993) and the concept of the self-made man as the autonomous builder of a career rose to unusual prominence (Burckhardt 1960). Despite sustained and cogent criticism of the latter claim,[2] considerable truth doggedly remains in it. Florentine social interaction was intensely competitive. Florentines sought upward mobility, honor, and protection from shame and isolation through patronage. The private patronage-seeking letters of Florentines looking to build or protect their careers, while informed by values (such as honor) and collective representations distinct from our own, remain recognizable to us in form and thrust. And many of the features of modern life deriving from embeddedness in multiple social networks are markedly evident there, such as the desire for individual autonomy, the tension between diverse roles and identities, and the quest for friendship.

Florentines sought each other out, face-to-face or through letters, to perform a multitude of favors. Such favor seeking was fraught with anxiety, ambiguity, and dissimulation on the part of both petitioners and patrons.[3] Petitioners asked for favorable tax assessments, offices for themselves or their friends and relatives, recommendations, marriage brokerage, rights to free passage through hostile territory, merciful treatment of their friends in prison, support in judicial disputes over property, and a host of other benefits. To a varying degree, the pursuit of each of these benefits was simultaneously a pursuit of relationships and of a relationally defined self. Petitioners moved, like rock climbers, from previously achieved network positional footholds to new positions and relations by means of accumulated resources and identities. Letters were a critical instrument for this tortuous mobility. Patronage letters contain many seemingly idiosyncratic petitions for assistance in fixing seemingly personal and unique problems. But when we examine letters in the aggregate, we find patterns: many practical cultural building blocks were available for use, institutionalized (Jepperson 1991) as rhetorical tropes and ideal typical roles by means of which individuals imitatively constructed and prosecuted their idiosyncratic preferences.[4] Florentine petitioners' agency lay not in idiosyncratic self-expression, nor in purely formal practice, but in the recombination, adaptation, and occasional violation of these exemplary practices.[5]

Thus, to understand how culture works in interaction, and to see both the strategic and constitutive faces of networking, a study of patronage-related interaction in Renaissance Florence is particularly apt. Clients self-consciously sought opportunities for building careers and obtaining prestige through their connections to powerful patrons, transforming themselves in the process. Networking, particularly in the form of patronage, was essential to the development of Renaissance art, but it was also essential to the process of social climbing and the operations of the Renaissance church, the Renaissance state, and the Renaissance economy. Florentines intuitively (and sometimes explicitly) understood that people could "make" each other—through marriage, through credit, through accounts, through careers, through patronage. They arguably had a deeper understanding of networking as a social process than we do.

The study of the Florentine case also reveals the inadequacy of simple dichotomous treatments of "traditional" versus "modern" styles of interaction. Both putatively modern and putatively traditional cultural elements co-existed in fifteenth-century Florence. Although no one in the social sciences seriously espouses a crude "traditional versus modern" distinction any longer, it remains an all too readily invoked assumption in even the best analyses of trust and culture in interaction.[6] Rich historical analysis is needed to put that crude analytical construct to rest.

In this book I will examine the strategic, career-making activity of the writers of Florentine patronage letters, showing how they actively constructed their social networks and presented credible portraits of themselves through a host of conversational and discursive techniques that appear with marked regularity in thousands of letters. I will illustrate the importance of discursive strategies in a specific setting of strategic interaction to make an argument about the importance of such strategies in general for the construction and maintenance of social networks. I will document variation in that strategic cultural work based in part (but only in part) on the relative social-structural position of those who ask for favors and those who receive requests. In so doing, I aim to provide sociologists of culture and students of social networks with a toolbox of concepts for analyzing how culture is deployed in interaction.

Where Is the Culture in Networks?

A second shortcoming in thinking about social networks has been the dearth of attention paid to the relationship between individuals and networks, and particularly to the cultural agency by means of which networks are constituted and maintained. The strategic and relation-building work of networking is quintessentially cultural.[7] This cultural work simultaneously seeks resources and constructs identities. Crucially, *both* elements filter through the practical cultural tools upon and out of which social interaction is constructed, making a study of these tools and their assembly imperative. The very importance of strategizing to achieve goals induces, in the first instance, careful self-presentation through culturally "safe" practices. Strategy tends to push people toward culturally proven means.[8] One tends not to experiment when seeking success; often it is better to use proven strategies. There are, then, definable rules for how one should go about currying favor to get ahead, and in this book (notably in chapter 2) I outline the rules Florentines understood to operate.

But such "rule following" is not enough. How can we distinguish ourselves from others if we merely follow the rules? That we do try to distinguish ourselves is indisputable. We do so by interpreting and implementing cultural practices improvisationally. When we seek distinction, we must assemble gestures, symbols, and other practical cultural elements—perhaps even transgressing the usual bounds of decorum in the process, and calling attention to such transgressions—in a way that separates us from the crowd and establishes our distinctive identity or "worthiness" (Lamont 1992; Lamont, Kaufman, and Moody 2000). So, for example, with the insertion of "my Averardo" into his letter, Nardi adds to the urgency of his request and purports to bind himself in a special way to his targeted patron (or more accurately, broker). Conversely, receivers of cultural signals have to interpret the assemblage of pieces with which they are presented, reading character from the form and beauty of the execution of the practices, or locating identity precisely where the veneer of rules is punctured and identity peeks through. Their task is to infer the nature of the "author" behind the construction (Goffman 1974, chap. 8). Receivers of cultural signals bring culture to bear as an exercise in classifying daily interactions or experience precisely in order to secure the trust necessary to the pursuit of interests. And all of this happens amid great uncertainty. As Giannozzo Alberti, a worldly-wise character in Leon Battista Alberti's *I libri della famiglia* ([~1430] 1969, 263) comments concerning favor-seeking interactions in particular, "We know well how to simulate good will or how to avoid friendship in order to suit our situation."

Consequently, strategizing induces convergence on proven practical culture, yet this convergence in turn motivates rule breakage on one side and active interpretation on the other—both vital forms of agency—as a means of establishing the particular identity, and therefore the interests, of interacting participants. This is the layer of motivation upon which trust is founded.[9] Identities are part and parcel of the texturing of frames put into play by networkers and likewise invoked by receivers of messages to understand what each other wants and what each other can do. Recipients of cultural signals try to read identities off of actors' embeddedness in social structures; but senders also actively represent that embeddedness in their messages.

The relationships that in the aggregate constitute networks are built, re-built, sustained, and transformed across time. Thus we have to think about social networks and networking dynamically—something that until recently network analysts have had a hard time doing. And each successive effort at networking takes place from a newly achieved position in a net-work. Consequently, agency within networks is ever adapting to an unfold-ing social structure as well as an evolving repertoire of discursive gestures. Understanding the nexus of culture, structure, and agency in this way leads us toward an *interactionist* theory of culture in general, and toward a deeper understanding of networking in particular.

I began by claiming that little attention has been paid thus far to the cultural aspects of networking. I pursue this complaint further here by ar-guing that a problem in our current appreciation of social networks lies in an oscillation between undersocialized and oversocialized conceptions of their significance.[10] For some scholars (and lay people), networks are simply resources for actors to use in pursuit of their self-interest. For another set of scholars, and certainly at the level of putting research questions into opera-tion, the identities (and therefore interests) of actors are simply read off of their location in social network positions. In the former approach, net-works are not understood to do as much socializing and self-constituting work as they do in reality; in the latter, they seem to do too much, with the identities of the actors all too readily equated with roles or structural positions. I suggest that in the vast body of sociological work concerning social networks, this oscillation has been embodied in the conceptually distinct (although sometimes conflated) perspectives of social capital theory and network analysis proper.

Social Capital

The term "social capital" has become immensely popular across many of the social sciences over the last decade—especially among those who hold out hope that it will explain the prospects for improvement of individuals or disadvantaged groups, and/or the prospects for economic development or democratization of one country or another.[11] Computerized searches on the term yield literally hundreds of citations. Specifically sociological applications run from studies of political and corporate elites (for example, Kadushin 1995; Anheier, Gerhards, and Romo 1995) to work on welfare recipients (Edin and Lein 1997), international migrants (for example, Aguilera and Massey 2003), international development (Woolcock 1998; Szreter 2002), and participants in the second economy (Portes and Sensenbrenner 1993); from job searches and promotions in America (Lin, Ensel, and Vaughan 1981; Podolny and Baron 1997; Burt 1997; Fernandez, Castilla, and Moore 2000) to job searches and advancement in China (Bian 1997); from the alleged decline of democracy in America (Putnam 2000; Brehm and Rahn 1997; Paxton 1999) to the supposed prospects for democracy in post-Communist Russia and elsewhere (J. Gibson 2001; Paxton 2002).

Formulations and applications of the concept by Nan Lin (2001; Lin, Cook, and Burt 2001), Pierre Bourdieu (1986), James Coleman (1990), Ronald Burt (1992), and Robert Putnam (1993, 2000) have been among the most seminal contributions to this burgeoning and variegated literature. Although there are important differences in their respective theories, there are some common threads and common shortcomings. Broadly speaking, the term "social capital" signifies a web of cooperative and trusting social relationships (that is, social networks and the norms that inhabit and sustain them) that provide individuals with emotional and/or material support and opportunities and help to coordinate their several actions (Brehm and Rahn 1997). How this web came to be, how to judge its most salient properties, and how to construe the relationship between social capital and individual action is where these theorists begin to part company.

For Coleman, although social capital is a structural entity, inhering in relations rather than owned by individuals, it nonetheless can be analyzed as a "resource" for individuals by means of which they "realize their interests" (1990, 300, 305, 308).[12] The kinds of dyadic obligations that make up a good part of social capital are treated by Coleman as so many insurance policies of self-interested actors (309), part and parcel of his general analytical framework whereby interdependence between individuals, and those individuals' desires for control, are construed in a narrow way (30).[13] The slide from social capital-as-relations to social capital-as-resource is part and parcel of Coleman's pragmatically justified methodological individualism, but it comes at a price. Although he acknowledges that trust, like social capital, presents both opportunities and constraints, and can have both negative and positive externalities, there is little sense in Coleman's writing that the relationships people enjoy in any way touch their identities. Moreover, the *mechanisms* by which trusting relationships between persons get interactively constructed are left completely unexamined (114).

The one-sided language of "resources" persists in a good deal of the literature on social capital. In a pioneering study, Lin, Ensel, and Vaughan (1981) adopted this orientation, seeing social contacts as resources individuals use to achieve better jobs. Lin, Fu, and Hsung (2001) and Lin's (2001) own formulation of the theory of social capital retain and sharpen this utilitarian orientation. In their study of a midwestern firm's hiring practices, Fernandez, Castilla, and Moore (2000) explicitly treat the social capital of employees as a resource that employers draw upon. Lee and Brinton (1996) treat it as a resource for career making in South Korea. And although Frank and Yasumoto (1998) neatly differentiate between self-interested actions that build social capital with particular others from those that build social capital in relatively dense and closed groups, they likewise see social capital largely as a resource. *How* actors make "efforts to accumulate and draw on social capital" (645) is not part of their analysis.

The relational nature of social capital is more fully emphasized in the work of Ronald Burt (1992, 1997, 2001). Burt sees actors' opportunities for action and competitive advantage as produced by social relations and positions in social networks. Whereas Lin and others emphasize the importance of "who you know"—the prestige of one's personal contacts—Burt (1997) adds that where you are, and how many others do what you do, contribute their own impact on one's prospects. In particular, profit, opportunity, and freedom come most to those actors who occupy "structural holes"—that is, to those who are empowered to act as brokers between otherwise disconnected actors in a network (see also Gould and Fernandez 1989). In an appreciative criticism of Burt's work, Podolny and Baron (1997) point out that in certain cases, occupying a bridge position is a distinct handicap. For example, promotion is often dependent on other actors' possession of a clear sense of who you *are*. In that case "smaller networks that display high closure and cohesiveness" (1997, 674) — where others can readily come to share a viewpoint on one's *identity* — are more advantageous. The bottom line is that analysis of network structure must be attentive to network *content*, and in particular to the way networks touch on and build upon actors' identities.[14] This becomes an explicit assumption in Burt's later work, where what is conveyed through social ties is not resources, but "gossip." To quote the later Burt (2001, 46), "Identity is at the heart of the broader motive behind gossip. Gossip is not about information. It is about creating and maintaining relationships. . . . Conversations about social structure are an integral part of building and maintaining relationships, with the primary effect of reinforcing the current structure." Hence even actors antagonistic toward one another or belonging to mutually antagonistic social circles will adapt the stories they tell about third parties to what they expect each other to want to hear. This is a matter of etiquette, not unbiased information flow. Burt thus invites us to investigate the terms of the etiquette that obtains in specific social settings, and the flow of conversations that occur there that build and maintain relationships.

Robert Putnam's work (1993, 2000) on social capital differs substantially from Burt's and Lin's research in its attention to macro issues — notably the connections between the volume of social capital and the vibrancy of democratic political culture. According to Putnam, social connections, both in the form of interpersonal networks and associational participation in civil society and local politics, support broad increases in the amount of trust in society and the amount of accountability of political leaders.

Despite the substantial splash it has made, Putnam's work has been subject to a number of criticisms: for its empirical conclusion that American social capital has declined (for example, Paxton 1999); for its empirical claim that northern Italian democratic vitality derives from a late medieval and early Renaissance legacy of participatory republicanism (for example, Cohn 1994); for its methodological foibles in measuring social capital (Jackman and Miller 1996); for its theoretical claim that a democratic political culture is a precondition for democracy and development (Jackman and Miller 1996);[15] and for its neglect of the role of the state in encouraging or stifling developments in civil society (Tarrow 1996). Notably, Putnam failed to recognize that networks can be highly destructive forces (for example, see Levi 1996). Thus, although some of the northern Italian city-states in the late Middle Ages and early Renaissance were participatory regimes, built around the ligaments of a variety of vibrant social networks, one could hardly call the virulent factionalism they periodically suffered an unadulterated benefit to their political stability and democracy.[16]

Putnam's account of social capital seems to err, not by treating actors as too instrumental with respect to their social capital "resources," as in Coleman's account, but by treating them as too simplistically constituted by the social structures in which they are embedded. The volume of associational memberships in the aggregate is taken as an indicator of political involvement. What is missing is an analysis of how people act in these associations: how they use and how they talk about (Eliasoph 1998; Walsh 2004) the political cultural repertoires they have at their disposal.

Of all these theorists, Pierre Bourdieu offers the perspective most similar to my own. Bourdieu correctly emphasizes the dynamic accumulation of capital rather than the simple possession of it (1986, 241). He also sees it not only as consisting of concrete social connections, but also as stored up in legitimate, credentialed categories of rank and social prestige, such as fatherhood or the aristocracy, which willy-nilly implicates the idea of social capital in the symbolic politics that inform all social interaction (1998, 119). Those with social capital are not only linked to others; they are "known by" others. Bourdieu (1986, 249) writes of the sociation (Simmel 1950) inherent in social capital:

> The existence of a network of connections is not a natural given. . . .
> It is the product of an endless effort at institution. . . . In other words,
> the network of relationships is the product of investment strategies,
> individual or collective, consciously or unconsciously aimed at establishing or reproducing social relationships that are directly usable in
> the short or long term, i.e., at transforming contingent relations, such
> as those of neighborhood, the workplace, or even kinship, into relationships that are at once necessary and elective, implying durable
> obligations subjectively felt (feelings of gratitude, respect, friendship,
> etc.) or institutionally guaranteed (rights).

Bourdieu explicitly denies that the benefits of social connections need be self-consciously pursued; rather, these benefits accrue through strategies and competencies that increasingly become habitual dispositions of the actor. It is this vision of social capital and its constitution that we should keep in mind, eschewing the more utilitarian construals. In short, where many analyses of social capital fail is in their insufficient attention, first, to the fact that individual (and group) identities are implicated in the experience of social capital, and second, to the processes by which social capital is created, maintained, and transformed. Researchers working within a social capital framework have largely failed to see networking's capacity to *constitute* us as social actors, changing our identities and preferences through interaction.

Social Networks

Although the literature on social capital has grown immensely in recent years, it remains dwarfed by the immense volume of quantitative and qualitative research on social networks. Much of this work has focused on the intricacies of network structure and measurement (see for example, Wasserman and Faust 1994; Watts 1999; Carrington, Scott, and Wasserman 2005). Additionally, however, network analysis has been an integral part of research in a variety of substantive fields, such as economic sociology (for example, Baker 1984; G. Davis 1991; Harrison White 2002), political and historical sociology (Adams 1994; McLean 2004), and immigration (Bashi 2007).

I could not possibly review this vast and diverse literature adequately here. Instead I will touch on applications of network analysis inspired by Harrison White in comparative historical sociology (Bearman 1993; Padgett and Ansell 1993; Gould 1995) and a recent statement of the state of social network theory (Watts 2003) to make three points.

First, any coding exercise in network analysis tends to presume that all ties of a given type are substantively identical, but this is not accurate. Just as memberships in formal organizations imply different meanings to different members and are experienced with different intensity, network ties of a particular type—say marriage (Swidler 2001), or friendship (Gould 2003)—can mean different things to the two halves of a couple, not to mention the sundry actors who participate—not together, but severally—in such a nominal type of relationship. Furthermore, the meaning of a relationship also undergoes profound alteration over time, as it is continually negotiated by interaction partners; yet the temporal dimension of networks and the variability of their significance have not been well handled by network theorists to date.

The variety of meanings given to any type of tie is practically indisputable, but it is also quite intractable the larger the network one wishes to examine. At some point, due to limitations in collecting and aggregating data, certain idiosyncratic elements of ties have to be elided. A second problem, however, is that social network analysts have been mistaken in assuming that persons enact courses of action according to roles that are strictly determined by the structural positions they occupy. This is the approach Roger Gould adopted, for example, in *Insurgent Identities* (1995). With characteristic clarity, Gould argues that whereas class provided the dominant "participation identity" for Parisians in 1848, neighborhood, or urban consciousness, animated protest during the 1871 Commune. The difference stemmed from "structural and material changes," such as the massive urban demolition and reconstruction project executed under Baron Haussman — changes that gave impetus to divergent sets of discursive practices that influenced insurgency (1995, 28). "The collective identity *as* workers only emerges if the social networks in which they are embedded are patterned in such a way that the people in them can plausibly be partitioned into 'workers' and 'nonworkers'" (1995, 15). Once particular structural patterns of ties are present, salient identities will follow. These identities intensify the cognitive significance of the boundary, but they hardly seem to create the ties. Nor is there any sense of multiple identities simultaneously coming into play in the construction of social ties. Structure is privileged here with respect to culture.

This primacy of structure is also evident in Peter Bearman's *Relations into Rhetorics* (1993). In the first place, Bearman argues that the breakdown of localistic networks prepared the necessary ground for the application of the "abstract rhetorics" (1) that ultimately animated the English Civil War. An important element in this structural transformation that precipitated ideological conflict was the forging of network ties — kinship and religious patronage — across social categories or classifications, such as occupation, status, and religious affiliation. Bearman suggests that over time these classifications have decreasing salience in directing marriage partners toward each other: "categorical attributes of individuals are not powerful predictors of subsequent action — at least not in this period" (8). Moreover, these social classifications are taken as "a priori defined categories" (52). Evidently the changing salience of these categories over time indicates changing meanings and significances attached to them. But these changes are not directly examined; instead they are only inferred by means of the methodological move of treating their meaning as perpetually fixed and only the frequency of their use as variable.

John Padgett and Chris Ansell's (1993) work on Renaissance Florence has been praised for giving more room to identities and less deterministic power to social networks than other historical sociological research (Emirbayer and Goodwin 1994). It is true that their treatment of social attributes as "'merely' cognitive categories" (Padgett and Ansell 1993, 1274; also see 1285 n. 38) is an advance over approaches that treat these categories as determinative of identities. But it also makes light of the value of these multiple categories in strategic interaction. It is true, the Medici come off as remarkably agile in using divergent elements of their overall identity to forge a party connected uniquely through them; but all others come off as remarkably unable to escape from these cognitive classifications in forging their social networks. Even though Padgett and Ansell provide a plausible historical account as to how these particular "oligarchs" fell prey to an extraordinary degree of lock-in of neighborhood and social prestige endogamy, the overall story they tell tends to close the "widely underappreciated gap between these macrocognitive (or cultural) operations and microbehavioral 'local action'" that is, theoretically, an important part of the Padgett and Ansell research program. Individuals' multivocality becomes an exception in this narrative rather than a commonplace. This tendency to re-hardwire identities recurs in some more recent work (Padgett 2001). Here dominant structural types of economic partnership become "modal logic[s]-of-identity" (Padgett 2001, 222). The distinction between categorical affiliation and cultural construction of ties is elided. Thus, for example, during the *popolani* regime of 1382–1434, among bankers "the distinct logic-of-identity was social class" (226). Empirically, individual bankers *did* choose partners most frequently from the same social class (Padgett and McLean 2006), but an examination of the rhetorics for forging such ties reveals a different cognitive basis for them. Notwithstanding the use of social class as a criterion of the search for partners, the actual mental and interactional representation of partnership may well have continued to be familial (and specifically brotherly) in nature.[17]

This brings me to my third point. The list of possible cultural framings of relationships is loosely coupled to the types of relationships forged. There is no simple one-to-one mapping of cultural logics of association to particular types of ties. Instead, the forging of any tie may well partake of multiple framings, borrowing the language of one kind of tie to construct a putatively different type. A striking example of this fact in the Florentine case is the widespread use of fictive kinship, and we need look no further than the letter from Francesco Nardi to Averardo de' Medici at the beginning of this chapter for an illustration of it. Although not positionally related to Averardo by blood, Francesco adopts the language of fatherhood to portray Averardo and thereby try to impose fatherly obligations on him. Similarly, fathers and sons could use economic metaphors of thrift, for example, to articulate their relationship. Political allies could use the language of friendship to articulate the meaning of their alliance. The concept of fictive kinship would make no sense unless actors took frames "normally" found in one sphere of life and adapted or applied them to relationships in other spheres. Friendship (*amicizia*) was the loosest and most ambiguous frame Florentines had at their disposal to apply to a multitude of different relationship constructions.

Thus, contra structuralist thinking that seeks to derive roles and other cultural features of actors from structural positions (classically articulated by White, Boorman, and Breiger 1976), types of networks do not have attached cultural logics. Instead, a handful of cultural logics get applied piecemeal and in combination in different network domains.

This insight has become increasingly clear to contemporary network theorists. Thus Harrison White writes (1995, 1042) not only that "the substance of a type of tie lies in what reflexive accountings are accepted in that network-domain as warranties," but also that "multiple alternative accounts are being carried along until temporary resolutions at disjunctions which I call switches" (1049). And Watts (2003, 151) has noted that humans routinely overcome intractable problems in communicating information across great distances in small world networks by drawing on their *multiple* identities to search for alters. Thus cascading across analytically distinct domains takes place not only in the sense that "moves" in one network domain (for example, business) have a significant impact on other network domains (for example, politics or marriage), as if individuals were playing multiple games that nonetheless retained mutually distinct sets of rules. Nor does cascading occur only in the sense that "moves in one domain are measured in the currency of other domains" (Padgett 2001, 233). We do not make unitarily conceived moves that are subsequently interpretable from multiple perspectives. We make multiply conceived (framed) and constructed moves that are interpretable from multiple perspectives. Thus cascading through-out the social space takes place in the sense that action in any one game will borrow self-consciously and relatively freely from multiple domains of meaning. We are embedded in multiple networks and multiple cultures, and accordingly we are cultural *bricoleurs* in each and all of these networks.

To sum up, network analysis has often fallen prey to an oversocialized and static conception of networks, treating network ties as simply con-stitutive of identities, without examining how they become constituted and how they are negotiated over time. As it is operationalized, network analysis often proceeds as if sharing an identity were an automatic trigger for subsequent action. But networks are places where action is happening, not where it has already happened. They do not simplistically determine mobilization, or alliance building, or career formation. They are more like congested, and therefore potentially fecund, arenas of persuasive social interaction (McAdam 2003). Although there have been some moves in the direction of studying the *construction* rather than the assumption of identi-ties in networks (Bian 1997; Yang 1994), network analysis remains inatten-tive in general to what happens in interaction to construct relations.

Enter the Practice-Oriented Conception of Culture

The oscillation I outlined earlier between undersocialized and oversocial-ized understandings of how individuals are embedded in social networks replicates a grand controversy affecting the social sciences writ large, namely that between *rational choice* approaches to social action and what we might term *culturalist* theory or *interpretivism*. Here the argument has been over the nature of individuals' relation to their culture and to other structures they inhabit. As with any set of antinomies, both sides persuasively offer fun-damentally sound and empirically grounded convictions. Rational choice theory correctly identifies the evident ability of actors to play roles instru-mentally, meanwhile attending to what seem to be their long-term private interests. Further, actors can talk about their culture reflectively with at least dissatisfaction, and occasionally with arm's-length impartiality.

At the same time, rational choice theorists have a hard time explaining why people operate at the level of cultural symbols at all if no one really takes culture seriously. Moreover, conflict seems very often to be precisely over the definition of a situation and the boundaries of a group, rather than simply the distribution of rewards within one. Explanations based on an abstract conception of rationality, subject to empirically variable but easily specifiable constraints and predicated of fixed and stable actors, have little to say about how strategic behavior grows from an emergent sense of *identity* of the actors, that is, an evolving constitution of the relevant actors and their self-conception.

Sociological research on the topic of culture over the last several years has sought to reconcile these two grand perspectives. I build on these developments. In particular, I will draw on the work of Pierre Bourdieu (1977, 1990a, 1990b, 1991, 1998, 2000), Ann Swidler (1986, 2001), and Erving Goffman (1967, 1969, 1974, 1981) to make better sense of networking as a strategic activity that is self-consciously constitutive of identities. The way actors pursue mobility through social structure (conceived as networks) is richly determined by the kinds of cultural repertoires they have available to them. Thus to pursue the connection of actors to networks requires a thorough treatment of the rituals, styles, and frames of social interaction. In short, it requires us to think about how culture operates, and how actors "use" their culture(s).

To be in a culture is, at least in part, to participate in a conversation. The image of being *conversant* in a culture is telling because it highlights the practical side and processual nature of culture, and it signifies the ability of actors to take multiple sides in a discussion and know what all sides stand for. Seeing it this way is to understand culture *interactionally*.

Pierre Bourdieu: The Logic of Practice

Undoubtedly Pierre Bourdieu has been among those most responsible for turning sociologists to the study of cultural practice. His views have been amply commented upon elsewhere (for example, Bourdieu and Wacquant 1992; Calhoun, LiPuma, and Postone 1993; Swartz 1997), so here I offer merely a brief and selective summary. As part of his explicit repudiation of rational choice theory, Bourdieu argues that social action is practical, by which he means that it is strategic but rooted in habitual dispositions and/or intuitive skills, not rational calculation. It is not executed according to rules, contrary to the structuralist anthropology articulated by Lévi-Strauss—although it does evince objective regularities based on actors' positions in social space and their corresponding ingrained dispositions (1990a, 37–38; 1990b, chap. 3). According to Bourdieu, it is critical to view these regularities through the lens of power. Power, and in particular what he calls symbolic violence, is ubiquitous in social life. There is an asymmetry in the opportunities presented to persons in different social positions, and an inequality of equipment (1985, 732) available to them with which to realize their objectives. He emphasizes this in contrast to scholars working in the American interactionist tradition, who he thinks largely neglect the issue of power, fail to explain why the substance of the social world appears to us as necessary (1990a, 52), and err in thinking they have an adequate grasp on social reality by virtue of participating in the processes they are observing (1990a, 34).

Social life is shaped by the dialectic between objective social structures and structured, structuring dispositions, or *habitus* (1990a, 40). These dispositions are "durable" and "transposable" cognitive orientations toward action (1990a, 53), applied to new situations and opportunities as they arise. Their durability and their determination by virtue of positions in social space render it likely that the bulk of social action results in a reproduction of the status quo (1990a, 95). Correspondingly, practical mastery means (in language borrowed from Goffman) having a firm "sense of one's place" (1985, 728). This sense of place is clearly not only (or typically) a sense of entitlement, but a sense of constraint: a sense of the difficulty of pursuing certain courses of action, and a feeling of discomfort or inferiority when placed in unfamiliar situations. Our practical relationship to the world is largely one of "immediate but unselfconscious understanding" (1990a, 19).

However, the frequent application of our dispositions to new situations and new settings lends the *habitus* the character not simply of reproduction, but of "regulated improvisation" (1990a, 57). Practical mastery, Bourdieu notes, is always a mastery of forms. Even the conversational exchange of stereotypical pleasantries requires an "unceasing vigilance" (1990a, 80). Yet these forms of action are not just rules or etiquette for proper play or proper gesture; they are also good ways of "getting around the rules," or for maintaining ambiguity about one's aims. Thus the sense of practical mastery also is characterized by a certain "fuzziness" (1990a, 12).

Virtuosic play in the games of social interaction resembles excellent athletic play (1990a, chap. 4)—first in the sense of having great anticipation about how the game will progress, and second, "being able to play the game up to the limits, even to the point of transgression, while managing to stay within the rules of the game" (1990b, 78f.). The best players' performances will systematically negate the simple formulae according to which the game is supposedly played (1990a, 81). The most successful strategies are those that appear to make the most spontaneous adjustment to changes in the field (2000, 139). And even though Bourdieu regards sport as an imperfect analogue for social fields, since in real life "one does not embark on the game by a conscious act, [but] one is born into the game, with the game" (1990a, 67), networking really is more like a sport than other aspects of social life, since actors *are* typically conscious of it as a game and have meditated upon and theorized about the "rules" (cf. 1990a, 73).

For Bourdieu, social fields and cultural practices are inherently dynamic and thoroughly relational. What makes for a class of culturally defined actors is not a set of "necessary and intrinsic properties," but a set of skills, practices, dispositions, tastes, and so on, that are oppositional to those currently adopted by other groups (1998, 4). An important element of this view is that the ruling elite is likely to adopt a succession of different values, practices, and styles over time as they seek ever renewed distinction from subordinate groups aspiring to become like them.

Finally, in his analysis of strategic interaction, Bourdieu emphasizes the importance of time (1990a, chap. 6). Structuralists eviscerate the temporal unfolding of social action and ignore the suspense that derives from not knowing with certainty how another actor will respond. This suspense about the appropriateness of one's actions and the nature of another's response is particularly urgent in games of honor (1977; also see Goffman 1969, 66). Indeed one reason Bourdieu's analysis of Kabyle society is so germane to an analysis of Florentine patronage interaction is that "honor" plays an important constitutive and communicative function in both societies. The culture of honor features a kind of tense double talk: participants have a shared understanding that ulterior motives routinely lurk behind elaborate gestures of self-presentation. Moreover, there are constant, often anxious allusions to interruptions and lapses in communication in Florentine letters, suggesting how much time (and in particular continuity) was a vital concern to them, an important element in their playing of the patronage "game." Nardi's letter at the beginning of this chapter illustrates this concern: "I wrote to you . . . and from you I have had no reply." He hastens not to blame Averardo for this time lapse but explicitly mentions it to add to the urgency of his request.

Sometimes Bourdieu's emphasis on *doxa* (1977) and *habitus* tends to overwhelm the notion of "improvisation." Erickson (1996) has argued that he overemphasizes the "categorical" side of social capital at the expense of examining concrete social connections that span status categories rather than simply reproducing them. He clearly does not anticipate much transformation of social systems or of symbolic orders, or even of actors within them. By contrast, I will show in chapter 3 that the symbolic order surrounding the meaning of honor was constantly changing in Florence. Action therefore was really taking place in a setting of significant cultural heterogeneity and dynamism. As Anne Kane (1991) has put it, culture is "messy" in a way Bourdieu's work does not quite capture.

Ann Swidler: Culture as Repertoires

Ann Swidler's 1986 article in the *American Sociological Review* marked a decisive turn toward studying culture in terms of practices instead of shared values, beliefs, or attitudes. Her recent book, *Talk of Love* (2001), elaborates upon her view of culture in action and offers a virtual treasure trove of observations about what culture is like in practice and how people are related to it. In the first place, she argues, her interviews on the topic of love demonstrate that people do not have a single unified set of beliefs about things, but instead they possess a "repertoire" (also see, for example, Steinberg 1999) or "toolkit" of cultural elements—ideas, symbols, gestures—that they appropriate and recombine in interaction. Even a common culture can be used in very different ways (Swidler 2001, 4ff.). Clifford Geertz's (1973) classic vision of culture as webs of significance—a cluster of historically generated, meaningful, and inter-related symbols that can be articulated through the method of thick description—was handy for turning our attention to the vast diversity of meaningful cultural practices, but Geertz ended up overstating the coherence of culture and the completeness with which it creates us (Swidler 2001, 12, 22, 75). Researchers have documented a great deal of contestation within cultures over what key concepts and symbols mean. And people themselves can enact quite disparate, or even contradictory (2001, 26), elements of the overall repertoire at different times, "trying various rationales, with little concern about coherence among them" (29).[18] Moreover, people vary (and individuals vary over time) in terms of the seriousness with which they play with culture. Not all play is "deep" (cf. Geertz 1973, chap. 15).

Culture, notes Swidler, is thus less a great stream in which we all swim, and more a kind of soup in which we float or drift about (2001, 24, 59). Within this soup, people know a lot more culture than they draw on in any one instance, and they are skilled at summoning a variety of interpretive frameworks to understand any given scenario or interaction (40, 81).[19] The incoherence of our cultural practices is made up for in the flexibility and adaptability a varied toolkit provides for us (182–83).

According to Swidler, cultural practices routinely cluster into sets, or "strategies for action" (83). These strategies strongly shape what people want and how they can conceive of asking for it, rather than being harnessed to preexisting goals. The multiplicity of strategies we can enact means we are truly multiple selves (Mead 1934). We learn to become a certain kind of self through the strategies we adopt in interaction. Especially when the use of particular strategies becomes problematic, we become an audience for ourselves, a moment of reflection on how we want to be related to different strands of cultural meaning (Swidler 2001, 31).

Once this understanding of culture is firmly established in our minds, it becomes possible: 1) to elaborate the toolkit of widely used but disparate repertoires (as I do for Florentine patronage interaction in chapters 2 and 3); 2) to show how and when particular tools in the toolkit actually get used (as I do in chapter 4); 3) to see what anchors the various rhetorical elements used and which circumstances trigger shifts or switches from one part of the repertoire to another (as I do in chapters 5 and 6); and 4) to see how micro-level cultural practices affect large and durable social institutions, such as the state (chapter 7), and the hegemonic conception of the self (chapter 8).

Swidler calls her theory "an identity model" of how culture operates. This is so because "people develop lines of action based on who they already think they are," and because "a great deal of culture operates by attaching meanings to the self" (2001, 87). I would expand on these observations with two of my own. First, these meanings of oneself are often constructed *in relation to* other selves, even in a culture that pretends to be based on individual autonomy and self-determination as much as ours does. Second, while people undoubtedly develop lines of action based on who they think they are, as Nardi's letter at the beginning of this chapter indicates, they also develop lines of action based on a *bona fide* strategic projection of who they wish to become.

Erving Goffman and the Interaction Order:
Frames, and How They Are Invoked Through Conversational Devices

Take the important structural realm of social relationships—their avoidance, creation, maintenance, deepening, attenuation, and termination, their linkages into networks of various kinds and func-

tioning. Since control of the state of a relationship is a mutually interdependent objective of the persons related, strategic analysis applies.
This analysis certainly adds something to our understanding of personal relating, especially . . . in regard to our model of the relating
entity, the individual. Nonetheless, a generalized picture of relationship formation and the resulting structures cannot be fully delineated
in strategic terms. (Goffman 1969, 137)

Although Swidler talks about "culture in action," it is not far from the
spirit of her thinking to proceed to a study of culture in *interaction*. Erving
Goffman was an indisputably masterful analyst of social interaction, identifying the "interaction order" as a distinct arena of social life with its own
rules, resonating with larger social structures, but also resistant to simple
determination by those structures (Goffman 1983; Malone 1997, 13). These
interactional rules are like traffic rules or maps (Malone 1997, 7; also see
Geertz 1973, 44; Cicourel 1973), not specifying where people go, but rather
how they might get there and how they should treat each other on the way.
Because the interaction order has its own rules of thumb and is only loosely
coupled to social structure or the institutional order, everyday interaction
has its own constitutive impact on the social order in general. So, for example, constructions of gender exist as institutional realities, but conversational interaction is a key mechanism by which gendered identities are
learned, and these identities may not be exact reflections of institutionalized conceptions. A routine element in the interactional aspect of patronage, for example, is that the reality of patronage is sometimes explicitly denied, even from within the practices that make it a reality. As Eisenstadt and
Roniger (1980, 50) have noted, patron-client relations feature "a peculiar
combination of inequality and asymmetry in power with seeming *mutual
solidarity* expressed in terms of personal identity and interpersonal sentiments and obligations"—a species of face-saving work (Goffman 1967).
Again we look to Nardi's letter. He is pleading for Averardo's assistance, but
he does so in such a way that communicates his expectation of being helped
and provides Averardo with a face-saving account as to why he has not yet
responded. Furthermore, he concludes ("You understand my meaning") by
alluding to an understanding he shares with Averardo as to what is at stake,
a conclusion that treats Averardo more as a fellow player of the game than
as a superior. These features are endemic to the Florentine patronage interaction order.

Interaction is specifically *strategic* (Goffman 1969) when actors find themselves in the joint production of fateful outcomes, where each actor's moves "are made in the light of one's thoughts about the others' thoughts about oneself" (101). The fundamental question (85) in strategic interaction is, "When a respectable motive is given for action, are we to suspect an ulterior one?" Often, some guarantees are available of how others will behave: when judges or referees monitor compliance; when an audience is present; when there is a definite understanding of the resources at stake; when the actions taken are transparently clear and/or provide material evidence of commitments; or when it is clearly useful for a given actor to comply with his or her promises (115–28). But what happens when these are not available? At least three times in *Strategic Interaction* (106, 112, 124), Goffman wonders how we find reasonable grounds for relying solely on one another's *words*. That we do so is evident. People act as if their assertions really are performative commitments. That an individual can commit him- or herself through words, and furthermore that the manner in which that commitment is expressed will confirm his or her position, "are fundamental, if misguided, assumptions of our strategic interactions" (127). This conclusion undoubtedly propelled Goffman (1974, 1981) and his successors toward the idea that talk in itself provides expressive frames and cues to commitment that demand empirical analysis. Shared meanings are a product of interactional frames, cued by particular conversational practices (Goffman 1974). Through the manipulation of these performative and interpretive frames in social interaction, agents aim to establish socially recognized identities for themselves. Certainly some sense of form and situation-specific etiquette is relevant here: we have "the belief that the very design of his construction provides a window into [the speaker's] intent, a window to a room that is lit from within by emotional expression" (Goffman 1969, 128).[20] Moreover, we act as if our speech involves *moral* commitments (127)—and indeed our speech *is* moral because it produces the joint construction of meaning and formulates a public image of the self implicated in interaction. Each gesture stands for the self that enacts it. Given that when we act, we are saying something both about the outside world and about ourselves—and often multiple things about the outside world itself—discursive action is inherently multi-functional. This multi-functionality or polysemy of practices must be explicitly attended to in studies of interaction.

In "Expression Games" (1969, 1–81), Goffman begins to enumerate a variety of techniques we might find employed by strategic actors. Actors

attempt to establish the meaning of a situation in the early stages of interaction (12). They will provide "accounts" to each other to alter the assessment each would otherwise make of their opponent (16). They will provide
nonessential information to each other about themselves to flesh out a more
nuanced and credible presentation of self (19). They will "split" themselves,
commenting upon their own feelings or vulnerability to exploit that vulnerability to good effect, providing a textured presentation of themselves
(47). They will avoid bluffs on which they could not possibly deliver (56).

Yet actors don't just use rules and maps to figure out cooperatively where
they are. They also manipulate the projection of cultural space with each
other. Actions or events are not given as normal or exceptional; they are
framed as normal or exceptional. Goffman's (1974) use of the notion of
"frame" was felicitous because it implied both the negotiation of meaningfulness (that is, sharing a common "framework") and the possible deceptive
manipulation of relevant resemblances and exemplars (that is, "he framed
me").[21] Thus framing involves primary frames but also keying (establishing which tone of interaction is in play at the moment, or switching between frames), fabrication (sustaining a frame which misleads another), and
lamination (the layering, texturing, or even melding of different frames of
meaning) (Goffman 1974, chaps. 2–4). Rather than an attitude toward an
object or another actor being a function of the full array of frames and characteristics predicated of it, frame theory suggests that attitudes in particular
settings are crafted through deliberate adjustment of what is lit and what is
shaded. Cues given in interaction guide the establishment of framing, since
it cannot be assumed that actors have from the outset the same idea about
where each other, or the event of their interaction, fits into their schematic
understanding of the organization of the world. And there is power in how
framing exercises unfold. For example, Maynard (1991) shows how doctors
take conversational turns with patients and express apparently sincere interest in patients' self-diagnoses but end up framing patient problems as symp-
toms, that is, as medically manageable phenomena, that they have specific
expertise to treat. Similarly, Sarat's and Felstiner's work (1995) on lawyer-
client consultations preparatory to divorce proceedings demonstrates that
clients depend on lawyers to recast their grievances—first expressed in pas-
sionate and personal terms—into a frame (or narrative) accessible to the
legal system and amenable to favorable treatment by it. But typification is
not the whole story. O'Barr (1982, 32, 34, 120f.) notes that practical manuals
for courtroom performance stress that cross-examinations must incorporate artful variation in tone, syntax, rhythm, and pace, as well as personal

touches in story narration (rather than simply hackneyed accounts) to be effective. Moreover, successful courtroom strategy often involves breaking at least the formal rules of presentation, as with the strategic introduction of inadmissible evidence (O'Barr 1982, 6). When expectations of procedural regularity are not met, or when the labels assigned to individuals or events are jarring, precisely then are participants (and audiences) in courtroom settings—or in patronage-seeking letters—called upon to assess what these breaks in form indicate.

Shared Themes

While differences exist among these three theorists, they do share themes that can guide empirical research. First, there is the definition of strategy as somewhere in between rational calculative action and the mere expression or execution of a structuralist logic. All three note the importance of marked violations of rules in practice for maintaining the salience of the rule, for practicing agency, and for presenting oneself. All three agree that routine, formalized practices need to be documented, but all three also see agency as richly improvisational. All three share in a search for rules and mechanisms by which multiple cultural logics, goals, and symbols are stitched together in interaction. While paying different amounts of attention to social structure and to the manner in which it impinges on action, all three agree that particular cultural repertoires will appear more or less legitimate and will be more or less available depending on the location of actors in social space. And all three see agency as deeply reflexive. Strategies cast light upon the self that is adopting them, with both others and oneself being audiences for these strategic performances. From Bourdieu, we can draw the additional idea that interaction is temporal and suspenseful, from Swidler the idea that cultural elements are used in a patterned but eclectic way, and from Goffman sustained attention to discourse and its ambiguity. Perhaps pushing beyond both Bourdieu and Swidler, however, I would emphasize that networking actors are *reflective*: they think about what they are doing, pursuing advantages self-consciously and crafting innovative presentations of self.

Enumerating a Repertoire of Discursive Strategies

Goffman's work in particular has inspired an abundance of research in symbolic interaction, discourse analysis, conversation analysis, and related fields. Although the historical data I have available is not strictly speaking unedited interaction (such as conversation analysts study), or even interaction episodes in the sense of back-and-forth communication, I draw on some of this sociolinguistic research for specific ideas about what to look for in my analysis of patronage interaction. A number of these techniques and markers are listed in table 1.

One important element of Goffman's agenda focused on "recipient design" (Sacks 1992), an outgrowth of early work on "altercasting" (Weinstein and Deutschberger 1963). There are a multitude of ways in which senders of messages attempt to characterize recipients favorably and to tailor recipients' sympathetic reception of these messages.[22] A blunt instrument in this regard is flattery, a strategy to which fifteenth-century Florentines were scarcely averse, although they were seemingly less inclined to indulge in it than favor seekers in later centuries. The more flowery the flattery, typically the more transparent its disingenuousness, so it must not be overdone. However, brief assertions welcoming the health and good fortune of one's alter—what medieval letter writers dubbed a *captatio benevolentiae*—functioned in this way. Once it is established rhetorically that favor seeker and recipient are on the same wavelength, it becomes possible to make open-ended, deferential offers of reciprocity that proactively align the interests of petitioner and recipient: "I am yours in everything"; "Advise me what you want and I will do it willingly"; "If there is any one thing to do more than another, let me know." At the same time, petitioners also seek ways to communicate that they are not only requesting but *expecting* assistance from patrons. I call this technique *rhetorical brinkmanship*: "you know well my need" (*sapete bene il mio bisogno*); or "I am certain that, on account of my love of you and your kindness, I will be served" (*sono certo per mio amore e per vostra benignità io sia servito*). The contrary elements of deference and desert, charity and merit, are commonly juxtaposed.[23] Together they construct a complex relationship between petitioner and patron, and concomitantly supply a complex construction of the patron's motives.

I noted above the double meaning of "frame" and the idea of "alignment" of frames. Both ideas are nicely handled in the research on frame alignment processes in social movement mobilization undertaken by David Snow and his collaborators (Snow et al. 1986; Snow and Benford 1988, 1992). Framing, they argue, is an ongoing and context-sensitive accomplishment. Providing a compelling motivation for action is necessary because, privately, individuals may attach a great variety of subjective meanings to objective situations (1986, 466).

Table 1. Selected Discursive Techniques for Building Relations

Concept/Technique	Selected Citations	Use/Purpose
Primary frames	Goffman 1974, chap. 2	Establishing the basic meaning of an inter-action
Keying	Goffman 1974, 43–44	"The set of conventions by which a given activity, one already meaningful in terms of some primary framework, is transformed into something patterned on this activity but seen by the participants to be something quite else."
Fabrication	Goffman 1974, chap. 4	Sustaining a frame that misleads another
Lamination	Goffman 1974, 82	For Goffman, a multiply re-keyed frame; more simply, employing diverse cues of multiple interpretive framings of a particular activity
Anchoring	Goffman 1974, chap. 8	Techniques for signaling the beginning or ending or authenticity of interaction, and specifically the way a role adopted signals the person behind it
Recipient design, Altercasting	Sacks 1992; Weinstein and Deutschberger 1963	The multitude of ways in which actors attempt to characterize recipients favorably and to tailor recipients' sympathetic reception of these messages
Bridging	Snow et al. 1986	Targeting appropriate new alters
Amplification	Snow et al. 1986	Repeated use of critical cues
Extension	Snow et al. 1986	Re-framing oneself to align with alter
Transformation	Snow et al. 1986	Recasting an event in terms of new goals or motivations
Identity qualifying	Mische 2003	Foregrounding/backgrounding of diverse roles/identities according to setting and interactant
Generality shifting	Mische 2003	Using ambiguous language with multiple plausible referents
Speaking for another	Schiffrin 1993	Providing accounts of what others have said, done, or felt
Pronoun manipulation	Muhlhausler and Harré 1990; Hanks 1992	Drawing social boundaries discursively through strategic pronoun use: "we" vs. "they," "my" vs. "his," etc.

Table 1. (*continued*)

Concept/Technique	Selected Citations	Use/Purpose
Politeness strategies	Brown and Levinson 1987	Marking social distance through the use of simple/elaborate prefaces to requests
Contextualization cues	Gumperz 1992; Duranti and Goodwin 1992	Providing evidence of the context of a request within the communication of that request
Deictic expressions	Hanks 1992	Use of locative expressions ("here," "there," "together") as indicators of distance between actors
Rhetorical brinkmanship		Communicating expectations of assistance
Stitching together, or switching between, frames	Harrison White 1995; Mische and White 1998; Schiffrin 1987	Expressions and/or grammatical devices for connecting frames

Snow and his colleagues describe four key processes of frame alignment brought to bear by social movement activists on potential movement participants: bridging, amplification, extension, and transformation. The logic of the first is "You may be like us." In the case of Renaissance Florentine patronage, potential patrons were explicitly targeted by virtue of their background attributes or connections to mutual friends and acquaintances. The second technique, amplification, involves the repetition of key words or phrases to instill some confidence in the recipient that the framing provided corresponds to reality. In the Florentine case, textual cues such as "*commune*" signal belief amplification, that is, "I believe the commune is primary and a symbol of our power." Other amplificatory devices include recurrent statements about the seriousness of outside threat or the efficacy of action, and the stereotypic depiction of enemies (for example, competitors for patronage in the Florentine case).

Extension is a tactic by which one claims that what one's organization or oneself does or is can fit what the target person does or is: not "you can fit us," but "we can fit you." Capitalizing on past favors, and rhetorical techniques for assimilating one's own preferences to those of the patron are examples. Frames invoked to establish a relationship in the first place are typically not the same as those used subsequently to explain allegiance or ongoing loyalty (1986, 473). Finally, transformation amounts more or less to Goffman's notion of re-keying, recasting an event or stream of events in terms of new goals or motivations. Any rhetorical switching device such as "Heretofore I have spoken one way; now I say thus," could be considered a transformational framing technique.[24]

Scholars such as Doug McAdam (2003) and Ann Mische (2003; see also Mische and White 1998; Polletta 2002) have recently sought richer treatments of the cultural, and sometimes specifically conversational, interactional mechanisms whereby participation in social movements is created, negotiated, and maintained. Here "social networks are seen not merely as locations for, or conduits of, cultural formations, but rather as *composed of* culturally constituted processes of communicative interaction" (Mische 2003, 258; emphasis in original). Mische discusses four such mechanisms, but I will highlight two in particular: identity qualifying, and generality shifting. The first refers to the cues actors use to indicate which aspects of their multiple identities are "active 'right now,' in a particular set of utterances" (Mische 2003, 269). This tactic involves the compartmentalization, or the strategic foregrounding and backgrounding, of motives associated with particular roles or network positions. For example, at any given time in Florence many individuals occupied official positions on behalf of the commune, but rotation through these offices was frequent. This meant that private concerns were frequently brought to one's purview and pursuable through public means, but private concerns also needed to be actively distinguished from public ones. The second of Mische's mechanisms, generality shifting, implies the use of referents that are ambiguous in the generality of their meaning. To say "students" were at the forefront of the Brazilian impeachment process might imply that a small band of politically active student groups were the main catalysts of the movement; alternatively it might imply that the movement succeeded because a broad, youthful, largely non-political swath of the Brazilian population indirectly supported it. Different audiences will hear the label "students" differently. Similarly, in Florence, the word *amici* (friends) has several meanings, from very general ones to very particular ones. It may mean Florence and its allies, it may mean all internal supporters of the commune, it may mean supporters of a particular policy within the commune, or it may mean the factional associates of a particular family. Readers of letters had to figure out which level of generality of *amicizia* was meant by letter writers who invoked it, but the wording also left the meaning ambiguous, to allow petitioners to reframe their intentions after the fact, to elide particularistic goals with communal ones, and to protect writers from incriminating evidence of factional activity should a letter fall into the wrong hands.

Intimately connected to the depiction of self and one's own motives in interaction is the depiction of the motives and identities of others. Petitioners speak for others as well as for themselves (Schiffrin 1993). They use pronouns strategically (Muhlhausler and Harré 1990), in at least two fundamental ways. First, formal or informal second-person singular pronouns (*voi* versus *tu*) signal the social distance between the petitioner and the recipient of the letter. Connected to this direct signaling of social distance are various strategies of politeness (Brown and Levinson 1987) that implicitly signal the type of relationship obtaining between interacting individuals. Second, petitioners use possessive pronouns strategically,[25] inclusively constructing boundaries around themselves and their patrons while excluding others from the circle. Alternatively they may remove themselves from a circle of clients whose motives are portrayed as less than honorable. Are the friends petitioners mention "our friends," "your friends," or somewhat more noncommittally, "the friends?" Each depiction reflects differently on the sender. The honor of my associates rubs off on me, while their dishonor taints me. In the former case, I actively emphasize my connection to them; in the latter, I actively distance myself from them. In either case, the proper context for understanding my message about myself does not merely exist independently but is communicated in the text of the message itself through the use of "contextualization cues" (Gumperz 1992; Duranti and Goodwin 1992). Critical to this discursive work that creates the contexts of interaction are "deictic expressions" (Hanks 1992; Bachnik and Quinn 1994, 107, 146) that identify key places and times in the social landscape. Pronoun use again fits in here, but so too do locative expressions such as "here," "there," and "together." Florentine correspondence teems with such words, undoubtedly in part because people corresponded, and asked for favors, across considerable distances. But these words also were used to emphasize writers' dependence on recipients for news of what was happening elsewhere, and to depict separate arenas of activity. When writers asked for help, they sometimes asked recipients to work together (*insieme*) with others to achieve a favorable outcome, once again constructing boundaries around groups through discourse.[26]

Schiffrin (1987) identifies a number of other markers in discourse that signal information management ("oh, . . ."), the beginning of a response ("well, . . ."), connections or disjunctions between ideas ("and," "but," and "or"), and efforts at positing agreement between the sender and the recipient of messages ("y'know"). Essentially, pieces of communication are stitched together, or switched between (Harrison White 1995; Mische and White 1998), by means of these seemingly innocuous devices. So, too, is the significance of communication marked. As Harrison White (1995, 1040) argues, "It is in conjunctions, pronouns, relativizers, and other grammatical gadgetry of a particular language that are to be found evidence of the basic mechanisms underlying sociocultural dominance."

Finally, scholars have increasingly sought to incorporate *place* into the analysis of the interactional mechanisms by which cultural practices are improvisationally utilized to generate and to maintain network relations. These places or spaces go by various names: Goffman publics (Harrison White 1995; Ikegami 2003), settings (Mische and Pattison 2000), group styles (Eliasoph and Lichterman 2003), or situations (Goffman 1967; Swidler 2001; Mische and White 1998). Here is where frame switching to couple and decouple networks takes place. Critical to the analysis of interaction is understanding the rules and/or regularities that cover interaction in particular places. Places limit what kinds of cultural practices can be articulated.

Coda: From Interactional Culture in General to Political Culture in Particular

I have sought to lay out some ideas about culture in interaction in this chapter. Further, I have sought to identify some particular techniques by means of which culture in interaction takes place. But in talking about patronage-seeking interaction, we are talking not just about culture, but about specifically *political* culture. Furthermore, understanding Florentine interactional culture as political points toward the important task of linking micro-political interaction dynamics to macro-political outcomes. Building on Bourdieu, Swidler, and Goffman produces a very different vision of political culture than has existed in the past (Somers 1995; Berezin 1997).[27] The pioneering work of Almond and Verba (1963) on "civic culture" began by viewing political culture as a hybrid entity, composed of diverse traditional and modern elements, but ultimately it abandoned this tack and instead emphasized the functionality of particular attitudes and values for maintaining political stability. Political culture was unduly limited to the relationship between people and their political structures, not to the relations they have among themselves when pursuing politically salient ends. And as the authors themselves have noted (Almond and Verba 1980), the tendency toward finding congruence between political culture and political structure wrongly treated individuals as mere mirrors of the political structures they face.

Other research on political culture is similarly problematic. Ronald Inglehart's work (1988, 1990, 1997) on changing attitudes seems to treat culture as a unitary independent variable and as a black box residual explanation for complex social processes. The work of Aaron Wildavsky (1987, 1991) and his collaborators (Thompson, Ellis, and Wildavsky 1990) represented a slightly different cut at the matter, but with similarly unsatisfactory conclusions (see Laitin and Wildavsky 1988). Wildavsky linked "shared values" to "the social relations they rationalize," an assertion that denied culture any independent explanatory import and denied actors' flexibility with respect to the culture they use. Despite his accurate claim that preferences and meaning emerge out of social interaction, and that actors test out cultural repertoires (1987, 7), his portrayal of the process of preference formation as a *prix fixe* menu in which only certain combinations of preferences are viable seems contrary to the richness of actual belief portfolios in the world.

Jeffrey Alexander has advocated a Durkheimian vision of political culture, to outline its structure or design, to depict agency within it, and to reinvest it with a normative component (Alexander 1990; Alexander and Smith 1993). He views culture as an autonomous, logically arranged system based on dualities or pairs of opposites: good/evil, truth/opinion, freedom/tyranny, and so on. These pairs are understood to be linked to each other via analogy and metaphor, stackable into a two-column "discursive structure" (Alexander and Smith 1993, 162). Such an effort to document the traits and dynamics of a culture is important, yet it falls prey to criticisms similar to those made by Bourdieu regarding Lévi-Strauss. The description Alexander and Smith offers is unrealistic in the way it leaps immediately to a very simple patterned order within the cultural sphere—order of a barebones, dichotomously structured sort. But the "structure" of culture can hypothetically take many different shapes: polarities of opposites analogically related; a grid of terms and concepts, polar or not, hard-wired to each other through a single path; narrative strings or sequences (Abbott 1992, 1995; Steinmetz 1992; Griffin 1993); mutually autonomous clusters of discourse, each obtaining in a different sphere (religion, politics, literature, the home, the business world, and so on); or overlapping discourses or language games that evoke each other.[28] Consistent with the Gramscian view that all life is political, a political culture provides a rich and deep reservoir of interconnected repertoires for people seeking better social positions, projecting themselves into more valorized identities, and, occasionally, achieving the transformation of political structures. At root, political culture is interactional and conversational (Eliasoph 1998; Walsh 2004).

Conclusion

The juxtaposition of agency and culture is succinctly posed in Leon Battista Alberti's *I libri della famiglia*, from Florence in the 1430s. One character, Piero Alberti, outlines the appropriate forms of behavior and outward signs of honor by which to seduce men of various ranks in life into friendship. In another part of the text, though, as I noted above, Giannozzo Alberti tells of how a powerful friend of his would elude such petitioners or flatterers, demurring to satisfy their requests through standardized excuses and exercises of foot-dragging. Agency is operative here in the desire to choose the optimal strategy (given expectations about others' behavior), and in the ability to detach practice instrumentally from intentions. Yet the motivation underlying the whole text is Adovardo Alberti's sincere plea for instruction concerning how to obtain and maintain *friendship*. On the one hand, therefore, the Florentine case forces us to give room in a theory of culture, and in particular political culture, to the actor as an undeniably reflexive implementer of culturally specific strategies. On the other hand, it also highlights the desire for relationships and the puzzle of how intrinsic relations can be secured through instrumental means. Where all agents are aware of the strategic subtlety of others, how can intrinsic relationships ever get locked in?

Actors negotiate their way into relationships by means of words. Even though words can be empty, they are the unavoidable instrument for this pursuit. As Allan Silver (1989, 288) has noted, "The conditions of Renaissance [that is, sixteenth-century] political life did not diminish the supreme importance of practical acts as forms of help between friends, but subtilized and complicated the relationship between acts and speech." And even if, as Silver continues, "speech became newly vulnerable to dissimulation" (1989, 289), "words—promises, oaths, undertakings—become crucial to assessing others' intentions."

In communicating with each other, actors express ideas about networks and comment on existing network ties, to identify where they are, who they are with, and where they want to go. Action in networks is simultaneously strategic, as the social capital perspective stresses, and constitutive of identities, as the network analysis perspective all too quickly assumes. Building a career depends not on rational action per se, but on socially and culturally embedded strategies, strategies that have to be derived from multiple identities and multiple network settings.

2

The Rhetoric and Design
of Florentine Letter Writing

When we communicate with others, we adopt recognizable styles or practices of interaction. When we work with multiple possible meanings of an interaction or relationship, we employ recognizable tropes for signaling switches in the pace and flow of conversation that demarcate which parts of our speech or writing ought to be attended to most. Likewise we employ devices for marking the beginning and ending of particular utterances or remarks. These devices "anchor" activity (Goffman 1974, chap. 8). In the last chapter I discussed some of these discursive tools in general sociological terms. In this chapter I describe the rhetoric—tropes and design—specific to fifteenth-century Florentine favor-seeking letters. I identify a list of regularities in the pattern of their construction and discuss some of the sources of those regularities. I see patronage letters as a corpus of patterned discourse,[1] a kind of local situation or style composed of "everyday interactional routines" (Eliasoph and Lichterman 2003, 779) with a distinctive form and character that constrains what writers can say and how they express themselves (Gibson 2000).

I locate this discussion of predominant designs against two major backdrops. One of these is Florentine social relations in general, which were highly strategic and frequently plagued by jealousy and anxiety. The other is the importance of proper form in Quattrocento religious, artistic, and literary culture. Strategy and formalism were inextricably bound together. I will draw on a variety of primary sources—*ricordanze*, advice books, religious and philosophical treatises, educational manuals—as well as secondary sources to make this point, sketching a map of key Quattrocento Florentine cultural practices, and adumbrating certain attitudes and values associated with those practices.

The pairing of strategy and formalism could perhaps also be expressed in terms of the pairing of patronage and rhetoric. Patronage is "a reflection of social norms and values, and . . . a determinant of individual and collective social and political behavior" (D. Kent 1987, 63). It was a pervasive feature of Quattrocento Florentine life, a basic means of achieving security and/or social advancement. Likewise, rhetoric and discussions of rhetoric were sites where Renaissance social "self-definition" was under construction; so rhetoric, too, speaks of and to a wider culture (Rebhorn 1995, 12). Indeed, one could plausibly argue that rhetoric—the art of verbal persuasion by means of clearly delineated figures and tropes—approaches being the defining feature of the Renaissance, an era of the emergence of humanism, enhanced social mobility, and decreased certainty concerning traditional moral authorities. Rhetoric was widely regarded as a tool with expansive application (Rebhorn 1995, 6). The issue, then, is to see how *patronage*, a constitutive principle of the everyday political world, and *rhetoric*, the master discipline and master topic of philosophical discourse, were conjoined. Rhetoric came to be seen as a critical device for seducing the powerful. Rhetoric, in short, was the art behind the construction and maintenance of Renaissance patronage networks. It was an art with fairly clear practical specifications. As a result, through rhetoric, letter writers converged on a set of procedural rules of thumb for presenting themselves to others.[2]

Chapter 3 will discuss in some detail a few of the dominant substantive frames used to give meaning—or more accurately, multiple meanings—to Florentine social interaction, to individuals' actions, and to significant events. In particular, I will document the multiple contents that were given over time to the inchoate notion of "honor." One has to talk about values and other meaningful points of connection when reaching out to others, and "honor" was a crucial touchstone for Renaissance Florentines. So, broadly speaking, this chapter is mostly about forms, and the next one is about content. However, the discussion cannot always be so clearly divided: some relational frames are almost ritually invoked, bleeding over into the area of formal design. These become not so much the flesh erected on the bones of stock turns of phrase, but the bones (or building blocks) themselves.

Procedural rules (how to proceed?) and inference rules (what to evoke?) are intimately connected. It is as much through the former as the latter that supplicants attempt to frame themselves legitimately in the eyes of would-be patrons. Sound procedure begets credibility—even granting that sound procedure is itself culturally defined. Nevertheless, failing the task of establishing rules of thumb for *inferring* what people really think or feel, it is hard for actors to get beyond surfaces. Whereas practices can signal *competence*, they rarely adequately signal *commitment*. The actors, and we observers, may see such strong convergence at the level of behavior (the use of certain rhetorical flourishes or other "tools") as to make it very difficult to infer meaningful differences between letter writers. We, too, often effectively hide behind formalized presentations of self. As Goffman notes, "Whatever it is that generates sureness is precisely what will be employed by those who want to mislead us" (1974, 251). Of this problem, Renaissance writers were acutely aware. Rhetoric was both medicine and poison (Rebhorn 1995, 132), available for good and bad uses. The distinction between "good" and "bad" rhetoric, that later authors sought to establish, could not be seriously sustained. As the rhetorician George of Trebizond knew in the 1430s, rhetoric was (and is) a dubious—but utterly indispensable—tool of communication and, inevitably, emotional persuasion.

And so, once we identify core practices and key frames, we are still left with the question: What does the style and substance of the composition of any particular letter or set of letters say about the person writing it? The presentation of a credible, trustworthy self needs to be subtly and repeatedly accomplished, not simply ritually reproduced. This is what later chapters will discuss in detail.

I begin with a very brief account of formalized practice in Quattrocento art and religion, examining notions of the meaningfulness and affective impact of formal representation, and then proceed to a brief summary of Florentine social relations. I next discuss the place of rhetoric, and in particular the rhetoric of writing letters, in the Middle Ages and the Renaissance, to identify structural and tactical elements that appear commonly in the letters I have examined. The rules of rhetoric that dominated official correspondence in the Middle Ages were hardly directly implemented in the personal correspondence of the 1400s. Further, the basic methods of letter composition changed significantly between the 1100s and the 1400s. Nevertheless, suggestive similarities between high rhetoric and everyday practices do exist. Quotidian letter writing was, to a considerable extent, a formalized, routinized, strategic interactional behavior. The culturally sanctioned practices that comprised letter writing were almost certainly part of the average patrician son's education (Grendler 1989). I conclude with some examples of letters. My goal is to identify a number of the specific threads Florentines owned before stitching them into a fabric of messages they wished to communicate to their alters. This fabric of messages would convey credible, trustworthy presentations of themselves.

Form in Art and Religion in Renaissance Florence

Michael Baxandall's discussion (1972) of an amateur's account of the differences among four painters—Ghirlandaio, Filippino Lippi, Perugino, and Botticelli—provides a convenient point of departure. We like to think of these artists as unique. But were these painters' styles their own, or more like "stocks of patterns, categories, and methods of inference . . . [for] visualizing what we have incomplete information about" (32)? Given that paintings were almost always commissioned by patrons (D. Kent 2000), for institutional locations and to facilitate certain kinds of institution-bound experiences, we should expect some non-personal regularity in artistic representation. This would be all the more true when considering specifically religious art. Various treatises such as the *Zardino de Oration* (Garden of prayer) of 1454 tell us that particular mental representations within prayer can and should kindle particular affects. Similarly, outward visual representations of an event such as the Annunciation will emphasize, by virtue of the specific standardized gestures they choose to depict, different emotional states of the persons depicted; and hence they also call forth those particular emotional states in the viewer. The parallel between physical gesture and mental condition was, for example, a central concern of Alberti's treatise on painting. A similar idea held for religious "drama": the gestural components of preaching (the *ars praedicandi*) were highly codified, first because of the difficulties involved with following the texts of Latin-only sermons, but also because such gestures were really thought to have precise affective impact.

This was the core idea behind a thirteenth-century prayer book, *De Modo Orandi*, still available in the fifteenth century, that articulated nine distinct modes of prayer: "one can precipitate a psychological state by assuming the gesture appropriate to it" (Hood 1990, 117). The book formed the basis of Fra Angelico's panels on the cell walls of San Marco in Florence. These panels accomplished two linked goals: 1) they depicted gestures designed to kindle affects of devotion in the self; and 2) they instructed viewers in the art of formal practices that would elicit a desirable response from God. They also helped to preserve the common bonds of the fractious members of the Dominican order who resided there (Hood 1990, 110). They did so, though, not by rigid stipulation of what behavior membership in the order entailed, but by skeletal representations of such behavior, thereby allowing individuals the freedom to discover their own psychospiritual path within those forms.

The case is similar in interaction. Actors need not directly express the values or norms of their culture but rather only infer or elicit them in some way or another. This elicitation is meant to have affective repercussions for both the *audience* (insofar as the writer is like an "artist") and the *self* (insofar as he is like a "supplicant"). This double impact was also stressed by early Renaissance rhetoricians. Speakers or writers must use vivid figures and tropes to elicit the appropriate emotional responses in their audiences, but they must also move *themselves* with their words — or at least feign being moved (Rebhorn 1995, 86–87, 232)! Proper form is an important component for eliciting the proper reaction.[3]

Examples could be multiplied many times over. Formalism was pervasive in Renaissance life (Trexler 1980). Formalized cultural practices were clearly understood to have affect-generating potential in self and audience. This is one way culture has both "tool" and "world" components (Wittgenstein 1958); we live in it, and we use it. These diverse aspects of culture — routine, cognitively supported practices, and values and affects called upon to shape or reinforce preferences — are not inherently separable from one another.

Other aspects of social life besides the artistic and the religious were also characterized by a flexible formalism. Peter Burke (1987, 81) has noted that early modern Italian culture was one in which speech and its accompanying gestures were of crucial importance in the presentation of self. The Renaissance city was the quintessential stage, Burke notes, for the kind of dramaturgy of the self that Goffman eloquently analyzed (Burke 1987, 8, 10). And as Burke writes in introducing his exploration of the elusive topic of the nature of spoken language in early modern Italy, "Language is a sensitive indicator of social relationships such as deference, familiarity, solidarity and so on, and also an active force in society, a vehicle for social mobility, for the assimilation of new recruits to a group, and so on" (79). In short, "talk" is an interactional vessel for making social connections (Harrison White 1992; Mische 2003), one sensitive to both standardized forms and affective, strategic bricolage and manipulation.

In what follows I will document the importance of formal, time-tested standardized practices in interpersonal relations and then discuss a number of these specific practices. But to do that, I must first present an account of the basic tenor and structural properties of these relations.

Florentine Social Relations

In a frequently cited characterization of Florentine social relations, Ronald Weissman (1982) has called the politics of everyday life in Florence "agonistic." The source of this contestation has been sought variously in holdovers from the Italian city-state's feudal past, the congestedness of the urban landscape, the ethos of the merchant, or the decline of corporatism, singly or in combination (Brucker 1983, 101). Among these, the decline of a corporatist political structure seems most compelling (Najemy 1982, 301; Brucker 1983, 97). The elitist, consensus-oriented regime that controlled the city from the late 1380s to the 1430s, and the Medicean regime that succeeded it, expanded the pool of eligibles for political office while simultaneously devising formal rules and informal strategies for limiting the participation of the vast majority of these eligibles and concentrating power in the hands of relatively few politically influential families. Individuals needed to pursue opportunities avidly in this world of limited resources and scarce (albeit varied) paths to upward mobility. Thus they engaged in behaviors designed to obtain favors from the influential few. Access to jobs, to marriages, to religious benefices, to tax relief, to recognition were all sought by the same means. Almost unavoidably, resources were obtained only through the intercession of others, frequently through relationships constructed across the boundaries of class and social prestige (F. W. Kent 2002).[4] Obtaining such intercession depended upon demonstrative displays of affection and expressions of loyalty, albeit often expressed in the midst of quite utilitarian, quotidian, vernacular letter writing (Najemy 1993, 18).

The chronicler Marchionne Stefani claimed in the fourteenth century that all conflict within Florence arose in contest for public offices and the status that they yielded. Neighborhoods were critical sites for this contestation, whether construed as the fiscal and administrative building blocks of the city (the *gonfaloni*) wherein office holders were nominated and tax burdens were assessed (see, for example, F. W. Kent and D. Kent 1982); or as the parishes (*popoli*) with their churches (Cohn 1980); or as the city squares (*piazze*) with their clusters of patrilineages that undoubtedly were central to the daily round of life (Eckstein 1995). Weissman's picture suggests strong intra-neighborhood allegiances forged on the basis of both strategic and unreflective behaviors; the rest of the city by contrast could not help but be a more hostile environment into which interpersonal links could be extended only with utmost care.[5]

Patrons occupied the interstitial positions within and among Florence's multiple social networks, affording information, materiel, services, and opportunities to disadvantaged clients on a dyadic basis, and often also brokering links to others through extended chains, either by linking their own clients to particular office holding or otherwise empowered third parties, or by delivering the goods to friends of their own clients. Using patronage required tact and circumspection but also a demonstrative, almost thespian virtuosity.[6] In most cases, cultivating friendships required "great patience" and "an almost incredible firmness of purpose" (Alberti 1969, 256) where "one slight error" (261) could engender fierce animosity or studied indifference. With the potential for so many cross-cutting loyalties, too, social ties were always in danger of disruption, or at least, in danger of yielding no payoff. Consensus and assurances of loyalty were sought, but always within a framework that permitted honorable exit. The ubiquity of instrumentality in friendship made intrinsic friendship that much more treasured, but also that much more difficult to identify—to parse out the intrinsic aspects from the instrumental. Intrinsically valued friendship without instrumentality was foreign to the Florentine consciousness (Trexler 1980; F.W. Kent 1991; Najemy 1993; Padgett and McLean 2002). Friendship was certainly idealized and formally demonstrated, but to the minds of suspicious Florentines it was rarely actualized.

This world of honor and shame, loyalty and deceit, was amply commented upon by contemporaries, notably by the diarist Paolo da Certaldo in the mid-fourteenth century, by Giovanni di Pagolo Morelli in his *Ricordi* begun in 1393, and by Leon Battista Alberti in his treatise, the *Della famiglia* of the mid-1430s. In the last of these, Giannozzo Alberti exclaims cynically, "Show me one whom you can trust with even the least of your secrets. The world is full of deceit" (Alberti 1969, 239). Likewise his nephew Adovardo remarks (1969, 266):

> The world is so full of human variety, differences of opinion, changes of heart, perversity of customs, ambiguity, diversity, and obscurity of values. The world is amply supplied with fraudulent, false, perfidious, bold, audacious, and rapacious men. Everything in the world is pro-

foundly unsure. One has to be far-seeing, alert, and careful in the face of fraud, traps, and betrayals.[7]

One craved friendship with another who was sincere and constant, but the environment ensured that dissimulation was chronic. As Giannozzo Alberti instructed his wife, "Call only him a friend whom I honor when he is present and praise when he is absent" (1969, 229).

A substantial chunk of the fourth book of Alberti's *Della famiglia* is given over to a discussion of different types of friendship, and of how to initiate such friendships—or "how to make ourselves well loved" (1969, 252).[8] Piero describes the various strategies by which he contrived to befriend the duke of Milan, Ladislas the king of Naples, and the pope. Each friendship required a different tactic. In the case of the duke, Piero first cultivated the friendship of a potential middleman, a lover of poetry who delighted in the recitation of Messer Antonio Alberti's poems, "which are full of ripeness and adorned with touches of much delicacy and grace" (253), and thence obtained an audience with the duke. Note here the aesthetic nature, if not precisely the formal properties, of Piero's solicitation. In the case of Ladislas of Naples, good fortune afforded Piero the opportunity to do the king a favor in the absence of any intermediary.[9] He resorted to praise and flattery to win the king's good graces: "I engaged in honorable and cheerful sport and was discreet in speech and *most decorous in every gesture*, so that I might continue to enjoy the good graces and benevolence of Ladislas" (261; emphasis added). Finally, in the case of the pope, friendship was strictly instrumental, based on a loan and conveying the appearance of openhandedness and generosity. Piero requested things that it was a priest's "duty" to provide—offices, benefices, favors—and did so repeatedly.

Paolo Da Certaldo offered advice of a similar kind, counseling his reader to seek out certain kinds of friends, especially when abroad—a doctor, a judge, a priest, one or two of the *grandi*—and to proffer them gifts once a year or so—a sword, a knife, falcons, a silk purse, and so on—in order to retain their favor (Branca 1986, 22, #113). He elaborated on the proper strategy later. One should become a friend of the secretary of the most powerful man, giving him something and asking for his help and counsel as a broker first (Branca 1986, 28, #133). Gift giving should accord with the status and virtue of the recipient, and it should be calibrated over time so that the well of gifts will not appear to run dry (Branca 1986, 87, #366).[10] Morelli summarily provided the same sort of advice: to acquire friendship with good and powerful men show them great love by serving them, flatter them by honoring their wisdom in consulting them concerning one's own affairs, and honor them in giving them good things to eat and drink and in baptizing their children (Branca 1986, 138f., 183).[11] Above all, he suggested, "Use courtesies toward them" (*usa verso di loro delle cortesie*) (Branca 1986, 182; also 111, 144, 168, 194).

Like Alberti, Morelli provides a laundry list of practices for developing *amicizia*, but through the use of *cortesia* he also encouraged the use of certain rules of etiquette, forms, or styles for engaging in these practices. "Make yourself an expert in speaking to citizens, to officials, to rectors . . . teach yourself the tenor of words, the kind approaches and flattering speech (*riverenze*) that one has to adopt" (Branca 1986, 198). Implicit here is a keen sense of how to use words properly, carefully being attentive to the audience addressed. Da Certaldo, too, connects praise and success to form: "In every affair of yours show decorum and you will be praised" (*in ogni tuo fatto abbi modo, e d'ogni tuo fatto arai lodo*). *Giusto modo* is a recurrent motif of this often disjointed work.

For all of these writers, in Alberti's (1969, 277) words, "to make friends it is necessary to study the gestures, words, customs, and conversations of others." They thought a fine greeting might be all that was needed to plant the possibility of friendship (273). Thus words, speech, and grammatical and rhetorical forms became the essential ingredients of making friends, especially in a world not conducive to identifying them with certainty. Even if reliable friends existed, they were not easily discovered. If persons, however, were not easily classified, at least Florentines could rely on codified behaviors by means of which to draw out those willing and able to be friends. This is the functional basis for the standardization of behavior in the interactions unique to particular cultures. Even if the forms themselves through which friends are discovered and confirmed are themselves ambiguous or polyvalent, like the flirtation gestures described by Peter Blau (1964, 76–85), they make interaction possible and recognizable.

That such regularities of strategic interaction existed is well documented using contemporary texts such as those of Alberti, Morelli, and da Certaldo. Yet these texts rarely indicate precisely what to say, the actual words and turns of phrase and styles to adopt in correspondence. To understand this, we must get to know the rules for the composition of letters, the dissemination of these rules, and the patterns with which we find particular verbal gestures deployed in actual correspondence.

The Medieval and Renaissance Letter-Writing Tradition

There were at least three distinct traditions of letter writing in Renaissance Italy: 1) the immense volume of private vernacular writing—by no means all of it patronage oriented—such as is studied in this book; 2) diplomatic and official letter writing; and 3) humanist writings in Latin that followed the form of the letter but had fictional recipients, or recipients incidental to their theme, and that were "generally intended for circulation and even publication in carefully arranged collections" (Najemy 1993, 18). The boundaries between these traditions could be fuzzy, but in the aggregate they were fairly distinct. Private letter writing is far more idiomatic, far less polished, far more often hasty in its composition, and so on, than the other types, although it is fraught with the presentation of complex motives through elaborate codes and conventions.

According to Ronald Witt (1983, 2000), the *ars dictaminis*—the medieval art of diplomatic letter writing—may have continued to dominate official correspondence down to the end of the fifteenth century, letter writing being one of the last genres to be influenced by humanistic currents of thought.[12] Nevertheless, some new styles and sensibilities invaded the composition of private correspondence beginning with Petrarch in the mid-fourteenth century. Petrarch deliberately distinguishes the plainness—studied though it undoubtedly is—of style in his letters to friends and acquaintances from a more ornate but artificial oratorical style (Najemy 1993, 27). The Florentine chancellor, Coluccio Salutati, writing around 1400, had received thorough *dictamen* training as a youth, and while this training was evident in his official letters, it is not clear to what extent it also animated his personal correspondence (cf. Witt 2000, 320–21). The boundaries between rhetorical genres were probably thought to be considerably more impermeable by Renaissance writers than they seem to us today. And the dissemination of detailed instruction in rhetoric was probably not widespread, even though young boys customarily did receive education in reading and writing, plus elementary business correspondence and notarial formulas, at a primary school or *botteghuzza* (Bec 1967, 383ff.; also see Rebhorn 1995, 236f.). Although it is tough to prove direct connections, nevertheless the patterned and persuasive quality of private letter writing is readily perceivable. Further, it is quite possible that "the importance of classical rhetoric in Renaissance culture had quite popular origins, rooted in the necessary verbal sensitivities required to negotiate the demands of everyday life" (Weissman

1989, 273). I will argue that something of the formal structure of medieval diplomatic letter writing—the so-called *ars dictaminis*—and the aims behind these formal properties carried over into the construction of private letters.

The Latin word *dictamen* comes from the verb *dictare* and in turn from the notion of dictation (Murphy 1974, 195 fn. 5). Thus the term implies a connection between oral communication and the letter as its written-down representation. Various extant letters from the 1400s comment on the imperfectness of the letter as a substitute for face-to-face communication, and yet Florentines saw it—or rather they deliberately constructed it—as an acceptable alternative.[13]

The *ars dictaminis* arose in the eleventh century with the monk Alberic of Montecassino, who applied rhetorical principles explicitly to letter writing and identified the genre explicitly as a written one, rather than a proxy for speech or oration. The letter was given a five-part organization: *salutatio* (formal greeting); *exordium* (also *proemium*, or *captatio benevolentiae*—usually an introduction to the content of the letter and a laudatory exhortation to the reader to capture his attention and goodwill); *narratio*; *petitio* (presentation of requests); and *conclusio*.

Pedagogically, the construction of the first two parts was emphasized most. In particular, salutations were constrained to show the appropriate sense of discrimination between sender and receiver. As the centuries progressed, sensitivity to such discriminations of status increased, so that with the florescence of feudalism, with its many ranks and variety of relationships, quite substantial collections of detailed (but thus inflexible and limiting) prescriptions for salutations and letter *formulae* became popular. These *formulae* seem to have a mechanical connection to the meaning they apparently convey; thus, where one might simply use the word "allegiance," one could enhance the effect by writing "due allegiance." Close friends could be identified as "the closest of friends," or the "dearest of favorites," or "linked together by an indissoluble chain of affection," or according to any of a number of other prescribed *formulae*, each with its own precise connotation. Minor distinctions in the perceived ranking of friends could be handled with minor changes of phrasing: a "bond of affection" could become "friendship," "fellowship," or "brotherhood," as the precise situation demanded.

The *exordium* was meant to render the addressee "attentive, docile, and well-disposed" (Murphy 1974, 205; Faulhaber 1978, 97); and certain *colores* (figures) were identified as proper for decorous beginnings of letters. Good-will could be secured by the sender "if he mention[ed] humbly something about his achievements or his duties or his motives," by the use of certain words (including notably "fatherly feeling" and "affection"), and most especially "if the extent of its [that is, the matter at hand's] future importance is openly set forth" (Murphy 1971, 17). Goodwill could in fact be expressed throughout the letter repeatedly, for example through the use of formal titles indicating the honor or glory of the recipient's office or rank. In a nutshell, the *exordium* presented the letter's "general, interpretive principle" (Shepard 1999, 6), or what I would call its "primary frame."

The third part, the *narratio*, was judged best if credibly genuine (*onesta*), and this could be best achieved by writing with brevity and clarity.[14] Guido Faba, the author of the *Summa Dictaminis* of 1228, instructed his readers here in the use of the *cursus*. The *cursus* was a system for placing words or phrases that followed one of three prescribed metrical cadences at the end of sentences to enhance the musicality and flow of the composition. Writers were instructed to vary their word order, in particular systematically varying the placement of the verb and selectively placing stress on important pronouns (Faulhaber 1978, 100). More elegant words were to be placed at the beginnings and ends of sentences where they could draw the most attention. The *dictatores* aimed—albeit through a fairly mechanical process—to instruct writers to the point that the rhythmic construction of clauses would become second nature.

Alberic, like many of the later Italian *dictatores*, largely ignored the last two parts of the letter, the *petitio* or *argumentatio*, and the *conclusio*, "concentrating on the psychological impact of the first parts instead" (Murphy 1974, 207). An important implication of this emphasis was that the nature of the letter was established—even determined—by the relative status of the addressee and the writer, rather than the subject matter, and the form of the letter would simply flow once the appropriate salutation had been chosen. Some writers accepted the possibility of shifting the order of the parts of the well-written letter, but for the most part the Alberician form stood (Witt 2000). Indeed it is a form recognizable to us today.

For the thirteenth-century *dictator* Bene of Florence, the *ars dictaminis* "increases eloquence, promotes favor, enlarges honors, and often enriches the needy" (cited in Seigel 1968, 209). Lawrence of Aquilegia (c. 1300) not only identified specific words as good (*bona*) or bad (*mala*) for use in letters, but also wrote, consonant with the dictaminal tradition, that "it is better to work from form than from material" (Murphy 1974, 259). Lawrence's view strongly suggests the routinizing tendency in thinking about letter writing in late medieval Europe. This tendency led directly to the *ars notaria*, dominant in Italy from 1250 on, a school that treated letters as official documents and was preoccupied with the physical, spatial representation of the letter on paper (Murphy 1974, 264).

The hegemony of the notary and his particular skills certainly had not ended by the fifteenth century (Martines 1968); in fact, the notary was frequently the filter through which written correspondence passed. "Lawyers, notaries, secretaries—all had to be familiar with the rules for drawing up formal documents as well as official and private letters (which accounts for the near-fusion of *dictamen* and *ars notaria* in later periods)" (Faulhaber 1978, 108). The tendency toward codified writing techniques meant that *dictamen* came to benefit urban leaders and merchants. It increasingly "allowed modestly educated laymen to produce acceptable petitions and official documents" (Shepard 1999, 9). Kristeller (1983) notes the existence of several *dictamen* treatises from fifteenth-century Italy: that of Gasparino Barzizza, who propounded the principles and techniques of Ciceronian rhetoric in the first decades of the Quattrocento (Monfasani 1988, 187ff.; Najemy 1993, 44; Fantazzi 1991); that of Jacopo Publicio, the author of a quite traditional 1460s dictaminal text; and that of Niccolò Sagundino, the clarity and brevity of whose manual pointed more ahead to the sixteenth century than backward to the fourteenth. The great humanist philologist Lorenzo Valla composed a manual on letter writing halfway through the fifteenth century (first published in 1503 in Venice) that was organized according to the hegemonic five-part structure, and Cristoforo Landino supplied perhaps the first letter-writing manual in the Tuscan vernacular in 1485 (Najemy 1993, 42ff.).

Beginning with Petrarch, but accelerating in the fifteenth century, a new rhetoric emerged, constitutive of Renaissance humanism and based on imitation of the classics, not the recipes or templates of the *dictatores*. The humanists dispensed with the idea of a strict linkage between verbal cues and the substance of requests, as well as a strict enactment of the role relationships between letter writer and recipient based on the design of opening salutations, replacing strict linkage with a mimetic technique of letter composition. This entailed the loose imitation of exemplary letter models and more playfulness with the conventions of letter salutations, the goal being to convey something like "individual personality" through writing

(Witt 2000, 317f.). This development seemed to parallel the loosening up of the Florentine corporatist political and social structure in the late Trecento and early Quattrocento, which precipitated increased interaction between favor-seeking individuals and potential patrons that cross-cut or stepped outside of traditional role relationships.[15] Notwithstanding this change in the concept of the letter, however, these humanists occupied the same occupational niche as the earlier *dictatores*, working as secretaries for principalities and communes, or as teachers, frequently using these positions as paths to upward social mobility. Additionally, the early humanists favored similar genres as their predecessors — treatises on rhetoric and letter writing, funeral orations, ambassadorial speeches, and so on (Seigel 1968, 213). They "elevated the letter to a favorite literary genre to be used for many purposes" (Monfasani 1988, 194), and in such letters decorum remained a prized standard. Consequently we may assume "a direct link between medieval *ars dictaminis* and humanist epistolography" (Murphy 1983, 8; Witt 1988, 54).

The *ars dictaminis* arose in response to the critical need in the late eleventh century for tools to present material clearly and concisely and for managing the practical exigencies of life, exigencies that only the rare letter-writing genius could negotiate without assistance (Murphy 1974, 199). By the late twelfth century and the early thirteenth, its aims included not only clarity and concision, but also persuasive power (Shepard 1999). This fact would have made it an apt model to be adapted later for strategic communication between clients and their potential patrons. The *dictatores*, like the artists who depicted standardized gestures to represent internal spiritual states, regarded the letter as capable of communicating intentions and establishing interpersonal bonds reliably and effectively.

Education: The Scope of Dictaminal Influence in the Fifteenth Century

How much were contemporaries from various urban classes exposed to an education in the kinds of compositional principles outlined above? Strictly speaking, very little, since *dictamen* was most fully taught at the university level. And yet, Paul Grendler claims (1989, 111, 77), the intensely rule-driven system of *dictamen* definitely colored pre-university educational principles, even if we cannot document its precise place or extent in the curriculum. The literacy rate in Florence was undoubtedly high; according to the chronicler Giovanni Villani (1935, 361), between two-thirds and five-sixths of Florentine male children in the mid-1300s had some schooling. This number is certainly inflated, and yet schooling was undoubtedly common. By 1480, Grendler (1989, 78) claims, many Florentine boys studied Latin grammar, with an overall literacy rate of more than 30 percent. This total included practically all sons of nobles and wealthy merchants, sons of professionals, and the sons of many craftsmen and shopkeepers.

We know that instructors hired by various communes were still teaching *dictamen* in 1410: in that year, Faenza advertised for a teacher skilled in such matters (Grendler 1989, 117). Until 1427 Spoleto advertised for a teacher skilled in grammar, and only in 1432 did a shift to the humanistic focus on oratory occur (137). As noted above, Gasparino Barzizza was among the notable teachers in this period, a transitional figure who endorsed humanistic scholarship but clung to medieval authors and methods and sought the reform rather than the repudiation of *dictamen* (126). The new humanists continued the dictaminal practice of tailoring their message to their audience; it was just that now greater flexibility was introduced into this practice of customization. Cicero's *Epistulae ad familiares* (Letters to his friends) was rediscovered in 1392, an event of great importance for the curriculum. Guarino Guarini compiled fifty of Cicero's letters into an anthology and used them in his lower-division instruction, perhaps as early as the 1410s in Venice, and certainly by 1430 (Grendler 1989, 122). In 1437, Stefano Fieschi compiled a phrase book (the *Synonyma Sententiarum*) for "boys and youths" wanting to learn to write eloquent letters. He structured the book by providing Cicero-inspired sample sentences in Italian appropriate for any *exordium* (as well as for other parts of a letter, presumably), and a variety of translations—simple and embellished—of each of these sentences into Latin. This allowed the student to paste together letters in a way very similar to the method provided by the *ars dictaminis*. Substantively, the work was classical in its reliance on Cicero and in its reduction of the raw number of *formulae*; but methodologically, it was largely dictaminal in spirit. This text enjoyed an extraordinary distribution throughout the fifteenth century. A letter of December 5, 1439, from Giovanni Cappelli to Agnolo di Palla Strozzi (*C.S.* III, 128: 130) explicitly mentions Cicero's "libro di amicitia," but whether this means his *Laelius de Amicitia* or the letters to his friends is not entirely clear.[16]

It is difficult to know how much lag time occurred between the introduction of such a curriculum into the schools and its concrete imitation in private correspondence. Grendler notes that those with humanist training received favor at the papal court from 1447 onward—some twenty or so years after the first significant changes in pedagogy (1989, 136). Only with the rediscovery of the full text of Quintilian, and of Cicero's *De oratore* in 1421, did change accelerate, and then predominantly at the highest levels of the humanist movement. Moreover, although we tend to associate the Renaissance with the development of primary rhetoric (that is, speech), or at least with writing strictly imitative of eloquent speech (Alberti's dialogue, for example), really secondary rhetoric dominated the schools: "few middle- and upper-class men would orate but all would have to write letters" (Grendler 1989, 209).

Such instruction complemented training in practical mathematics using the abacus (Grendler 1989, 160). This is essentially what Morelli counseled (Branca 1986, 192). Morelli further suggested reading certain of the classics—the works of Boethius, Seneca, Cicero, Virgil—almost certainly key authors in the primary education canon, as well as Dante and other poets. One needed to learn how to read in order to examine notarized documents for oneself, and especially to know how to read letters and to write properly composed letters with proper grammar (Branca 1986, 199).[17] It is this practical focus of the merchant-writer tradition, as discussed by Bec (1967) for example, that ultimately most cogently suggests that time-tested principles inculcated via primary education were followed at least in some way in letter composition.

Da Certaldo counseled his readers about business correspondence in his compendium, noting that it was always wise to read the incoming mail before sending anything out oneself (Branca 1986, 49, #251). Giannozzo Alberti (Alberti 1969, 197) advised his protégés always to have a pen in hand to record transactions and to respond quickly when circumstances required, and Morelli also suggested writing everything down clearly and at length in account books (Branca 1986, 178). The practical rules of thumb that evidently guided merchant behavior, including the distinct *mercantesca* script in which nearly all non-diplomatic correspondence of this period was composed, no doubt also contributed mightily to the convergence of merchant favor-seekers on particular (and expected) forms of self-presentation. The vocabulary, structure, and style of extant late-fourteenth-century commercial correspondence, such as that of the Datini company in Milan (Frangioni 1994), is sufficiently like that of patronage correspondence from the early and mid-fifteenth century to suggest considerable continuity with the past.[18] In short, although most educated men would not have had dictaminal training strictly speaking, it was a sufficiently time-honored discipline that some of its compositional rules and strategies must have infiltrated patrician educational curricula.

Actual Practices

In sum, letter writing was an important element of the Florentine patronage system, and training in the canonical structure and techniques of letter writing had a long and distinguished history. In addition, the valorization of rhetoric and the expansion of its application in the Renaissance supported the strategic use of persuasion in interpersonal interaction. Now we turn to an enumeration of some of the concrete techniques and framing devices found in patronage correspondence, attending where possible to how these practices resonate with the dictaminal tradition and the wider spectrum of Florentine cultural practice. In what follows, I put my labels for these tactics and devices in boldface type.[19]

Common letter salutations included "dearest friend" (*amico carissimo*), "my honored elder" or "superior" (*honorevole maggiore*), and "respected sir" (*spectabilis vir*), but these could be adapted to liken the patron more to an honored family member: "honored as an elder brother" (*MAP* II, 154), or "noble brother and friend" (*C.S.* III, 120: 317), or "eminent and honored one, uniquely like a father to me" (*MAP* III, 151). One "rule" of patronage correspondence, thus, was the use of the rhetoric of **fictive kinship** and/ or **marking status relationships** to indicate connectedness. Even this most ritualized of letter-writing techniques was calibrated to construct the social distance between writer and recipient, and thereby establish a role relationship that would guide the would-be patron in his evaluation of how (or whether) to offer assistance.

Another vital means of marking social distance between writer and recipient was the **choice of personal pronouns**. *Voi* indicated not only some lack of familiarity, but typically also some degree of respect. The use of *tu* was somewhat more complicated, signaling familiarity and intimacy on many occasions, but potentially also signifying a kind of superiority or condescension. Sometimes, indeed, writers choose to qualify their use of particular pronouns in order to hedge their bets on how much letter recipients shared their understanding of the social distance between them.

As part of the introduction, letter writers routinely indicate the date or occasion of their last letter to the recipient, and indicate when or if they received the last correspondence from the recipient. While practically oriented,[20] this device also constructed a kind of **interactional continuity** and permitted writers a formulaic entry point into their requests. It was also a stock device for explaining the beginning of a new interaction. "I have not written to you recently, there not having been any need" (*non essere suto di bisogno*, or *non essere acaduto il bisogno*) is an extremely common opening to letters in the 1420s and 1430s.[21] This opening is sometimes abruptly, sometimes not so abruptly, followed by the phrase, "And the reason for this letter is . . ." (*e la cagione di questa è*)—a blunt move that is far less frequently made in letters to Lorenzo the Magnificent later in the century. By means of this phrase, the writer signals a turn from the preamble of the letter, including a summary of the past, to the specific, present problem the client faces. The abruptness of this transition seems to be typically a function of the social distance between the writer and the recipient: it is immediate if the writer and the recipient are intimates or equals, delayed if they are not.

The request for favor is almost always signaled by the use of the phrase, "I pray that it be pleasing to you that . . ." (*vi priego che vi piaccia*). The second half of this formula is in the **subjunctive tense**. Consequently, the choice of wording highlights the conditionality of requests and communicates deference toward the recipient of the request. This is an important way that subtle signs of writers' experience of vulnerability in their requests for assistance are inscribed into the very grammar of patronage correspondence.

Another stock element is the closing **generalized reassurance** of loyalty or commitment: "If you see anything for me to do, advise me of it and I will do it *willingly*" (*volentieri*; for example, *MAP* II, 112), or "I am yours in everything and recommend myself to you" (*sono vostro in ogni chosa e a voi mi raccomando*; *MAP* II, 311), or "I pray this of you *as much as I know and am able*" (*quanto so e posso*; for example, *MAP* II, 243). These closings often indulged in the use of **superlatives**: for example, "I am your *least servant*" (*minimo servidore*; *MAP* II, 328), or "so shall I always be completely faithful to you" (*MAP* XIII, 27). It is hard to convey how standardized these expressions actually were, but in a sample of over 1,100 letters, the expression *quanto so e posso* ("as much as I know and am able") or its variants appears in 132 letters; the promise to take care of business "willingly" appears in 97 letters; and on more than 24 different occasions writers used the exact formula of referring to themselves as "your least servant." Clearly these were widely disseminated phrases.

As with opening salutations, these expressions of commitment were often (though not always) calibrated in accordance with the relative social status of letter writer and recipient (D. Kent 1978, 86; for a detailed argument to this effect, see McLean 1998). Yet running alongside these expressions of commitment were expectations of assistance, or what could be called **rhetorical brinkmanship**: for example, "you know how great my need is" (*MAP* II, 185), or "I'm sure you will be successful [in obtaining a position for me]" (*MAP* II, 78), or "you know how much I was treated unjustly" (*Conv. Soppr.* 78, 324: 108). In fact, one could argue that the pretend naiveté adopted by writers who reported that they had not received responses in the beginning of their letters combined an outward gesture subtly giving the patron the benefit of the doubt with an inferred expectation of assistance. The tactics of rhetorical deference and rhetorical brinkmanship, so curiously mixed in the practices espoused by Morelli, are frequently combined in these letters, melding two key cognitive components of client-age—deference and reciprocal obligation—into a single interaction.

Letters were often transported by means of intermediaries, and it was common practice to identify these intermediaries in the first sentence of letters. More tellingly, in the body of the letter, clients often referred to "the friends" (*gli amici*), or referred to "friends of our friends" in their letters. In doing so, they indicated their expectation that supporters of the Medici would work as a more or less coherent group attentive to the needs and the honor of all its members (D. Kent 1978, 91). In both instances, writers self-consciously understood the relations of patronage in terms of a social **network** that they **actively constructed** in the course of making each request. Thus to Averardo de' Medici, Bartolomeo Ridolfi identified a potential recipient of assistance as follows: "a friend and relative of your and my own dearest friends" (*MAP* III, 126). Likewise, Cosimo de' Medici wrote to Pazzino di Palla Strozzi in December 1436 on behalf of Rienzo di Biagio del Cascina: "[He has been] a dear friend to me, and likewise his father always was a friend of our company here" (*C.S.* III, 120: 138). And Domenico Bartoli wrote to Lorenzo de' Medici on June 5, 1472: "I have seen what you wrote to me, and for love of you I will take it as recommended to me, for you know that your friends are my friends" (*che sai che gli amici tuoi sono miei*) (*MAP* XXVIII, 205). Recall also that in the first chapter I discussed the use of indexical language in discourse to locate speaker/writer and hearer/recipient in relation to each other and to draw relevant social boundaries. **Pronouns** were essential ingredients in this task of drawing boundaries: again, he was "a friend and relative of *your* and *my own* dearest friends; "*your* friends are *my* friends" (emphasis added).

A laundry list of standardized letter chunks and phrases for signaling them is admittedly difficult to follow in the abstract. Identifying them as they operate in particular letters is therefore an important means of proceeding. For example, then, a number of these devices and regularities appear together in the following letter of February 4, 1429[30] from Francesco di Michele degli Arrighi to Averardo de' Medici in Pisa (*MAP* II, 175):

> Dearest and great father, Since you left here I have not written, there not having been any occasion. However from your [friends or relatives] there, I hear all the news that you are well—Thanks be to God! I think that you know how Giovanni d'Astore left the cash account, and that Papino di Gerozzo overdrew [it] in his exchange [transaction], such that I pray of you that it be pleasing to you to write two verses down there to Andrea de' Bardi [Averardo's banking partner], if he sees fit to place me in the position where Papino was, that is, at the salary he had, and that I be recommended to him. For you know well my need to earn something now more than ever. So, for the love of God, do not neglect to write to him a couple of lines that I might have as soon as possible that place or another. I have nothing else to say except this, if there is anything I can do [for you], advise me of it and I shall do it willingly.

Note this letter's rough correspondence to the formal structure of the *ars dictaminis* guidelines: 1) an opening salutation (again invoking the image of fatherhood); 2) a kind of *captatio benevolentiae* with the expression of thanks to God for Averardo's health; 3) a brief narration of the case at hand; 4) a petition for a favor, in this case a promotion in the firm; and 5) in conclusion, a kind of repetition or continuation of the *captatio benevolentiae*, claiming willingness to carry out any task that Averardo might request of him. In addition, this letter features the "I pray of you that it be pleasing to you" formula (*vi priego che vi piaccia*) for phrasing the actual request, and the "There is nothing more to say except that" formula (*Nè altro a dire se non che . . .*) to begin the final sentence. Both are stock phrases in fifteenth-century patronage letters. As I noted above, the first directly signals the arrival of the moment of request. The second signals its end, as well as occasionally marking a shift from the specific favor requested to a generalized assurance of loyalty or friendship. As with the first letter cited above, the phrase "you know well my need" introduces an assumption of long-term friendship or intimacy between petitioner and addressee. Finally, we find here the functional trope of beginning letters with an account of when the most recent correspondence had occurred, in order to assure the other that no letter had been lost, and that the relationship between sender and recipient, client and patron, had not been ruptured.

Consider a second example, this time a letter of December 12, 1438, from Johannes de Ghivizzano in Lucca to Cosimo de' Medici (*MAP* XI, 193). Here the writer responds to an earlier request for a favor rather than posing his own. Thus we see here how a connection previously forged is strengthened through interaction, and specifically how the phenomenon of calling in a debt is managed.

> Magnificent and generous sir, honor[ed] like a father, Recently I received one of your letters from your Barto[lomeo] Baldovini, which I saw quite willingly and heard with delight, and regarding what Bartolomeo told me of your part, I am responding to you briefly: that even as I recognize your request to be (as you say) most just and reasonable, and you have no need of entreaties, I am struck by no less than your great humanity and mildness in asking and begging [a favor of] me, where one mere notice would be enough. I will willingly work to provide every (*ogni*) favor in this your affair and any (*ogni*) other affair where I were to see and were to recognize my ability to do profit and honor to you and every (*ogni*) other friend of yours. I promise you (*Prometandovi*) that where there is a need I will not tire[?] of being asked—as though it were my own affair. I pray (*Pregandovi*) in conclusion that when anything should occur for your comfort and honor where you should see that I may do anything, only make that I should hear it and be advised of it, and the work shall demonstrate my spirit and intention. Advising you (*Avisandovi*) that, likewise in every (*ogni*) matter that touches me, I will place in you the confidence such as in my own honored father and elder, and to you I recommend myself.

First note the salutation, which contains two components: 1) a heightened version of the standard "Respected sir" formula, stressing Cosimo's magnificence and generosity, and 2) an additional clause treating Cosimo metaphorically as a father. Both parts posit a role relationship between recipient and sender, one that emphasizes the protective and nourishing functions of the patron. The fatherly imagery is repeated at the end of the letter (what in the *ars dictaminis* would be called the *conclusio*), a closing parenthesis to the father frame used in the salutation. Patron-client relations in many different contexts employ father-son imagery (Eisenstadt and Roniger 1984), and it was abundantly used in papal diplomatic correspondence in the Middle Ages (Shepard 1999).

In addition, a number of other techniques and expressions are found here that are spread more diffusely throughout the bulk of Florentine patronage correspondence. First, we find, at the outset, the assimilation of the aims and intentions of the writer to the aims and intentions of the addressee (Shepard 1999). Johannes received Cosimo's letter "with delight," and he agrees with Cosimo's previous framing of the request as "just and reasonable." Here is imagery suggestive of long-enduring friendship and trust, as in the public letters of the Florentine chancellor, Coluccio Salutati (cf. Witt 1976, 45). Second, Johannes explicitly dedicates himself to Cosimo's honor and profit, or advantage—in Italian, *onore et utile*. We typically expect tension between these two goals; what is conducive to our advantage is often achieved in dishonorable ways, and what redounds to our honor often provides us with no direct material benefit. In the first place, this tension was somewhat foreign to medieval and Renaissance persons. *Amicizia*—friendship—inherently conjoined instrumental assistance with emotional attachment (Silver 1989, 1990). Second, the substantive connection between honor and advantage did not completely obliterate the analytical distinction between them. Cognizant of the possible tension between honor and advantage, medieval and Renaissance authors routinely followed Ciceronian tradition and paired these two words as a stock phrase in their rhetorical practice, as if to persuade the reader that they converged serendipitously in this particular request.[22] This, in short, was a **stock lamination of frames** for persuading a patron that a particular course of action was the best one, or for indicating the multiple bases of one's loyalty. Third, note the structural rhythm of the last three sentences, each beginning with a gerund in the Italian, lending a kind of natural cadence to the letter—a hint of the *cursus* used in diplomatic correspondence in previous centuries. We see other repetitions as well, such as the repetition of the word *ogni* (every, any) to stress the unconditionality of the writer's promises.

Finally, the following letter of August 12, 1459, from Stagio Barducci to Pier Francesco di Lorenzo de' Medici (*MAP* V, 748), provides an interesting commentary on the concern with social distance between writer and recipient, as well as highlighting certain techniques for capturing the goodwill of the recipient.

> Dear to me as an elder brother, I know that one could ascribe it to presumption (*imputare a presunzione*) that I am asking you (*tu*) for something with such familiarity (*alla dimesticha*), not yet having had occasion to do anything easily for you, although I wish that you would find yourself in need of me. And considering your nature and

fine manners (*buona usanza tua*), that you are a generous and liberal provider of whatever benefice you can, I am confident—not by my merits as I said, but because of your kindness (*gentilezza*)—that I may pray of you that it be pleasing to you for love of me to be the means by which the bearer of this letter, who is Bruno di Lorenzo di Panutio, my good friend, that he, by means of you, be served with a position with the Sei della Rocca da Valiano for one year. . . . which to us is little, but to him will be a singular favor, and to me also, for the love I have of him. And again I promise you that this is my special interest, and thus I am asking it, obligating myself to you however you will want satisfaction—although in every way, as you must believe, I am most prepared to do you pleasure.

Stagio allows that it may appear presumptuous to use the familiar *tu*, especially given that the exchange of favors has not yet proven to be reciprocal. Thus he must mark his adoption of informality in such a way that he does not give up deference to Pier Francesco entirely. Beyond that, many of the stock compliments of the time—your *buona usanza*, your *gentilezza*—are introduced to win Pier Francesco's favor. And finally, although it is not explicit, Stagio melds utilitarian and intrinsic valuations or framings of the request. Repeatedly he asserts the importance of love—love of Pier Francesco, and love of Bruno—as a motive for granting the request. Yet at the same time, he reminds Pier Francesco that granting the favor will be relatively costless to him, but well-nigh priceless in Bruno's estimation. It is an opportunity to get something for nothing.

Conclusion

There are regular patterns of practices in Quattrocento favor-seeking letters. This regularity even became a serious problem. Dale Kent (1987, 74) notes that frequently different members of the Medici family would sponsor different potential clients indistinguishably from one another, recommending several persons with the same enthusiasm. While summoned by Kent to indicate the density and complexity of Florentine patronage networks, this fact might as easily be summoned to support the claim for the regularity of cultural practices in Renaissance Florentine letter writing and the decision-making problems such standardization posed.

In this chapter I have argued how form and regularity mattered to Renaissance letter writers, and I have described some of the routine techniques and phrases letter writers adopted to pursue the favors and offices that were the substance of their social and political careers. To conclude, I present a summary of the structural features and some of the stock phrases and turning points used in letters as a kind of checklist for readers as we proceed to more detailed analyses of letters in subsequent chapters.

In reading patronage letters as a corpus of patterned discourse, we should attend to the following general properties:

1. Salutations: a starting point for constructing the role relationship between writer and recipient.
2. Banal preamble material: recapitulating the history of the relationship or accounting for gaps in that history and identifying relevant third parties.
3. Insertions of (often stock) phrases designed to curry favor with the recipient before the narration of the problem.
4. Typically a brief narration of the problem, introduced with the phrase "E la cagione di questa è" ("And the reason for this letter is . . .").
5. Cobbling together multiple justifications for receiving assistance, a tactic captured most notably in the "honore et utile" formula but present in other forms as well—most notably in letters of recommendation.
6. The petition for assistance, typically and most forcefully signaled with the "E pertanto vi priego che vi piaccia" formula ("And therefore I pray of you that it be pleasing to you").
7. Conclusions: often begun with "Non altro a dire" ("Nothing more to say"), and typically involving reassurances of a general willingness to be of service, and an explicit recommendation of oneself to the recipient of the letter.

To the extent any of these elements is dropped, or to the extent an element is more elaborately developed, we will see departures from the standard form. Then we can seek the significance of these departures, possibly in the status relationship between sender and recipient, and certainly in the strategic choices the writer is making in his presentation of self.

3

The Socially Contested Concept of Honor

Lacking credit, it was necessary that we gather our resources and withdraw into ourselves to pay everyone, and to beg money from friends and to contrive with every means (*operare con ogni ingegno*), with losses and interest charges and expenses, not to go bankrupt and not to have shame (*vergogna*). And although my partner would have liked to go bankrupt so as to avoid losses and charges, I decided I was more willing to be ruined economically than to lose honor (*disfatto dell'avere che dell'onore*).

Goro Dati, *Libro segreto*

I am certain, for as long as you will be alive, never will I neglect to do what is satisfying to you. Moreover, I am stirred to say that I would hold dear your honor more than my own profit.

Ciaio di Pagolo dalla Scarperia to Averardo de' Medici, April 30, 1430

To round off these instructions, let me say what has always seemed to me the most important thing in anyone's life. It is one thing without which no enterprise deserves praise or has real value. No authority or dignity can be maintained without it. It is the ultimate source of all the splendor our work may have, the most beautiful and shining part of our life now and our life hereafter, the most lasting and eternal part—I speak of honor (*onestà*).

Leon Battista Alberti

There is little doubt that Renaissance Florentines were mightily concerned with honor (Kirshner 1977; Trexler 1980; Weissman 1982; Weinstein 2000). The resolve that Goro Dati expressed in his personal memoirs—to protect his honor rather than run away from his commercial obligations—exemplifies one aspect of it. Economic life was imbued with a calculus of honor and shame, as well as a calculus of profit and loss (Weissman 1982, 35; Padgett and McLean 2002).

The elective and appointive offices of the commune were referred to as *onori* (honors), an etymological indication of how considerations of honor were essential to official Florentine political life. *Onori* were integral elements in the construction of an honorable career. Furthermore, factional loyalists such as Ciaio di Pagolo dalla Scarperia, a lifelong client of the Medici, could express their devotion by adapting the rhetorical pairing of honor and profit—*onore et utile* being a stock phrase of the time—to their own ends. I am more committed to the protection and increase of your honor, Ciaio claims here, than I am concerned about my own well-being. Thus honor was also essential to unofficial political life, in the workings of patronage.[1] Indeed, making a claim to hold someone else's honor dear is itself an implicit claim to a special kind of honor for oneself.

The last passage cited above, which appears toward the end of Book II of Alberti's *I Libri della famiglia*, presents honor strikingly as the cardinal orienting moral concept for Florentines. Alberti's character Lionardo, his spokesman of moderation, reason, and the new humanist culture, goes on to claim that honor is our "shadow" from which we take counsel, always beside or inside us weighing and judging our actions, and standing by us as a public and private evaluative or normative measure of those actions. When we behave dishonorably, we feel as though this dishonor is made public—we feel the shame of our bad behavior. Honor gives us our sense of integrity.[2]

"Honored" and "honorable" are ubiquitous elements of salutations in Renaissance correspondence, and evocations of the notion abound in the texts of those letters as well. Meanwhile, the closely associated concept of nobility became a stock topic of disputation among Quattrocento humanists (Rabil 1991). But while the words *onore*, *onestà*, and *nobiltà* were repeatedly used, the content ascribed to them could vary rather widely according to time, place, and user. What exactly did honor, or acting honorably, entail? Writers seeking favors or recommending their friends to powerful patrons often asked for help according to the demands of honor, or within the limits set by honor. But what concretely made an "honorable" person feel obliged to assist others? And what exactly did the Florentines mean when referring to action that would be within the limits prescribed by honor, or, as they would say, "saving" honor (*salvando l'onore*)?

This chapter addresses these questions by adumbrating the history of honor as a social idea in late medieval and Renaissance Florence.[3] It introduces various concepts and cognitive frameworks associated with and giving significance to the notion of honor and honorable practice that appeared in Florentine culture over a period of roughly two centuries. I make three basic claims.

First, I posit that discussions of the concept in philosophical treatises, advice manuals, and *ricordanze* (personal memoirs) comprise a set of collective representations about a key moral principle of late medieval and early Renaissance life. These representations are not completely consistent. Indeed, particular texts can be somewhat confused, and certainly multivocal, about what honor is and what it entails. In the aggregate as well as within particular texts, the culture of honor is a dialogue among competing claims—a conversation revolving around shared points of contention rather than a coherent vision (Laitin and Wildavsky 1988; Bourdieu 1998, 78). Not surprisingly, many of the Florentine humanists adopted the dialogue genre to discuss honor and nobility, to reflect faithfully the disputes over the meanings of these terms (Marsh 1980).

Second, I track changes in these collective representations over time, and I suggest that these changes are rooted in the balance of status among competing groups in Florentine society during these different periods of social and political development. As Eiko Ikegami succinctly states in her research on the culture of samurai honor in Japan, "From this mutuality of symbolic and social-structural realms there follows an important understanding: structural changes in this community inevitably affect its style of honor" (1995, 24). Still, this mapping is not a simple one. The meanings, or connotations, of honor do not simply succeed one another. More accurately, additional innovative meanings are agglomerated onto preexisting ones. Sometimes, too, the content given to honor does not simply reflect the characteristics of the group that sponsors it. Instead, a group crafts an innovative notion of honor in a field of preexisting contending meanings that shape what it can legitimately and uniquely claim. Thus honor is a relational field of contending meanings (Bourdieu 1998, 4–7; Bourdieu 1984, passim), and these meanings can become somewhat detached from their original proponents.

Third, I suggest that these changing and accumulating representations of honor are referred to, combined, adapted, and transformed when used by actors in everyday interactional settings such as patronage letters. Since honor is inherently a relational concept—that is, the sense of self-worth that it encapsulates is integrally tied to the image others have of us—tracking its changing meaning is particularly urgent for understanding the construction of relationships between individuals that written correspondence aimed to accomplish. We need to become acquainted with honor to discern how Florentines accomplished the presentation of themselves as worthy recipients of favor in the patronage-based Florentine state of the fifteenth century. That is because honor, and from the late fourteenth century, *amicizia*, represented master tropes for crafting relations in a variety of interleaved domains of life, whether economic, social, political, marital, or diplomatic.

Some General Points about Honor

To comprehend honor as a cultural complex, we must attend to certain ironies inherent in it. One of these concerns the interplay of individual and group. Frequently making a claim to honor involves an implicit assertion of self-reliance, and yet the culture of honor often resides in societies where patronage is widespread and one has to be constantly running to others to get what one needs! Autonomy can be something of a fiercely preserved fiction. Alberti presents this irony in his *Della famiglia*. Lionardo Alberti argues that a good father should strive to "leave behind for his children so much of fortune's goods that they might never need to speak that most bitter word, most hateful to a free man's mind: 'I pray of you'" (1969, 65).[4] But this phrase—*io ti prego*—was a defining element of Florentine patronage interaction.

Further, contention over the group versus individual basis of honor was a chronic feature of the Florentine debate over nobility. Nobility, I suggest, is the group (or lineage) counterpart to the individual concept of honor, precisely because it is in practice often predicated of a whole class (or line) of people rather than of any one in particular, and the duties of that group come to be imposed on its members. The stock response to this attribution and desire to treat nobility or virtue as coterminous with social group boundaries in the Florentine milieu was to insist upon personal merit as the foundation for nobility, while arguments about its biological, social, or juridical basis were attacked and refuted.

A second irony is that despite the fact honor talk can be quite demonstrative, it also provides a set of gestures that in their standardization shroud one's true intentions and help forestall overt conflict. "Talking the talk" may delay forcing one to "walk the walk." Furthermore, in a patronage-based system, honor talk provides patrons with respect and clients with respectable grounds for their subordinate status (Eisenstadt and Roniger 1980, 1984). A good deal of the culture of honor revolved around standardized gestures, or etiquette (cf. Arditi 1998).

Undoubtedly etiquette was extremely important in late medieval and Renaissance Florence. Countless manuals gave advice on how to write letters, how to win friends, and how to handle countless other problems (Bell 1999). But Florentines could not simply use the recommended words in their own writing. They needed more than a superficial set of practical guidelines of what to say and do to win acceptance and gain friends. As Adovardo Alberti remarks in Book 4 of the *Della famiglia*, they needed a subtle sense of the multiple meanings or significations of those practices. This knowledge could guide them toward a deeper understanding of each other, thus making the relationships they forged more durable and genuine (Alberti 1969, 264–67):

> I certainly agree, Lionardo, that the things Piero said [about recruiting friends] all seemed to be wise and sound and full of prudence. . . . But it seems to me that I want some other sort of thread and texture in talk on this subject. . . . To deal with human wickedness in all its boldness, daring, and greed one must be able to remain constant, temperate, and full of inner strength. These are the qualities I would like to see actually practiced by a man whose friendship I hoped to gain and enjoy. These are qualities not just to be learnedly categorized and almost diagrammed.

In short, Florentines wanted to know that their friends were true friends and would deal with each other honorably. Formulae of self-presentation were one kind of signal, as I outlined in chapter 2, but using significant and widely understood frames of meaning—conceptions of honor—in the appropriate contexts communicated more about how friends should (and could) construe the content of their relationship with each other. Different definitions of honor have conflicting significances for conduct. Thus, we need to trace out different views of honor at the macro-historical level to know which meanings of honor might be in play at any given time.

The Changing Contours of Honor in Renaissance Florence

For the balance of this chapter I outline—briefly and selectively—competing accounts of what constitutes nobility or honorability from Trecento and Quattrocento Florence. To assist the reader, I provide table 2, which lists major framings of honor in Florentine life over a period of two hundred years, along with the names and dates of their major advocates, and a

Table 2. Conceptions of Honor, Their Advocates, and Corresponding Important Themes

Frame	Advocate/Period	Key Ideas or Themes
Patriarchal	1250–	Family solidarity, fatherhood, vendetta, *cortesia*
Virtue	Dante, ca. 1305	Virtue, *gentilezza*, *vita contemplativa*
Legal	Bartolus of Sassoferrato (ca. 1350), Coluccio Salutati (ca. 1400), 1350–1400	Legal privilege → an innate disposition
Early merchant	Lapo da Castiglionchio (ca. 1360), Paolo da Certaldo (ca. 1383), Giovanni Morelli (ca. 1405), Goro Dati (ca. 1412)	Mercantile trades, caution, honor + profit, *giusto modo*, political conservatism, piety
Late merchant	Buonaccorso Pitti, ca. 1412	Family, *amicizia*, knighthood vs. wealth
Civic humanist	Leonardo Bruni, ca. 1400–1420s	Civic virtue, honor vs. profit, patriotism
Albertian	Leon Battista Alberti, ca. 1430	*Diligenza*, autonomy, debate among family, thrift, and civic virtue
Early humanist	Buonaccorso da Montemagno (ca. 1429), Poggio Bracciolini (ca. 1440)	Virtue, learning, wealth
Later humanist	Carlo Marsuppini (ca. 1440), Lauro Quirini (ca. 1449), Cristoforo Landino (ca. 1475)	Magnificence, generosity, virtue, *vita contemplativa*

brief list of key concepts or ideas they emphasized. A key mechanism driving the evolution of these accounts lies in the efforts of outsider classes or groups to tell a story about themselves or to define themselves positively and differently from contemporary ruling classes or groups, and occasionally in the efforts of mature ruling groups to naturalize their own claims to honor. These efforts eventuated in a heterogeneous mix of notions of honor available to be read into the term *onore* as it appears in personal correspondence on various topics. Honor gives life and property meaning—but which meaning?

The Deep Backdrop: Family Honor and the Duties of Fatherhood

We start with the stereotypical view of politics in late medieval Florence in terms of factional fighting and vendetta. Honor appears to have had a more **martial** character in mid-thirteenth century Florence than would be the case in the fourteenth or fifteenth centuries. In fact military participation, or tracing descent from the heroes of Montaperti and Campaldino, was considered a matter of personal honor and glory. In the late thirteenth century, some Florentine families displayed courtly manners lavishly and strategically to signify their honor. Villani noted in his chronicle that the Rossi family, a magnate (but not ancient noble) family, held a great festival in honor of St. John the Baptist in 1283, in which such displays took place (Lansing 1991, 159f.).

Lansing argues that the magnate families, whether noble in origin or not, suffered from an exaggeratedly **patrilineal** conception of honor (1991, 164). The abundance of young members of lineages not profitably employed but organized into *brigate* (groups of youths who rode together according to the chronicler Dino Compagni) created a labor pool for the day-to-day production of clan-based violence.[5] This corporate, patrilineal conception likely emerged out of the peculiar circumstances of Florentine contestation for influence, where families that operated successfully as cohesive corporate groups to obtain control over offices, benefices, tax collection, and the administration of justice were emulated by the rest. Indeed, Najemy (2002) argues that what seems like a timeless Mediterranean notion of patriarchy-based honor was in fact a fourteenth- and early-fifteenth-century development. Within this patrilineal frame, offenses perpetrated on any member of the lineage would impugn the honor of all members of that lineage and spark acts of vengeance that had to be public in order for honor to be demonstrably restored. Certainly an integral and abiding component of this picture is the centrality of the chastity and material elegance of women to the honor of the Florentine family (Klapisch-Zuber 1985b; Fabbri 1991; Molho 1994; Kirshner 2002).

Over time the familially based notion of honor expressed through vendetta moved toward the background but did not disappear. Various commentators (Goldthwaite 1968; F. Kent 1977; Cohn 1980; Fabbri 1991; Molho 1994) point to transformations in the structure and meaning of family over time. The family memoirs, so richly explored by Christiane Klapisch-Zuber (1990), that began to emerge in the 1300s and became prominent in the 1400s effectively invented the connection of present actors to a familial past and originary places, while typically reducing the importance of violent conflict as the hallmark of family honor. Early communal statutes, plus the important redaction of 1415, stipulated appropriate forms of retribution against family-based violence. One important upshot of communal regulation was the legal definition of the magnate class, a group displaying a set of increasingly stigmatized behaviors, conspicuous possessions, identity markers (heraldic insignia), and political culture orientations (Lansing 1991, 209). Once so labeled, the magnates had their allies defined for them—namely, other magnates—so they emerged with a new sense of shared identity and perhaps more coherence as a group than had been the case before.[6]

While the magnates were the "carriers" of this familial, vendetta-based code of honor, they were not its only practitioners. Public order remained a delicate balance of mutually suspicious families attentive to even minor affronts. Kuehn (1991, chaps. 4–5) shows that vendetta sensibilities were still present in the early 1400s and beyond, even among non-magnate families.[7] Buonaccorso Pitti wrote openly of his family's vendetta against the Ricasoli family (see Branca 1986, 448ff.). Remigio Lanfredini violently repudiated his father for having unilaterally reconciled with Giacomo Pascilocha, the family's enemy. Indeed, Remigio invoked a corporate, familial notion of honor when he wrote to his brother that their father "does not look after our honor" (Kuehn 1991, 137). Thus the conception of family honor survived, even as there was abiding, integrity-threatening tension within the family as to who would determine when that honor had been damaged.

By the 1500s, a number of treatises adumbrated rules for the settlement of attacks on one's honor by means of dueling (Weinstein 2000). The state, while trying to curb the spread of dueling, had to acknowledge the presence of the code of honor that motivated it. This particular code of honor remained "too important to their way of being to be relegated to the lumber room of an earlier feudal age" (Weinstein 2000, 54). Street fighting over honor was punished in the courts according to the letter of the law, yet judges recognized as legitimate the informal context of honor, vengeance, "gentlemanly obligation," and family solidarity that prompted the fights (Weinstein 2000, 140ff.). Thus the courts did not so much reduce honor talk as provide new forums for it.

As family was essential to this notion of honor, the role of **fatherhood** took on an especially prominent place. Alberti's *Della famiglia* and the works of da Certaldo and Morelli provide ideal-type specifications of the good father's role. The setting for Alberti's work is the gathering of Alberti family members for the impending death of Lorenzo (in 1421), Leon Battista's own father. This provides the catalyst for a discussion of the merits and respons-ibilities of fatherhood as well as, later, the obligations of friendship beyond the household.

The dying Lorenzo is the first character to address directly the duties of fatherhood. Using language that will appear often in patronage correspon-dence, he avers that a father must "stand ever prepared and ready to foresee and to know everything. For these duties they must undergo fatigue and anxiety, exerting the greatest care and effort" (Alberti 1969, 38). Then Lio-nardo takes up the theme. A father cares for his sons' welfare, and incites his sons to contend for honor, mindful of every act and gesture (65f., 85). He should not be overly familiar, yet kind, for love lasts much longer than fear (88). Lionardo further claims there is more honor and value in helping your own family than outsiders, simultaneously exalting the family and provid-ing an incentive to frame non-familial interaction as though it occurred within the boundaries of the family. This fictive kinship was ubiquitous in letters; for example, "Honorable like a father" (*Honorevole come padre*) or "Dearest as much as a father" (*Carissimo quanto padre*) were widely used salu-tational forms. Requests formally framed this way, Lionardo's remarks sug-gest, had to be taken seriously by a father-like patron.

Next, the image of the practical man of affairs working on behalf of his family and friends is brought home vibrantly in the person of Giannozzo Alberti.[8] In a metaphor powerfully suggestive of the demands of clientage networks, Giannozzo portrays the ideal father as a spider who sits at the center of the web he has spun outward from the center in all directions (206). Should any filament be disturbed he feels it immediately and in-stantly moves to rectify the disruption, alert to the needs of everyone in his web.

As Kuehn (1982) notes, the concept of *famiglia* in Florence was polysemic. Not only could it signify either the household proper or the extended family, but it could have more symbolic meanings. Among these was the notion of a group subject to one directive, paternal will. Fathers were sup-posed to be the primary teachers of practical insights invaluable for a son's life in both domestic and civic spheres. Because of this belief, Giovanni di Pagolo Morelli characterizes his own orphaned status as a curse: "whereas sons receive training and advancement and status and good habits from their fathers, we remained without a leader and without guidance" (Branca 1986, 166; my translation). Good merchant fathers instruct their sons, helping them to avoid wily deal makers and parasitic relatives seeking tax help (173, 184, 187). Particularly when a father is lacking, a man should contrive to obtain familiarity with one or more noble men, and to learn from them through imitation (*t'ingegna di somigliarlo*; 205). Thus a patron directly replaces a lost father.

The result of this analogizing tactic was that a network of clients or *amici* could be likened to a family, and the patron to a *padre* or *padrino* (that is, father or godfather; see Molho 1979). Institutions such as godparentage were employed to give sons additional fathers (godparents were overwhelmingly male)—often out of respect and love for the chosen godparent, but also with an eye to the political connections thus forged (Klapisch-Zuber 1985a). Likewise the language of fatherhood was used to interpret civic obligation. Thus Piero degli Alberti, in the report of his speech to Gian Galeozzo Visconti, the duke of Milan, remarks that to attack one's country "is as deep a sacrilege as to do violence to one's own father" (Alberti 1969, 255).

There were also analogies working in the opposite direction, likening fatherhood to some other role. Thus Marsilio Ficino and Giovanni Cavalcanti each likened a son to a debtor with respect to his father the unrepayable creditor (Kuehn 1982, 60). The transposability of these rhetorics of connectivity was a critical element stitching together the multiple social networks that made up Florentine society. Yet most commonly, fatherhood remained the dominant metaphor. Whereas the honor of patronage per se could hardly be the formal, overt ideology or culture of Renaissance Florence, legitimate honorable roles such as fatherhood (and presumably friendship) could be substituted and used strategically as proxies in the discourse whereby plaintiffs sought favors from their powerfully situated superiors.

Dante and True Nobility

While vendetta and family had an abiding significance for the rhetoric and practice of honor throughout the late Middle Ages and the Renaissance, we cannot neglect Dante's high-cultural distillation of medieval and scholastic arguments concerning nobility and his focus on *gentilezza*. In Book 4 of his *Convivio*, Dante explicitly sets forth a **virtue-oriented** definition of nobility and takes issue with views that base it on "ancestral wealth / Together with fine manners," or worse, on either of these criteria separately (1990, 138). Dante calls nobility the error that he condemned more than any other, seeing bad people "honored and exalted" (4.i.7). It may be appropriate to speak of fine athletes or women and children with a fine bearing as "noble," so that outward manners or forms may be part of nobility, but the true foundation of nobility is virtue, since wherever virtue is, nobility must follow (4.xix.5). In particular he rails against wealth or riches (4.x.2), an attitude that places him in the position of criticizing "the contemptible merchants who travel about the world," fearful of having their money stolen and resented by those who envy their wealth (4.xiii.11).[9]

Dante outlines the component parts of a noble life: obedience and a sense of shame in youth; temperance, courtesy, and loyalty in maturity; prudence, generosity, and affability in old age. One who bears false witness deserves reproach rather than honor, just as one descended from noble men but who himself forsakes virtue is not worthy of the honors paid to his family (4.xxix.4). He praises the Aristotelian virtues, among which are liberality and love of honor, but these should ideally be wedded to the *vita contemplativa* rather than the *vita activa* (4.xvii.4, 9), a distinctly medieval (but also late Renaissance) preference. Dante's love of knowledge and of his lady Philosophy, the entire underlying motif of the *Convivio* and the motivation for his attack on the impure, debased conception of nobility that spurns knowledge and contemplative wisdom, will find an echo in the writings of the early humanists 120 or more years later, although then knowledge will be joined much more closely to the active life and a positive evaluation of wealth. A deferential bow to the virtue-centered view of honor became a stock rhetorical trope for the next two hundred years.

The Juridical Viewpoint: Bartolus

In the dialogical works of the fifteenth-century humanists, a proponent of the Dantean view always appears. His customary opponent usually adopts, or at least adumbrates, a radically different viewpoint that can be traced to the great Trecento jurist Bartolus of Sassoferrato. Briefly stated, Bartolus argued in favor of a legal definition of nobility, recognizing that this definition would vary from locale to locale. For example, military functions were handled by the so-called nobility in Perugia, even as they were handled by the *popolo* in Florence. There was no consistency to roles and labels in different places (Rabil 1991, 13; Donati 1988, chap. 1). In a somewhat similar vein, in his treatise on arms and insignia, Bartolus argued that there was little to prohibit persons (or commercial partnerships) legally from adopting coats of arms as markers of their identity and, as it were, self-styled guarantees of quality (Cavallar, Degenring, and Kirshner 1994). Essentially there was no "inherent" standard distinguishing just from unjust claims of nobility. Only when that claim had damaged another party might the injured party appeal to the courts. In general, Bartolus argued from de facto conditions rather than from juridical or philosophical niceties: if legal status as a noble was not in fact revocable upon vicious behavior, then it made little concrete sense to claim nobility was based in reality upon virtue.[10] Conversely, noble status might be conferred for dubiously virtuous service to the state; honor frequently rests more on a kind of post hoc accounting of materially successful action than intrinsically "honorable" behavior. Nobility as legal privilege was a public affirmation of a right to be treated as (though) noble.[11]

Bartolus's definition of nobility, which had a de facto orientation rather than an essentialist definition, could only have arisen during a time when it was no longer clear—not only between locales, but within them—who qualified as noble and who did not (Rabil 1991, 16). The pre-Bartolan ambivalence toward the meaning of true nobility is exemplified in Dino Compagni's descriptions of key *magnati* in the late thirteenth century. Corso Donati, Rosso della Tosa, and Pazzino de' Pazzi all were aristocratic in temperament, beautiful in body, and/or practitioners of elegant courtly pastimes who failed to be virtuous and, in particular, caused the commune grief by arousing factions and creating civic discord (Lansing 1991, 226). Dante, who stressed interiority, virtue, and self-discipline, and Bartolus, who stressed visible, verifiable legal claims to being honored, both in their own way helped assuage this contestation.

The tone and substance of Bartolus's thought reached its climax in a slightly perverse way in the writing of the great Florentine chancellor Coluccio Salutati around the year 1400. According to Salutati, nobility was based on proprietorship of prerogatives, either feudal or communal according to how circumstances varied. Not the least of these prerogatives was the active support of a clientele, again either in the feudal (vassalage) or communal (patron-client) sense of the word. Just as Bartolus had realistically reflected upon the diversity of noble classes in the world and found that juridical entitlement was the only common denominator, so Salutati paints a realistic picture of the Florentine ruling class in the post-Ciompi era, going beyond its legal entitlement to political power to include the de facto relations it enjoyed with other social groups and individuals. Remarkably, although he deferred to Dante in one place that virtue rather than privilege or blood is the mark of true nobility, he argued in 1403 that nobility rests on a **natural or innate disposition.**[12] Legal proofs of privilege give way to a predestination-style argument that such proofs tend to betoken or imply a particular inner drive or cause. Now no clear outward signs of nobility exist, nor can nobility be linked to virtuous deeds. Effectively Salutati accepts a definition that makes nobility not only juridically based, but both unchallengeable and so completely artful that those who aspire to it can scarcely follow practical precepts for achieving it.

Lapo da Castiglionchio

The positive valuation of the term *nobiltà* is pronounced in the late Trecento work of Lapo da Castiglionchio (the elder). Lapo ostensibly accepts Dante's arguments, adopting in a preliminary way the conventional stance that virtue is the first support for nobility, but in the process of writing he demonstrates such pride in the seigneurial past of his own ancestors that one recognizes his strong attachment to the abidingly significant familial concept of honor.

> And thus all of them together had great status, and in all the country-side they were held to be and reputed the greatest and most noble men of the territory. There were still in this country, both around and inside this fortress, many of their vassals and faithful followers; and they enjoyed jurisdiction in civil and criminal matters. . . . (Quoted in Donati 1988, 8; my translation)

Lapo was a member of one of the early consular families, and the lineage was honored by ascending to the priorate first in 1289 (Mecatti 1754). Consequently, Lapo exemplifies a late Trecento Florentine class with a multivalent concept of honor: behaviorally civic but also disposed toward pre-civic and ultra-Florentine measures of status.[13] Particularly noteworthy in the correspondence of Lapo and his son Bernardo is how they make favorable assumptions about who possesses nobility that go beyond Bartolus's realist but also cognitively conservative position. Bartolus accepted de facto assignations of nobility, while eschewing generalizations about nobility across localities. But Bernardo da Castiglionchio asks how one should consider families that do not possess juridical proof of their noble status of the sort that Bartolus would have regarded as indisputable. Lapo's answer is that, having possessed their privileges for such a time that no one can remember their origins, one may safely presume that they are justly and legitimately entitled to the nobility they claim (Donati 1988, 8). He thus heads down Salutati's path. He goes on to assert, somewhat awkwardly, that even were such families to lose their outward signs of power, they could not suffer such poverty that they would surrender their honor, nor lose their reputation for nobility.

To the extent members of their own family had changed lifestyles, it was to take up the ways of the merchant—but not just any merchant. Bernardo upholds the distinction, quite common to Florentine writers, between the "noble and honorable" occupation of the international cloth merchant, and the "vile" occupations practiced by members of the minor guilds (Donati 1988, 9). This post hoc redefinition of noble activity is consistent with Lapo's recurrent reference in his letter to what is "profitable" (*utile*; Castiglionchio 1753, 6, 13). Still, Lapo makes clear that once families asserted their claim to ancient nobility—an increasingly popular activity in the late 1300s (Klapisch-Zuber 2000)—that assertion evidently could be persuasive. Encountering a descendant of one of the vassals of the da Castiglionchio family in 1353, Lapo tells how he used his family's legacy of ancient landed wealth to advantage. Though the vassal family had become rich and had achieved Florentine citizenship, Lapo contemptuously reminded the descendant of his family's prior status as servants of the da Castiglionchio (and showed him the papers to prove it); whereupon the descendant became "humble and reverential, and always honored me as his superior, in a way that appeared to him conventional, considering his former servile condition; and we were thereafter always friends" (Donati 1988, 22).

To sum up, nobility in Lapo's view is based on a juridical claim to ancient noble ancestry increasingly naturalized through a particular lifestyle involving **landed wealth** and the pursuit of the **highest mercantile vocations**.

The Merchant Writers of the Late Fourteenth Century

We get a somewhat more ground-level view of the issue of honor and nobility in turning to the merchant writers of the late 1300s and early 1400s, as they employed the term honor in certain ways without theorizing about it explicitly. For example, Paolo da Certaldo asserts in his opening paragraph that, following the precepts he sets down, his reader will attain for himself "much good and honor" for both body and soul (Branca 1986, 3; my translation). Da Certaldo, Giovanni Morelli, and Buonaccorso Pitti by no means represent a unitary position. And their differences of viewpoint may be expressive of personal quirks rather than societally shaped dispositions. Nonetheless, as Branca argues (1986, xliii), they epitomize an important trend from "reasons of business" to "reasons of family" to "reasons of state," and they reflect the overall importance of *constructions* of biographies in the fluid context of early-fifteenth-century Florentine politics (Connell 1990).

Whereas the Florentine economy of the early Trecento had been constituted by far-flung, family-based firms with huge start-up capitals, by the mid- to late fourteenth century these had been succeeded by much smaller companies.[14] These guild-ensconced Florentine merchants were newly cautious, prudent, and frugal in their operations. Some of the greatest merchant-bankers retained a kind of mercantile sobriety in the conduct of life. Merchants were to have Guelf sentiments, long-standing civic status, and a demonstrably stable domestic and business life.[15] For da Certaldo **caution** becomes paramount: secrecy is perfectly compatible with honor (Branca 1986 #96f., #370); a good and solid marriage reinforces honor (#156); deal courteously with others (#141); take the middle way. Maintaining honor means walking softly. Even where a **mildly civic** sentiment appears—"love the honor and well-being and good condition of your city . . . and never take the side other than of your own commune" (#353)—one senses that this sentiment is expressed under the guiding light of a generally cautious, bourgeois ethic. Concerning vendetta, though he does on one occasion praise it as one of life's joys,[16] he generally regards it as dangerous and misdirected (#276; cf. #44, #119, #334). Da Certaldo (and Goro Dati, too, with whom we began) thus offers a low-profile, bourgeois ethic of honor involving repayment of debts, Christian charity, and unimpeachable (if somewhat boring) character.

Morelli also praises the honorable life of the *buono mercatante* (Branca 1986, 123, 131), but he stretches the Certaldoan standpoint in a variety of directions to generate a variegated (though implicit) portrait of honor. On the one hand, Morelli extends da Certaldo's praise of secrecy to a form of downright theatrical duplicity, especially when it comes to taxes. Honor lies in not being cheated or fooled (*ingannato*). On the other hand, he clearly internalizes the importance of **Guelf** loyalties to a greater extent than da Certaldo: his ancestors always desired the honor of the commune more than anything else, and they filled its offices honorably (Branca 1986, 111, 162, 273, 145). And following da Castiglionchio rather than da Certaldo, Morelli seeks to demonstrate the nobility of his ancestry by attributing to them particular physical beauty and aptitude. He claims that among their strengths was an abundance of *cortesia* and the ability to hunt and fowl — qualities typically associated with medieval courtly virtues (Branca 1986, 111). Self-reliance and suspicion on one side, solid cultural and political **conservatism** on the other: this is a rough but fairly accurate cultural sketch of the post-Ciompian Florentine state. Trexler calls Morelli "the classical inside outsider" (1980, 164) — seeking favors with enough guile to mask both his inferiority and his ambition. The bourgeoisie adopted certain pre-bourgeois practices or values as a means of self-valuation, as talismans of upward social mobility, and as old cultural capital newly appropriated (Bourdieu 1984). The *ricordanza*, so popular in the late fourteenth century, insofar as it takes the form of a (re-)construction of the past, precisely highlights ancestry (and biography) more than any compendium of proverbs possibly can, again leading to emphasis on a family's political standing (but not vendetta).

It is important to add to this portrait the peculiarly **Christian** tone of Morelli's worldview. God and Providence figure much more pervasively in his thinking than in, say, that of Alberti, writing twenty-five years later, in part because the humanists imitated classical models in composing their dialogues. Morelli's accounting of the lives and deaths of his children in mid-1403 (Branca 1986, 163), and his surrender to the inscrutable desires of God upon the death of his first son (294) reveal at first glance a deep **faith**. "Everything has proceeded from His will," including "every honor and increase of stature of our city" (297). However, Morelli reads purpose into Providence, which lends a distinctly **transcendent** tint to his theology and a **formalist** tint to his viewpoint on interaction: events or opportunities, whether advantageous or damaging, come not by chance nor simply by human agency, but as a sign and verification of God's judgment of our words and deeds (139).[17] This view yields a meaning-rich, anxious, anti-predestinarian ethic based on rigorous ritual enactment, and therefore on a conception of honor ripe with the aim of imitating particular patterns of behavior and particular human exemplars. For example, the death of his eldest son haunts Morelli and eventually spurs him to an elaborate ritual of prayers and self-scrutiny in order to see his son well-buried, and therefore well-accepted into heaven. Honor consists in a life spotlessly conducted and well-concluded—a life marked by doing all the right things. This requires considerable **circumspection**. Morelli was more conscious than any other merchant writer that this meant pursuing business, being frugal, obtaining wealth, residing in Florence, and being loyally Guelf, politically active, and well-liked.

Buonaccorso Pitti begins his *ricordi* letting us know quickly both that he and his brothers succeeded to the most honored offices in the commune, a fact that excited envy from a certain misanthropic relative (Branca 1986, 351). **Office** and **ancestry** are keynote features in the design of family honor, an honor reinforced by the extensive enumeration of family members and their particular services to the commune. But if Pitti seems to construct his honor on the basis of these institutional facts, he also bases it extensively on a particular type of conduct, controlled and yet impassioned—in short, a courageous, chivalric ethic. The biographical nature of his *ricordi* stresses his own individuality. In his youth he expressed his devotion to a woman and in the folly of love traveled to Rome and back to demonstrate his obedience to her command. A similar quiet yet mildly reckless courage pervades his interactions with the *difensore* of Pisa, the duke of Brabant, and others (373ff.). In each case he disports himself enviably, conquering that inferiority complex in the face of authority and foreign nobility that Trexler finds constitutive of the Florentine psyche (Trexler 1980; cf. Brucker 1983, 18).

Pitti achieved nobility for himself and for his family in 1401 through his interaction with Rupert of Bavaria, the Holy Roman Emperor. Rupert had obtained assurance from German merchants that they would provide him with fifty thousand ducats in Augsburg, but the merchants were unable (and probably unwilling) to finance him once it was known that the emperor intended to march beyond Lombardy to Rome to be crowned emperor by the pope. Pitti reluctantly embarked on a series of missions to secure these funds. Before the most perilous of these missions, he requested that he be knighted as a sign of his service: "I would be more content to die in battle in his service, than to die being sent for money, as a much better reputation would remain as a result for me, and honor for those of my family (*casa*)" (Branca 1986, 424; my translation). Rupert bestowed on Pitti the right to place the emperor's golden lion on his coat of arms. Nobility was gained through response to the imperilment of the emperor's honor. And evidently honor here is viewed as more desirable and laudable in a martial context than in an economic one.

Even if the Pitti were status inferiors with respect to the ancient magnate families, they were representative of the most politically prestigious
families in the city: the Albizzi, the Strozzi, the Guicciardini, the Medici.
In some sense, da Certaldo, Morelli, and Pitti represent gradations on the
scale of the cognitive and practical limits of honor. That is, the practice of
honor becomes less defensive and more assertive, founded less on economic
stability and more on documented ancestry and political status, as we climb
the social hierarchy and as the post-Ciompian ruling oligarchy matured.

Leonardo Bruni's Civic Conception: The De Militia

Leonardo Bruni's early-fifteenth-century viewpoint on nobility and honor
may be regarded as seminal to the development of humanism, but it may
also been seen as transitional between an earlier, energetic, unreflective,
participation-oriented civic or patriotic conception and a later refined,
humanistic one. This emerges particularly in two of his works, the *De Militia* and the *Laudatio* of the city of Florence. The former is written as a letter
to Rinaldo degli Albizzi, the mainstay leader of the post-Ciompi oligarchic
regime in the city. Albizzi headed a commission in 1420 to revise the statutes of the Guelf party. Bruni acted in a secretarial capacity for this commission and so was prompted to compose this work contemplating the origins,
function, and essence of knighthood (Griffiths, Hankins, and Thompson
1987, 108). Knighthood was "an honor and dignity" still bestowed upon
"outstanding men" (127) in his day, yet it could absorb a great variety of
different connotations and locality-specific customs, just as Bartolus had
noted. Though acknowledging the importance of virtue, he denies that it
has any special role in defining nobility: "for virtue is common to all" (128).
Likewise, whatever distinguishing marks the knight might adopt, these in
no way epitomize his actual superiority. Rather than defining a noble class
in regard to its particular privileges, Bruni first invokes a Platonic model,
defining it in relation to its role in defending the city, such that nobility's
specific virtue is **patriotism**. Nobles have no authority independent of or
superior to the city of which they are a part.

But Bruni quickly turns to a different model, the Roman one, whereby
a man is *miles* only so long as he is actually fighting on behalf of the city. In
Rome there was no *miles* class, but only a militia that those in different occupations joined periodically (132). This model Bruni offers as most suited to
the system adopted in contemporary Florence; and yet, he faces some diffi-

culties in settling upon its applicability. First, despite the temporary nature of the Roman militia, there were evidently different ranks within it. The cavalry, or *equites*, de facto enjoyed a superior honor, he notes agnostically, "either because of their property or their family or their accomplishments in life" (133). Being an *eques* tended to become an abiding mark of rank even during peacetime. Bruni accepts this, even coming to regard this fetishized form of honor as a reasonable distillate of other, possibly more original forms. Therefore, while the people must be free, the *equites* still must stand above them in honor.[18] Bruni ends up awkwardly appropriating both Platonic and Roman models: knights (or more strictly speaking, the *equites*) form a coherent and abiding group with elevated status, yet they should enjoy this distinction strictly in regard to their wartime function.

If knights are part of a militia that reverts to quotidian tasks when not in battle, what then is their specific peacetime function? Certainly they should engage in their own affairs preserving **justice, temperance,** and **liberality.** They should be vigilant in peacetime, protecting the weak and the powerless from the violence of the powerful. But this set of criteria—vigilant guardianship of orphans, offering service and good advice to the commune, cultivating friendships, generosity, and justice with neighbors—far from being essential to the knight alone, ends up being applicable to any good man and citizen. A more serious problem is that the introduction of the knight's military function and the tools of his trade in peacetime will lead to injuries inflicted on fellow citizens that can only be described as "shameful," "infamous, impious and detestable" (143). There is no doubt whatsoever that Bruni refers to a distinctly vivid issue in contemporary Florence: the noble man must internalize the norms of knighthood, accepting the standards of honor his office imposes while refraining from the *practice* of his profession at any time while his city is at peace.

In accepting that knights enjoy an abiding status (and vocation), Bruni is led to separate the pursuit of money from the occupation of the knight, calling it "sordid and unnatural" (143). More correctly, he wants the noble man, qua noble, to be unconcerned with money and acquisition, strongly forbidding the knight to engage in commerce and instead exhorting him to find greater "honor" and "dignity" through military service.

> Since it was the dignity of the office that made me what I was not before, shall I out of folly and cowardice remain engaged in the same activities as before, and not be ashamed, after having been raised to

the heights and decorated by marks of distinction, to slip down once
more and so, in sordid pursuit of profit, to tarnish the purity of my
gold medal? . . . I shall conduct myself as my rank requires in peace
as well as in war, and shall never set profit or even my very life before
my honor. (144)

Here again "honor" and "profit" are explicitly paired, but in this case the
two concepts are opposed to one another. This oppositional pairing appears
again in the remonstrance delivered by the city to the derelict knight: "It
was my will that my *milites* should be characterized by fortitude rather than
by cowardice, that their objective should be glory rather than the accumulation of money" (145).

Consequently, Bruni's position is that honor is rooted in virtue, but
also in **defense of the community**. This in turn entails a **devaluation of
the pursuit of profit**, and it places the knight in the bind of being unable
to express his honor, for which he has such great concern, in peacetime.
Further, despite being framed as an etymological or quasi-historical essay,
Bruni's work is actually ideological: nobility ought to derive from one's
position with respect to the city, not from monarchically granted powers,
land ownership, wealth, or even the insufficiently exact principle of virtue.
The knightly class effectively epitomizes the primacy of the city and the
honor founded on the duties of citizenship. Its members obtain through
office, but also retain apart from office, a special purity that obligates them
strictly to uphold a certain type and quality of conduct (**civic virtue**). This
is consistent with the view of political participation as the supreme honor
expressed in Bruni's *Oration for the Funeral of Nanni Strozzi* and in his *Laudatio*
of the city of Florence (117), and it is consistent with the praise expressed
in the latter for the work of members of the Guelf party as defenders and
guardians of the republic.[19]

Alberti's Views on Honor

I began with a quote from Book 2, originally the pivotal book, of the
Libri della famiglia. There it was evident that Lionardo Alberti considered
honor the basic metric of value. Honorable action therefore historically
achieves its deserved praise; honor in fact is what is publicly praised, even
as Alberti (like so many others) bows to the old claim that honor coincides
with virtue.[20] But the question of precisely which sorts of action produce

honor and its concomitant praise is left unresolved. Whereas Lionardo the humanist says honor is most durable when it is based on the real possession of virtue, a property more durable than wealth, the old businessman and pragmatist Giannozzo stresses the importance of flexibility, experience, and prudence, rather than virtue, in the face of fortune (Alberti 1969, 13). Later, Piero Alberti emerges in Book 4 as a kind of political version of his contemporary Giannozzo. How many competing views of honor can we distill out of this text?

References to honor (*onore* and *onestà*, as well as some variants or associated concepts such as *gloria, fama,* and *laude*), and to *fortuna* and its counterpart, diligence (*diligenza, industria, fatica*), completely saturate the prologue, and much of the rest, of Alberti's work. Honor, in the form of glory and fame, is the desired end, and diligence in action its shield against threats from *fortuna*. Diligence here is the application of energy or effort (often called *fatica*) and intellect or imagination (*ingegno*), through constant works (*opere, esercitazioni*), for the pursuit of honor. Albertian honor in a sense consists in **diligence** itself. All of these terms, common in patronage correspondence, come together in Battista's short laudatory remarks to Lionardo in Book 2, after Lionardo has spoken in praise of honor and virtue over love:

> Neither work nor diligence (*diligenza*) shall be lacking in us, Lionardo, on this and every other occasion, to be obedient to you and like you. And as you further assure us that even ordinary friendships may be most useful not only to us but to the whole family, we promise you, Carlo and I, always in every [matter touching its] honor and profit (*onore e utile*), you shall see us with all strength and cleverness (*ingegno*), wherever necessary, contriving to exercise ourselves (*adoperarci*) against whatever threat were a bother (*fatica*) or danger to it, most readily and preparedly. (119; my translation)

Nonetheless, the substance of honor is not concretely and univocally specified in the text. First, as to the family, Adovardo comments that its honor depends on the recognition by outsiders that the lineage looks after the needs and honor (*utile e onore*) of even its least (*minimo*) member. Honor correlates with clan size and unity (128), even if warlike tournaments are now repudiated (157, 174). Honor requires different actions of us depending upon whether one is dealing with a family member or an outsider: the former deserves all that he asks, while the latter must be handled circumspectly.

Family members are far more trustworthy as agents and employees than are outsiders (200). Thus the family, especially for the older Giannozzo, marks a cognitive boundary distinguishing what kinds of people are worthy of particular kinds of treatment. Further, the anthropological view of women as the potential Achilles' heel of the family is fully represented in Alberti's dialogue (213ff.; Najemy 2002). For example, a wife should be chosen from a family of wealthy practitioners of an occupation comparable in honor to one's own. Here honor is clearly relational, its rate in part determined by the amount of honor of those around you. Overall, the intricacy and length of the discussion of family suggest it is a primary vehicle for attaining and maintaining honor.

But there are extenuating circumstances to the praise of family. Adovardo had experienced directly the pain of exile that the Alberti family had endured. Small wonder, remarks Lionardo, that he prized his dedicated family over friends (Alberti 1969, 93f.). Further, Lionardo accepted the first book's praise of family, he admits later, more out of respect for Adovardo's authority than on account of the logic of the argument. Finally, Battista himself is ambivalently related to the Alberti, an illegitimate child and a youth probably more focused on friendships than on family.

When it becomes Giannozzo's turn to dominate the discussion, a new **thrift-centered**, ambiguously bourgeois ethic of honorable conduct comes to the fore. Honor now coincides with self-sufficiency in the sphere of economics as much as in the sphere of virtue. Honor consists in proper time management and care of the household so as to avoid dependency. For this reason Giannozzo praises the farm as a great and honorable place where diligence should be practiced. Furthermore, he praises operating a firm in the wool or silk industries—trades at once "*onestissimo* and *utilissimo*" (249)—and he repeats da Certaldo's praise of the merchant with ink-stained fingers. Living independently, spending wisely, engaging with moderation in an honorable trade—these are the components of Giannozzo's conception of the honorable life implicit in his advice to Battista and Carlo: "Live honorably (*vivete onesti*; 317). Giannozzo also repudiates international trade (196) and finance (234). These are too susceptible to the vagaries of fortune and to the vices of dissoluteness and deceit.

Lionardo, however, repeatedly resists Giannozzo's one-sided praise of the countryside and leads the conversation back to a civic conception of honor. In the city, men "taste the sweets of praise" and are "awakened to the pursuit of excellence" (194). "Glory springs up in public squares; reputation is nourished by the voice and judgment of many persons of honor, and in the midst of the people" (178). In Book 4, added in the late 1430s, Piero Alberti speaks of his family as one renowned for putting the welfare of the country above its private wishes. And Ricciardo notes that it is necessary that wealth should be added to virtue to adorn it and make it shine (250).

Thus **civic responsibility** and an **adequate wealth** both become components of the conception of honor in later parts of Alberti's work. The many voices in this rich and masterful work distinguish it as a distillation and juxtaposition of a variety of strands of honor stretching from Dante to the Medicean humanists. What distinguishes Alberti uniquely, however, is the preoccupation with *diligenza*, a component of honor understood as the property of an **agentic** individual.

The Humanistic Conception of Nobility I

Beginning with Buonaccorso da Montemagno's treatise *De nobilitate*, written in 1429, and continuing throughout the fifteenth century, Italian humanists repeatedly returned to the question of nobility to inquire about the kind of actions and profile of attitudes that best characterized the honorable man and/or his social class. The humanists' treatises are distinctly classical, both in form and content, betokening the cultural shift in play over this period. In particular, as Rabil notes, works by Buonaccorso, Poggio Bracciolini, Leonardo of Chios, Cristoforo Landino, and Bartolomeo Sacchi (Il Platina) are all cast as dialogues, a quintessentially classical form; meanwhile their near universal praise of virtue, particularly in this-worldly deeds rather than other-worldly contemplation, places them squarely in the tradition of Aristotle's *Politics*, and in some tension with the more medieval and Christian praise of virtue expressed by Dante in the *Convivio* (Rabil 1991, 3). Perhaps paradoxically, while these treatises generally tend to exalt virtue over birth, they were written in Medicean Florence under a regime that was de facto less egalitarian and participatory a republic than it had been in the Trecento (Najemy 1982; Rubinstein 1997).

Buonaccorso da Montemagno was a jurist, an esteemed instructor at the university in Florence in the 1420s, and a communal diplomat. His treatise, widely disseminated in Latin, in Italian, and later in French, English, and German, takes the form of two extended monologues by Publius Cornelius and Gaius Flaminius, two young Romans competing for the hand of Lucretia, the beautiful, wise, and virtuous daughter of a wealthy and virtuous scion of an ancient Roman senatorial family. She agrees to marry the nobler of the two, with each representing respectively ancient familial descent (Cornelius) and personal virtue (Flaminius). The debate, unresolved save that Flaminius is allowed to speak second (and then more eloquently), is cast as a debate between these two conceptions of nobility.

Cornelius belongs to an excellent family and has interests that anachronistically seem distinctly courtly in nature: hunting, singing, and playing instruments (Rabil 1991, 34). Therefore, though he is himself Roman and the setting is Roman, he embodies the appropriation of a transformed feudal conception of nobility. His claim rests on his ancestors' deeds and virtue, but especially on the gift of nobility bestowed by the republic for their military service. Their nobility—their daily customs, habits, and conversation—penetrated into the very bones of their progeny. "Certainly everyone regards this as nobility. Do the people call any others noble except those whom the noblest parents generated?" Later he asserts that the nobility of his ancestors inheres in him "by nature" (38). He therefore rhetorically adopts a Salutatian point of view.

To these factors Cornelius crucially adds **wealth**, by means of which household magnificence is augmented, the virtue of generosity is exercised, and one's circle of friends is expanded. "Nobility shines through generosity and becomes more notable through the favor and kindness rendered to many" (37). Wealth also makes possible a life of leisure that provides protection against the pains of daily business. Birth and riches thus go together in Cornelius's view of the naturalized attainment of honor and nobility.

Flaminius opens his oration by expressing indignation at the dishonor shown toward him in Cornelius's speech. He apologizes that he shall have to speak with uncustomary and unseemly immoderation in his own defense. Flaminius then proceeds to express the Dantean stance that the nobility of a man resides in his own virtue. It rests particularly on unselfish (and level-headed and loyal) service to the state and military courage—a practical, manly, and civic form of virtue. Thus Flaminius reframes the leisure that Cornelius had praised as "idleness." Such service must be one's own service, not one's ancestors, and to substantiate this requirement he offers a devastating summary of the "shameful" (50) deeds of the children of noble families. To this portrait of honor, Flaminius adds **learning**, a distinctly humanistic value (40f.):

> When a mind long trained in the best arts has distinguished itself in
> justice, piety, perseverance, greatness of soul, restraint, and wisdom;

when it has deserved well of the immortal gods, parents, friends, relatives, and the commonwealth; when it has been raised in the most hallowed traditions of literature; then indeed it is to be regarded as noble, exalted, illustrious, and renowned above others.

Thus he cites Socrates, Euripides, and Demosthenes as noble, despite their humble births, a stock set of examples that, for all their typicality, Cornelius could never have invoked. In contrast to Cornelius's country estates, Flaminius proposes his library as the epicenter of the home and the fountain of his virtue.

The Humanistic Conception II: Poggio Bracciolini

The lines between a humanistic, virtue-centered conception of nobility and a traditional wealth- and inheritance-based conception are starkly drawn by Buonaccorso. They are still present in Poggio Bracciolini's treatise of 1440, but more ambiguously so. Rabil (1991, 60) cogently speculates that Poggio himself was considerably more undecided than Buonaccorso about which position was superior. Poggio was from Arezzo, but he moved to Florence as a youth wherein he joined the humanists' circle around Salutati and later Bruni. Most of his career was spent in the papal curia, but his fame is mostly due to his rediscovery of ancient texts by Quintilian, Cicero, and others in 1415 and the following years, discoveries that revolutionized philosophy and philology.

Poggio's treatise takes the form of a dialogue between Lorenzo di Giovanni de' Medici, the brother of Cosimo and a merchant and patron in his own right, and the humanist Niccolò Niccoli. Niccoli begins by asserting the Flaminian position: "Wisdom and virtue alone elevate one to nobility." Lorenzo follows immediately with the Bartolan position: "Nevertheless, we know that those who have paintings, varied and elegant sculptures, wealth, and abundance of possessions, or who hold public office and positions of power, have nobility bestowed on them, even though not noted for their virtue" (Rabil 1991, 65). The word "nobility" derives from *notus*, notable in any way (an etymology that, incidentally, Dante explicitly rejected), and this, says Lorenzo, conforms to the commonsensical way of thinking about the term. Niccoli's response is that, on the contrary, there is no consensus regarding the question of what is noble according to outward signs. In Naples, it includes languor and sloth and excludes business; in Venice, it emphatically includes business; in Genoa only birth is relevant; in Greece, service to the crown is key; in the Ottoman Empire, military prowess is key; in Rome, Britain, and France, nobility is rural and virtue-oriented. Since these forms of nobility are founded on custom or force alone, they do not merit the term "nobility." Lorenzo by contrast distills from this diverse list of nobles a few plausible bases of nobility—wealth, leisure, arms, splendor, virtue—and takes this diversity as a fundamental indication that local judgment is the final criterion for what constitutes nobility.

In fact, Niccoli critiques the very concept of nobility. There is no specific virtue that ennobles, while virtue should in fact be its own justification and end, not dependent on the purely contingent trait of nobility. In particular, wealth depends on *fortuna*, whereas nobility must be based solely on the will (Rabil 1991, 80)—a point made as well by Landino and other humanists later in the century. The properly exercised will, following the Stoics, rests on a sense of honor, the stable and enduring determinant of our conduct. Niccoli continues to expound this Albertian view: accomplishments result from one's own "exertion and diligence." Honor and nobility, inextricably linked to the conduct of life, rest on respect for, and the cultivation of, virtue.

But Lorenzo outlines a claim that **wealth** is integral to the practical exercise of nobility. External goods in fact bring public esteem, parentage imbues individuals with habits of conduct conducive to nobility, and engagement in civil life is praiseworthy. Certain virtues such as **magnanimity, generosity**, and **defense of one's country** are not practicable without wealth (Rabil 1991, 86). Niccoli has the last word in the text, but it is more important for present purposes to note how an explicitly Medicean perspective finds expression in this work. Wealth linked to magnanimity and civic magnificence plays an integral role in the construction of nobility and the maintenance of honor, defined in terms of virtue, knowledge, or any other criterion. Poggio's own career was notably advanced by his connection to the Medici; he and the early civic humanists before him all came to grips with how their own social mobility was rooted in the city, and even in the politics of the city, whether in the rise of a rationalized administrative chancery or in the support of private patrons who funded the city's celebration of itself. This was even more true of Carlo Marsuppini, a favorite of Cosimo's, than it had been of Poggio. In his poem based on Poggio's work, Marsuppini asserts that "virtue and goodness alone / are the marks of true nobility," yet Cosimo and Lorenzo, his patrons, are his modern paragons of all the virtues (Rabil 1991, 109).

The Humanistic Conception III: The Later Humanists

The Quattrocento preoccupation with nobility did not expire with Poggio and Marsuppini. Leonardo of Chios took up Poggio's argument but challenged the supposed Florence-centeredness of its definition of nobility as resting on participation in the administration of the commune. Leonardo remarks that nobility lies not among those sharing a certain legal or political status, but secretly in the hearts of the just (Rabil 1991, 120). Yet he also claims that it is unlikely that the working classes possess virtue, and that their political participation "deforms the beauty of the republic" (125). The humanists had to admit the overriding importance of virtue for a satisfactory philosophical definition of nobility, but they were extremely reluctant—whether for reasons of patronage or from a sense of their own superiority to inferior social groups—to dismiss the boundaries between social strata as meaningless to this definition.

A more thorough-going (if solecistic) challenge to Poggio was offered by Lauro Quirini in the late 1440s. Quirini, a patrician Venetian by birth, understandably was piqued by Poggio's mild disparagement of Venice and sought a philosophical defense of Venetian practice. Through some rather arcane philosophical invective he claims that much more often than not nobility reproduces itself, generating a "natural disposition," such that "from the careful education of nobles children of exceptional mind necessarily emerge, well-adapted to excellence, honor and virtue." Furthermore, "virtue stands in need of wealth" (Rabil 1991, 163, 166, 174f.). In this way, Quirini's position is characteristically Venetian, yet it also seems appropriate to a Florentine regime increasingly conscious of its superior elegance and increasingly closed to entry from below.

The final text I will consider here is Cristoforo Landino's dialogue, *De vera nobilitate*, composed around 1475, a text that Rabil (1991, 185) asserts reconciles civic virtue with the newly emerging contemplative ideal of Platonism. The dialogue is floridly dedicated to Lorenzo de' Medici (that is, Lorenzo the Magnificent—Cosimo's grandson, not his brother), whom Landino personally tutored. Lorenzo had been one of the interlocutors in Landino's earlier *Camaldulensian Disputations* along with Leon Battista Alberti. (One can see that a number of persons end up being both real and virtual participants—actors, exemplars, and authors—in this long-term debate on nobility.) There Lorenzo is made to claim that both (civic) work—the *vita activa*—and reason—the *vita contemplativa*—must be balanced, while

Alberti argues that reason or speculation is superior because clear thinking is a precondition for proper action. The latter position clearly wins out in the extended Platonic allegorical reading of the *Aeneid* with which Landino concludes that work.

This position is roughly restated in the dialogue on nobility. The most noble figure is the one who excels over others in the most distinctively human traits: the mind and contemplative reason (Rabil 1991, 217, 249). Merchants cannot be among the ranks of the philosophers (222). Following Plato, it is those with the most virtue who should administer the city. The eloquence of orators is connected inherently to wisdom and harnessed naturally in the service of the unity of the city. Passages from the ancient writers suggesting otherwise show merely that they knew how to adjust their speech to popular opinion. Recalling the structure of the *Disputations*, we should expect the Albertian position to triumph, and in some sense this is the case. Still, the dedication of the *De vera nobilitate* is telling: the Medici have always been known to have studied letters and the liberal arts, yet Lorenzo surpasses all of his ancestors in this regard. In his palace and in his accommodation of guests, too, Lorenzo surpasses all others. Even though Landino suspends his panegyric to the Medici lineage, remarking that genealogies are often abused by the powerful to support their claim to superiority, he more than adequately succeeds in portraying Lorenzo as the natural heir to the Medicean disposition. Thus in the person of Lorenzo we have a new model for emulation, a return to a more contemplation-infused picture of nobility, one emerging out of a quasi-hereditary, aesthetically graceful disposition toward letters as well as politics. Lorenzo the Magnificent is the Florentine expression of Quirini's portrayal of Venetian nobility, a hypertrophied version of Poggio's earlier Lorenzo (di Giovanni) de' Medici.

What motivated these texts and their choice of content? Perhaps the humanists experienced anxiety over their own status (Rabil 1991, 17). Perhaps their vision of a new civic conception of virtue and honor was driven by changing political circumstances (Baron 1966; cf. Skinner 1978), particularly the emergence of a secularized, elitist, republican Florence. Perhaps the humanists thereby found a niche as the conscience of the man of wealth (Martines 1963). They were supported by the Medici, who saw their administrative importance and their value in securing political appointments for clients and friends (Hankins 1992, 81, 89). But most compelling, perhaps the humanists viewed honor/nobility as a "winning" cultural strategy in a field of contending meanings (J. L. Martin 2003), or an ecology of nested games played by the elite, their opponents, and by the humanists themselves. The ethos of knighthood belonged more to the Medici's enemies than to themselves: Rinaldo degli Albizzi was known as "the Knight," while men such as Palla Strozzi had more legitimate claims to "nobility" than the more commercial Medici. The Christian ideal also ran afoul of Medicean commercial and financial activities. By contrast, neoclassical discourse accommodated wealth as a virtue, as a strengthener of the perpetually important family, and as sinew of the body politic (Hankins 1992, 84). Thus it worked not so much on its own merits but in contrast to the alternatives. Ultimately, humanism channeled political challengers' energies into the pursuit of cultural accomplishments and made that pursuit sufficiently arcane that it effectively created a "class barrier preventing 'inferiors' from learning the gestures and language of the in-group" (Hankins 1992, 89). In addition, its appropriation as an ideal by the ruling class co-opted the intellectual class, which otherwise might have challenged much more openly the legitimacy of elite authority.[21]

Conclusion

As I indicated at the beginning of this chapter, the term "honor" could signify a variety of substantively different values and behaviors in Florence, depending on one's social status, position, time period, and presumably, interlocutor. As a result, there was a vibrant and long-lasting debate about honor, rather than a unitary "culture" of honor. The different connotations of honor were available as background understandings, and they could be invoked in interaction as cognitive and normative cues, although there could be residual uncertainty about which particular "honor" was being invoked at any given time. Their use implied the invocation of some frame of meaning for action, structuring pleas for assistance or claims of self-worth and aiming at eliciting desirable responses from friends and enemies alike. Claims to honor by diarists or by letter writers, or assertions of the interdependence of the writer's honor and that of his audience—heirs, friends, or patrons—implied expectations about that audience's behavior. Inferences about which definition was operative could be made on the basis of the nature of the request, surrounding vocabulary, and social understandings of the kind of person making the request.

The various conceptions of honor or arenas in which honor is most properly displayed appear, disappear, reappear, and combine in a variety of ways over the two centuries roughly from 1280 to 1480. A family-centered conception of honor had effective strength not only in the late medieval period but also throughout the Quattrocento, even if the state made efforts to regulate it and curb its destructive impact. As service to the commune shifted from providing military service to filling legislative, administrative, and ambassadorial positions, the focus of honor changed accordingly.

Both Dante's and Bartolus's views were bred from the social upheaval over dissatisfaction with the vendetta-obsessed ruling classes of the late thirteenth century. As the *popolo* emerged, their own claims to nobility and to being honored, increasingly coincident with their role as the *classe dirigente* of the commune, led to a progressive naturalization of the status of this class as "noble," which theretofore had had to be justified from a Barto-lan standpoint. In Salutati's strained account, nobility is defined in terms of political position and dispositions that one must assume to be innate, even though recently constructed. We see this also in Lapo da Castiglionchio's arguments in favor of his own ancestry, in Morelli's praise of his family's heritage, and in other late Trecento *ricordanze* (Klapisch-Zuber 1985a). The easy attitude of nobility appears in its most naturalized form only with Pitti, an exemplar of the Florentine *reggimento* in its mature and satisfied self-recognition. With Bruni, the civic humanistic version of honor comes to the fore. Political activity is now clearly considered ennobling, although subtle differences continue to distinguish this attitude from the earlier strand of patriotic Guelfism.

Virtue had to become a rhetorically or tropically recurrent theme once Dante had "codified" it, but virtue—almost as polysemic a word as honor—could be teamed with a variety of different contents. There was a notable trend toward signifying by it the active life—either politics (as in Morelli or, more purely, in Bruni) or commerce (as in da Certaldo and even da Castiglionchio)—around the end of the fourteenth century, despite the un-Dantean quality of this move. *Virtù* obtains the consummate, proto-Machiavellian meaning in Alberti, where it is grouped with *diligenza* to signify something like practical capability and supreme self-reliance. All the same, a gradual rearguard action by the humanists (da Montemagno, Poggio, and Landino, supported by the stability-seeking Medici in the mid-fifteenth century) shifted the idea of virtue and honor into line with the contemplative life.

Wealth had a less illustrious relation to honor in the late Trecento and early Quattrocento than did political participation. Although a necessary means (perhaps following Aristotle's view), the drive for wealth was not integral to honor. But in the Medicean period wealth shifted from being a safeguard against shame and a manifestation of unimpeachable ethics to being a way of expressing magnificence, munificence, and civic philanthropy. The estimation of wealth therefore traverses one of the most tumultuous paths in this period in relation to honor, at first challenging the conception of honor based on flamboyance, later helping to sustain such a conception.

These shifting representations of honor emerge more or less in conjunction with underlying structural changes, but far from simply succeeding each other, they persist in overlapping ways. As a result, they comprise an array of usable frames for understanding a term of constitutive importance in the forging of personal relationships and the forging of a sense of self and self-worth, in a formative period pointing toward modernity.

4

What Gets Said When
in Patronage Letters

In the last two chapters, I presented evidence, first, of the "toolkit" of letter-writing techniques in early Renaissance Florence, and second, of a variety of cultural meanings, or frameworks, that those techniques could activate. The theoretical idea is that rhetorical techniques erect a fairly generic scaffolding upon which particular meanings or sets of meanings may be supported. Agency lies in the use of sanctioned practices to position oneself, for others, in a nexus of meaningful cognitive, moral, and aesthetic frameworks, or sensibilities. Patronage letters were one of the critical Florentine milieux in which that agency occurred.

This chapter moves beyond an account of the origins and existence of these practices and frameworks to an examination of when and how frequently particular practices and frameworks were used in actual patronage letters. By way of analogy, consider this: I have quite a nice, adjustable, right-angled, claw-like plumber's wrench in my toolbox at home. It is in quite good shape—undoubtedly because I hardly ever have occasion to use it! It belongs in the toolbox, but it is a low-frequency item. Next to it lies my hammer—a very frequently used item. One would ill judge the critical importance of a hammer, and the abundantly various uses one can make of it, without actually observing how and when a given person or type of person uses it in various kinds of home repair. Similarly, one cannot really understand culture only by looking in the toolkit. One must observe it "in action" (Swidler 1986). Consequently, this chapter is about patterns in actual letter construction, examined from three angles. First, I will present quantitative data on how frequently certain turns of phrase and critical keywords appear in different kinds of letters. Second, I will examine changes in the use of critical keywords over time. Third, I will examine whether or not letter construction differs in identifiable ways across different social distances between sender and recipient. Throughout, I will provide an abundance of examples from the letters themselves illustrating how these building blocks of patronage discourse actually got used. Sometimes I will point out the artfulness of particular letter constructions, so that we can begin to see specifically "the art of the network" in action, but more of that will come in the next two chapters.

It should be obvious that the contents of letters will differ somewhat according to the primary aim of their writers, although these differences may not be apparent to someone unfamiliar with the Florentine cultural milieu. Quantitative changes in usage over time will be of particular interest to historians as they point to qualitative differences in the construction of patrons and of patronage between the pre-Medicean and early Medicean period on the one hand, and early Laurenzian Florence on the other.[1] I also quantitatively examine certain differences in letters according to the relative positioning of the letter writer and the recipient in critical status categories (age cohorts, income brackets, prestige groups) and in different social spaces (neighborhoods, marriage networks, economic networks). Examining these usage patterns provides us with an inductively generated, composite portrait of an average letter (of a given type, or a given time). It also allows us to identify departures from the average. This information, although not sufficient in itself, does bring us closer to knowing how and when tools are used in combination. It brings us closer to knowing how and when particular cultural meanings are juxtaposed. It brings us closer to knowing which tools typically get used in fashioning which kinds of raw materials. In short, it brings us closer to understanding the work of "doing culture" strategically.

Sampling the Corpus of Florentine Patronage Letters

The Florentine State Archives contain literally thousands upon thousands of letters written to the Medici, the Strozzi, the Sacchetti, the del Bene, and a handful of other families. But no previous study has made a substantial effort to document the language and codes of this "epistolary production" (Boschetto 2003, 253; also see Molho 1979; F. W. Kent and Simons 1987). A key reason for this lack is that no single scholar could possibly read all of the available documents; nor could anyone offer a comprehensive examination of all possible substantive and rhetorical components of the letters. Many of the letters are well-nigh illegible. Spelling and grammatical idiosyncrasies abound. Even were one able to read, transcribe, and code all of the available material, he or she could have no confidence that such an effort would produce a representative picture of Florentine correspondence in general. The families to whom correspondence was addressed are not average representative families.[2] The letters they saved are probably on average fundamentally different from the ones they failed to save. Letters survive in vastly different numbers for different time periods. For any number of reasons, then, we have to settle for a very imperfect empirical study of content. Nevertheless, such a study is valuable for providing benchmarks about the letters, and for seeing that observed cultural practices can differ substantially in content from what we might expect based on other documentary sources.

Toward the goal of providing a composite portrait of Renaissance Florentine patronage correspondence, I read thousands of letters. Furthermore, I transcribed more than eleven hundred of these letters in two major waves. In selecting letters for transcription, I was unabashedly biased. Letters between family members are underrepresented in my sample because career-building dynamics are typically less visible there (although such letters may well provide other critical insights into the operations of patronage networks). Letters had to be legible—not a negligible consideration. I targeted letters of modest length (typically no more than one full page), with an eye toward selecting a sample that would include: 1) letters between both politically allied and non-allied people; 2) rich people and poor people, as well as those of high and low status; 3) foreigners and Florentines; and 4) letters covering a range of topics and types of requests.

I coded the transcribed letters for date of composition, names of the sender and the recipient, the degree of formality used in the letter (*tu* or *voi*), and their primary theme or content. In addition, whenever possible I included information on key social and personal attributes of each sender and each recipient: the social status of his family, his family's neighborhood of residence, his age, his household wealth at a time close to the date of the letter, the family name of his in-laws, his family's place in the Florentine marriage market, and so on. This enabled me to place sender and recipient relative to each other in social space. Further, I searched through all of these transcribed letters for several dozen keywords that seemed, on the basis of my reading, and on the basis of the secondary historical literature, to be critical elements in the construction of a patronage letter, and critical elements for portraying a situation, for construing one's relationship to another, and for presenting oneself.

These keywords can be divided roughly into two classes: substantive expressions and idiomatic expressions. The substantive expressions are those that say something directly about the content of the relationship being constructed or about the character of the participants in it. For example, does the writer talk about honor—his own, or that of the patron, or that of the person he is recommending—in the course of his letter? Is the writer prepared to portray himself as the "servant" (*servidore*) or "slave" (*schiavo*) of the patron? Is he prepared to be "obligated" (*obligato*, *obrigato*) to his patron, and how much? To what extent is "virtue" or "excellence" (*virtù*) discussed as a relevant criterion for assessing how "capable" (*valente*) a person is, and thus how worthy of a "favor" (*favore*)? When are particular virtues stressed, such as courtesy (*cortesia*), generosity (*generosità*), benevolence (*benevolenza*), humanity (*umanità*), or mildness (*gentilezza*)? Is a favor construed as a "favor" (*favore*, *grazia*) or a "duty" (*dovere*) for the patron? And when is a favor or obligation demanded by "friendship" (*amicizia*) as opposed to "honor" or virtue, or the "need" (*bisogno*) of the person requesting "help" (*aiuto*)? We can begin to answer these questions of letter construction by examining letter content—quantitatively in this chapter and more qualitatively in subsequent chapters.

The idiomatic expressions I consider to be regular features of a wide variety of letters, features that seemed to perdure across situations and over time as relatively generic techniques of favor seeking. They are elements of etiquette, and they are filler material, often used to round out a letter in its proper form and with an agreeable cadence: for example, "Prepared to do what is pleasing to you" (*apparechiato a vostri piaceri*); I ask this "as much as I know and am able" (*quanto so e posso*); "I will feel emboldened to ask you" (*piglierò sicurtà chiederti*); and so on. However, they have varied uses, including qualifying role relationships, and they vary in the frequency with which they are used over time. Consequently, some of them seem also to carry substantive significance, as I will describe below.

Differences in Content across Types of Requests

Florentines wrote to powerful others for any number of reasons: seeking help in securing offices; requesting help with tax problems; securing recommendations to others; getting out of prison; seeking help with legal disputes; passing along critical information; as an accompaniment to gifts by means of which they tried to ingratiate themselves. The list goes on.

But the modal elements of different kinds of requests differed somewhat. Table 3 pools the patronage letters I have transcribed and coded according to their primary content and then indicates the number of times selected keywords or phrases occur per letter.[3]

A quick examination of the table makes it clear that any given keyword by no means appears in all letters of a given type. Fifteenth-century Florentines were not writing according to inflexible forms or templates. I also acknowledge that it would be difficult to assess the statistical significance of these findings, although the number of cases of each type is substantial. Nevertheless, some noteworthy differences do exist in how different types of requests get framed, and differences of usage appear between various keywords, even ostensibly synonymous keywords. These differences can be seen by comparing the global average frequencies in the last row of the table with the averages for particular letter types, and by comparing the columns for different keywords.

For example, the word *onore* (honor) appears on average in one out of three letters in my dataset, but it appears in more than half of all the letters related to office holding or eligibility for the scrutiny. And it is used in almost half of the letters whose primary goal is to assure the patron of one's loyalty and those related to the negotiation of marriages and other kinds of family ties. It is used far less in different kinds of letters having to do with money. Surely this slant is in part based on the etymological connection between the words *onori* (honors, offices) and *onore* (honor). Honor was clearly a relevant concept in political and familial matters, but not so much in economic matters. Thus, in one of the earliest letters in my sample, Rosso de' Ricci wrote to Francesco di Iacopo del Bene on February 13, 1392 (*Carte del Bene* 49, 174): "Dearest friend, I heard that you are the one doing the new scrutiny, so that I pray of you that it be pleasing to have recommended to you my honor (*l'onore mio*), and that of Bernardo and Salvestro my sons, which on every occasion I repute to be your own, and concerning this operation that you see what is necessary to do. Prepared always to do your pleasure." In a similar vein, Taldinus di Buoncompagno di Visso wrote to Simone Strozzi (*C.S.* III, 131: 13): "I would dearly love to be honored (*honorato*) with the next election of the office of *podestà* of Florence, and because I am informed of how much you know and are able to do for your friends, humbly I pray of you that you would wish to be the man (*essere operatore*) to bring this about, which would be to me such a great service." And Giovanfrancesco Panciatichi wrote to Cosimo de' Medici on August

24, 1435 (*MAP* XII, 17): "I recommend myself to you, that you contrive with the pope that I be elected *podestà* of Bologna, or another honorable place—at Prato, or Perugia, or wherever it pleases him. . . . In everything that they will work out for me, I will do honor (*farò l'onore*) to you and I will serve well." In the first example especially, honor comes off as a kind of personal property, but it often was also assigned group consequences, as in Panciatichi's promise to do honor to Cosimo. Carlo di Bonaiuto Biliotti expressed a similar trope to Averardo di Francesco de' Medici on January 21, 1432 (*MAP* III, 13): "I pray of you that you exercise your most clear intellect and ingenuity and your sublime help that I may remain here as castellan. . . . Honor I will give you for sure. Bartolomeo Peruzzi knows, when he was commissioner in the other war there was in Sant'Agnesa whether I did honor to him or not." And Palla di Nofri Strozzi expressed the idea succinctly in a letter of September 17, 1416, to his kinsman Simone di Filippo Strozzi (*C.S.* III, 132: 32): "The occasion of every honor to you gladdens me, as much as my own do."

An old Ciceronian trope paired what was honorable with what was "useful" or "advantageous" (*utile*), as if the two goals could be simultaneously served.[4] We see this, for example, in a letter that another of the Panciatichi, Antonio di Giovanni Panciatichi, wrote to Pazzino di Palla Strozzi on March 13, 1437 (*C.S.* III, 120: 193): "In this country there is no greater servant [than I], with such loyalty (*con tanta fede*) will you be served by me . . . Do not forget me. And if there were any office of honor and advantage (*d'onore et utile*) that you would wish to give me, I would hold it dear on account of both the advantage and the honor (*per l'utile et per l'onore*) it would bring."

In certain respects, not all that much changed by the early Laurenzian period. The same sense of doing honor to others through office holding is expressed in many letters.[5] Tommaso Minerbetti wrote to Lorenzo de' Medici on July 30, 1471 (*MAP* XXIII, 375) to express his especial commitment to honor, and the dependence of his honor on Lorenzo's favor:

> And so, dearest confrere of mine, I am sending you these little verses to recommend myself to you, praying of you that my honor be favored by you, and that if you had not written to me that I should give an account of myself, I would desire death more readily than life, because, being left behind, each would speculate that it were on account of some defect of mine. . . . And so, once again as much as I

Table 3. Average Incidence of Selected Keywords by Letter Topic

Primary Topic Addressed	Number	*Onore* Honor	*Virtù* Virtue	*Bisogno* Need
Assurance/Flattery	125	0.46	0.05	0.46
Information/Request for Info	89	0.37	0.02	0.61
Military News/Supplies/Diplomacy	118	0.35	0.02	0.58
Office Holding/Scrutiny	154	0.60	0.10	0.41
Recommendations	216	0.31	0.06	0.46
Unspecified Requests for Favor	59	0.29	0.08	0.71
Requests: Money, Property	109	0.19	0.02	0.61
Requests: Release from Prison	57	0.23	0.12	0.33
Tax Relief/*Licenzie*/*Bollettini*	78	0.19	0.03	0.64
Thanks/Gifts	55	0.16	0.09	0.22
Benefices/Church-related Offices	25	0.08	0.16	0.44
Dispute Resolution (e.g., *Differenze*)	32	0.34	0.03	0.50
Marriage/Friendship/Family	29	0.45	0.14	0.52
For All Letters	1146	0.34	0.06	0.49

	. . . issimo Superlatives	*Singulare* Singular	*Certo* Certainty	*So e posso* I know+can
Assurance/Flattery	0.48	0.14	0.34	0.08
Information/Request for Info	0.19	0.03	0.12	0.04
Military News/Supplies/Diplomacy	0.19	0.05	0.20	0.07
Office Holding/Scrutiny	0.54	0.21	0.32	0.12
Recommendations	0.59	0.19	0.19	0.17
Unspecified Requests for Favor	0.22	0.10	0.17	0.15
Requests: Money, Property	0.27	0.06	0.28	0.16
Requests: Release from Prison	0.44	0.16	0.26	0.11
Tax Relief/*Licenzie*/*Bollettini*	0.26	0.12	0.22	0.13
Thanks/Gifts	0.36	0.13	0.27	0.25
Benefices/Church-related Offices	0.52	0.24	0.32	0.08
Dispute Resolution (e.g., *Differenze*)	0.41	0.13	0.16	0.09
Marriage/Friendship/Family	0.24	0.10	0.14	0.17
For All Letters	0.39	0.13	0.24	0.13

Amico Friendship	*Amore* Love	*Affezione* Affection	*Servidore* Service	*Fede* Faith/Trust	*Volentieri* Willingness	*Obligato* Obligation
0.39	0.32	0.03	0.56	0.41	0.14	0.21
0.29	0.19	0.01	0.24	0.20	0.11	0.02
0.25	0.08	0.01	0.23	0.12	0.04	0.06
0.44	0.21	0.07	0.60	0.25	0.09	0.24
0.52	0.24	0.08	0.53	0.24	0.09	0.20
0.39	0.36	0.02	0.39	0.24	0.17	0.15
0.25	0.17	0.00	0.59	0.17	0.08	0.28
0.56	0.44	0.02	0.81	0.32	0.07	0.21
0.32	0.12	0.01	0.41	0.14	0.06	0.15
0.25	0.20	0.07	0.27	0.11	0.07	0.27
0.64	0.36	0.08	0.52	0.64	0.16	0.12
0.50	0.34	0.00	0.56	0.16	0.06	0.06
0.45	0.45	0.07	0.14	0.24	0.07	0.10
0.39	0.23	0.04	0.47	0.23	0.09	0.18

Favor Favor/Prefer	*Grazia* Favor/Grace	*Adoperare* Contrive	*Pregare* To Pray	*Gravare* To Beg	*Supplicare* To Entreat
0.10	0.45	0.28	0.67	0.06	0.02
0.08	0.17	0.15	0.30	0.04	0.00
0.03	0.04	0.16	0.49	0.10	0.02
0.10	0.23	0.53	1.05	0.12	0.03
0.32	0.26	0.28	1.02	0.09	0.00
0.12	0.32	0.39	1.14	0.10	0.10
0.11	0.11	0.27	1.39	0.11	0.01
0.16	0.61	0.39	1.23	0.16	0.04
0.08	0.21	0.37	1.10	0.28	0.01
0.05	0.35	0.25	0.65	0.09	0.00
0.48	0.32	0.52	1.24	0.04	0.20
0.19	0.31	0.19	1.34	0.25	0.03
0.03	0.31	0.31	0.86	0.18	0.00
0.14	0.26	0.31	0.92	0.12	0.02

can I recommend my honor to you, such that having the scrutiny to do, you not abandon me.

Alessandro Martelli summed up a widespread sentiment when he wrote to Lorenzo the Magnificent on January 31, 1473, in defense of his request for favor: "Wherever I have been always have I pushed myself to have honor" (*perche dove mi sia stato sempre mi sono sforzato de havere honore*; *MAP* XXIX, 25). And Fruosino di Lodovico da Verrazzano wrote to Lorenzo on August 21, 1472 (*MAP* XXIII, 488) to say

> As the time of the *imborsazione* [i.e., determination of the pool of eligibles for communal office] is approaching, I pray of you, my Lorenzo, that it be pleasing to you to have me seen for gonfalonier of justice. You know how much I have desired it, and I am most certain that for you it is not [difficult?], but I know that in your kindness (*tua humanità*) you have always done honor to me (*m'ai sempre fatto honore*). Now on this occasion do not abandon me, and let it please you to give me this happiness, for never will I forget it.

These examples could be multiplied many times over.

Consider *virtù* next. Here is a richly evocative and polyvalent term one might expect to be used often given its prominence in the work of Florentine writers from Dante and Petrarch to Alberti and on to Machiavelli (Pocock 1975; Skinner 1978). In fact, it is rather scarcely used in patronage interaction. Like *onore*, it is particularly relevant to marriage and family issues, but unlike *onore*, it is invoked more commonly in letters pertaining to ecclesiastical offices than communal offices.[6] Indeed, in one communal office-related letter, sent by Cristofano di Guerrante Bagnesi to Forese Sacchetti on October 8, 1407 (*Conv. Soppr.* 78, 324: 132), *virtù* is introduced only to discount its importance: "I wrote to you, dearest and honorable confrere, recommending to you my affairs—not because it were necessary, but because I desire to be honored there, which I am certain I will be, not on account of my virtue, but because of your good and caring efforts (*operatione*), which you have always undertaken for me."

In letters about ecclesiastical offices, *virtù* is typically predicated of the person being recommended. Thus Morello da Panzano wrote to Lorenzo de' Medici on May 8, 1472 (*MAP* XXVIII, 165) to recommend someone for a position at a chapel outside of Monte Varchi: "The singular trust and devotion that I have in your Magnificence moves me to write to you, and also the virtues and goodness (*le virtù e bontà*) of him who has made a request to me." Alternatively, it may be applied to someone else intimately connected with the recommendee, as when Simone Granzini recommended a certain Ser Bartolomeo to Lorenzo de' Medici on September 13, 1472 (*MAP* XXVIII, 513):

> I pray of your Magnificence as much as I can that it please you to write a note in your name to the syndics of San Piero in Palco in Napoli, that it please them to elect as rector of their said church a certain Ser Bartolomeo, priest and son of the departed Gherardo Gherardini. He has a brother named Ser Giovanni, my notary in the shop, whom I love very much for his virtues and his goodness (*le virtu e bontà sue*); and he and his brothers have always been most loyal to your family (*fedelissimo di casa vostra*).

Virtù is also used more commonly than average in letters written by persons seeking release from prison, typically to emphasize the virtue—the goodheartedness, or generosity—of the patron. This letter written by Lodovico Manfredi to Averardo di Francesco de' Medici (*MAP* LXVI, 36) is typical: "I have a firm hope of being liberated from such a great misery by your grace/favor and effort (*gratia e operatione*), especially considering that there aren't the same obstacles now that you told me there were before. God has given you grace (*v'a fatto gratia*), and hoping continually to go from good to better, please deign to exercise your virtue (*la virtù vostra*) and help me." Similarly Lionardo Fantoni wrote to Averardo de' Medici on March 15, 1432 (*MAP* III, 106): "[I]recommend to you Luigi di Lando, whom I am certain on account of your virtue and grace/favor (*tuo virtù e grazia*), and for love of me, will be made free."

Certainly when requesting help, it was possible for Florentines to speak in terms of need (*bisogno*): that a request should be granted based on necessity, not favoritism. To write in terms of *bisogno* was to provide a construction of desert in objective terms. But such constructions predominated precisely in letters where expressions of friendship (*amicizia*, to be an *amico*), or service (more accurately, servanthood, that is, to be a *servidore*) were relatively scarce: military letters, informational letters, and money-related letters. Friendship and servanthood, by contrast with need, were crucial tropes used in patronage letters strictly speaking. They were tropes that rhetorically constructed a particular abiding role relationship between writer and recipient, a critical element of patronage interaction. They thus proactively supplied justifications to patrons for whatever help they could or would provide.

By no means were these two framings clear in themselves, nor were they always distinct from one another. For example, Vicino Orsini wrote to Lorenzo de' Medici on June 10, 1472, in favor of a certain Romanello, calling him both "a long-time servant and excellent friend of our family" (*MAP* XXVIII, 217). Similarly, Domenico Attavanti signed off in a letter of November 14, 1472, to Lorenzo de' Medici (*MAP* XXVIII, 217) calling himself Lorenzo's servant, although in the body of the letter he offered himself and his brother Carlo to Lorenzo as his "good and faithful friends" (*buoni et fedeli amici*). Indeed, in terms of aggregate patterns of their usage, the two framings seem quite correlated: they are "overused" (assurance letters, office letters, benefice letters, and recommendations, for example) and "underused" (tax letters, informational letters, thank you letters, for example) in the same kinds of letters.[7] But the similarity in the aggregate is a bit misleading. Often they are *alternative* framings rather than complementary ones. An interesting example in this regard is the following letter of November 27, 1472, from Bernardo Corbinelli to Lorenzo de' Medici (*MAP* XXVIII, 707):

> It occurs to me to write to you because I have heard that ser Barone, [notary] of the *Mercanzìa* [the Florentine commercial court], is on the verge of death. And I have an intimate friendship (*intima amicizia*) with Ser Bartolomeo Lioni, . . . a good man and one to do honor to you (*farti onore*). In his old position [as a tax official of some sort] and in every position where he might find himself, [he would be] a friend of ours and of our friends. I would like, inasmuch as it were pleasing to you, that you would contrive (*essere operatore*) that he come into the position that Ser Barone will be vacating. This would be most gratifying to me, and he will offer himself to you forever as your good servant (*t'offerò per sempre buono servidore*).

Note here how Lioni is identified as a friend of "ours," but a "servant" to Lorenzo in particular—indicated by the use of the informal second-person pronouns in the expressions "he will do honor to you" and "he will offer himself to you." Thus Lioni is both friend and servant, but friend and servant to somewhat different constituencies.

Because *amicizia* can include the notion of friends of friends, and given that the Medici were critical brokers in the task of supplying church-related perquisites in particular, Florentines talked about friends disproportionately in pursuit of church benefices. Further, because *amicizia* frequently had an instrumentalist tinge, it was used relatively frequently in letters of recommendation. A letter of Andrea di Matteo of Verona to Cosimo de' Medici on March 3, 1439 (*MAP* XI, 161) is especially saturated with this talk of friendship:

> Because I consider myself among the number of your oldest friends, as my forebears always were with yours, and desiring to maintain this good old friendship, I have written many letters to you as your friend . . . and now I am writing to you as your friend praying of you that it please you to write and pray to the illustrious doge of Venice, who I hear is very much your friend, that it be pleasing to him for love of you to look upon me favorably, that I be seen as their good and upright servant, which I desire to be like the good old friend I am to you. . . . I have hope in you in the greatest possible way.

The term *affezione* (affection) was somewhat similarly emphasized in recommendation letters, but by contrast, the superficially similar keyword *amore* (love) was not so used. *Amore* was instead often tropically paired with the idea of trust or loyalty (*fede*), as in a letter from Piero de' Ricci to Giovanni di Cosimo de' Medici on April 1, 1445 (*MAP* V, 568) to signify more intimate relationships. Piero asked Giovanni to write a letter of condolence to Piero's recently widowed sister Camilla de' Ricci Peruzzi, concluding, "Whenever you see anything pleasing that I could do for you, I will do it with love and loyalty." He signed the letter, "your brother" (*tuo fratello*).[8]

Fede and *amore*, separately or together, also were used to communicate a special commitment to one patron. Certainly this was signaled from the outset in a letter of August 21, 1472 written by Raffaello Bonciani to Lorenzo de' Medici (*MAP* XXVIII, 440), and it was reiterated toward the end:

> I am certain that your humanity could consider it presumptuous, but rather the love and loyalty I have for you led me to write these few words. This is a matter which I neither could nor would want to address to anyone but yourself, and this I will do with that confidence and boldness given to me by the love you have borne toward me. . . . I pray of you as much as I can that it please you that this time I receive satisfaction. If this cannot be, nevertheless always I will re-

main patient with every decision of yours, believing that you were keeping me in reserve for the best place, because the love and loyalty that I have borne toward you, and still bear, proceeds more from your goodness and virtues (*più dalla bontà e virtù vostre*) than your stature (*vostro stato*).

Note the careful representation of "network density" and social distance here: no one but Lorenzo matters, and Raffaello's attachment to him is not only based on love, but is a reciprocation for Lorenzo's earlier gesture of love. He also sees fit, given that Lorenzo received dozens upon dozens of daily requests (F. W. Kent 1992), to deny explicitly that his love is motivated by Lorenzo's position.

Next let us look at trust or loyalty (*fede*) and being obligated (*essere obligato*). Florentines used these terms in somewhat different contexts. To reassure someone about one's motives, one would stress loyalty by using the language of *fedeltà*; but to ask for a specific favor—an office, or help getting some money or property—or to express thanks for a past favor done, then one would more likely say "I am obligated to you."[9] Whereas *fede* expressed positive and indeterminate commitment, *obligato* expressed commitment more negatively and in the framework of tit-for-tat trading.[10] Thus a letter from Vanni de' Medici to Averardo de' Medici of June 7, 1428 (*MAP* II, 104) is a quintessential "assurance" letter:

The trust/faith I have had in you has always given me success, and in many ways. I would like only to be more yours than is a son, or anyone in whom you have the most trust (*più fede*). May God grant me grace (*Idio mi dia grazia*) that I may demonstrate this to you. Concerning my election, which you have brought about, I cannot thank you here because I would have too much to say, but I am more yours than I can say, offering proof of myself (*faccendome pruova*) when I have occasion. I will strive to do honor to you (*sforzeròmi di farvi onore*) in every way. If there is anything I may do that is pleasing to you, command me.

The words *favore* and *grazia* had overlapping meanings, both being used to talk about the favors done that were a core currency of the Florentine patronage system. Nevertheless, their connotations were somewhat different. *Favore* connoted "preferring" someone, as when Donato Acciaiuoli wrote to Lorenzo de' Medici on June 14, 1472: "Andrea Verdelli or his deputy will be the bearer of this message. He would desire to have the favor of a letter of recommendation to the *podestà*" (*MAP* XXVIII, 236). *Favore* appears more often than usual in recommendation letters and in requests concerning ecclesiastical offices (which often required that the Medici intercede with church officials on behalf of particular candidates). It was frequently paired with the term *aiuto* (help), as in the following excerpt from a letter written by Cosimo de' Medici and sent to Pazzino di Palla Strozzi on December 4, 1436 (*C.S.* III, 120: 138)—a letter that incidentally also illustrates the use of the language of obligation to represent the reciprocity of *amicizia*:[11]

> Rienzo di Biagio del Cascina, a Roman, [is the] bearer of this letter, dear friend to me and so his father was always a friend of our company here. And as the father has just died, he has left in our hands the affairs of Rienzo his son. For that reason it appears I am obligated in all senses (*obrigato in tutte sense a llui*) to give him my every favor and help (*favore et aiuto*). And because it happens that he has to come there and will have need of your help and favor (*aiuto et favore*), I comforted him that he might come to you, and that, on account of my love, you will give him your help and favor (*aiuto et favore*) in all honorable and reasonable things.

By contrast, *grazia* connoted bestowing one's favor upon someone in a way much more in line with the notion of grace than favoritism. To be favored with the *grazia* of God or a patron was much more like enjoying the benefits of Providence; it was to receive an undeserved, perhaps even miraculous gift. Hence the frequent use of the term in letters requesting help in getting out of prison, as when a church official wrote to Lorenzo de' Medici on March 18, 1484: "Magnificent Lorenzo, my most singular lord and benefactor, I pray of you and entreat you that you deign to do me this singular favor (*grazia*): to contrive that the said Ridolfo be set free" (*MAP* XXIX, 108). Or when a certain Giovanni wrote to Lorenzo de' Medici on June 20, 1472 (*MAP* XXVIII, 246): "I pray, by the mercy of His mother, the Virgin Mary, that you should wish to bestow upon me such favor (*tanta grazia*) to get me out of here"—that is, out of a jail cell he called "this miserable place."

Table 3 also provides information on the differential use of various important semantic elements. For example, consider the use of superlatives, often enacted in Italian by adding *-issimo* to the end of an adjective. For example, generous (*generoso*) becomes "most generous" (*generosissimo*); "I am certain" (*sono certo*) becomes "I am most certain" (*sono certissimo*). It is not hard to see where this inflationary tactic gets used: precisely in those types of letters where network tie construction (office letters, benefice letters, recommendations) or tie strengthening (assurance letters) is most salient. For instance, consider this letter written by Bartolo Mori to Lorenzo de' Medici on July 28, 1472 (*MAP* XXIII, 476) concerning the upcoming *imborsazione* (the selection of persons deemed eligible for holding the most prestigious offices in the city and the wider Florentine administration). The *imborsazione* was a moment, one might say, of incredible fatefulness and consequentiality (Goffman 1967); hence the superlative language used to talk about it.

> You know that when I left there I came to you and reminded you of my concern, and from you I have had the most gratifying/gracious (*gratissima*) response. Now, with this letter and with the greatest faith (*fede grandissima*) in you, I pray of you that in the placing of names in bags, or when they come to put the names in the bags, that you have me in mind, for all my trust (*tutta la fede mia*) is in you. . . . I have faith you will do this, and in everything I will remain most obligated (*obligatissimo*) to you.

Virtually the same pattern of usage according to letter purpose holds for the adjectives *singulare* (unique, different from all others), which is a discursive marker of distinction, and *certo* (certainty), which is a discursive marker of emphasis.[12]

The last several columns in table 3 list the frequency with which certain critical verbs were used in patronage letters. The verb *pregare* (to pray of someone) appears on average nearly once per letter across the entire dataset. As I noted in the last chapter, it was practically the sine qua non verb of Florentine favor seeking, despite Alberti's wry suggestion that one should like never to have to use it. However, occasionally other verbs could be substituted. Florentines begged (*gravare*) for tax relief and begged for help in getting out of legal jams of various sorts. However, they entreated (*supplicare*) their patron for assistance when it came to ecclesiastical offices. Also, one should note the abundant use of the verb *adoperare*, which had the connotation of "pulling strings"; hence its use whenever one asked for help in obtaining an office that required backstage machinations of one sort or another.

Other verbs could supplement *pregare* for emphasis, as in this letter of

Antonio Ferrucci written to Lorenzo de' Medici on June 12, 1468 (*MAP* XXIII, 207):

> Respected youth and my most beloved son, My Lorenzo, these few verses I am writing to you, trusting in your customary humanity, love, and benevolence, which you have always demonstrated toward me; and I will have confidence in you, requesting of you a service greater than any other you could do for me in this world. And this is that, being in the midst of the drawing for gonfalonier of justice, and not having seen my name yet[?], and I, desiring that which every man desires, I can only pray of you, beg of you, and entreat you (*prieghi gravi et supplichi*), that it please you to pray, beg, and entreat your magnificent father Piero (*ti piaccia pregare gravare et supplicare el tuo magnifico padre piero*), that it please him to console me by having me seen for gonfalonier . . . for the love and great affection you show me emboldens me intimately to request this service of you, which more than any other I esteem, holding this one to be more than the other matters I have with you. I remain forever your good and faithful servant.

Note how this letter uses *pregare, gravare,* and *supplicare* rhythmically and repetitiously, and note how Ferrucci actively distinguishes this favor from others he has requested before, while likening himself to others, "desiring that which every man desires."

Finally, table 3 can be read across the rows to get a sense of the most "typical" elements of particular kinds of letters. "Typical" assurance letters incorporate honor, service, obligation, love, trust, certainty, proof, sincerity, and willing choice to a disproportionate degree, while generally failing to actually make requests (the verbs *pregare, gravare*). The letter of Vanni de' Medici presented above (*MAP* II, 104) is a good example. Office letters "typically" emphasize honor, service, obligation, sometimes friendship, and the certainty of being favored. They do make requests and especially emphasize the capacity of the patron to bring satisfaction. Recommendation letters emphasize friendship and affection (but not love), and the granting of favor (*favore*) to capable (*valente*) others by means of (*per mezzo di,* or *mediante*) the actions of the patron. I will offer examples of these types in the next two chapters. Requests concerning money and property tend in the aggregate to focus on need, not honor, on obligation and indebtedness rather than loyalty. They sometimes request that the patron put out some effort or endure some strain (*fatica*) on their behalf. Requests for help from prison emphasize virtue, friendship, love, trust, and grace, and stress the writer's humility (*minimo*) and presumption (*presunzione*) in asking for help. Still, variations in letter composition do blur the boundaries between these types.

Changes in Keyword Usage over Time

It is widely understood by Florentine historians that various elements of Florentine patronage changed over the course of the fifteenth century (D. Kent 1978; F.W. Kent 1992; Connell 1994). Early in the 1400s a number of different families clearly cultivated clienteles, but there was a shift to a period in the 1430s when the rhetoric of letters written to the Medici in particular took on an added urgency.[13] With Cosimo, with his son Piero, and with his grandson Lorenzo the Magnificent, the Medici were increasingly near monopolists in the dispensation of favors to Florentines, and they were critically important to foreigners as well. Even when others were understood to be powerful, it was often because of their perceived closeness to the Medici. As Francesco Sassetti wrote to Lorenzo de' Medici on November 27, 1472 (*MAP* XXVIII, 706), "It is so widely known to everyone the love and kindness you bear toward me, that I am constrained to intercede on behalf of many, which, however, I do willingly, seeing your generosity, and how much it is gratifying to you to serve your friends and servants, especially in honorable matters." With favors increasingly monopolistically supplied, it would be reasonable to expect an increasing intensity in the practices by which they were sought. Table 4 presents some findings on changes in keyword usage over time that support this theory and contribute additional nuance to it. Table 5 will provide a different look at the issue, controlling for letter type and comparing usage across three eras of Florentine patronage for which I have sufficient data: the late Albizzi regime, the period of Cosimo's dominance, and the early stages of Lorenzo the Magnificent's supremacy.[14]

Because the rows of table 4 are arranged chronologically, the findings emerge clearly. The term *onore*, which is undoubtedly a resonant one throughout the fourteenth and fifteenth centuries, nevertheless was clearly used less frequently by favor seekers over time. Trends are less clear for *amicizia*, which appears to persist as an omnibus conceptual framework for thinking about how to distribute favors. But clearly a whole slate of terms—some old, some newly adopted—arose in the Laurenzian period for the pursuit of favor: assertions of affection became more common; service and claims of servanthood surged; expressions of obligation (the 1460s notwithstanding) multiplied; expressions of faith, trust, loyalty, and trustworthiness began to abound. New terms expressing ever more deeply dependent roles vis-à-vis the patron came into use, even if they remained somewhat uncommon. Hence letter writers came to identify themselves or others whom they recommend, not merely as servants, but as slaves (*schiavi*) of another.[15] The term *creatura* (dependent), while not unheard of in the mid-1440s, became slightly more common. For example, in writing about Messer Geronimo Geraldini, a certain Braccio of Perugia declared in a letter of February 3, 1474, to Lorenzo de' Medici (*MAP* XXIX, 35) that

> I have always loved him, and still love him as a dearest brother, and every honor of his is as dear to me as one done to my Bindo or my Ridolfo. Thus, as I regard him as my most beloved dependent (*mia creatura amantissime*), I recommend him to your Magnificence, regarding every good done toward his person not otherwise than if it were done for me personally.

Thus, there is clear confirmation in this table that dependency in social relations — certainly rhetorically, and quite possibly materially — increased under Lorenzo. There is also a trend in these letters toward replacing political talk of "the commune" and "the honor of the commune" with "the state," and especially identifying the state with Lorenzo or calling it "your state."[16] This also confirms what historians already know from other documentary sources.

We turn next to the idiomatic expressions that qualify assertions and/or qualify the role relationships writers portray. Here too we see fairly clear trends. The use of superlatives increased dramatically in letters written to Lorenzo, even when counting separately the ubiquitous *vostra magnificenza* term of address and the use of superlatives in letter salutations.[17] Writers increasingly referred to a particular person or request as "maximally" (*massimamente*) important. In a letter of March 27, 1468, Niccolò Berardi wrote to Lorenzo de' Medici (*MAP* XXIII, 180):

> From a letter of yours of the 24th, I learned how avidly you desired that Iacopo di Giovanni d'Arrigo be elected chancellor of the people and city of Cortona, and because my desire is always to divine how to please everyone of your family, and especially you personally (*indovi-*

Table 4. Average Incidence of Selected Keywords by Decade, All Types of Letter

Period	Number	*Onore* Honor	*Amicizia* Friendship	*Affezione* Affection	*Servidore* Service	*Fede* Faith/ Trust	*Obligato* Obligation
1360–99	36	0.22	0.44	0.00	0.39	0.03	0.06
1400–09	14	0.57	0.21	0.00	0.00	0.00	0.00
1410–19	38	0.24	0.24	0.03	0.34	0.16	0.11
1420–24	35	0.49	0.66	0.03	0.34	0.17	0.09
1425–29	111	0.38	0.26	0.01	0.33	0.15	0.09
1430–34	304	0.39	0.44	0.01	0.33	0.13	0.12
1435–39	124	0.44	0.41	0.08	0.56	0.27	0.19
1440–49	123	0.25	0.31	0.02	0.34	0.21	0.19
1450–59	40	0.30	0.41	0.03	0.72	0.11	0.25
1460–69	34	0.18	0.35	0.09	0.35	0.29	0.12
1470–79	275	0.29	0.43	0.08	0.68	0.42	0.28
1480–89	14	0.21	0.21	0.07	0.57	0.29	0.57
All letters	1148	0.34	0.39	0.04	0.45	0.23	0.17

	Grazia Favor/ Grace	*Adoperare* Contrive	*Pregare* To Pray	*Gravare* To Beg	*Supplicare* To Entreat	*Degnare* To Deign	*Prestare* To Lend
1360–99	0.17	0.22	1.03	0.06	0.00	0.00	0.00
1400–09	0.07	0.64	0.79	0.36	0.00	0.00	0.00
1410–19	0.16	0.24	0.79	0.21	0.00	0.00	0.00
1420–24	0.17	0.54	1.00	0.11	0.00	0.00	0.00
1425–29	0.15	0.22	0.80	0.13	0.00	0.01	0.00
1430–34	0.12	0.28	0.78	0.10	0.01	0.02	0.01
1435–39	0.23	0.41	1.11	0.15	0.02	0.06	0.02
1440–49	0.17	0.28	1.02	0.19	0.00	0.02	0.00
1450–59	0.23	0.28	1.21	0.20	0.00	0.08	0.00
1460–69	0.15	0.18	0.51	0.09	0.09	0.09	0.03
1470–79	0.55	0.33	0.97	0.05	0.07	0.12	0.08
1480–89	0.36	0.21	1.07	0.21	0.07	0.14	0.07
All letters	0.26	0.30	0.91	0.11	0.02	0.05	0.03

Schiavo Slave	*Creatura* Ward	*. . .issimo* Superlatives	*Massimo* The Most	*So e posso* I know+can	*Apparechiato* Preparedness	*Favor* Favor/ Prefer
0.00	0.00	0.19	0.00	0.17	0.11	0.03
0.00	0.00	0.43	0.00	0.21	0.21	0.00
0.00	0.00	0.18	0.00	0.18	0.34	0.13
0.00	0.00	0.20	0.11	0.17	0.11	0.11
0.00	0.01	0.10	0.05	0.14	0.11	0.14
0.00	0.01	0.20	0.06	0.13	0.06	0.07
0.00	0.01	0.44	0.05	0.12	0.10	0.16
0.00	0.00	0.22	0.02	0.09	0.10	0.13
0.00	0.00	0.27	0.08	0.13	0.05	0.05
0.00	0.00	0.32	0.09	0.18	0.00	0.06
0.07	0.02	0.81	0.11	0.09	0.01	0.27
0.00	0.00	1.29	0.29	0.07	0.00	0.36
0.02	0.01	0.39	0.07	0.12	0.07	0.14

Commune Commune	*lo Stato* the State	*Mezzo* By means of	*Presunzione* Presumption	*Pruova* Proof	*Prudenzia* Prudence	*da Bene* Merit
0.03	0.03	0.00	0.00	0.00	0.00	0.00
0.00	0.00	0.07	0.00	0.00	0.00	0.00
0.00	0.00	0.00	0.00	0.00	0.03	0.00
0.14	0.03	0.00	0.00	0.00	0.03	0.00
0.12	0.00	0.00	0.00	0.03	0.05	0.01
0.16	0.01	0.01	0.01	0.02	0.01	0.01
0.07	0.03	0.00	0.02	0.02	0.02	0.02
0.02	0.00	0.00	0.00	0.03	0.01	0.04
0.05	0.00	0.03	0.13	0.00	0.00	0.03
0.18	0.06	0.00	0.00	0.03	0.03	0.03
0.09	0.05	0.07	0.04	0.05	0.02	0.09
0.00	0.00	0.00	0.00	0.00	0.14	0.07
0.10	0.02	0.02	0.02	0.03	0.02	0.03

nare di compiacere a qualunque di cotesta casa e massimamente a tte), today I
have had the syndics and counsel of this city elect the said Iacopo chancellor with all the black beans [that is, unanimously]. I would not be
able to tell you with what great enthusiasm these men have learned[?]
that I first had your letter, and they prayed of me that I would write
to you and recommend him to you, and thus I am doing.

By contrast, the old idiomatic expressions "As much as I know and am
able" (*quanto so e posso*) and "prepared to do your pleasure" (*apparechiato ai vostri piaceri*) declined in fashion after the mid-1420s, appearing least frequently
in the Lorenzo letters of the 1470s and 1480s.

Writers also much more explicitly signaled the importance of the
patron's favor (in both senses) in the 1470s letters. This conforms with the
idea that by that time patronage had indeed become not so much the sub-
terranean machinery of the Florentine system, but its constitutive principle. To a lesser extent than in the past would Lorenzo have had to engage
in machinations to make things happen. They would happen instead as a
function of his own will. In addition to praying and begging for assistance,
writers took up a new verb by means of which to "implore" or "entreat"
Lorenzo to help them (*supplicare*). This was part and parcel of the expanded
and inflated toolkit of rhetorical equipment of mid- to late-fifteenth-
century patronage. In addition, two other verbs of request began to appear.
The first, *degnare*, stressed the arbitrary gracelike favor of Lorenzo, as when
a certain Niccolaio Nosseto of Lucca wrote to Lorenzo on behalf of a friend
of his (February 13, 1474; *MAP* XXIX, 92):

> Because I have been requested by a very dear friend of mine, I should
> like to write to your Magnificence for the reason you will hear from
> the bearer of this message. He has a certain dispute with certain men
> in Barga, as he will tell you more fully. I pray of your Magnificence
> that you should wish to deign to operate that a truce be worked out
> . . . I pray of you that for my sake you deign to do this pious and
> laudable work for which I will remain, above and beyond my other
> obligations, most obligated to you, and you will acquire such fine
> servants in perpetuity.

The second verb, *prestare*, which hardly appeared in the context of favor
seeking previously, was used to ask Lorenzo to *lend* assistance or lend favor.
Its vaguely economic connotation resonates with F. W. Kent's (1992) argu-

ment that Lorenzo had come to be widely regarded as *maestro della bottega* (literally, master of the shop; more figuratively, something like "the boss"). An early instance of the term occurs in a letter of Archbishop Giuliano di Giovachino Ricci to Averardo de' Medici, dated August 19, 1431 (*MAP* IV, 57). Ricci sent Benedetto di Marcuccio degli Strozzi to clarify an issue regarding a man from Santa Maria in Trebbio and asked Averardo "to lend him favor for the honor and advantage of the commune" (*prestargli favore per honore e utile di commune*). And in a letter of September 1, 1435 (*MAP* XII, 26), Duccio Mancini wrote to Cosimo de' Medici with some military news, but he began his letter by saying, "You have lent me such boldness and daring (*voi m'avete prestato tale ardire e audacia*) that I will speak to you with complete confidence." However, the term became much more commonplace in Lorenzo's time. Thus in a letter of November 16, 1472, Giovanni di Taddeo dall'Antella asked to be given an office in lieu of his brother Lodovico, who was excluded from accepting it by the *divieto*[18]: "May you be content to lend me your favor (*volermi prestare il tuo favore*), for you know . . . one could not feel more love and trust toward you than I do" (*MAP* XXV, 228). And similarly on November 5, 1472, Archbishop Filippo de' Medici recommended Lorenzo di Gherardo Galletti to Lorenzo (*MAP* XXVIII, 651); "As much as I can and know I recommend him to your Magnificence, praying that in matters just and honorable (*nelle cose iuste et honeste*—a phrase of very long standing) you lend him (*li presti*) every opportune favor and help such that he be secured in his affairs."[19]

A number of these trends in content and rhetorical framing—the increased use of *favore* and *grazia*, more expressions of obligation—come together in a letter of December 18, 1471, from Giovanni di Salvadore del Caccia to Lorenzo (*MAP* XXV, 124). Giovanni asked that his very close relative Antonio di Lorenzo Spinelli be seen for the gonfalonier of justice in his quarter of Santa Croce:

> Work your grace (*aoperare la vostra grazia*), because without it we will reap no fruit whatsoever. He is a very worthy man (*un uomo molto da bene*), most friendly toward the state (*amicissimo dello stato*), and capable and good. I recommend this case to you as if it were my own, that you extend yourself and that you lend him every favor of yours (*si distende gli prestiate ogni vostro favore*), and so much honor will follow to him, which I will consider as if it were given to me personally, remaining toward you supremely obligated (*restandovi sommamente obligatissimo*).

In addition, there was a slight semantic shift in the terms people used to talk about brokerage in patronage networks. In the first three decades of the fifteenth century, writers used the word *mediante* to express the idea of "by means of." For example, on May 7, 1414, Filippo di Andrea di Antonio wrote to Averardo de' Medici (*MAP* LXVI, 10) to express his gratitude: for "the more and more benefits that my brother Papi and I have received by means of you (*mediante voi*)." On December 12, 1427, Puccio di Antonio Pucci wrote to Averardo (*MAP* II, 69) concerning the work of the Medici party and mentioning some success that had been achieved "by means of one's friends" (*mediante le opere degli amici suoi*). Others sought help "by means of your virtues" (for example, *MAP* II, 13; XII, 7), "by virtue of your innumerable virtues" (*C.S.* III, 130: 194), or by means of specific virtues with which the patron was reputed to be endowed, such as prudence and attentiveness (*MAP* XI, 169), or humanity (*C.S.* III, 150: 111). While the word was still used in the 1470s, the way in which it was used largely changed, and a new word took its place in patronage talk.[20] The new word was *mezzo* (now meaning "means," not "half" or "halfway," as it had been used in the first part of the fifteenth century), and more specifically the phrases *per mezzo di* (by means of) and *per tuo mezzo* (by means of you). A letter that Cosimo de' Medici wrote to his brother Lorenzo on March 17, 1432 (*MAP* VI, 4) offers an early example, but the new word is seen much more regularly after 1450. More precisely, in the later letters the sense is that favors will be bestowed by means of the patron personally, not "indirectly" on account of his virtues. Thus, for example, on August 12, 1459, Stagio Barducci wrote to Pierfrancesco di Lorenzo de' Medici: "[May] Bruno di Lorenzo di Panutio, my good friend, be served by means of you" (*per tuo mezzo servito*) with a particular office (*MAP* V, 748). Similarly, a certain Captain Mariano wrote to Lorenzo de' Medici on August 28, 1472 (*MAP* XXVIII, 474): "The magnificent Marquis Messer Gabriello Malaspina, upon his departure from here, begged me very strictly that I recommend to you Ser Andrea dalle Rici, your servant and bearer of the present letter, because he desires to be elected as an official of the Wool Guild by means of you" (*per vostro mezzo*). And in a letter of May 23, 1473 (*MAP* XXV, 253), Francesco da Colle wrote to Lorenzo asking for an office for himself:

> Although I am aware I have not paid my debt, you having shown toward me such goodwill, . . . and recognizing in you so much humanity that every day one sees, and especially as it is shown toward your most faithful servants, . . . I pray Your Magnificence that, there

not having yet been assigned a *podestà* of Arezzo, that I may go there by means of (*per mezzo di*) Your Magnificence, offering myself always to do honor to you in whatever place you put me.

Other changes signaled a new representation of the social distance between Lorenzo and favor seekers, such as the emergence of expressions of presumption (*presunzione*) in asking for help. Antonio Boscoli wrote on February 8, 1473, asking for Lorenzo's help in recovering some money he was owed, with the following apology: "If I am bothering you too much, I pray that you pardon me, but the trust I have in you makes me be presumptuous" (*MAP* XXIX, 59).[21] Nello Ciunughi of Siena began a letter to Lorenzo on August 4, 1472: "Reminding you of the long-standing kindness always shown to me by the rich and happy legacy of Piero your father, to whom I was a servant and friend in many affairs, now I will be presumptuous to place trust in your Magnificence" (*MAP* XXVIII, 354). And in a remarkably poetic instance of this self-conscious talk of presumption—and overcoming or explaining away presumption—Niccolo di Giovanni di Sernigi, the *podestà* in Castello Fiorentino, wrote on August 10, 1472, to request Lorenzo's assistance with the *imborsazione* for himself and his brother (*MAP* XXVIII, 385): "My Lorenzo, if my writing were full of presumption (*copia di presunzione*), consider it to be driven (*sforzato*) by a sincere love (*sincero amore*) and charitableness (*carità*) that presses me toward you, hoping in your humanity that you will tolerate this like one who is drunk with love."

Finally, we see the hesitating emergence of a handful of words—proof (*pruova*) of oneself, characterization of oneself or others as sincere (*sincero*), talk of prudence (*prudenzia*), and depiction of recommendees as worthy or meritorious (*da bene*)—that bespeak increased competition for favor, an increasing intangibility in the criteria that qualify a person for favor, and an increased feeling of the gap between words and actions, between appearances and reality, and between outward expressions and inward thoughts. These terms arise to express concern over, but also reassert, the authenticity of patronage ties. These terms I will discuss at some length in chapter 8.

Given that there are different patterns of usage for letters of different types, and changes in usage over time, table 5 presents within-type changes over time for a handful of letter types in which the number of cases is adequate to draw some conclusions. Very briefly, the use of the term *onore* drops across all major categories of letters, but particularly in office-related letters after the Cosimo period. Strictly opposed to that pattern are the profiles for "service," trust/loyalty, and the use of superlatives, all of which surge

Table 5. Comparing Keyword Content in Certain Types of Letters Across Periods

Period	Number	*Onore* Honor	*Servidore* Service	*Fede* Trust/ Loyalty	. . . *issimo* Superlatives	*Virtù* Virtue
I. Assurance Letters						
Late Albizzi Regime	32	0.66	0.38	0.38	0.19	0.03
Cosimo Period	27	0.59	0.30	0.41	0.41	0.04
Lorenzo Period	51	0.35	0.78	0.47	0.75	0.08
II. Office and Scrutiny Letters						
Late Albizzi Regime	45	0.76	0.42	0.11	0.33	0.16
Cosimo Period	29	0.79	0.59	0.17	0.48	0.14
Lorenzo Period	57	0.37	0.68	0.46	0.81	0.04
III. Recommendations						
Late Albizzi Regime	61	0.33	0.38	0.18	0.18	0.03
Cosimo Period	43	0.42	0.37	0.16	0.56	0.07
Lorenzo Period	89	0.24	0.64	0.34	0.96	0.10
IV. Property-related Requests						
Late Albizzi Regime	50	0.18	0.56	0.12	0.12	0.02
Cosimo Period	27	0.19	0.63	0.04	0.19	0.00
Lorenzo Period	13	0.08	0.85	0.54	0.85	0.08

in usage across all letter types, and particularly so after the Cosimo period. Obligation surges in use across all types, but the major increment here appears to be between the late Albizzi period and the Cosimo period, rather than after Cosimo. Expressions of willingness to cooperate (*volentieri*) and talk of advantage or profit (*utilità*) do the opposite, falling in frequency during the Cosimo period. The use of the verb *adoperare* increases over time in assurance letters, but it falls dramatically in office letters, perhaps supplanted by the more deferential verb *degnare*. Finally, some of the most striking changes are the flow of superlatives into property-related requests and the flow of the language of grace (*grazia*) into assurance letters, both during Lorenzo's time.

Linking Rhetoric to Social Distance

Undoubtedly our upbringing and our economic and cultural milieux subtly and at times dramatically affect our identities and impinge on the way we

2
11

Amico Friendship	Obligato Obligation	Volentieri Willingness	Utilità Advantage	Favor Favor/ Prefer	Grazia Favor/ Grace	Adoperare Contrive	Degnare To Deign
0.59	0.13	0.28	0.31	0.06	0.19	0.19	0.00
0.37	0.22	0.15	0.15	0.07	0.11	0 26	0.04
0.33	0.25	0.06	0.06	0.14	0.86	0.37	0.12
0.67	0.16	0.11	0.16	0.09	0.11	0.64	0.02
0.21	0.34	0.21	0.28	0.17	0.38	0.79	0.00
0.33	0.30	0.05	0.04	0.12	0.26	0.28	0.09
0.46	0.08	0.13	0.13	0.16	0.10	0.33	0.00
0.70	0.19	0.07	0.12	0.37	0.19	0.16	0.05
0.51	0.34	0.07	0.09	0.49	0.44	0.31	0.08
0.32	0.24	0.06	0.10	0.10	0.10	0.34	0.00
0.15	0.37	0.19	0.07	0.04	0.11	0.19	0.00
0.08	0.38	0.00	0.08	0.23	0.15	0.15	0.15

try to adopt public roles. The main message of Bourdieu's work may well be his stress on the tendency for people to (be constrained to) choose particular social practices—and to enact those practices in particular ways—that reproduce their structural position and reconfirm their cultural *habitus*. I would like to be a little more specific and suggest that people's "choices" of cultural practices in interaction are dependent not only on their own position, but also on their position vis-à-vis those to whom they write. This notion of position, or better, social distance, can be thought of in two ways: in terms of the "distance" between the social categories that writer and recipient instantiate—for example, lower-middle-class writer versus upper-class recipient; and in terms of patterns of concrete ties between writer and recipient or the groups to which they belong—for example, proximity in a marriage network. The content and style of presentation of self in favor seeking and the degree of familiarity expressed directly (through terms of address) or indirectly (through the assembly of frames and idioms) are likely to depend on both of these kinds of social distance.

Of all historical cases, the Florentine one is quite possibly best suited to put this theory to the test. The Florentines bequeathed to us more information about themselves than any society prior to the nineteenth century. Office-holding records, birth records, records of marriages, and data on household wealth and patterns of neighborhood residence are amazingly voluminous.[22] Transcripts of communal political deliberations (the *Consulte e Pratiche*) and texts revealing personal sensibilities such as the *ricordanze* of Morelli, Pitti, and others (Branca 1986) provide vivid insights. Listing these particular sources of information barely scratches the surface of the diverse body of materials available. I used some of this data to code letter writers and recipients for the social status of their families, their approximate household wealth, the neighborhoods in which they lived, their ages, and the kinds of marriage and/or economic ties that obtained between them at the time the letter was written.[23] Writer and recipient positions were compared to compute a rough measure of distance between them. These measures were then used as independent variables in models designed to predict certain compositional features of the letters: average usage of key terms, as above; whether formal or informal terms of address would be used, for example; whether or not writers would be likely to invoke honor in their writing; and the extent to which writers would be likely to use inflationary rhetoric.

The results partially rather than powerfully confirm the Bourdieuan argument. To begin, it is difficult to discern meaningful differences in keyword usage according to several of these dimensions of social distance. Economic networks seem not to matter, nor does path distance in the marriage market.[24] Age effects are diluted by the inflationary rhetoric used in letters written to Lorenzo the Magnificent by petitioners who were much older than he. The clearest effects are for status differences, neighborhood proximities, and number of direct marriage ties, as reported in table 6. The frequency with which inflationary rhetoric (the *-issimo* words), expressions of faith/trust (*fede*), talk of favor/grace (*grazia*), and talk of honor (*onore*) are used all increase as one moves from letters in which senders have higher status than recipients through those where there is status parity to those in which senders have considerably lower status than recipients.

Letters written to patrons who reside in the same neighborhood of the city as the letter writer are relatively light on inflationary rhetoric and brinkmanship, on expressions of faith/trust, obligation, and service, and on explicit discussion of favors (both *gratia* and *favore*). The use of each of these terms grows among letters written to patrons who reside in the same quarter (but different neighborhood) of the city, again in letters written to those patrons who reside in other quarters of the city, and yet again in letters written by foreigners. Further, the use of the weak-tie term *amicizia* increases, although modestly, as neighborhood distance increases.

Finally, consider the case of direct marriages between families. Average usage of *-issimo* keywords, of the terms faith/trust and obligation, of favor in both senses, of brinkmanship-like expressions of certainty, and of the deferential verbs *degnare* and *supplicare* all decline as the number of direct marriages increases. Particularly noteworthy here is the fact that many keywords are least used, not in letters between family members, but between individuals whose families are joined by three or more marriage ties, suggesting these are the most intimate and informalized relations of all. The following letter from Giovanni Rucellai to Lorenzo de' Medici of August 22, 1472 (*MAP* XXVIII, 448) provides a sense of how unadorned—even self-consciously merely obligatory—letters between intimates often were.

> Dearest relative, Another time in the past few days I recommended to you Zanobi da Ghiaccetto for *gonfaloniere di giustizia*, and knowing that he has loved your house as much as any citizen of our city has, and being a strict relative of ours, I can do no less than recommend him to you as fully as I can, considering that you would be doing for me as much as you will do for him.

Nevertheless, the link between social structural positioning and cultural practices is statistically significant only in a weak sense, for several reasons. First, statistical models involve considerable simplification, especially on the side of cultural practices. It is one thing to predict how many particular works of art or music a person will recognize on a survey based on her social structural position (Bourdieu 1984). It is another thing to classify a more complex piece of cultural production like a letter and to identify higher-order structural components in it. Second, even when we try to predict simple things, such as whether or not formal terms of address will be used, whether or not inflationary rhetoric will be used, whether or not writers will invoke honor, or friendship, or other core frames, structural positions afford modest insight. For example, a logistic regression analysis of patronage letters seeking to predict whether formal or informal terms of address will be used can correctly classify about 72 percent of the cases, with direct marriage ties, age difference, and wealth-level difference each having sig-

Table 6. Average Incidence of Selected Keywords by Social Distance between Writer and Recipient

	Number of Cases	. . . *issimo* Superlatives	*Fede* Faith/ Trust	*Obrigato* Obligation	*Grazia* Favor/ Grace
1. Difference in Political Status N = 1076					
Writer's family much more prestigious	22	0.09	0.14	0.14	0.18
Writer's family more prestigious	38	0.08	0.08	0.21	0.18
Relatively equal prestige	365	0.31	0.19	0.15	0.18
Recipient's family more prestigious	239	0.34	0.22	0.18	0.18
Recipient's family much more prestigious	146	0.44	0.27	0.16	0.38
Recipient's family vastly more prestigious	121	0.41	0.21	0.14	0.21
Foreigners	145	0.54	0.36	0.27	0.41
2. Neighborhood Proximity N = 1025					
Inside the gonfalon	170	0.25	0.11	0.09	0.15
Outside the gonfalon, inside the quarter	185	0.31	0.14	0.18	0.16
Outside the quarter, inside the city	532	0.34	0.27	0.16	0.23
Outside the city	138	0.61	0.34	0.25	0.41
3. Number of Direct Marriage Ties N = 1017					
No-last name Florentines, no direct ties	74	0.53	0.24	0.19	0.42
Last-named Florentines, no direct ties	604	0.41	0.24	0.16	0.24
One direct marriage tie	148	0.28	0.18	0.14	0.18
Two direct marriage ties	54	0.29	0.26	0.09	0.22
Same family	125	0.26	0.11	0.18	0.17
Three-plus direct marriage ties	12	0.25	0.00	0.08	0.08

nificant predictive effect. But the rate of accurate prediction is not high, and other dimensions of social position confound prediction. No model based on social position that I have tried seems able to predict other features, such as whether or not inflationary rhetoric will be used, or whether or not talk of honor will be employed. When information on primary letter content and date of composition is added, prediction becomes harder still. Thus, while social positions can be shown in the aggregate to affect the cultural production of patronage-related letters, these distances hardly will determine those practices. Agents skillfully manipulate their social structural

Favor Favor/ Prefer	*Amico* Friendship	*Onore* Honor	*Servidore* Service	*Certo* Certainty	*Degnare* To Deign	*Supplicare* To Entreat	*Amore* Love
0.00	0.18	0.14	0.45	0.14	0.09	0.00	0.09
0.11	0.32	0.32	0.32	0.21	0.00	0.00	0.16
0.14	0.42	0.35	0.37	0.25	0.02	0.02	0.17
0.12	0.41	0.35	0.33	0.19	0.02	0.01	0.21
0.13	0.39	0.34	0.42	0.18	0.08	0.02	0.24
0.11	0.26	0.39	0.57	0.21	0.07	0.01	0.22
0.23	0.41	0.28	0.77	0.37	0.11	0.06	0.35
0.11	0.31	0.36	0.32	0.18	0.02	0.00	0.15
0.11	0.38	0.41	0.38	0.21	0.05	0.02	0.29
0.12	0.41	0.31	0.39	0.23	0.04	0.02	0.17
0.25	0.43	0.28	0.71	0.38	0.12	0.08	0.38
0.21	0.42	0.35	0.89	0.24	0.09	0.04	0.44
0.13	0.37	0.34	0.43	0.23	0.05	0.02	0.21
0.14	0.45	0.39	0.26	0.21	0.01	0.01	0.20
0.06	0.54	0.21	0.35	0.19	0.02	0.00	0.04
0.12	0.34	0.39	0.34	0.19	0.02	0.00	0.11
0.00	0.42	0.17	0.17	0.17	0.00	0.00	0.25

profile, foregrounding certain social positions and backgrounding others in defiance of a simple structural determination of their fate. Finally, despite the wealth of positional information available for the Florentine case, critical aspects of social structure—confraternity co-membership, parish-based activity, godparentage relationships, employment relationships, and much more—remain largely unobservable. But these kinds of ties may well have been more important than the social structure measured in this study. However much sociologists aspire to link social network structure to cultural production, a cogent and coherent mapping often eludes us.

Conclusion

This chapter has established important patterns in the construction of Florentine patronage letters, examining them by virtue of their primary aim, the period of their composition, and the social attributes of the people sending and receiving them. It has also introduced the reader to a large number of letters and letter fragments that begin to provide a sense of what patronage discourse was all about. The idea was to present letter elements that one might typically see, even though the letters may not seem "typical" to untrained eyes. This is precisely the point of observing culture in action in the aggregate: to establish patterns empirically in order to know when we are seeing something different. For each type of letter, this chapter established a kind of typical "parts list." But what kind of machine gets assembled out of those parts? There may be many different answers to that question. The next two chapters will examine particular letters in detail to see the art of letter construction, and therefore the art of the network, truly "in action."

5

The Dynamics of Office Seeking

> I pray of you that you should wish to contrive for me, as your servant, that I be among the number of those eligible for office, and although I were already most obligated to you, this would be of a quality to provide a reminder that would last eternally, and something to esteem more than life itself—for life without honor/office is a true death (*la vita sanz'onore e un vero morto*).
> Piero di Giovanni Capponi to Lorenzo de' Medici, August 10, 1472

I have argued that Renaissance Florentine patronage letters constitute a corpus of patterned discourse. There were standardized practices for assurances of loyalty, for the presentation of self, for the framing of requests, and so on. Chapter 2 discussed the provenance of some of these practices, arguing for seeing patronage letter writing as a distinctive genre, or in sociological terms, a kind of flexible institution (Jepperson 1991). The last chapter identified continuities and changes in actual usage over time, and similarities and differences across types of letters. In this chapter, I turn my attention explicitly to variation and improvisation, and hence agency, in the construction of one kind of letter in particular: office-seeking patronage letters. The letter quoted at the beginning of this chapter (see figure 2 for a photograph of the document) gives a good sense of the value placed on office by Florentines. But that valuation of office made efforts to seek it particularly urgent and competitive. What messages does a letter communicate? And what makes a particular request distinctive?

Letters, or sets of letters, like relationships, are not static objects: they flow, they narrate a story, they pose contrasts. In short, they dynamically construct a relationship and an image of the letter writer. As a result, there is no substitute for examining letters in textual detail in order to articulate sociologically how people act strategically using available cultural frames and practices. I discuss many letters, but I focus ultimately on two streams of letters—one from Ormanno degli Albizzi and another from the supporters of Tedaldo Tedaldi—to Averardo de' Medici in 1430 regarding the staffing of a Florentine galley, comparing and contrasting their approaches

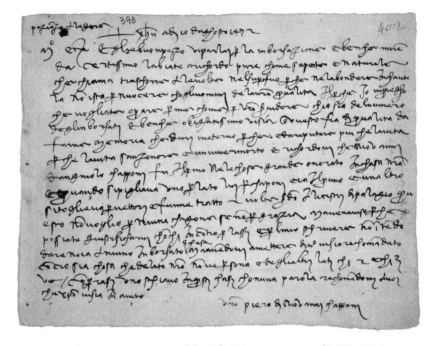

Fig. 2. Piero Capponi to Lorenzo de' Medici, August 10, 1472 (A.S.F., *MAP* XXVIII, 393r). Used by permission of the Ministero per i Beni e le Attività Culturali, Italy.

to favor seeking. I utilize the discourse analysis tools presented in the first chapter to analyze letters in various ways: for keyword content; for the construction of frames and techniques of frame alignment, frame lamination, and switching; for strategies by which the reader's attention is steered in particular directions; for rhetorical brinkmanship—communicating that one *expects* to be assisted; for contextualization cues; and for the inclusive and exclusive use of pronouns and other boundary-marking devices. These are interactional devices for the achievement of objectives, the portrayal of self, the representation of networks, and the erection of relationships.

Mapping the Rhetorical Space of Office Seeking

The fact that there is variability in the use of stock grammatical particles, rhetorical gestures, and substantive frames implies that the institution of patronage letter writing is rather like a rhetorical *space* in which writers act strategically. One handy technique for representing such a space is multi-dimensional scaling (MDS). I hypothesize that letters roughly resemble or differ from each other in terms of the patronage keywords, images, and phrases used to compose them. Thus the distance between letters in some patronage-seeking space may be represented graphically by means of a systematic, pairwise comparison of the arrays of keywords of which they are comprised. In short, letters are distinguishable from each other by means of their composition, just as persons are distinguishable from each other by virtue of the distinct webs of group affiliations they occupy (Simmel 1955). Conversely, keywords and the frames of meaning they evoke are distinguishable from each other by virtue of their usage in some population of letters—just as groups are distinguishable by means of the people who comprise them (Breiger 1974). Dispersion in the placement of patronage keywords helps us to distill the key rhetorical dimensions within which requests for patronage (in this case, offices) took place. Dispersion in the placement of letters can be usefully compared to underlying social structural and temporal factors.

I use MDS heuristically. This is so for a variety of methodological and substantive reasons. First, it would be impossible to define a bounded population of office letters to graph, and any change in sampling will alter the placement of letters in the MDS stimulus space.[1] Second, the boundaries between types of letters are blurry, so extracting a set of letters specifically concerned with attaining office involves judgment. Third, it would be impossible to define in the abstract all of the components available for composing a patronage letter. The selection of keywords must be guided by an extensive and recursive reading of the documents themselves, but conceivably some critical components may be missed. Fourth, collapsing the multitude of dimensions into two or three dimensions, as MDS does, inevitably distorts the "actual" rhetorical space.

More interesting are the substantive problems. First, as noted above, dispersion in the placement of letters can be usefully compared to differences in the relative structural placement of writer and recipient. But the correlation between the location of a letter in rhetorical space and the relative structural attributes (class, neighborhood, age, and so forth) of writer and recipient is imperfect. Indeed, it is inherently imperfect, in that writers are adept at not merely reproducing their structural position, but *improving* it by discursively foregrounding useful aspects of their profiles and backgrounding vulnerabilities. Second, since letters are measured in terms of

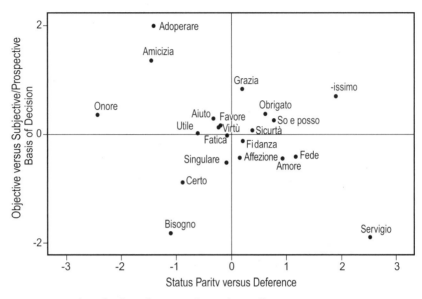

Fig. 3. MDS Plot of Selected Keywords Used in Office Letters

the keyword components out of which they are constructed, MDS cannot easily discern the "keying" (Goffman 1974, chap. 3) of these keywords. One can imagine a letter being written between friends that apes the style and content of obsequious patronage letters, yet by means of tone, exaggeration, or other subtle cues signals that it is to be understood ironically. Irony is better discerned through textual analysis than graphical analysis. Moreover, as I described in chapter 3, keywords such as *onore* can have multiple possible connotations — connotations that can only be discerned contextually. Consequently, MDS is largely a springboard for a more detailed, immersive analysis of the actors and discursive moves operating in the space it graphs.

Figure 3 is a plot of selected keywords used prominently in office-seeking letters, based on counts of the number of times they appear in each letter. Note first that friendship (*amicizia*) and service (*servigio*) are placed on opposite sides of the space. The verb *adoperare* — to contrive to make something happen, and in particular to engineer a favor for someone — is commonly used in conjunction with *amicizia*.

The *amicizia* frame implicitly treats self and other as equals — at least equally committed to a partisan project, and often engaged in a reciprocal exchange of favors. It is to recognize each as a helper of the other. By contrast, the service framing is deferential and explicitly clientelistic in nature. Identifying oneself or another as a servant is to suppress one's autonomy. Both, then, are constructions of relationships, but friendship in the Florentine case was often a fairly weak-tie relationship, whereas servanthood implied a strong, hierarchical, ongoing connection to a patron. Service articulates a deeper kind of commitment, a commitment often discursively sealed with a more inflationary rhetorical style.

Honor also lies diametrically opposite service. Framing oneself in terms of the pursuit of honor was to highlight one's autonomy and to claim equal membership in an elite that shared a sense of the importance of office holding and obligation to the city. Honorable men should be reluctant to self-identify as servants of another. The relation between honorable men is neither hierarchical nor affective, as is the servanthood relationship. Furthermore, honor typically meant that one was willing and worthy to hold office on the basis of one's own character and abilities, not on the basis of one's loyalties. Insofar as it implicitly stresses parity, honor is like *amicizia*. But insofar as it postures toward autonomy and eschews favoritism, it comes into contrast with *amicizia*. Thus the horizontal, or more precisely the northwest-to-southeast, axis of figure 3 measures rhetorical representations of status differences: parity on the left side, deference on the right.

Next consider the keywords toward the bottom of figure 3. Speaking in terms of *bisogno* (need) is to identify a problem that objectively merits attention. To express certainty about being helped is to expect that it will be performed, that it is demanded by the merits of the case. By contrast, to stress the favor/grace (*grazia*) of the patron, or to stress that one is obligated (*obrigato*) to the patron, is to admit that the patron has considerable discretion about how to proceed. Further, to argue in terms of need may be to put matters in a relatively unadorned framework. This is in contrast to the use of superlatives (*-issimo*) to raise the pitch of a request. Thus, the vertical (or more precisely, the southwest-to-northeast) dimension of figure 3 measures the degree of rhetorical inflation and the amount of patronal discretion implied in a request: low at the bottom of the figure, high at the top. Requests are objectively justified in the former case and, one might say, prospectively justified in the latter. This helps make further sense of the relative placement of honor versus friendship. Certainly, the man of honor craves a position; he does not strictly speaking "need" it. But as noted above, he eschews the favoritism associated with *amicizia*-based decision

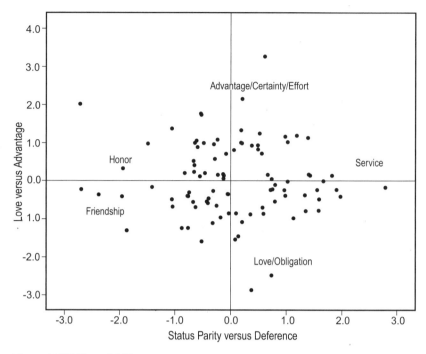

Fig. 4. MDS Plot of Office Letters

making. He believes that honor makes objective demands and he welcomes those demands. He is unwilling to identify himself as obligated (*obrigato*) to anyone. This tension between *amicizia* and honor, in terms of the degree to which decisions should be made objectively, is played out at length in the correspondence between Ormanno degli Albizzi and Averardo de' Medici discussed later in this chapter.[2]

Many of the relatively scarce, closely clustered keywords near the center of the plot can also be interpreted by means of these dimensions. Trust and loyalty (*fede, fidanza*) and expressions of love (*amore, affezione*) veer toward the poles of deference and patronal discretion. Note that love and affection are not typically associated with friendship, with its instrumentalist hue. "Objective" criteria such as virtue (*virtù*), effort (*fatica*), and advantage (*utilità*) tend toward the poles of status parity and objective need. Thus, different keywords and the frames they evoke calibrate the social distance between sender and receiver in different ways and construct the meaning of a request in different lights.

Table 7. Relative Positions of Writers and Recipients of the Letters Plotted in Figure 4, Averaged by Sector

Type of Relative Position	Core	All Outlying	Outlying Sectors			
			West *Parity*	East *Deference*	North *Need*	South *Obligation*
Marriage: Direct Ties	0.71	0.26	0.87	-0.22	0.36	-0.50
Marriage Path Distance	1.81	2.32	1.71	3.00	1.91	3.25
Difference in Social Status	1.11	1.00	0.79	1.50	0.80	1.17
Difference in Age	-0.63	-0.59	0.00	-0.86	-0.63	-2.00
Members of Same Family	0.09	0.02	0.07	0.00	0.00	0.00
Difference in Wealth	1.26	1.19	0.50	2.00	1.86	1.40
Neighborhood Proximity	2.49	2.76	2.29	2.89	3.08	3.00

Note: Number of direct marriage ties equals the number of ties between sender's and recipient's families from thirty years before to two years after the date of the letter. Low-status senders with no chance of marrying into recipient's family were coded −2. Marriage network path distance equals the actual distance between sender and recipient families in the marriage market. Differences in social status, age, and wealth, plus neighborhood proximity, are based on constructed scales, not raw numbers. For all, larger numbers betoken greater social or geographic distance. Negative average scores for age difference indicate sender was older than recipient.

Figure 4 presents a sample of one hundred office-seeking letters, distinguished from each other by their use of critical keywords.[3] Here the mapping is harder to interpret. Honor is clearly the predominant (though not exclusive) frame for letters on the left side of the figure, and it appears also in those toward the top of the figure. But letters invoking *amicizia* (friendship) also tend to cluster toward the left side. Service is clearly the predominant frames in letters on the right side, but expressions of obligation are found in letters in the southern periphery of the picture and even bleed over into the honor sector. Expressions of advantage, certainty, and effort (*fatica*), plus egalitarian letter salutations, all seem to predominate toward the top of figure 4, although explicit expressions of need are not particularly abundant there.[4] The critical keywords that anchor office-related patronage discourse are often used in conjunction with one another rather than alone, so letters do not cluster so neatly.

The question arises as to why each of these different available framings would get chosen by particular writers. The answer is partially rooted in the placement of writers in social structure, as reported in table 7. Letters located in the core of figure 4 (I categorize "core" letters as those having both x and y coordinates with absolute values less than or equal to one) are more often written by family members, and by persons with more direct marriage ties to the patron's family, greater proximity in the Florentine marriage market, and closer proximity in terms of the neighborhood geography of the city. Their social structural proximity allows them to be less excessive in framing their letters. Certain positional differences are even more clearly present when we examine the outlying letters sector by sector. In particular, those located in the "status parity/honor" sector of the diagram (that is, those letters located outside the core and toward the left side of figure 4) are written by persons from families with, on average, more direct marriage ties to the patron's family, closer proximity in the marriage market, greater social status parity and wealth parity with respect to the patron's family, and closer residential proximity, than is the case for any other sector.

There is also a temporal element to figure 4. That is best seen by examining figure 5, identical to figure 4 except each letter is labeled with the period in which it was composed. Clearly letters written before 1434 predominate on the left-hand side of the figure, while letters written to Lorenzo the Magnificent predominate on the right-hand side of the figure. Letters written during the intervening Cosimo and Piero de' Medici periods are sprinkled throughout. Figure 5 thus depicts a drift in the composition of the Florentine office-seeking letter over several decades.

The patterns in table 7 are suggestive, but they are only averages. There are several core cases where relatively low-status writers write in intimate terms to high-status recipients. This intimacy across social distance is endemic to the performative part of clientelism (Stokes 1995; Auyero 2001). So to better understand this world of office-related favor seeking I turn now to a qualitative examination of particular letters.

The Qualitative Analysis of Office Seeking: Patronage Letters as Exercises in Framing

First I will present some fairly simple examples of different sorts of framing of motive and castings of relationships in office-seeking patronage letters. I will then proceed toward more complicated forms of laminating together different frames of meaning to produce textured public presentations of self. Throughout, I will show how individual writers use the substantive frames I have described so far, but also how they construct their letters to

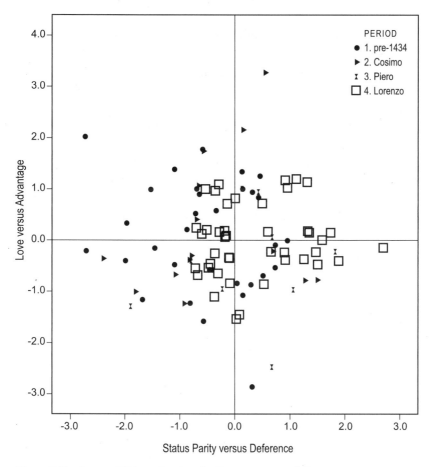

Fig. 5. Office Letters Written During the Pre-1434 Era and the Lorenzo Era

achieve a portrait of themselves and their motivations by amplifying certain themes through repeated use of keywords, by communicating their confidence in being well served, by adjusting the limits of their politeness, by linking their interests rhetorically to those of their would-be patrons, by ranking their preferences, by stitching together or contrasting multiple frames justifying their requests, and by providing the context for their requests in the course of their writing. These techniques for self-presentation and "networking" appear rather modern, even if they are harnessed to building relationships in substantive terms rather different from those we might seek.

Arguably the simplest way to request assistance in obtaining office is to ask for it bluntly, as in a letter of Francesco di Niccolò Baldovinetti to Forese Sacchetti written on October 12, 1409 (*Conv. Soppr.* 78, 324: 172; case 10 in the core of figure 4): "I pray of you as much as I can, that if you were to see yourself able to provide me with some office or other commission, either keeping track of your soldiers or inspection or some similar thing, I pray you advise me of it, for it would be singularly pleasing to me . . . And I pray that you keep me in mind in whatever you might see that would increase my honor." There are stock elements here ("as much as I can"; "singularly pleasing"), but the tone of this letter, written using the informal *tu*, suggests that the two men were already well acquainted with each other, so that hardly any framing of Baldovinetti's character or situation needed to be provided in the letter, nor hardly any rationale for Sacchetti to take action on Baldovinetti's behalf.

Sometimes informality, however, takes the form of "positive politeness" (Brown and Levinson 1987) and becomes an explicit part of the framing, as in another letter from the core of figure 4 (case 6), a letter from Marcello Strozzi to his kinsman Simone Strozzi (*C.S.* III, 131: 12):

> Speaking with such familiarity (*dimestichezza*) as we may together, I pray of you that you be the agent (*operatore*) whereby Giannozzo Cavalcanti, my brother-in-law, who has need of earning a little money, and also of having some office (*onore*), receive from you the office of inspector, so that this May he is sent out. I pray this of you considering it to be a singular pleasure of mine.

The opening clause here provides a particular "keying" (Goffman 1974, chap. 3) of patronage interaction. Marcello does not simply follow the form of asking for a favor, but more or less detaches his request from the typical form (which is thus constructed as inadequate and not to be taken at face value) and instead casts his request in terms of the intimacy he already shares with Simone.[5] This keying justifies the candor of the request that follows. "Yes, I am asking you for help," acknowledges Marcello, "but *we both know* this is a different situation than most patronage interaction." Further, different rationales for granting this favor—*parentado*, need, honor— are stitched together by Marcello as jointly conducive to Simone taking action on Cavalcanti's behalf. Marcello rhetorically presents a multitude of common ties and motivations he and Simone share to deepen Simone's sense of commitment to him. A letter from Iacopo di Ugolino Mazzinghi to Lorenzo de' Medici of May 29, 1472 (*MAP* XXV, 159; case 67 in the core of figure 4) similarly stitches together multiple justifications: personal loyalty, a legacy of familial loyalty, and *parentado*.

> The great faith I have in you gives me confidence (*mi fa pigliare sicurtà*) to write to you to remind you that it would give me great pleasure were it to please you to contrive that my son Giuliano were one of the priors for July and August—as much as it pleases you and when you can—reputing it a very great pleasure because he is my eldest, with the youngest being twenty-eight this coming August. And he is loyal[?] as I and my family have always been to your family—for other families and other loves I have not known, and also being born of your flesh (*essendo nato del vostre carne*) [Iacopo's mother was a Medici]. For all of these reasons (*per tutte queste cose*), may it please you to do as I ask, insofar as it appears to you, for always I will be content with what seems best to you.

As we often see in these letters, here the writer actively distinguishes his feelings for the Medici from his feelings for all others, and, especially through the trope of *parentado*, he aligns his identity with Lorenzo's (Snow et al. 1986).

As noted above, *amicizia* was an important frame used in office-seeking letters, although it was often used in juxtaposition with other frames. Consider the following excerpt from a letter of July 25, 1472, written by Matteo Buonaguisi to Lorenzo de' Medici (*MAP* XXVIII, 329; case 76 in the core of figure 3). Buonaguisi requests that he be considered for the upcoming *imborsazione* on the personalistic grounds of his loyalty and desire to serve Lorenzo's friends. However, he also deliberately distinguishes his claim on the basis of *amicizia* from a claim on the basis of virtue or merit:

> I recommend myself to you, praying of you that it please you to want to give this start to my family, advising you that you will find many more more expert than I, but more faithful to you and your affairs, none. And although I were not worthy (*sofficiente*) of such a distinction, I would desire to be seen as are many others, to be able to find myself in such places where I could please you and your friends.

Again, the effect of this composition is to make friendship the dominant motif, but that effect is strengthened by contrasting *amicizia* with Matteo's self-professed insufficiency on the grounds of objective merit.[6]

By contrast, in a letter of May 14, 1431, from Bartolo Ridolfi to Averardo de' Medici (*MAP* III, 126; case 37 on the upper left side of figure 4), the dominant frame of *amicizia* is supported and supplemented by other criteria. Bartolo writes on behalf of a certain Benedetto da San Miniato: "[He] is a person for whom I would always exert myself to do good, both because he merits it and I am obliged to him, and because he is a friend and relative of your, and my, dear friends." Benedetto was in search of a new position, and Bartolo was urging Averardo to help him obtain one with a different *signore*. He went on to write:

> For this reason if there is any favor or pleasure whatsoever you can do for me, as much as I am able I pray of you that it please you to fix him up with Signore Michele as his chancellor. . . . He is an able person in this and everything, and if you will do it, as I know you can, you will be many, many times thanked by Signore Michele; and to me, especially, among whatever pleasures you may afford me, this is one of the greatest ones. I will not express myself further on this, because I know it is not necessary, and because things will be arranged in the way you want, and your will and mine are the same thing.

The boundaries of friendship and the confluence of interests are actively constructed in this letter: yes, Benedetto is an able person, but more important he is a friend of the friends of both of us, and so a circle of *amicizia* is drawn around him and Averardo. Bartolo urges Averardo to consider the consequences of providing this assistance, "speaking for another" (Schiffrin 1993) by anticipating for Averardo the kind of gratitude he could expect to receive from Signore Michele, and from Bartolo himself. Bartolo explicitly ranks the awarding of this favor against others past, present, and future. Consequently this request is contextualized and prioritized in light of others, intimating where Bartolo's deepest preferences lie. Further, he gives an account of how Benedetto has chosen not to go home: "For you know all the offices there are rotten and the country is in darkness." This short narration of the reality of the situation gives greater justification to Benedetto's plan and Bartolo's portrayal of his need, and it draws writer and recipient into shared knowledge of the context of the request. Finally, Bartolo actively communicates an expectation of being assisted by claiming an identity between his and Averardo's will, and confidence that Averardo can bring to pass whatever he wishes to have done. This amounts to a kind of rhetorical brinkmanship that is commonly found in these letters.[7]

Under certain circumstances, the request for favor on behalf of friends had to be hedged with rhetorical concern for honor. A letter of Palla di Nofri Strozzi to Simone di Filippo Strozzi of August 11, 1421 (*C.S.* III, 132: 50; case 8 in the friendship sector of figure 4) demonstrates such a texturing of motivations:

> I wrote to you praying that you contrive, within the bounds that honor requires, that Galeotto di [?] be elected to the constabulary of this place, telling you of his *virtù* and gentility, and also that he would be cognizant of his place as I understand it. And although I hear at the constabulary there is no place because the electors have deliberated, still the captain has not been provided. It would be dear to me if concerning this you might operate for my friend. May it not be bothersome to you to arrange the consent of Raffacane, who is one of the electors. And recommend him to him, and contrive some action in this matter as much as you see possible, while retaining honor. He is a man of such *virtù* that I do not doubt that he would honor those who were to elect him, and who were to perform any favor for him.

Palla offers this recommendation for his friend, but he does so in the context of honor. Twice he emphasizes that pulling strings should be done within the demands of honor, and although Galeotto can be expected to be loyal to those who would help him, Palla tries to suggest that this loyalty is a product of his sense of honor, as though returning favors were a matter of objective personal integrity. This letter highlights the potential tension between acting with an eye to honor and acting with an eye to *amicizia*. The expression *salvando l'onore*, which afforded the recipient an opportunity to save face if he failed to satisfy a request, became a stock element in the way Florentines went about making requests and recommendations. Here the expression is particularly apt, for Palla is inviting Simone to intervene illegitimately in a political process that has already been decided.

These different manners of invoking *amicizia* can be contrasted as a whole with examples in which supplicants portray themselves as servants of their patron. For instance, we have a letter of Francesco di Luigi Benintendi to Cosimo de' Medici of September 1, 1435 (*MAP* XII, 25; case 50, between the service and love/obligation sectors of figure 4):

> My honorable elder, This letter only for the reason that I find myself in Pisa as you know, and I am searching for some occupation with

which to sustain myself until the galleys leave, but still I have been able to find nothing—nor will I obtain anything without your help, such that I pray of you, as your faithful follower and servant, that in service to me you write a short note to the Marchese Malaspini, who is here as you know. . . . And further if you were to see another place in which to situate me with your letter, I pray of you, that wherever you put me, I will do you honor. Perhaps I use too many words, but the great faith I have in you moves me, such that I pray of you that I be recommended to you, as I am in a bad sort of state at present.

This letter, signed "your least servant," goes to considerable length to stress the dependence of the sender on Cosimo for help, as he claims implicitly to have no other source of assistance. But it also implicitly suggests that this assistance is warranted on the basis of a standing relationship: I have been "your faithful follower and servant." Moreover, various cues are used to communicate simultaneously Cosimo's power and Benintendi's confidence in being helped. Rather than the letter communicating much in the way of news to Cosimo, Benintendi frames it as though Cosimo no doubt were already aware of his circumstances. He enacts shared understandings with Cosimo. Rather than the strong framing betokening his desperation, Benintendi tries to suggest it is a function of his enthusiasm for Cosimo. As a result, Benintendi sets up his relationship to Cosimo as though assistance should flow automatically from the letter.

Compare that to the framing of the following letter from Luca Carducci to Giovanni di Cosimo de' Medici of February 3, 1454 (*MAP* I, 252; case 15 in the love/obligation sector of figure 4):

Thinking of how many times we have bothered you, requesting of you favors for us and for our friends, through the mediation of Antonio degli Strozzi your brother-in-law and our honorable brother in love, it is not without trepidation I thought to write to your Magnificent Lordship to ask a new favor (*gratia*) and service, but provided it is an appropriate matter[?], noble and generous souls are in their magnanimity no less ready to grant what anyone were to demand. Considering the *virtù* and benevolence of your Lordship, I presume with great confidence to ask of your Lordship a favor, which is that Matteo Carducci my brother, at present *podestà di Piccioli*, by your *virtù* and efforts (*operatione*) be reappointed for one year or for six months, for the election has been postponed[?] for one year . . . Such that to your Lordship in this instant I recommend this matter, hoping that thus

Matteo will carry himself to better things, and always we will remain obligated to your magnificent Lordship, whom may God in His grace always maintain and prosper.

Various messages are being communicated here. Luca and Giovanni share an intimate connection with the same individual, a contextual fact that Luca himself provides for us in the body of the letter. And Luca is writing on behalf of someone for whom he feels personal affection. But the stress on bother, presumption, and trepidation, and the circumlocution they effect, quickly distances Luca from his own request; he seems to self-impose limits on his relationship with Giovanni. The personalism inherent in this request is actively portrayed as slightly distasteful, so that the reading of it as an opportunity for the exercise of magnanimous generosity takes center stage.

Finally, a straightforward distinction between motivations occurs in a letter of May 22, 1434, from the notary Iacopo di Antonio di Salvestro to Matteo di Simone Strozzi (*C.S.* III, 112: 175; case 3, in the core of figure 4):

> Honored like a father, I heard that Messer P[iero] your relative was elected captain of Cortona, such that I beg of you that, if he is not so furnished, you speak to him about me being his notary. And if he wants information about my affairs, I went with Antonio di Tedice degli Albizzi to Pisa when he was *podestà*, and with Buonaccorso Pitti to Prato. I am not concerned with the salary so much as with acquiring friends. I say no more for the moment. May Christ always watch over you. And if I can do anything in Pistoia, I am ready to do whatever is pleasing to you.

In some respects, this writer adopts customary practices to present his request. For example, the letter uses a customary *vi priego* formula; the salutation partakes of both honor and fatherhood frames common in office-seeking letters; and it ends with a formulaic expression of generalized reciprocity that is typical in favor-seeking letters. The mention of friends suggests in a fairly standardized way Iacopo's desire for reliable connections with an eye toward advancement, and, ultimately, his desire for relationships.

Then how do we read through this letter to a credible portrait of the writer? First, note how this claim for friends is framed: "I am not concerned with the salary so much as with acquiring friends." This is an answer to an unposed question: Which is more relevant to understanding Iacopo's motives in obtaining this appointment: friendship or money? Iacopo's writing contextualizes his request for favor reflexively through the very text by means of which that request is made, assertively establishing the relevant frame for understanding his request. In this publicly constructed image of his private motivation, Iacopo claims his role in *amicizia* corresponds to his true self, his "real" motive.

Second, the letter foregrounds critical social networks discursively. Actors are positioned in networks, in status groups, in relationships. Yet in discourse relevant past relationships can be highlighted and problematic ones can be cast in shadow. Iacopo here invokes his connection to two powerful and prestigious Florentine families. In effect, Iacopo is saying, "These are the kinds of relationships I have sought and found in the past." Writers presented themselves through patronage letters, attempting to establish their worthiness discursively while constructing a context of relationships with relevant others—again discursively—by which their worthiness could be inferred and tested. They manipulated words to present a textured public picture of their "private" motivations, and this framing was integral to the achievement of network positions.

Framing across Letters: The Dynamic Construction of Relationships

As the project of self-presentation is inherently designed to change one's structural position for the better, it is essential to trace the ways in which this change was accomplished across a series of letters, rather than simply asserted in one. We can do this for the case of Ormanno di Rinaldo degli Albizzi, the son of one of the commune's most prominent politicians, who wrote a series of letters in early 1430 to Averardo de' Medici, requesting assistance in securing an office in the naval service of the commune, in particular focusing on the arms he would be allowed to command in the war effort against Lucca. At this time, Averardo was *consolo del mare* in Pisa, a position with considerable influence over such appointments. Ormanno's difficulty was that while he was equal (if not superior) in social status to Averardo, the two found themselves on opposite sides of the factional battles shaping up in the city. Consequently, Ormanno had to begin by making a claim of being served with an office on the basis of honor, not on the basis of *amicizia*. Any claim he might eventually make concerning *amicizia* would have to be actively contextualized.

Six of the ten extant letters Ormanno sent to Averardo are included in figure 3: *MAP* II, 148, 152, 168, 180, 225, and 226, in chronological order (cases 17, 18, 19, 21, 28, and 29). The first five of these appear on the left periphery, where talk of honor predominates, while the last is situated very near the origin. Ormanno's framing shifts during this stream of letters in a way that dynamically constructs his motivations. Custom dictated that he frame himself as of inferior status, but as we shall see, the rhetoric of the letters often suggests parity of status between himself and Averardo. Meanwhile, the intimacy of talk in the letters contrasts oddly with Ormanno's unwillingness to commit himself personalistically to Averardo and his friends. In a sense, then, all of the cardinal poles of the rhetoric of office-seeking identified in figure 3—status parity versus deference, strong versus weak ties, objective merit versus personalistic favor—are activated in this complex correspondence.

Two basic issues arise: 1) How does Ormanno go about framing an image of himself through the narrative, imagery, and cuing in these letters? 2) Why is the ultimate image he constructs a credible one? As to the first of these, the presentation of Ormanno's "true" self follows this basic trajectory: 1) I, Ormanno, assert that I am basically unconcerned with money (salary); 2) more importantly, I openly disparage the crass politics of *amicizia*, that is, favoritism; I eschew it as a base motivation; 3) I repeatedly adopt the implied high ground of concern for personal honor tied to the destiny of the commune; but then 4) I re-key my ostentatious rhetoric as mostly playacting and quietly and "self-revealingly" adopt the language and tone of *amicizia*—which I had disparaged—as an acceptable portrait of my motivation, my interests, and my understanding of the way things work. We could not know how extraordinary Ormanno's writing is in the absence of a quantitative analysis of many letters, yet we could also not fully understand Ormanno's self-presentation and the nature of its change across letters without observing his rhetorical strategies closely using concepts borrowed from discourse analysis.

These letters are too long and involved to be reproduced in full here (see McLean 1996; Guasti 1873). Some aspects of them are standard. For example, Ormanno repeatedly expresses certainty that he will obtain Averardo's assistance, as if to create through the construction of the letter a view of the facts and his alter's character that would of themselves demand that the favor be supplied: "My honor I know I do not have to recommend to you" (case 17); "I have faith in you as in a dear father" (case 17); "I know that you desire that I have honor" (case 18); "I will have entered a new labyrinth if you do not help me—as I have a firm hope you will" (case 18); "I am most certain, wherever you find yourself I cannot have anything other than honor" (case 19); "You being there, [the galley] cannot be other than well armed" (case 21). This is particularly noteworthy near the beginning of the first letter in a place where medieval dictaminal writers would have inserted a *captatio benevolentiae*—a rhetorical gesture designed to flatter and curry the favor of the recipient. Ormanno writes, "You are on the job: I think for all of this the galley will be furnished." Further, Ormanno portrays his relationship with Averardo using the customary imagery of a father-son relationship. The opening salutation of the first two letters and the fourth is "Dearest like a father." In the first letter he writes, "Consider it as if this affair were touching your son, although I don't want so much, but I do have faith in you as in a dear father"; in the second letter he writes, "In you I trust as in a dear father." This likening of the patron-client role relationship to the father-son role relationship was ubiquitous throughout Florentine popular culture, perfectly appropriate when the recipient of a letter is considerably older than its sender, as is true here. Finally, Ormanno offers the customary assurances of a willingness to respond to his patron's wishes: "I would be next to you at your every command" (case 17); "I am at your disposal" (case 17); "In conclusion, again I recommend myself to you" (cases 18, 19, and 21).

But Ormanno is inordinately adamant at the end of his first letter that he is concerned about his personal honor: "You hear the need of my honor, for you initiated it, and likewise you may give it its fulfillment." In so writing, Ormanno links his own sense of honor to that of Averardo, drawing a boundary around the two of them and claiming they are linked by a common motivation leading to a common path of action. This is the third time honor has been mentioned in the first letter, but its salience is increased further in the second letter in which Ormanno alludes to his honor fully six times.[8] This amplification (Snow et al. 1986) of the honor frame gives the first two letters a certain urgency: "Perhaps it would be well now more than ever to start, I don't say to conclude things, but to show our intentions and to write to officials, comrades and also the sailors that they take up no other exercises away from here such that when the time comes none of them will be missing."

Whereas in the first letter Ormanno makes the stock claim, "[I will do] what I think will be pleasing to you and others and do from now on what goes toward my honor and advantage," in the second letter he exclaims, "I would rather die than turn back at the expense of my honor." Honor now apparently exceeds life itself as a value; how inappropriate it would be now to speak openly of "advantage." The second letter also contains more extravagant pleas for assistance and more interpretive effort from Ormanno concerning the motivations and opinions of various actors.

> For certain, Averardo, if this galley be armed with men well-chosen and well-tested, we will have honor; if the opposite, we will face great danger, and you are aware of this. The best thing is always to be prepared. Rinieri Lotti and Banco [Bencivenni], who is here in the *galeotta*, conspire in not taking care to arm the galley, and use dishonorable words against the last consuls, and against me. It's all wrong, and God knows that nothing but honor pulls me here.

Here Ormanno paints the alternatives starkly: we will have honor if you follow my advice, shame and humiliation if you do not. And here also is an example of generality shifting (Mische 2003): "we" the commune will succeed, but also "we"—Ormanno and Averardo—will share in the honor of having done what is best for the commune. The pronoun "we" is used inclusively to link Ormanno's private destiny to that of Averardo, and to the publicly prized destiny of the commune. By contrast, Rinieri Lotti and Banco Bencivenni are represented by Ormanno as being outside the circle of respect for honor (cf. Lamont 1992). They speak disrespectfully of the previous set of officials, and of Ormanno himself.

In the postscript to the second letter, Ormanno further distinguishes himself from Banco Bencivenni:

> I have from Ser Mariotto Bencini, your notary here, that Banco writes a long letter to the consuls, which contains many things at my expense, etc.; and everything he says is the will and opinion of you consuls. I know they are his own; he is a man who sows scandal. I believe he will return here soon; how much more of his bad morals have your friends heard. He is a person who has done badly for himself, and does not take care of the honor of his companion more than his own.

Banco, says Ormanno, misrepresents the opinions of others and treats honor selfishly. His character failings are made out to be directly detrimental to the execution of communal policy. Implicitly, Ormanno suggests that he is a different sort of person, and more trustworthy than Banco. Ormanno speaks for another here (Schiffrin 1993), and he relies on the spoken authority of someone whom he can be reasonably sure Averardo will trust, the notary Bencini. Thus his speaking for another is distinguished from Banco's. Again he draws an inclusive boundary around himself and Averardo and excludes Bencivenni from the circle of "honorable people," using the re-narration of gossip in the city to buttress his claim.[9]

Ormanno writes later in the same postscript: "For you were the reason I was elected chief of this blessed galley, I know you desire that I have honor, which I hope to have by the grace of God, if it be made well-armed, and with experienced men, and not dictated by friendship, as it seems to me Rinieri and Banco wish it." Ormanno here asks for a decision in favor of honor, and therefore a decision against friendship (*amicizia*): deserved patronage over partisanship. This juxtaposition and ranking of relevant motivations is actively introduced by the letter's author; honor is rhetorically made into the "deeper" motivation. Ormanno argues that a sense of honor, which he possesses in spades, is the prime requisite for the task at hand. Patronage is acceptable, if based on the merits of the candidates and their prospects for performing their assigned duties well.

The same message is conveyed slightly differently in the third letter. Where Ormanno does mention friends here, near the beginning of the letter, they are "your" friends, not "our" friends. Toward the end of the letter, "we" (Ormanno and his soldiers, the commune, Ormanno and Averardo) is used inclusively to link Ormanno's personal honor to Averardo's, as it had been in the second letter. A similar use of pronouns occurs in the fourth letter (*MAP* II, 180):

> I think, by the grace of God, if I go up, I will do honor to whomever has done it to me, and I will make a believer of anyone who speaks badly; for everything proceeds from envy. It pleases me that Messer Rinaldo and you have been together; he wrote of this to me. Some desire his return, and those who wish him ill will desire it most. Even so, there appear to the *Dieci* for now proofs that he can do some good in this blessed enterprise, in which consists the exaltation of all your friends, and especially considering that it is by the *Dieci*: what a great reprisal it is to the adversaries, and does them quite a lot of damage.

Ormanno is "inside" with respect to Averardo's honor calculus, but he is outside his circle of "friends." Implicitly, Averardo is entitled to a friendship (read "politically partisan") network, but Ormanno is not in it. Partisanship and patronage networks, based respectively on favoritism and merit, are constructed as divergent in these letters.[10]

Finally, these letters show us something concerning the issue of making and breaking frames. In three letters, Ormanno frames Averardo as a father, as a superior; but halfway through the second letter, he momentarily steps out of this deferential role and says, "For certain, Averardo" (*per certo, Averardo*). This is an address to a peer, not a father, and it cues a plea for honor. So despite the "patronal" beginning, this is not a letter sequence about favoritism, but about honor and honor's due. Ormanno breaks through the frame set up in the salutation, as if his true self must speak through the decorous forms with which he began. It may seem that this insistence stems from his impetuous and arrogant character, just as he claims in a later letter that all criticism of him stems from envy (*invidia*). But whatever its source, it is as if his inner self is being sincerely represented here. The way this self and its aims are linked to those of Averardo evolves across episodes. At the beginning, Ormanno practices a kind of extension technique (Snow et al. 1986); his promise, "I will await whatever they and your companions there will say, and immediately I will obey as much as is assigned to me," communicates the message that he can conform to Averardo's plans and expectations. But later, he seems to say, "Do well by me and you will discover your reward in the honor I will reflect onto you"—that is, "Assuming you are an honorable man, you cannot fail to act in the way I request of you." Stated thus, his approach resembles more the discussion of bridging by Snow et al., where the recipient of a message is invited to bend so as to conform to the sender's expectations. Overall, Ormanno fluctuates between these modes of bringing Averardo's interests into congruence with his own, rather as clientage typically oscillates between gestures of deference and defiance.

Although the first letters set up honor as Ormanno's cardinal motivation, a motivation that implies he will dependably pursue certain kinds of action, this frame is noticeably adjusted in the last two letters here. The opening of the first of these marks a critical moment.

> Until now I have written to you concerning the matter of the galley in one manner, and now I speak in another. It seems to me they intend not to arm the galley for now, which is a great happiness to me. And if my father was not returning, I did not see a way of being able to leave earlier anyway. It seems to me the affair has transpired well, and according to my wishes (*desiderio*). I did not want to refuse, so as not to give pleasure to our enemies (*nostri nemici*), for they would have

said that I had done it from cowardice or fear that someone else might be put in my place. If this had been the case, I would not have given so much trouble to our[?] friends (*agli amici*). The fact is, with time, everything comes. I thank you very much for everything you have contrived (*aoperato*) on my behalf.

"Until now I have written . . . in one manner, and now I speak in another." This sentence betokens a change in frame, a different tactic for speaking, and seemingly a yet more honest representation of his motivations. Here Ormanno modestly reconstructs an interpretation of his earlier presentation of self—a new keying, or more precisely, a "re-keying" of his already keyed performance of the patronage letter idiom (Goffman 1974, 81). Earlier he had taken a stand against threats to his honor. Now he shows himself more patient and willing to let the affair develop as Averardo had contrived it should, and he even claims this accords with his private wishes. Suddenly, Ormanno offers a backstage explanation to the effect that his onstage zeal for honor was wrapped up with sustaining appearances, to quell gossip in the city.

Take note: this is the gossip of "our" enemies within the city. Unless his quest were fully justified in his own eyes, Ormanno now claims, he would not have given so much trouble to his and Averardo's friends. This is post hoc accounting—frame construction on the go—and through it, Ormanno subtly suggests a drift to a more intimate relation with the Medici, whether sincere or not. He says, in effect, "I spoke to you, Averardo, in a way consistent with how I had to act with others in order to maintain my reputation." Like his father before him, Ormanno felt damned if he did and damned if he didn't. If he refused to go unarmed, his enemies would call him a coward; if he proceeded rashly, they would accuse him of having too much concern for status and too little sense of civic responsibility. This situation required subtle management. In the last letter, Ormanno simplifies the request: "Concerning the talk one hears here about this galley, I want to beg that you arrange through your office that I be called there. Give me the spirit to make Messer Rinaldo happy, and to see that everyone who has exerted himself (*s'è aoperato*) on my behalf will have satisfaction." And only in this last letter does Ormanno use the verb *pregare*, the primary verb in patronage supplication. Its absence in earlier letters could hardly fail to communicate to Averardo his expectation of satisfaction and his effective treatment of Averardo as an equal. Only at the end does his writing turn into a "properly" framed request and come into line with the filial framing used in the earlier letters, by which time, however, he has traversed considerable terrain in laying bear his complex motivations, far surpassing Piero Alberti's simple formulae for dealing with different alters. Throughout, Ormanno communicates the context of his action and motivation. This is not something simply given outside of the text of the letters, but rather it permeates them. It is through discourse as a form of agency that placement in social and cultural space is communicated. Conversely, through the complex representation of the relationship between Averardo and Ormanno, we can sense the tensions and conflicting significances that particular network ties could have.

Was this elaborate rhetoric about honor credible to Averardo? The answer is a qualified "yes." We do not know if Ormanno went to sea, but we do know three things: 1) that Averardo had responded to Ormanno's letters (*MAP* II, 168); 2) that other sources (that is, Ormanno's letters from his own father) indicate that people were talking about his appointment, and that Averardo was trying to do something; and 3) that some of the Medici partisans whose correspondence to Averardo survives thought that Ormanno's request was worthy of being satisfied.[11]

Ormanno came from a family inordinately attentive to honor, and he likely thought that Averardo would respond to an honor-based plea. Yet the emerging tensions between the two families meant that Ormanno's request could not be credibly based on a self-portrait claiming partisan *amicizia* with Averardo. The change of tone in the last two letters is not something planned from the outset, but rather it emerges in the course of the interaction in response to external constraints: threats to his honorable reputation from a group of enemies who wanted to find fault with him goaded Ormanno into seemingly rash statements. Inherent in his situation is that Ormanno must orchestrate an image of himself for two audiences simultaneously, offering to only one of them (Averardo) a theatrical aside about his "true" feelings. Once his reputation for honor is salvaged, Ormanno revises the presentation of himself to assure Averardo that they are on the same wavelength. Throughout, the relationship between Ormanno and Averardo is framed through words that texture the image of the letter writer and shape or construct the proper attitude of the reader. Ormanno sought a determinate favor that would allow him to execute his self-image as a man of honor and a patriot of the commune through a studied activation and structuring of his relationship with an important gatekeeper for favor. In these cases and others, frame assemblage, frame breaking, and narrations of one's experiences and motives comprise techniques that had evolved, in the context of a fluid clientelistic politics of opportunities and favors, to depict motivation and support interpersonal credibility.

Seeking Office through Partisanship: The Tedaldi Correspondence

Ormanno's letters were not the only ones addressed to Averardo during this period. A whole host of other correspondents wrote to him seeking assistance with appointments. I will examine one subset of these letters in the balance of this chapter.

On February 7, 1430, Tedaldo Tedaldi, a petitioner from Averardo's own *gonfalone* of Vaio, wrote on behalf of his son, Papi, supporting him for a position with the galley (*MAP* II, 185; case 22 in the core of figure 4). This was followed by a letter from Papi himself on February 10 (*MAP* II, 198; case 24 in the core of figure 4), another letter from Tedaldo on February 23 (*MAP* II, 239), a letter from Bartolomeo Tedaldi on March 2 (*MAP* II, 253), a third letter from Tedaldo on that same day (*MAP* II, 256; case 30 in the core of figure 4), a fourth letter from Tedaldo on the following day (*MAP* II, 257), and finally, a fifth letter from Tedaldo on March 12 (*MAP* II, 276). I will briefly discuss these letters here, demonstrating how differently office holding is construed and how differently the motives of office seekers are constructed in them. I will also document the way that networking involves the coherent efforts of a number of supporters and the discursive *representation* of a community of supporters. I will begin by presenting the text of the first of these letters (*MAP* II, 185).

> Honored like a brother, By your Giuliano was shown to me a [letter] in which you write concerning the matter of the *galeotta* for Papi Tedaldi, concerning which I immediately came to Giovanni di Antonio Pucci, and he tells me they have deliberated to prepare the galley and the *galeotta* and to you they will have committed the task of arming it, and to you remains the task of placing on the galley and the *galeotta* whomever you would please. And if it were necessary to do anything here in service to Papi, would you advise me of it and of what one were to do. And because I am certain there is no need to remind you of our affairs, I say no more, except advise me if I have to do any one thing rather than another, just as I am certain you would

do concerning your affairs. I say no more for now. May Christ watch over you. You know my need.

Tedaldo's self-presentation here only makes sense given his family's Medicean partisanship. First, he uses the familiar *tu* and the salutation "Honored like a brother." Immediately we see a less deferential tone, prompted both by the Tedaldi family's established Medicean sympathies (D. Kent 1978), their indebtedness to them (*Catasto* 81: 36), and Tedaldo's age—roughly the same as Averardo's.[12] Tedaldo also indicates his communication with the hard-core Medici partisan Giovanni Pucci. No wonder, then, the tone of the letter is so forthright. Especially striking is the last sentence, actually standing alone after the closing material of the letter: "You know my need" (cf. D. Kent 1978, 94). This is effectively a bald statement of tit-for-tat reciprocity and an expectation of assistance, the basic elements of patronage. It is also worth noting that, at first, Tedaldo includes few of the customary phrases of patronage seeking: there is no version of the verb *pregare*, no subjunctive form of the verb *piacere* (to please), no *non vi sia grave* (let it not be burdensome to you), no *quanto so e posso* (as much as I know and am able), no mention of effort (*fatica*) or cleverness (*ingegno*), no reference to honor, *amicizia*, or even virtue. If anything, need is the *leitmotiv* of this letter—need already known.

After his father's letter of introduction, Papi follows up with a brief request for consideration in his own voice (*MAP* II, 198): "Honorable and dearest father, From Tedaldo I have heard that you have been charged with arming certain vessels there, and for this reason I remind you that if you see that in any way I were able to be good for you, make of it as if I were your son, for thus I believe you would do. I recommend myself to you. May Christ watch over you."

Again we have a very terse letter from an individual known to be already politically intimate with the Medici. Papi adheres to the more formal *voi* term of address. Likewise he substitutes "father" for "brother" in his salutation to reflect his youth. Yet even as the framing was slightly different from his father's, the substance stays much the same: no inflationary rhetoric, a simple promise of reciprocity, and a tropic casting of himself in the role of Averardo's son.

A similar style holds for Tedaldo's next letter (*MAP* II, 239).

From Giuliano I have heard how much you have been doing for the affairs of Papi. Now I have heard that the *Dieci* have placed into your hands the election and everything else concerning it. Let it be up to you to resolve it. I know I need not remind you of his honor (*onore*) and his salvation (*salvazione*) and his advantage (*utile*), because I know you consider him to be a son. What I want to say to you is that, in carrying out the election, have regard that he be, or able to be, furnished with good officials, or companions.

Again Tedaldo informs Averardo that he has heard news from the most unimpeachable source, Averardo's own son. Thus his narrative is contextualized and authorized through, in a sense, speaking for another. Tedaldo completely expects to be satisfied in his request, and he communicates as much through the tone of his letter: since Papi is like a son to Averardo, his honor and his advantage are together close to Averardo's heart.[13]

Papi's uncle Bartolomeo, a man tightly tied economically to the Medici and their allies (*Catasto* 81: 25), weighed in on March 2 (*MAP* II, 253):

My Honored Elder, Without recalling the love and affection you have borne toward us, I have turned to writing to you concerning the affairs of Papi. And although dangers to honor and to advantage in this enterprise have moved me, all the same, having confidence in your prudence, and knowing that you make no other account of Papi than as your son, I want to align myself with your opinion and advice. Only I pray of you and remind you that the troop be appropriate to a task of such importance. One trusts that he have such companions that they will do honor to you and to him. I pray that it be pleasing to you to give him such advice and warnings that would be to his advantage for the time you will be there and for the future, and that they not depart from the will you have imposed.

We have here Niccolò di Lodovico Tedaldi, and he is in need, as you know. We would like it if you were to exert yourself, placing him there, collecting either the *gabelle* taxes or the gate taxes or in some other service in which he might occupy himself. He is an excellent and good writer, and willingly would do well to the extent he is able.

Here, as in Tedaldo's letter of February 23, the writer claims *not* to be bringing up a topic that nonetheless, precisely by that device, *does* get introduced. In Tedaldo's letter, "I know I don't need to remind you" constitutes a reminder of Papi's honor and well-being; here Bartolomeo's denial of the need to mention the "love and affection" connecting the Tedaldi and the Medici is a reminder that he really does understand their relationship in these terms.

The most interesting element of this letter is that Bartolomeo piggy-backs a recommendation for his kinsman, Niccolò di Lodovico Tedaldi, onto his plea on behalf of his nephew. Niccolò was a fairly poor relation of Bartolomeo living in the same neighborhood. The difference between the two men recommended is palpable in the letter, and consequently so too is the implicit justification for helping them. Whereas Papi is worthy of consideration for a position of great honor, Niccolò is merely "a good writer" fit for a minor bureaucratic post. Here again boundaries of competence and moral fiber are actively constructed in interaction.

Tedaldo wrote again on March 2 (*MAP* II, 256), using almost identical language as in his letter of February 23—that is, denying the need to speak at length, highlighting the need for good companions to ward off the dangers Papi would otherwise face, and speaking of Papi's honor and advantage as joint objectives. In fact, honor is *always* conjoined to advantage in these Tedaldi letters, never standing alone as it had been in Ormanno degli Albizzi's correspondence. But Tedaldo further heightens the paternal framing that his brother Bartolomeo had used in his letter of the same day, noting to Averardo: "You know it gives one little status (*grado*) to leave one's loved ones to the commune [that is, orphan your children by dying in service of the commune]. I pray that it be recommended to you in this way, for you know his little girls will want to get married." In other words, supply Papi with the means to survive this office successfully, because, "you know" (Schiffrin 1987), other things in life—such as family and marriage connections—are equally important. Again the contrast with Ormanno's letters is clear. Rather than offering dedication to the commune and an inherent sense of honor as primary motives, office holding here is a means—albeit a perilous one—to obtain personal prosperity. It is inconceivable that Ormanno would bring up this seemingly base or ulterior motivation as an encouragement to Averardo to work more diligently on his behalf, yet it fulfills the framing of familiarity with which the rest of the Tedaldi-Medici correspondence is endowed.

Two more letters arrived from Tedaldo, one on March 3 and another on March 12. I conclude my discussion of the framing of favor seeking in the Tedaldi case with a discussion of two sections from the first of these (*MAP* II, 257). The letter opens without any opening salutation: "If I believed you did not have regard for filial love, I would not have felt comfortable wearying you so much with reading my letters; but because I know you do consider and recognize it, take note that while you are there you will have something to read every day; therefore please have patience." He continues:

> Averardo, when I decided Papi should take up this challenge, I considered very well his endangerment, but I considered that you, being there, would have a due regard for everything, and I took him to be under your guidance. So, I pray of you that you might wish to have him before your eyes whatever choice you make and however things proceed. And so I told him that he should do whatever you tell him to. For now I say no more. Christ be with you.

This letter begins with a classic *captatio* in the form of an apology: however much I may bother you, it arises from love, and I take confidence in the love you have for me. It concludes with a direct attention-getting address to Averardo, not unlike the ploy used by Ormanno in his second letter (*MAP* II, 152). Here, however, it introduces a plea, not for honor, but for parental guardianship. The whole tenor of Tedaldo's framing of self is different from Ormanno's, guided more by considerations of partisanship and its legitimacy than by honor and the more objective justification of assistance it entails. The letters accordingly occupy a different rhetorical space than the bulk of the letters of Ormanno. Is this difference based on status attributes of sender and recipient? In part, yes, for the comparability of Tedaldo's and Averardo's ages is important for how Papi's need gets framed. Yet the Tedaldi and Albizzi lived in the same quarter of the city (in adjacent neighborhoods). Both had households of considerable substance, and both were esteemed *popolani* families. The difference between these cases lies in different constructions of underlying networks of relations. Undoubtedly the cultural work we see here has been prepared over a long period of time through past interactions. These different discursive constructions of relatedness permit different presentations of self and legitimize different motivations for the pursuit of what appears to be, from the standpoint of social network analysis, the same goal.

Conclusion

Social scientists nowadays are keen on the idea of mechanisms (Elster 1989; Hedstrom and Swedberg 1998). We may know that certain phenomena are highly correlated—for example, that social actors in certain structural positions have a higher probability of achieving upward mobility than others. But we also want to know more about precisely *how* structural position gets translated into mobility, the means by which strategic actors try to achieve the gains that they may (or may not) be structurally prepared to obtain. The cultural work we do to represent our positions, our networks, and our capabilities is a crucial translation mechanism. Then again, it is not simply translation, but more like imaginative, improvisational representation. Was writing a patronage-seeking letter a sufficient condition for obtaining a communal appointment or obtaining any other kind of favor? Undoubtedly not. Was it a necessary condition? Also, undoubtedly not; Florentines thought face-to-face communication was much more efficacious than letter writing and would have employed it whenever possible. Nevertheless, patronage letters were devices for putting oneself in front of powerful others, for putting others in mind of oneself, and for constructing a plausible image of oneself that might trigger a positive reaction from a patron. It was in such interaction that social and political networks were built and/or maintained.

This chapter has examined in detail a number of such constructions of self, constructions of alter, and representations of the surrounding world, particularly with regard to communal office holding, which was certainly among the most important aspects of a Florentine's "career." I have outlined crucial dimensions of the rhetorical space within which these strategic efforts took place and demonstrated that particular letters cobble together elements of the available rhetorical toolkit in distinctive ways. The toolkit Florentines used was distinctive to their own culture, and yet something of the way they expressed themselves is evocative of the same techniques we use today to accomplish some of the same kinds of goals.

6

Friends of Friends

Raccomandazione as Rhetoric
and as Constitutive Principle

Respected and generous sir and my honored superior, In the past days I had
your letter in which you recommended to me Migne, a blacksmith from Mar-
radi, and his family. This was not necessary because it is a long-established
habit of our families (*case nostre*) to serve and to recommend worthy persons,
especially your friends, who are [therefore] also mine (*gli amici vostri, i quali
sono miei*).
Lorenzo di Antonio Ridolfi to Lorenzo de' Medici, November 26, 1472

The letter of recommendation was an utterly ubiquitous feature of the
Florentine social and political scene in the fifteenth century across a variety
of contexts, from wartime situations to the personal politics of the distribution of papal benefices, from the settlement of judicial proceedings to
the conduct of commerce. The need for frequent communication across
distances, the need to share information, the large number of offices that
needed to be staffed, the importance of choosing one's allies carefully in an
agonistic social setting, and the moral imperative of coming to the aid of
one's friends, all conspired to make it so.

Several important points about this cultural institution must be noted.
First, the letter of recommendation, strictly speaking—more than the
office-seeking letter, more than the tax-relief letter, indeed more than most
other kinds of communication—was typically terse and utterly formulaic.
No better type of letter could be found than this on the basis of which
to assert that Florentine patronage interaction was a thoroughly patterned
corpus of discourse.

Second, however, virtually every Florentine letter was, in one way or
another, a letter of recommendation! While the verb *pregare* (to pray, to ask)
was virtually the sine qua non of patronage requests, even more so was the

language of *raccomandazione* the sine qua non of Florentine interpersonal correspondence in general. Letters might not include explicit requests for favor, but they almost always include expressions of desire for *raccomandazione*, even when they have for the most part communicated largely innocuous information. The meaning of being *raccomandato* is not as transparently clear as it might seem. By it, Florentines did not mean simply being recommended to others, and certainly not only being recommended to others for specific tasks (although this was very important). Instead, *raccomandazione* was equally, but more profoundly, a plea for recognition. To recommend oneself to another, as Florentines so formulaically did in the conclusions of their letters, was to ask *to be remembered* by another, to be kept in mind by another, to respect and be respected by another. A recommendation letter from Luigi Guicciardini to Lorenzo de' Medici on August 10, 1472 (*MAP* XXVIII, 386) nicely illustrates the memory and recognition part of *raccomandazione*:

> Although I am certain my relatives and friends will be recommended (*raccomandati*) [that is, approved for political eligibility], nevertheless with this letter I remind you and pray of you that you keep Piero Velluti and Piero di Gino Capponi in mind, that their names be put in the bag for *gonfaloniere di giustizia*.[1] I spoke with you about this another time, and you promised me you would do it, and I do not wish to bother anyone besides you. I hope you will comfort me with this. You have never informed me if you had spoken with Messer Francesco Brunacci, and also what response you have had from Giovanni Tornabuoni. If there is anything of which to advise me, I pray of you do so now. Nothing else occurs to me. I recommend myself to you (*Raccomandomi a te*) and I pray of you that you not forget about me (*non mi mette nel dimenticario*).

To be in a circle of *raccomandazione* could surely yield material benefits, but it also signified in a manner similar to the case of honor one's membership in a community of people who promised to act responsibly and supportively toward each other.[2]

As F. W. Kent (1991, 10) has noted, the letter of recommendation in conjunction with personal visits "engineered a flow of patronage, of reciprocal services between the grandees whom contemporaries called the 'gran maestri' and their friends (*amici*) and 'friends of friends.'" Clients, as Kent (11) goes on to note, were also "agent[s] of friendship" between the patrons they served, while powerful patrons connected their friends and followers with powerful friends of their own through correspondence, building interpersonal relations and communicating information through weak-tie networks (Granovetter 1973). Such friendship networks as we can see operating in recommendation letters routinely extended across social class categories (F. W. Kent 2002). Florence indeed was a society of friends (Trexler 1980, 139), even as the complement of this network structure—one might even say woven directly into its fabric—was an ecology of enemies (*nemici*) and cross-pressured neutral citizens (D. Kent 1978; F. Kent and D. Kent 1982; Weissman 1982; Padgett and Ansell 1993).

Florentine friendship (*amicizia*) was more ritualized and stereotypical and less a unique meeting of unique souls than we believe modern friendship to be (Silver 1989, 1990). It was a relation in which both affection and interest were implicated. Because it was both instrumental and affective, *amicizia* as a cultural form resonates with the view of culture and cultural practice I have been presenting in this book. Different characters in Alberti's *Della famiglia* articulate these analytically separable but practically conjoined aspects of friendship: obtaining favors, but also engendering love and mutual sacrifice (McLean 1998). And as Trexler (1980, 132) has noted in his reading of the friendship between Francesco Datini and the notary Lapo Mazzei in the late 1300s, sentiment and advantage, inward feelings and outward societal forms, coexisted, contrapuntally driving their relationship. He points to an example of this (Mazzei 1880, I, 5), a letter in which Mazzei proposes the terms by which his interaction with Datini should be conducted: "I thank you with much joy, so much you have given me in your letter, and especially in wanting me for a friend, even if it were disadvantageous to you. And I pray of you from now on, in writing and in action, that you treat me as befits a friend, and leave off those honors and praises which I in no way merit—even if it all proceeds from love." Here Mazzei distinguishes love from friendship: love may well infuse friendship in some way, even to the point of pursuing friendship at a disadvantage to oneself. But in the actual practice of friendship, Mazzei encouraged Datini to bracket the love part. He insisted that the valency of their interaction be lowered from one of overt expressions of affection to a more business-like tenor, thereby allowing advantage to return to the foreground. In his letter, instrumentality and affection were not simply conflated. Rather, the intertwined relationship between them was discursively handled.

The Datini-Mazzei correspondence also reveals some of the various valencies of *amicizia* when pursued with multiple others. Datini and Mazzei regarded Guido del Palagio and Niccolo da Uzzano as men with justified reputations for nobility, and their dealings with them accordingly retained a respectful tenor. Others failed the test of unbesmirched integrity and gracious impartiality, but made up for it in political energy and partisan effort: Francesco Federighi fit this category, one of only two individuals called *padrone* by Mazzei. Mazzei advised Datini concerning "what posture to assume with each individual in any given situation, what he should and should not do and what he could not effect" (Trexler 1980, 142). Since Mazzei himself wrote letters in Datini's name, it is evident that Mazzei himself was not only assessing and inferring the motivations of those whose aid was needed, but was also imputing legitimate motivations to Datini himself, constructing images of both "sender" and recipient of these letters (Mazzei 1880: I, 337ff.). He provided appropriate salutations and appropriate expressions of emotion and framings of Datini's self in these texts.[3]

Thus *amicizia* could have multiple meanings, "keyed" differently (Goffman 1974) in different contexts. But beyond that, while friendship talk figured prominently in letters of recommendation, recommendation was not only about friendship, and *amicizia* was not the only frame used in such contexts. Recommendation letters could also be for worthy people (*uomini da bene*, or *valenti*), or good citizens, or family members, or "servants." This brings us to a third important point to consider about *raccomandazione*, one that is directly germane to the framing of interpersonal correspondence. Recall first that letters through which people sought office, like those examined in the last chapter, required that the writer frame himself and his relationship with his alter in a manner most likely to make his request for favor credible. There the single dyadic relationship between writer and recipient was the primary, and sometimes sole, focus. This dyadic relationship was sometimes supported by the discursive invocation of a reference group that lent the writer a patina of reliability, but the request for favor for oneself did not inherently involve others.

However, precisely because most recommendations connect friends with other friends, or friends with patrons, or one's family members with one's patron, or worthy people with one's patron, they are routinely attentive to at least two and often three separate efforts of relationship construction or framing. The basic unit of analysis in them is the triad, not the dyad. This is important theoretically. In most statistical analyses, we assume that separate cases really are independent. But a fundamental premise of social network analysis is that a connection between any dyadic pair of actors is probably dependent on the existence of some other tie or ties. Indeed, a considerable amount of energy over the last decade has been put into modeling social network structure while recognizing the interdependence of ties (Wasserman and Pattison 1996; Anderson, Wasserman, and Crouch 1999). Florentine recommendations were always implicitly (and often explicitly) attentive not only to the motivations and character of the letter writer, and the discursive construction of the proper attitude of the letter recipient, but also to some third party, the recommendee. They were devices by means of which network ties—and indeed ties across multiple *types* of networks— were interdependently constructed on the ground. In other words, the recommendation letter genre, routinized though it was, was the quintessential locus of brokerage.

How, then, was the relationship between sender and recommendee described or constructed through the letter? How was the proper understanding of the relationship between recipient and recommendee to be construed? And what was the recipient to expect to gain by granting a favor to the person recommended? These are the main questions explored in this chapter.

Different Framings of Recommendation Letters

In the previous chapter, I suggested that we could think of patronage letter writing as a rhetorical space. That proved to be instructive. Office-seeking letters were not necessarily constructed out of one frame only, but laminating or stitching together different frames was a little more exceptional than typical. Thus multidimensional scaling (MDS) could provide a fairly clear picture of the space, and we could make some sense of the placement of letters in the space in terms of the social attributes and social positions of writer and recipient. Such clarity does not hold for recommendation letters, precisely because recommendations often put together persons who knew the recommender on different terms. The relationships among them were accordingly framed in different terms.[4] Thus, rather than presenting a picture of the general landscape of recommendation, I will present a series of examples, each of which illustrates a different variant of the triadic relationship between self, recipient, and recommendee.[5]

The "Single-Mode" Triad

The letter at the outset of this chapter supports the idea that recommendation was about supporting the friends of friends, and even identifying those friends as your very own through the economical and trenchant use of possessive pronouns. Certainly we should be able to find letters in which friendship—between writer and recipient, and between writer and recommendee—provides practically the sole framework of the letter. The following example is a case in point. Zanobi di Pinello wrote to Giovanni di Cosimo de' Medici on March 3, 1459 (*MAP* LXVIII, 36):

> Dearest friend, like a father to me, The bearer of this will be Arcagnolo di Maestro Antonio da Modigliane, who comes there to you for certain needs of his, about which he will inform you fully. I pray of you that he be recommended to you as much as my own self, for he is a great friend, like a brother, to my Betto. And so I pray that he be served if it is possible, and if I can do anything for you, let me know. At your pleasure. I say nothing more.

Amicizia is really the only frame here, not only because Zanobi calls both Giovanni and Arcagnolo "friend." The explicit tit-for-tat reciprocity it invokes and its low style fit this same frame. The rhetorical move of recommending someone "as much as my own self" (*quanto la mia persona propria*) is extremely common in all sorts of recommendations, but it also suggests that this favor will eventuate in a similar kind of friendship between Giovanni and Arcagnolo.

The following letter of January 31, 1430, from Cosimo de' Medici to his cousin Averardo de' Medici (*MAP* II, 308), also mentions *amicizia* practically exclusively.

> I have not written to you while you have been there for not having had any need. The reason for this is that Piero Gaetano, the bearer of this letter, who is very much my friend, desires that you recognize him as yours, and has prayed of me that I recommend him to you, and so I am doing (*desidera lo conosca per tuo, e a mi pregato te lo raccomandi, e così fo*). He is a capable man, and a good merchant, and among those that one would want to be close to in that place, and to have as friends.

Of course, Cosimo and Averardo were family, not friends, but this letter capitalized on their intimacy to state baldly the dynamic of "friendship begetting friendship." Gaetano himself used one friendship rather instrumentally to forge another. In the same vein, Cosimo gave a predominantly instrumentalist justification to Averardo for pursuing the friendship from his end.[6]

Letters of recommendation could also focus singularly on a frame other than *amicizia*. Among such frames were, for one, kinship (*parentado*),[7] and especially brotherhood (*fratellanza*), and for another, servanthood. Concerning the first, symbolic brotherhood (and fatherhood) was very often signaled in letter salutations: for example, "Dearest to me like a brother," or "Magnificent sir and honored brother." But sometimes the body of a letter went further in using kinship symbolically to rhetorically align the interests of the various parties. The following letter of Cristofano Bagnesi to Forese Sacchetti, written on October 21, 1407 (*Conv. Soppr.* 78, 324: 131) illustrates this nicely. This letter is one of the many between Bagnesi and Sacchetti that are extant. Their familiarity with each other is indicated by the use of informal pronouns, and perhaps also by the absence of an opening salutation set off from the main body of the letter.

> Even as you well know, dearest and honorable confrere (*compare*), that there is no need to recommend to you my affairs any further, because you have always acted with such consideration and such love, as a singular brother (*singulare fratello*) would, toward every honor and advantage of mine (*ogni mio honore e utile*). Concerning this may God permit that I merit it, and may I put myself in such a position that I may demonstrate that I well remember the many benefits that I have received from you. When I took leave of you I recommended these my brothers (*questi miei fratelli*) in these things that must be done, and so I pray that you proceed for love of me, that they know and be able to rely on you as on their own elder [brother] (*loro maggiore*). I recommend them to you tenderly (*teneramente*) as much as I can.

Undoubtedly there is talk of honor here, and of advantage. These are frames that signal possible outcomes that may be anticipated from doing something for Cristofano's brothers. But notice in particular how Cristofano identifies Sacchetti as a special brother before going on to talk about his own blood brothers. The triadic solidarity of all parties in *fratellanza* is then sealed when Cristofano signals that his brothers will think of Sacchetti as an elder brother, too. The brotherhood frame is extended here (Snow et al., 1986) to incorporate others explicitly. It defines a community of mutual support inclusively.[8]

Concerning the second kind of non-*amicizia* framing I mentioned above—servanthood—consider the following letter from Donato dall'Antella to Giovanni de' Medici and Betto Rustichi (*MAP* LXVI, 541; December 1, no year given):[9]

> My magnificent Signore, I will proceed with such confidence with you that a good servant must observe toward his lord. I wrote something in the last few days to your Signorìa, but about my own [affairs] in particular I did not write to you, because I know without saying anything, you have them in mind. . . . Now once again I want to recommend to you a faithful servant of my commune, who comes to you for a certain just cause in my opinion, and also everyone who praises him will tell you the issue and need he has. May it please you, my Lords, to defend and help in reason and justice your subjects and your good servants, and not leave them to be violently exploited. First, you will do justice; next you will serve your servants as you justly must, and finally you will take away the daring of the wicked to slide or run into similar errors[?]. And also, my Lords, beyond the holy works that you will do for Giovanni, if you please, I will consider as if they were done by your Highness for myself.

Dall'Antella begins with a kind of *captatio benevolentiae*, establishing his role as a servant of Medici and Rustichi in their official capacity as representatives of the commune. The good master is perfectly attuned to the needs of his servants, without needing reminders. But as he proceeds to the second half of his letter, dall'Antella retains or even extends (Snow et al. 1986) the servanthood frame, implying that Medici and Rustichi must apply the same care and concern to this new case as to his own. To do so is, again, not at their own discretion, but demanded by their role.[10] Multiple motivations for providing assistance are stitched together or laminated toward the end of the letter. First, some objective measure of justice will be done; but also the role relationship between servant and master will be properly realized.

Because in these examples the same kind of frame is used to represent the tie that joins two of the three pairs of actors in the triad, and because the language used suggests that the same kind of tie applies to the third pair, we can speak of "single-mode" triads. The top two rows of diagrams in figure 6 depict a number of these triads. Furthermore, note that the friendship and brotherhood triads look like they are "balanced," or heading toward balance, in Holland and Leinhardt's (1970) sense: friends encourage their friends to become friends with their other friends; two brothers of

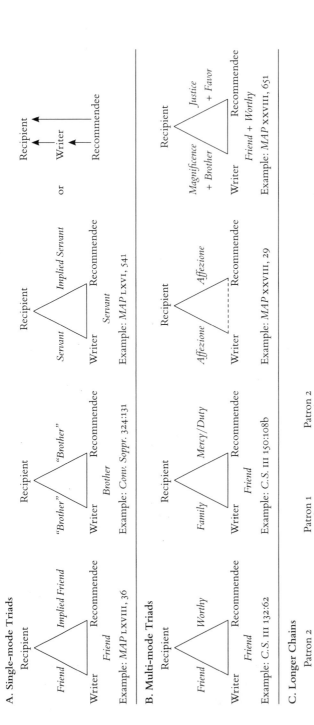

Fig. 6. Recommendation Letter Triads and Chains

A. Single-mode Triads

Recipient
Friend / Implied Friend
Writer — Friend — Recommendee
Example: *MAP* LXVIII, 36

Recipient
"Brother" / "Brother"
Writer — Brother — Recommendee
Example: *Conv. Soppr.* 324:131

Recipient
Servant / Implied Servant
Writer — Servant — Recommendee
Example: *MAP* LXVI, 541

Recipient ← Writer ← Recommendee
or

B. Multi-mode Triads

Recipient
Friend / Worthy
Writer — Friend — Recommendee
Example: *C.S.* III 132:62

Recipient
Family / Mercy/Duty
Writer — Friend — Recommendee
Example: *C.S.* III 150:108b

Recipient
Affezione / Affezione
Writer — — — Recommendee
Example: *MAP* XXVIII, 29

Recipient
Magnificence + Brother / Justice + Favor
Writer — Friend + Worthy — Recommendee
Example: *MAP* XXVIII, 651

C. Longer Chains

Patron 1   Patron 2
   Client 1   Client 2
      Brother of Client 2

Writer — Friend + Worthy — Recommendee
Example: *MAP* LXVI, 18

Patron 2
Recipient
   Worthy
Writer — Friend + Worthy — Recommendee
Example: *C.S.* III 150:108b

the same person are perforce brothers themselves. The servanthood triad may be a little different because it sets up a kind of hierarchical structure, whereby my servants become your servants if I am your servant. This, too, is presented in figure 6.

A letter of Francesco della Stufa to Lorenzo de' Medici on April 30, 1472 (*MAP* XXVIII, 29) also has a kind of single-mode triadic quality in terms of keywords used, although in fact it is referring to two different kinds of relationships. Writing on behalf of two non-Florentines, Francesco commented, "Knowing I am so affectionate (*tanto affezionato*) with your household, they have prayed that I should wish to write to you in their favor about how very affectionate (*affezionatissimi*) they are toward you, and that I should recommend them to you." Both the dyadic relationship of Francesco with Lorenzo, and that of the non-Florentines with Lorenzo, are portrayed as relationships of affection, although the superlative form used in the latter case represents the non-Florentines as even more asymmetrically dependent on Lorenzo than della Stufa was. In fact, although the word *affezione* aesthetically unifies the letter, it is clear that it means two different things here: intimacy in the case of Francesco, enthusiastic loyalty in the case of the non-Florentines.[11]

Thinking about the double meaning of this term *affezione* leads naturally to consideration of other cases in which there was a single primary framing of a recommendation, a framing that was nonetheless qualified in one way or another. Florentines were adept at indicating discursively when *amicizia* was special and when it was to be taken with a grain of salt. They sometimes recommended particular friends while discursively signaling their relative *lack* of commitment to them. More precisely, in several letters that I have seen, recommendations were explicitly identified as obligatory rather than heartfelt. For example, in a letter written in the 1440s to Agnolo di Palla Strozzi (*C.S.* III, 150: 111b), Nofri Parenti writes on behalf of the sons of Giovanni Gaetani, claiming that he knows there is no need for him to write, but that he is writing all the same "to satisfy friends" (*per sodisfare agli amici*). A similar example is afforded by a letter of February 17, 1432, sent by Cosimo de' Medici to Averardo de' Medici (*MAP* III, 71), in which Cosimo writes on behalf of a certain Antonio, but explicitly says he is writing because he had "been asked to do so by many friends." In this case, one friend appears not to matter very much, but other ones clearly do.

The opposite distinction, or keying, is illustrated in a letter of February 22, 1473 (*MAP* XXIX, 121), in which Piero di Lutozzo Nasi wrote to

Lorenzo de' Medici on behalf of a certain Piergentile di Folco Bifolci of Borgo San Sepolcro. Piergentile had approached him, says Nasi, "having heard of the goodwill (*benivolentia*)" that had always existed between the two men. But Nasi went on, expressing in a rather unusual way his own attitude toward having been asked to write this letter: "I willingly went along with giving you this present letter (*sono volentieri concorso farti questa presente*), by means of which I recommend him to you as much as I can, considering every benefit that flows to him by your means a benefit to me personally." This seems to have been a way to mark a recommendation as more enthusiastic or sincere.[12]

A simpler way to heighten the impact of a recommendation was to express deeper commitment to, or intimacy with, the person recommended. This would involve using expressions such as *mio intimo amico* or *mio caro intimo* (my dear friend). For example, in a letter of February 8, 1422 (*C.S.* III, 132: 33), Palla di Nofri degli Strozzi wrote to his kinsman Simone di Filippo, saying, "I am most certain (*certissimo*) I do not need to press you greatly to recommend to you a friend of ours there, the intimate [friend] of one of our close relatives" (*intimo d'alcuno nostro stretto parente*). Another example occurs in a letter of Roberto del Mancino Sostegni to Agnolo di Palla Strozzi on April 5, 1445 (*C.S.* III, 150: 82b), in which Roberto identifies Giovanni Falcucci as his "intimate and most congenial friend" (*intimo e cordiallissimo amico*). On February 13, 1427, Giovanni di Tommaso Luti asked Forese Sacchetti (*Conv. Soppr.* 78, 325: 440) to help Giacomo di ser Giovanni da Castiglione, his "intimate and singular friend" (*intimo et singulare amico*) in a legal matter affecting him. The sense of the *intimo* modifier is conveyed by a similar usage in a letter of Filippo Giugni to Forese Sacchetti (*Conv. Soppr.* 78, 325: 473), in which he claims of the recommendee, Rosso Botticelli of Pisa, "[He is] very much my friend" (*molto mio amico*). And yet another similar kind of superlative is found in a letter of Amerigo de' Medici to Averardo de' Medici of May 18, 1431 (*MAP* III, 130), where he describes Lodovico de' Rossi as "more than a brother" (*più che fratello*). All of these are special positive markings of the *amicizia* frame.[13]

One could say that both positive and negative markings appear in a letter written by Giovanni Rucellai to Lorenzo de' Medici on August 22, 1472 (*MAP* XXVIII, 448).

> Dearest relative, Another time in the past few days I recommended Zanobi da Ghiaccetto to you for *gonfaloniere di giustizia*, and knowing that he is affectionate toward your household, as much as any citizen

that our city has, and being a close relative of ours, I can do no less (*non posso fare di meno*) than completely (*di tutto*) recommend him to you quite strictly as much as I can (*tanto strettamente quanto posso*), considering that you would do for me the same I will do for you.

While Giovanni's recommendation is strong ("completely," "quite strictly," "as much as I can"), he imparts some feeling that he is doing his duty, more so than expressing his heartfelt commitment, in recommending Zanobi. Multiple factors conspire to necessitate this recommendation: Zanobi's commitment to the Medici, and his kin connection to the Rucellai. But this only means Giovanni must, at minimum, write the letter.[14] The chances of its being efficacious seem, on the surface, to be compromised. This means, once again, that the gap between having a friend or neighbor, and bringing about results on the basis of that friendship or proximity, could be substantial. Cultural work mediated the relationship between persons, and thereby between networks.

Multi-mode Triads

At a rhetorical level, however, Florentines did not show themselves to be so comfortable with justifying recommendations solely and explicitly in terms of *amicizia*. They often seemed to want to offer some objective reasons that favor should be extended to new recipients. The following letter of Niccolò di Bartolo di Giovanni, a *setaiuolo* (silk merchant), to a *podestà* named Baldo on April 22, 1422 (*C.S.* III, 132: 62) is almost entirely framed in terms of *amicizia*, but Niccolò felt obliged to endorse the recommendee also in more objective terms:

> Honorable and dear friend dearest [*sic*], I wrote to you a while ago via Cucinochio, your house servant. I have not written for not having any need, and from you there have been no more letters so that in this one I have little to say. The reason for this letter is that you must know how much Simone di Filippo di Messer Lionardo degli Strozzi is one of the greatest friends we have in this territory . . . We desire to honor him and his family on every occasion as much as were possible for us. He has a son whose name is Matteo, who is one of the most virtuous young men this city has. Thus we want to pray of you as much as possible that he be honored with the office of the *podesteria* of Città di Castello, and this we will consider one of the greatest favors we could

have, such that by God, contrive as much as is possible for you, and immediately with letters to the friends announce our intention.

Niccolò identifies Baldo as a friend, perhaps even a "dearest" friend as an afterthought to intensify the salutation. Likewise he identifies Simone Strozzi as a great friend, and he alludes to setting in motion a network of friends to achieve his objective. Nevertheless, the actual beneficiary of the favor is to be Matteo di Simone, who is framed as deserving because of his exceptional *virtù*. Whether understood as "virtue" or as "virtuosity," this is still a different kind of justification from *amicizia*.

Niccolò's letter adds *virtù* to the mix in the writer-recommendee pairing. The following letter of November 14, 1427, from Giovanni Corbizzi to Averardo de' Medici (*MAP* II, 53), more or less changes the framing by draining the *amicizia* out of the writer-recipient pairing.

> My dearest respected elder, The reason for this is that the bearer of this letter, Salvestro di Giuliano Torrigiani, my intimate and good friend, comes there to see one of his relatives, who left there with a good quantity of his money. For this reason I pray and beg of you that it please you that, finding him there, you were to act favorably toward him so that he gain satisfaction, considering whatever you do for him like it were done for my own self.

The salutation of this letter suggests a distant, respectful relationship between Corbizzi and Averardo. Both were bankers, although only modestly connected to each other through credit relations. Corbizzi appears to have been neither a Medici partisan nor a foe (D. Kent 1978). Salvestro Torrigiani, however, is described as Corbizzi's "intimate and good friend." Two different types of relationship are discursively established here: esteem for Averardo, attachment to Torrigiani. Corbizzi's indebtedness to Averardo is framed in terms of weak-tie reciprocity rather than strong-tie expectation, cordiality rather than intimacy.

The backgrounding of *amicizia* is more fully engineered in the following letter from Mariotto di Piero della Morotta (*C.S.* III, 150: 108b), sent on May 31, 1445, to Agnolo di Palla Strozzi:

> Dearest like a father, It seems that you have in your hands a certain dispute between the commune of Soiana and Curadoccio di Ceato of Soiana concerning [pay for] several days work the said Curadoccio is requesting from them. Truly he is a very poor person, such that I pray of you quite as much as I am able that, while retaining your honor

(*salvando l'onore*), the said commune be made to do its duty (*dovere*), for as much as you do for him, I will consider it as if you had done it for me personally, because he is my great friend (*mio grande amico*).

Mariotto represents his tie to Strozzi as quite strong by means of his opening salutation. But the terms used to portray the recommendee are largely objective: Curadoccio deserves help because he is very poor; it is implied he really did the work and naturally is owed for it; asking the commune to pay is thus only to ask it to do what is right and proper. Further, this is a request in which, as part of a politeness strategy (Brown and Levinson 1987), limits are imposed on Mariotto's expectations of Strozzi. He is to do only as much as honor permits—honor here meaning staying within the bounds of courtesy, respect, tact, and legality. Only at the end does Mariotto indicate that he is equally, if not more so, motivated by his friendship with Curadoccio.

The various justifications for seeking assistance are more balanced, but also more abundant, in a letter written by Filippo de' Medici, the archbishop of Pisa, to Lorenzo de' Medici on November 5, 1472 (*MAP* XXVIII, 651):

Magnificent sir, like an honored brother, The bearer of this letter will be Lorenzo di Gherardo Galletti, citizen of Pisa, who is a worthy man (*uomo da bene*) and a great friend of mine (*amicissimo*). He told me that he has there a certain lawsuit on account of some of his goods, concerning which I doubt he was treated justly, and for this reason he has prayed of me that I recommend him to you, being a good citizen and a virtuous (*costumata*) person and worthy (*da bene*), and toward whom I bear singular affection. As much as I can and know I recommend him to Your Magnificence, praying that in just and honorable matters (*nelle cose iuste et honeste*) you lend him every suitable favor and help (*favore et aiuto*) that he be preserved in his affairs, and even if Your Magnificence were prompt in this, nevertheless adding these my prayers, so much more easy will it be. And thus I pray this of you extremely, since for every favor and help you will lend to the said Lorenzo I will have such pleasure and consolation, as if Your Magnificence were to give this to me and to my own affairs, and I will remain most obligated to Your Magnificence.

The salutation here combines familial and respectful forms. The person recommended is both "a worthy man" and "a great friend." His request involves overturning an injustice, but he is also someone toward whom Filippo feels "a singular affection." Filippo asks for "favor and help," two words that tend to suggest the more instrumentalist side of patronage. Yet he also frames this instance as a matter of justice and honor, and in effect permits Lorenzo not to offer assistance should the matter *not* be considered one of fairness.[15] In other words, at virtually every turn the letter plays up both objective and personalistic justifications. This letter and some others in this section are diagrammed in figure 6, along with those of the previous section.

Longer Chains of Recommendation

As I have emphasized throughout this chapter, the letter of recommendation highlighted the construction of a triadic relationship. Nevertheless, it is widely understood by historians that patronage could involve many steps and more than three parties, such that in effect the Florentine social and political landscape was thatched with multiple, crisscrossing chains of patronage. Some hint of that structure appears in individual letters, as I will show briefly in this section.

Consider first the following letter from a certain Andrea in Lucca to Averardo di Francesco de' Medici of February 19, 1410 (*MAP* LXVI, 18), quoted in full here and diagrammed in figure 6:

> The bearer of this will be Meo Buongiovanni of Lucca, my great friend (*mio grande amico*). He is coming there on account of a property he has there, and also he is being sent there to consult with Messer Riccardo del Bene. For this reason, I pray of you as much as I know and am able, in great service to me, that you speak with the said Messer Riccardo, and recommend to him the affair of the said Meo. And so much am I begging this of you, be clear that this affair touches on me, for so I consider it. I know that the said Messer R[iccardo] is very much with you, and always his [friends] have been your friends, and I believe he would do for you whatever he were able to do with his honor. And this is a matter of both honor and advantage. If you were to recognize what this Meo is like, and to recognize his worthiness[?], you would say that he is a man to serve. He is the best of persons and best of friends. Contrive what you can in this matter, as if you were doing it for my own, and from him you will be more fully advised of his need. I say no more for now. I am yours.

The writer is Andrea; the recipient is Averardo; the recommendee is Meo. But a lot of this letter has to do with Riccardo del Bene, with Averardo being sought as an intermediary to gain Riccardo's favor. Andrea doubly identifies Meo as "the best of persons and best of friends," while claiming certainty about drawing a tight boundary of *amicizia* around Averardo and Riccardo: "I know that the said Messer R[iccardo] is very much with you" (*so chel detto messere R. e assai di te*). The connection proposed between Averardo and Meo is one based on Meo's worthiness, although Andrea also seems to promise it will redound to Averardo's honor and advantage (*questa è cosa d'onore e d'utile*).[16] In fact, the relationship that is least clear here is that between the writer and the recipient of the letter. Perhaps Andrea is Andrea de' Bardi, Averardo's longtime business partner, but that is not clear. He does use the informal pronoun *tu*, and he expresses in a direct manner the connection of this particular favor to his own well-being using the informal imperative tense: "Be clear that this affair touches on me, for so I consider it" (*fa ragione questo fatto tocchi a me, che così lo riputo*).

Through the technique of extension, Andrea draws Riccardo del Bene into this cluster of *amici* who mutually assist each other in strategic, advantage-seeking ways.[17] "I know," he says, that Riccardo and Averardo indulge each other; his family, or perhaps his followers, have always been friends of the Medici (*sempre i suoi sono stati vostri amici*).[18] In expressing his opinion that Riccardo would do for Averardo whatever he could within the limits of his honor, Andrea "speaks for" Riccardo (Schiffrin 1993), encouraging Averardo further to be of assistance. We may think that the phrase "with his honor" (*con suo honore*) or "within the limits of honor" connects honor to the idea of personal integrity: action is *limited* by a sense of honor, or by a desire to maintain one's character. Andrea's assertion here that this is a matter "of honor and of advantage" retroactively suggests that what he means by honor is linked to the approval of followers. Thus what Riccardo would consider doing is limited more by his concern for building reputation than by a reflective concern for personal integrity. Finally, again note how objective considerations of virtue and subjective considerations of friendship are united rhetorically in the end. Above all, it seems unlikely that Meo would be known to be worthy of favor independent of this letter. His potential value to Averardo and his group is accomplished in part through Andrea's constructions of him, and in part through the information provided contextually in the letter that Meo is seeking assistance from Riccardo del Bene, the leader of a group sympathetic to Averardo's interests.

It is hard to document quantitatively, but it seems pretty certain that longer chains of recommendation became more abundantly used later in the fifteenth century, during the time of Lorenzo the Magnificent. This is certainly in keeping with the idea that Lorenzo exercised more extensive arbitrage than did any of his predecessors. Otherwise, however, not that much differs in the construction of these letters over a period of eighty years or more. Consider, then, the following letter written to Lorenzo by Donato Acciaiuoli on August 27, 1472 (*MAP* XXVIII, 466):

> Magnificent, generous, and honored brother, Ser Piero Francesco da Santo Miniato has been with me as notary and chancellor in many places and I have found him to be faithful and capable, in such a way that I consider myself to have been very well served. At present it happens that the governors and the Volterrans have need of someone to be notary and chancellor, and because I have seen the experience of this [assistant] of mine (*di questo mio*), I would like that he were elected by them and therefore I pray of you that it please you to require of your chancellor that he send a letter of recommendation to these governors, for you will give me a great pleasure, and the Volterrans will be well served.

Here Donato first reestablishes his deep relationship with Lorenzo in terms of brotherhood and the delight one receives from having a favor done. He uses informal pronouns throughout, something increasingly uncommon in letters written to Lorenzo in the 1470s and 1480s. He frames his relationship with Ser Piero quite differently, though, on the basis of his experience, expertise, and loyalty. Note that Donato is asking Lorenzo not to provide a favor to Ser Piero, but to recommend him in turn to the Volterrans.

In a recommendation letter written to Lorenzo by Matteo Palmieri on June 29, 1472 (*MAP* XXIII, 469) we see a chain with one additional link. The writer sends a messenger, Andrea, who is the brother of the recommendee. The recommendee is being supported by Luca Capponi, but Luca evidently feels he needs Lorenzo's support to get his candidate for a church appointment approved. Palmieri is the intermediary trying to get everything worked out accordingly.

> Magnificent sir, Andrea di Antonio di Commuccio, blacksmith, is the bearer of this message and one of yours in San Piero a Sieve. He says he has a brother who is a priest in the house of Luca Capponi. And this Luca finds himself a consul of the Guild of Merchants and they control a certain church, and this Luca asks for this priest, and he de-

sires that he have your favor. I recommend him to you because it were very dear to me that he were served.

This is more or less what F. W. Kent (1991, 11) meant in saying that clients were also "agent[s] of friendship" between the patrons they served. But an even more complicated landscape of *raccomandazione* may be glimpsed in a letter of Bernardo di Antonio Boverelli (*MAP* XXV, 181), sent to Lorenzo de' Medici on July 13, 1472.

> Respected sir and honored brother, I will have confidence in you as you seem to take in me, for you know I consider it a singular pleasure to be able to do things gratifying to you. Ser Antonio di Giuliano Ferrucci da Pescia, my cavalryman here in Palazuolo, desires to go with the *podestà* of Librefatta, who it seems is Francesco di Messer Biagio Niccolini, and because I know that Antonio Infangati spoke to you about this, I will not go on at too much length . . . but I pray of you, as a singular pleasure, that you contrive that the said Ser Antonio be placed with him, for you will make me most grateful, and I will put this at the feet of the other obligations I have with Your Magnificence.

This letter has little in the way of framing of what is at stake in bestowing or not bestowing a favor on Ferrucci, but it is the kind of letter that goes some way toward representing a network of friends acting on behalf of one of their own. Boverelli writes on behalf of Ferrucci, asking that Lorenzo seek to help him get a position with yet another person. In addition, Boverelli indicates not only that another person—Antonio Infangati—has written to Lorenzo, but that he knows Antonio has written. There was always an incentive to make recommendations seem to be backed up by the multiple recommendations, and recognitions, of others. This is another example of how networks were not only constructed through letters, but were actually represented through those letters.

Conclusion

Were these letters of recommendation efficacious? And what made one more efficacious than another? I will conclude with excerpts from four linked letters written to Lorenzo de' Medici in 1471 and 1472 to try to address these questions. In the first letter, dated December 17, 1471 (*MAP*

XXVII, 572), Donato de' Medici, the bishop of Pistoia, wrote in favor of Ser Antonio di Iacopo di Giorgio for the post of chancellor of Fucecchio.

> Ser Antonio is a worthy youth, good and capable, and very well known by us (*a noi familiarissimo*) in such a way that one could not say any more. And because now we have heard this chancellery is once again vacant, . . . once again with this letter we say that for our satisfaction and for our pleasure, may you be content to contrive by means of your letter that the said Ser Antonio be rewarded with this chancellorship, for we are certain that to you and to us he will do honor.

Of course, this letter has a very familiar (may I say *familiarissimo?*) form. Both friendship and objective merit give warrant to Ser Antonio's case. It is claimed that Lorenzo and Donato will share in the honor his appointment will bring. But about seven months later, it is clear that things had not been quickly resolved. In a letter of July 13, 1472, Donato wrote again (*MAP* XXVIII, 298) on behalf of Ser Antonio, reminding Lorenzo that he had written before but this time slightly upping the ante by referring to Ser Antonio as "a singular friend" of his. The commune seemed unable to come to a decision about whom to pick as chancellor, and the matter had been resolved by putting the election in the hands of Lorenzo himself. "You would be able to give me a singular favor (*grazia*) if you were to elect the said Ser Antonio, for he is a person who will do you honor." Here Donato expresses his desire to see Ser Antonio rewarded a little more baldly than before by referring to the favor (*grazia*) it would be to him personally.

Donato apparently did not leave matters at that either, for fifteen days later, on July 28, Gualterotto Bardi sent a letter to Lorenzo about the same matter (*MAP* XXVIII, 312).

> Magnificent sir and most beloved honored one, I would not be able to stand it were I not to recommend friends, and especially good ones, as is the bearer of this letter, who would desire that one of his sons, whom I have brought up, were elected chancellor of Fucecchio, a matter that has been pursued other times by means of the bishop of Pistoia, from your family, with a similar avidity[?]. I recommend him to you. He is a person from whom to have honor, and it would be a singular pleasure to me.

It seems evident that Donato had impressed upon Gualterotto Bardi the need to write another letter in support of Ser Antonio and, again, to make clear that Ser Antonio enjoyed a network of support. The terms by which Bardi recommends Ser Antonio are very similar to those used by Donato, commenting on his ability to deliver honor, and the "singular pleasure" the granting of this favor would supply to the person writing the recommendation.

However, in a letter of August 1, 1472, Cosimo di Salvestro Pucci wrote to Lorenzo (*MAP* XXVIII, 345) asking him to finalize his choice between the two contenders for the job, one a certain Ser Marchionne, the other a certain Ser Filippo. Ser Antonio's name is not there. It seems, then, that Donato de' Medici's work was ineffective. Undoubtedly these efforts at recommendation were frequently ineffective. It would be wonderful to know what made one request more compelling, more persuasive, than another. But that can only be reconstructed after the fact, and then only rarely. What we can know, however, is that Florentines believed such letters would help. They may have believed that although they were not a sufficient condition for obtaining favor, they were well-nigh a necessary condition.

Florentine recommendation letters were generally rather formulaic. Nevertheless, they were an integral tool for gaining mobility and stitching relationships together across subdomains of the field of Florence's multiple social networks. We are accustomed to thinking of these efforts at constructing weak-tie networks and achieving mobility as predicated on the language and practices of *amicizia*, a *mentalité* in which issues of honor and advantage are assumed to be conflated. I have suggested instead that in the course of their letters, Florentines did not so much conflate honor and advantage, nor simply confuse regard for worthiness with the pursuit of group interest, as contrapuntally shift the emphasis back and forth between these aspects, pulling them together or pushing them apart to different degrees. It is this subtle shifting, in the context of whom they were writing to, and whom they were writing for, that shaped the terms of their concrete interactions with each other.

7

Patronage and the Stalled Transformation of the State

Dearest honorable friend, Since I last wrote to you I have heard that you are among those who have been assigned to rearrange the tax burden, that is, these new taxes of the new distribution for our *gonfalone*. And therefore I pray of you most dearly, even though I think I need not, for you have me in mind already as recommended to yourself . . . truly that in the new distribution I am still [charged] one florin and a half. I believe you know more than enough of my feeble condition, and for this reason as much as I am able dearly I pray of you that in this matter you help me, and be the operator with your companions in such a mode as appears to you, that this half-florin assessment be lifted from me, so that I remain with the one florin, to pay *a perdere* [at a reduced rate, with loss of claim for reimbursement]. Concerning this I write no more, except that I have such hope in you, ~~encouraging myself~~ [*sic*] that I am certain on account of your discretion and our intimate friendship, you will endeavor that the right and proper thing be done for me. Until now, I have always had the help and benefit of paying *a perdere*, and if this were not the case I would be undone, and I would not do in this office such good as one might otherwise believe; however, that law they made of April and May that anyone could see is barbarous did me the greatest ~~great~~ [*sic*] damage. I say no more. May Christ watch over you always. Prepared always to do your pleasure. In Florence, the 1st of August 1409.

Donato Acciaiuoli to Riccardo del Bene, August 1, 1409

In this letter, Donato Acciaiuoli, a politically prominent but not particularly wealthy member of an esteemed Florentine family, writes to Riccardo del Bene, a richer but younger co-resident of the neighborhood of Vipera, looking for an insider's assistance in keeping his tax burden down. Donato paints his economic position bleakly, unwittingly conforming in detail with prescriptions provided in the now famous contemporaneous memoir of Giovanni di Pagolo Morelli, written to urge his own heirs to hide their wealth and dramatize the fiscal injustices done to them:

Run to the Signori and lodge a petition to pay one-third or two-fifths [of your tax assessment] *a perdere*, or that the Signori and Collegi must correct your assessment, informing all of them of your incapacity to pay, and also advertising this to their friends; and thus put up a good fight. And if you're not able [to do this] at the time of a particular priorate, wait as long as it takes, since these are matters wherein he who persists in pursuing them, will have matters come around his way; or if they don't come around, demonstrate to everyone that you have been overburdened, and are unable to pay, and with that the next occasion you will have an easier time of it. (Branca 1986, 197, my translation)

However, Acciaiuoli's relationship to the state is not so one-sided as Morelli's advice would lead us to believe. In fact, Acciaiuoli's letter exemplifies the widespread Florentine strategy of relying on personal relationships *both* as a defense against the demands of the state *and* as a means of remaining an active member of it. Florentine citizens were not merely subjects or "victims" of the state, but also its custodians. Thus, although Acciaiuoli protests that "anyone could see" the newly instituted tax law was simply unfair, he also alleges that he needs and wants del Bene's favor to continue to serve the commune honorably. He actively links personal and collective destinies: a favor to him is simultaneously a benefit to the commune. Loyalty between friends and loyalty to the collectivity are represented as mutually consistent.

Friendship and citizenship, patronage and the state — these were inextricably connected in a variety of ways in the Renaissance Florentine polity. One cannot adequately write the political history of fifteenth-century Florence without attending to the emergence of the state (or at least the *reggimento*) as an autonomous actor (Fubini 1994) on the one hand, and a surge in patronage politics (D. Kent 1978, 2000; Rubinstein 1997) on the other. To put it succinctly, everyday micro-political practices affected macro-political institutional outcomes (and of course, vice versa). And as I shall discuss in chapter 8, everyday micro-political practices affected the macro-cultural emergence and development of a new conception of selfhood. Thus these two chapters together address the micro-macro link (Collins 1981).

In this chapter, I shall highlight two aspects of the state-patronage nexus, specifically as it pertains to taxation, by common agreement a critical component in the development of the early modern state (Tilly 1975; Levi 1988).

First, fiscal pressures and fiscal institutional innovation in fifteenth-century Florence were very much interwoven with the consolidation of clientage-based politics. The *catasto* of 1427 (Herlihy and Klapisch-Zuber 1985), the plethora of ingenious schemes for encouraging citizens to pay back-taxes (Conti 1984), the *Monte delle doti* (or Dowry Fund; see Kirshner and Molho 1978; Molho 1994)—were arguably "modernizing" innovations. They certainly depended heavily upon the sophistication of Florentine accounting practices (de Roover 1966; Melis 1991; Epstein 2000a, chap. 2), and were premised (in communal debates) on understanding the state as having needs aligned with, but also distinct from, the needs of the citizenry.

But to deal with the burdens imposed by these schemes for tax collection, Florentine citizens frequently and routinely turned to their fellow citizens for assistance (Conti 1984, 115; Molho 1987, 207). And of course, patronage letters were an indispensable venue where these pleas for help in return for loyalty were expressed. The Acciaiuoli letter at the beginning of this chapter instantiates many of the stock elements of this patterned, even institutionalized Florentine patronage discourse cum political culture (Somers 1995; Eliasoph 1998): the opening words (*di poi ch'io vi scrissi*); the rhetorical turn that initiates the request for a favor, "And therefore I pray of you" (*Et per tanto vi prego*); the superlative framing of the request, "as much as I am able" (*quanto più posso*), the open-ended nature of the specific actions the recipient is to take ("in such a mode": *in quello modo*); the abrupt, almost embarrassed closing of the request (*Sopra di ciò non scrivo più*); the expression of hope in the recipient (*o tanta speranza in voi*); and the closing salutations, "May Christ watch over you always" (*Christo vi guardi sempre*) and "Prepared always to do your pleasure" (*Apparechiato sempre a vostri piaceri*). Acciaiuoli also explicitly portrays del Bene as his *operatore*, a noun linked to the verb *adoperare*—to contrive, to make happen—and found often in Florentine patronage letters. Furthermore, Acciaiuoli sends mixed signals here typical of patronage interaction, mingling expressions of deference with claims to desert. He claims friendship, but he denies the need to have invoked it. He writes, but he denies the need to have written, since the two men's intentions are so naturally harmonious.

To sum up my first claim about the state-patronage nexus, putatively "modernizing" fiscal institutions of the state met with putatively "traditionalizing" innovations in the conduct of interpersonal interaction—"traditionalizing" insofar as it was built upon personal loyalties that compromised the autonomy and efficiency of the state. Allegations of favoritism in the distribution of the tax burden in turn prompted renewed rounds of search for more equitable methods of taxation. In effect, trends towards "modernization" and "traditionalization" *at the level of social institutions* developed simultaneously and in constant response to each other.[1]

The second aspect of the state-patronage nexus I wish to highlight is the way individual Florentines participated in both domains and managed these domains' disparate demands. As Conti (1984, 119ff.) has documented, administrative change in the commune was accomplished within the constraints of a contest, not between state actors and civil society, but between citizens in their role as custodians of the state and the same citizens in their role as subjects to the state. Members of the Florentine *reggimento* were fully implicated in, and had roles and identities based on, *both* sides of the state/civil society conceptual divide (Epstein 2000a, 32). Patronage letters are critical for evincing the way clientelistic loyalty and commitment to the state were interwoven *at the level of individual cognition and action*. This combination of roles—custodian and subject—was empowering to some extent. The very modest separation of the state from the citizenry allowed tax exactions to be extraordinarily high, since citizens tended to identify the viability of the state with their personal well-being to a greater extent than was true, or even conceivable, in more predatory states. But it also posed problems for state autonomy. As fiscal pressures grew, the rhetoric of personal loyalty among citizen "victims" of state policy grew stronger. And however desirable Florentine state makers considered reform, they found it impossible or inconceivable to establish fiscal relations with the citizenry that would definitively decouple taxation from political participation. No sufficiently affluent group was sufficiently removed from political participation as to be viewed as the legitimate victim of a predatory state.

Consequently, the evolution of the early modern European state stalled in Florence, as many historians and comparative historical sociologists recognize. But this was not simply because of Florentines' overzealous commitment to capital or their lack of enthusiasm for erecting a territorial state, as Charles Tilly's (1992) model may suggest. Nor was it simply a function of the composition of classes and their distinct interests, as Hendrik Spruyt's (1994) model and, occasionally, Richard Lachmann's (2000) might lead us to believe. The stunted Florentine counterpart of the early modern state was not the product of a set of necessary and/or sufficient conditions, but the outcome of a number of concrete *interactions* (Molho 1996, 103; Najemy 1991), both contentious (as emphasized by Tarrow 2004) and cooperative.

And again, these happened at both the institutional and the individual levels. Administrative innovations at the macro-level emerged and then were dismantled as an incremental and hesitant response to culturally shaped patterns at the micro-level of interaction in civil society. State institutions and interpersonal interaction styles co-evolved (Elias 1978; Ikegami 1995).

The next section summarizes the vicissitudes of Florentine fiscal policy throughout the 1400s. Tracing the increases and decreases in state demands year by year provides a roadmap for selecting important periods in which to search for tax-related patronage correspondence. The correspondence so selected reveals, by means of changes in the content and style of the letters over the course of the fifteenth century, that the state and interpersonal relationships developed in a conjoined way. In particular, the correspondence offers crucial evidence of how Florentines were both actors *in* and subjects *of* the state, a critical factor in Florentine state development.

The Ups and Downs of Florentine Taxation in the 1400s

The landscape of fifteenth-century Florentine fiscal policy is littered with innovations and reversals, all produced by a need, well recognized by citizen-legislators, to distribute the tax burden equitably and effectively. Molho (1971, 1996) and Conti (1984) provide outstanding detailed accounts of this history, and so here I will present only an analytical summary, highlighting two pairs of contrasting points.

First, to be eligible for communal office, one had to have contributed to the *Monte Commune*, the city's funded public debt, and paid one's taxes in full. Because the city was continually unable to pay off its debts,[2] contributors to the *Monte* were effectively creditors of the commune, and hence they were implicated in its fiscal and political health. Regarding taxes, being in arrears (*allo specchio*) could cost one a chance at office for three, five, or even more years until another scrutiny to determine eligibility was organized. Those who anticipated being seen as fit for office by virtue of their family's status had to keep their tax record clean by whatever methods available. For these reasons, Florentines feared and had to defend themselves against the *individual* effects of taxation.[3]

Second, however, many Florentines also feared the *collective* social and political consequences of taxation. Debates concerning the *catasto*—a method established in 1427 to assess taxes on the basis of extensive written inventories of household liquid assets *and* landed wealth (Herlihy and Klapisch-

Zuber 1985)—reveal that leading citizens valued the plan not only for its equity and efficiency, but also because, in the words of Francesco di Lorenzo Machiavelli, after its implementation "the conspiracies, false pretenses, and clienteles of the most powerful citizens will come to an end" (Conti 1984, 132; my translation). Averardo de' Medici, a banker deeply embedded in the patronage networks of the Florentine establishment, praised it because assessments would be determined on sure evidence rather than uncertainty clouded with favoritism; thus it would contribute to domestic peace. The debate over the *catasto* was undoubtedly marked with inter-elite, class-like tensions (cf. Lachmann 2000). For example, a number of merchants were afraid that including liquid capital in the estimates of wealth would burden them extraordinarily. However, the cleavages in the debate did not follow class lines in any simple way. Later in the century, too, Cosimo de' Medici would oppose tax plans—for example, the *diecina graziosa* of 1442— that might have benefited him personally but would have destabilized the regime. Nicolai Rubinstein (1997, 161f.) reports that Florentine leaders considered backing off on electoral controls in 1458 in order to facilitate passage of a new tax bill; evidently they saw the two issues as intricately connected. And in 1480, in the aftermath of an attempt on Lorenzo de' Medici's life, when the regime proposed the adoption of yet another *balìa* (an executive body with extensive but fairly short-term powers that short-circuited participatory government), they secured consent for it with the promise of tax reform (Rubinstein 1997, 226). The point is, it was not state officials standing outside of and acting upon society at large who debated fiscal policy, but rather citizens, discussing the apportionment of the tax burden among themselves. Theirs was a protracted effort to solve a key collective action problem of the polity, not a simple class battle.

The third point I will make is that one may postulate a certain governing dynamic to Florence's fiscal history. When the need for cash became more urgent, the imposition of forced loans grew, fewer citizens could meet these demands, and more of them had to pay discounted assessments and forego the interest owed to them. Alternatively, they could rely on others to pay on their behalf.[4] This tended to mean declining state revenue in the present (even as it reduced the state's long-term burden), which in turn increased the commune's desire for full-payment loans and forced the state to offer more appealing terms to those citizens capable of surrendering large sums (Molho 1971; Conti 1984, 237). The result was that influence was consolidated in the hands of a few solvent citizens, a number of whom (at least in

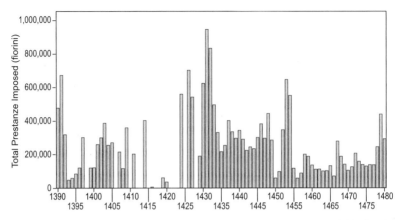

Fig. 7. Florence's Fluctuating Tax Burden, 1390–1480. Data is not available for the following years: 1398, 1406, 1410, 1412–13, 1415, 1417–18, 1421–23, 1425, and 1428. Sources: Molho 1971, 10, 62; Conti 1984, 81–83.

1427) combined public administration of the fisc as *Ufficiali del banco* with private speculation on the future value of *Monte* stock.[5] Cosimo de' Medici came to embody this dependence. On the verge of exile he addressed the Signorìa: "Ask your soldiers how many times they were paid with my own funds, the Commune subsequently repaying me when it was able to do so!" (Molho 1971, 188).

My fourth point, however, is that this elegant governing dynamic over-states the clarity and unidirectionality of actual developments. The city faced dramatically different constraints over time; innovations did not stick. This led to a history of oscillation back and forth between different off-the-shelf taxation procedures, between tax collection and tax relief,[6] between innovative and traditional strategies for increasing tax revenues, and between periods of duress and relative ease for taxpayers. Figure 7 graphs this history succinctly and provides an important context for the letters that follow.

The figure records the year-by-year fluctuations in the volume of forced loans imposed, which in turn correspond fairly closely to annual variability in military expenditures.[7] Clearly, the most severe crisis was faced in the early 1430s, during and in the aftermath of the war with Lucca. This crisis was exacerbated by having followed closely on the heels of the war against Milan in the mid-1420s. Other peak periods include the early 1390s (again a war against Milan) and the early 1450s (more wars, against Milan and King Alfonso of Aragon). There are smaller but significant jags upward in 1403,

1409, 1414, 1437–38, 1440, 1446, 1448, 1467, and 1479. I proceeded by assuming that these would be apt years in which to look for letters documenting how the tax situation affected interactions among citizens, and how communication about taxation signaled continuity and change in the texture of the state over time.[8]

Ground-Level Responses to Fiscal Demands

> All of my said goods have been sold for the Commune . . . in my absence, since I took off so that I wouldn't find myself put in prison; and besides these goods, all my shares in the *Monte* were sold; and besides this, I find myself debtor of the Commune! . . . So that one can see what justice this is, that everything I had has been taken, and remaining in such debt that if I were not supported by my uncle Francesco, I would die of hunger. And I am [only] twenty-five years old. (Conti 1984, 310; my translation)

> We have brothers trying to scratch out a living abroad, not being able to stay in Florence on account of the taxes. (Conti 1984, 343; my translation)

These laments made to tax officials by Filippo di Benedetto dei Nerli in 1442 and Matteo di Giovanni Strozzi in 1451, respectively, demonstrate how Florentines felt about the periodically egregious tax assessments of the commune. They also provide some evidence of the state's tactics and of certain strategies Florentines adopted to cope with the state's demands. Expropriation and imprisonment are hardly the benign acts of a weak state. And yet the state's often ingenious efforts to collect funds from the citizenry continually drove citizens to seek financial help from their fellow citizens, with the consequent reinforcement of interpersonal attachments that posed a challenge to the state.

In the rest of this chapter I present a dozen or so letters, all in one way or another about problems with taxes. They are presented in chronological order so that readers can follow several changes that occurred over time. One was a shift from citizens being proactive in reducing tax assessments to their becoming more reactive, asking for assistance in paying debts already owed. A second was that the balance between expressions of desert and expressions of deference shifted toward the latter after 1434, at least in letters addressed to members of the Medici family. Third, there appears to be a move away from writing to people who were directly involved in the taxation process and toward seeking help from those only indirectly involved.

The latter two changes jive well with what historians have recognized for some time: that there was a concentration in the personalistic practice of power in Medicean Florence. Extra-institutional channels had arisen to challenge state administrative control over fiscal outcomes, thus weakening the autonomous power of the state.

However, we will also see that there was over time a consistent pattern whereby the problem of tax collection was linked to performance in office and/or the desire to hold office. This link existed at the level of communal policy, and consequently it is found also in the substance and rhetoric of interpersonal interactions. The relationship of Florentines to the state was both adversarial and participatory, and this is an absolutely critical factor in understanding why rationalization and autonomization of the Florentine state stalled. The margins for state action were always tightly constrained by the competing (but shifting) involvements of Florentine citizen participants.

This chapter began with Donato Acciaiuoli's letter of 1409, a year of heightened taxation. The next such year for which data is available is 1414. Data are missing for 1413, but the following excerpt from a letter of October 17, 1413, from Filippo dall'Antella to Pippo di Franco Sacchetti, suggests that similar pressures were in play (*Conv. Soppr.* 78, 324: 108). Like Acciaiuoli's letter, this one is redolent with sensibilities akin to those of Morelli:

> My honorable elder and dearest father, I wrote another letter to you in the past few days, a letter which I do not know if you received. Now [again] I recommend to you my affairs concerning the *prestanzone*, that I not be treated as I was with the *prestanze*; you know how much I was treated unjustly. And I hope to be to you, Pippo di Franco, everything that you would like.

Note here the combination of familiarity, or aspirations to familiarity, in the body of the letter, with rather deferential framing at the beginning and at the end. The tactics of rhetorical deference and rhetorical brinkmanship ("you know how much I was treated unjustly"), so notably mixed in the practices espoused by Morelli, are combined here. The letter melds the two cognitive components of clientage—deference and reciprocal obligation—into a single interaction. Also present here is something quite common throughout Florentine correspondence—the metaphorical equation of the patron with a father, with the attendant implication that patrons are expected to carry out the same duties of protection and guidance in public life that a good father ought to provide. Nevertheless, this letter's rhetoric is not particularly florid.

Moving ahead a decade, the next example provides evidence that patronage *networks* had become activated to deal with the tax burden. Pagnozzo di Bartolomeo Ridolfi, a member of a distinguished patrilineage and the head of a moderately wealthy household (*Catasto* 66: 97), wrote a letter to Averardo de' Medici dated February 18, 1424 (*MAP* I, 64), not about his own tax problem, but about that of an underling:

> Thanks for working that favor for me. I might seem ungrateful, but I am informed it was the cause of my being able to come back to Florence, which is a great consolation to me. Now the reason for this letter is to recommend to you Antonio di Niccolò Benucci, this little guy (*fata*) whom I recommended to you another time. He is coming to lodge his petition concerning the *prestanze*, as in person he will advise you. He is poor and cannot pay; may he be recommended to you. . . . Say hello to Giuliano and Alessandra for our part.

This letter lacks the somewhat indignant tone of the previous examples, undoubtedly because Ridolfi is writing primarily concerning someone else's peril rather than his own. Ridolfi portrays himself as close to Averardo and somewhat distant from Benucci. Benucci is "this little guy" who is poor (*in miseria*); by contrast, he addresses Averardo using the familiar *tu* and makes a point of his personal acquaintance with Averardo's son and daughter-in-law. Although Ridolfi says that returning to Florence was a great consolation, he does not express his thanks dramatically.

The Medici were not the only targets of requests for tax help in the 1420s, as the following letter of June 26, 1427, from Marco di Simone Strozzi to Giorgio Cristofani, attests (*C.S.* III, 132: 277). Note how social distances are constructed rather differently here than in the Ridolfi letter. For one thing, Strozzi makes explicit that he is writing at the behest of his *friend* Ferrantini, not some "little guy."

> Dearest elder brother, My friend Mariotto Ferrantini has heard that I have trust in you. I myself am certain of this and so in service to him I am writing to you, praying that it be pleasing to you to look favorably on him, to collect certain monies he is owed by debtors of his employed at your court. For he cannot take care of his needs, nor contrive to remit his *prestanzoni*, which, if not paid, will prohibit him

from leaving the country. When you write to me about anything, write to me concerning this. Nothing more. I am always at your disposal. . . .

Strozzi deliberately addresses Cristofani lovingly and deferentially as a dear older brother, using formal terms of address throughout. He begins the letter by putting the responsibility on Ferrantini for initiating the request and claims that he himself is motivated by his desire to do what friends do for each other. Only secondarily does he assert his certainty that Cristofani will be willing to help. "I am always at your disposal" is a typical stock letter ending, and "praying that it be pleasing to you to look favorably on him" is a typical deferential framing of requests for help. Still, these are not counterbalanced in this letter with forceful claims of *deserving* assistance.

There can be little doubt that the early 1430s were the period when Florentine taxes were most onerous. Accordingly, the rhetoric deployed in requests for assistance became more florid and urgent. In a letter written on November 14, 1430, by Federigo Sassetti to Niccolò di Iacopo di Ubertino Strozzi (*C.S.* III, 113: 94), Federigo explains how Lionardo and Bartolomeo di Ser Tino had formerly paid his expenses "out of kindness" (*per loro benignità*), but now they would not pay them any more. Consequently, he wrote,

> I have no other recourse but to you, and for this reason I pray that you do your best in any way that occurs to you, that on the 8th of December, which is the day the rent for my place is due, that you make to pay the money there at Florence where Lionardo Gondi indicates, and this I pray of you as much as I know how, such that if the need [I have] and the adversity [I face] were not so great, I would not beg this of you.

Now we are getting to the core patronage-style language that appears across the board around the time of the *catasto*. "I have no other recourse but to you"; the recipient is portrayed as the only possible helper available. "I pray that you do your best in any way that occurs to you," and "I pray of you as much as I know how": the repetition of the verb *pregare* was certainly a stock element of requests for help. Finally, "need" and "adversity" are identified as motivating this request, rather than the fairness or justice cited in Acciaiuoli's letter. Thus Sassetti writes from a relatively supine position, one emerging directly from the extent of his need and the extremity of fiscal pressures, but one also considerably determined by the changing culture of requests for favor in the 1420s.

More of this change is evident in the following letter of May 23, 1431, written from the prison in Pisa by Giovanni di Pagolo Cantucci to Matteo di Simone Strozzi (*C.S.* III, 112: 65). Cantucci requests that Strozzi act in such a way that he be saved from undeserved injury and shame (*il danno e lla vergogna*), and that he be served with a *grazia* or *licenzia* to set his financial affairs straight.[9] He continues:

> And so I pray of you for grace and for the love of me and on account of reason, that you contrive with the friends and the Ten that in some way we are released from this place, and we will be obliged to you. . . . I pray of you that you recommend me to our friends, and to Luigi di Piero Guicciardini, that he pay my *catasto* assessments, because I hear that it would be advantageous; I pray that if he doesn't take care of it that you will.

His follow-up letter of May 26 is similar, begging Strozzi to recommend his case (to "our other friends"), and continuing that he had himself written to Marco degli Strozzi and Luigi Guicciardini. "Help me, for God's sake," he concluded (*C.S.* III, 112: 66).

As in earlier letters we have examined, Cantucci proposes multiple justifications for demanding assistance—here both love between writer and recipient, and the reasonableness of the request. But there is, in addition, a direct expression—even a promise—of *obligation* and future payback attendant upon receipt of assistance. Unlike the first letters we examined, this writer explicitly invites the recipient to activate a network of friends (*amici*) on his behalf. In the first mention of the word, Cantucci refers to "the friends" (*gli amici*), suggesting a more or less impartial group of potential helpers. But in the second instance he asks to be recommended to "our friends" (*agli amici nostri*), suggesting a more bounded, exclusive, and potentially partisan grouping of loyalists. With the references to Luigi Guicciardini, we find explicit reference to a pattern that had by this time become widespread: that of enlisting others to pay taxes on one's behalf.

No doubt it was prudent for those making requests to develop as many potential friendly contacts as possible, hoping that one of them might come through, or even that the more patrons back home in Florence who were apprised of one's situation, the greater the likelihood that one's need would be discussed in their conversations. In this way, too, those making requests sought to frame their problems in terms of matters of collective importance. Surviving letters of the Strozzi make clear how much that family cooperated to ensure that taxes were paid on time.[10] The patronage network assimilated itself to a family network in its effort to meet the public financial obligations of its poorer clients. In so doing, the patronage network did not always completely frustrate the state's efforts at raising revenues, but it gained another purpose that rendered its adherents more completely attached to it than to the collectivity as a whole. Practitioners of patronage also became increasingly adept not only at managing their members' resources, but also at hiding sources of wealth from communal officials.

Tax difficulties began to affect ever higher echelons of society. The Tornabuoni family, in-laws of the Medici and among the very richest households in the city in 1427, experienced a 45.4 percent drop in their net fortune between 1427 and 1431 (Conti 1984, 88). It is no wonder, then, that Francesco Tornabuoni wrote to Averardo de' Medici (his niece's father-in-law) from Cascina on June 19, 1432 (*MAP* V, 229), using the same kind of urgent language that Federigo Sassetti had used with Niccolò Strozzi, asking Averardo to help him with a pressing financial problem:

> Respected and honored brother, Yesterday I received a letter of yours of the 16th of this month, to which I respond now, praying that it be pleasing to you to contrive by all means available that I obtain permission (*licenzia*) to return to Florence because the necessity of tending to my affairs presses me to be there. I am still mindful of what you write concerning the *Monte* money. For this too it is necessary for me to be there. . . . Nothing else for now, except that I pray and beg of you as much as I am able that you contrive that I may come back there.

This letter was followed by another six days later (*MAP* V, 232):

> Respected and honored brother, Many letters I have written to you praying you to contrive by all means at your disposal that I may leave this place with permission, because I am under pressure with so many matters as you surely are sufficiently informed. And yet I still have heard nothing. And for this reason, again, as much as I am able and know how to, I pray that you act in this matter as much as is possible for you, since I am not able and do not want to stay here any longer. And advise me if you believe that coming back without permission were tantamount to throwing myself in the jaws of the *podestà*. I say

no more except that I pray of you and plead with you as much as I am able that you act so that I may come back to my home there.

Yet another letter was written three days later, virtually identical in character (*MAP* V, 234). In all of these Tornabuoni seeks a *licenzia*—a document signifying official permission of the commune to return to Florence in order to tend to one's financial affairs and cover one's debts to the city. Although he does not indicate that he was acting in any official capacity on behalf of the commune at the time, Tornabuoni's letters from this period suggest that he was aware of and even involved in Florentine troop movements and needs. Thus, at least in an implicit way, his correspondence sits astride the goals of service to the commune on the one hand, and evasion of state coercion on the other. Note how Tornabuoni begins each letter with a standard opening salutation that emphasizes Averardo's obligation to him through the trope of *parentado*. All three letters repeatedly employ the "I pray of you" (*ti priego*) or "I pray as much as I am able and know" (*priego quanto posso e so*) formulas to achieve a plaintive quality. The superlative quality of the latter phrase was undoubtedly intended to heighten the impression made on Averardo.

In a letter of November 5, 1431 (*MAP* V, 14), another Medici partisan, Bartolomeo Orlandini, wrote to Averardo seeking assistance on a financial matter pertaining indirectly to the crushing level of taxation in effect in the city. This letter demonstrates another facet of the link between taxes and political partisanship: some writers asked bankers to purchase government bills or borrow state revenues on their behalf for the purpose of meeting impending private financial obligations.

> Magnificent sir and honored like a father, The strong storm affecting my city, together with the unbearable taxes that our citizens face, forces them and you and I to adjust our intentions. And the reason [for this letter] is that the heirs of Filippo Fagni are owed by us approximately 170 florins and Davanzato [Davanzati] about 80 florins all because of the dowry of Luigi my brother, and that we still have to return to them this amount. They put me one night before the *ufficiali dei pupilli* and accused me. To defend myself any more I cannot do without great shame and injury, and going *allo specchio*. And because I am certain that you repute my honor to be yours also, I pray that you be content to write to Giuliano or to Piero who holds the ledger, that they purchase some of the advances from the *acatti* [forced short-

term, reimbursable loans to the city]. And that they record a *promessa* [written obligation to pay] in my name, such that at the time they need this quantity of money back, they will be paid. Do not touch any of my principal, because this is owed to Rinieri del Fiogia. I pray that you do this quickly because from day to day I am trying to keep the *podestà* from banishing me. And he has given me only a few days to give him a response. And for all of this I pray of you that you relieve me of this shame. May God in all things concede to you that honor that we and your friends desire. All of your family are healthy here.

Orlandini's large household had listed significant debits in its 1427 *catasto* declaration, but its gross assets placed it among the top four hundred of the city's 9,780 households (*Catasto* 79: 151). Clearly, the tax burdens imposed by the state drastically reduced liquidity in the city and caused citizens to fear for their own standing, forcing them to resort to ever more complicated strategies and manipulations of the tax system. As with earlier examples, this request is first framed in terms of family ("Magnificent sir and honored like a father"), although here we see a far more deferential rhetoric than dall'Antella or Tornabuoni used. Orlandini acknowledges the great shame (*vergogna*) that he faces.[11] Then, adopting a fairly standardized formula, he equates his honor with Averardo's own. Orlandini strategically invites Averardo to infer the worthiness of his petition, and the trustworthiness of himself, from the coherence of his reference to widespread understandings of honorable behavior. Were he not desperate, Orlandini would not make this request—he would not jeopardize what honor he presently enjoyed on the basis of his wealth, political position, and moral independence. This disclosure of earnest desperation enlivens the letter, but it also is animated by and in turn revivifies the sense of honor on which the whole system ultimately rests. Orlandini concludes his letter in a rhetorically conventional way. However, he also refers supportively to the *amici* of Averardo—seemingly indicating the political clients of the Medici and their collective agenda, even as he distances himself from them by referring to himself and/or his family as somehow distinct from the rest of the *amici*. Thus here we have examples of stock forms of patronage correspondence, but also evidence of how the state's inventive tax programs infiltrated private relationships.

After 1432 the burden of forced loans tapered off dramatically, and yet the high taxes left an indelible mark that became more evident with successive small increases in tax exactions from the late 1430s into 1440. This comes through in a letter dated February 4, 1439, from Lionardo di Antonio de' Nobili to Cosimo de' Medici (*MAP* XI, 218):

> Dearest honorable brother, One may say that I and my son, your god-son (*tuo figliaccio*), have become country dwellers. For a long time, I have not been able to enter the city on account of the enormous taxes I owed in the past, and if it had not been for the *novina* and the *ven-tina* [of 1434 and 1437 respectively, procedures for tax collection res-urrected from the early 1400s, prior to the adoption of the *catasto*] one would no longer have any recollection of me or my son. . . . I am often not able to make my payments, so that often I find myself *a specchio*, and for about sixteen years, one could say I have found myself and find myself [in that condition]. And I have a great hope in this new distribution of the *settima* [of November 1439], that they will give good and perfect consideration of my impossibility of paying.

Nobili continues, explaining that his family has often had to resort to living off of the woods. But soon he comes to his main point:

> I hear that it has been arranged that a new *imborsazione* concerning the offices of the palace, both domestic and abroad, is to take place. I am certain that you and your sons need expend little effort (*bisogna durare pocha fatica*) by honest means, and so I want to pray of you, with your friends, that you contrive that your godson not be consigned to oblivion (*dimenticatoio*).

Despite the decline in tax pressures, many citizens still suffered on account of them. Sometimes they bore this suffering for a period after taxes were levied, but eventually the strain caught up with them. Consequently the techniques for overcoming tax problems in pursuit of communal office re-mained in place, arguably with a heightened rhetoric of deference toward those whose influence had grown enormously. More intriguing still, Nobili openly suggests in his letter that he believes he owes his survival to the dismantling of the *catasto* and its replacement with more traditional meth-ods of collection. These methods—the *novina*, the *ventina*, the *settima*—en-hanced the exercise of favoritism. Nobili may have believed that the Medici themselves were instrumental in this change. Now he reminds Cosimo (who appears to have had no direct role in the distribution and collection of the new tax) of his terrible situation, hoping once again to get relief and, more than that, re-enlistment, for his son if not himself, in the register of potential office holders. To accomplish this he flatters, writing that he is certain that it will require "little effort" on Cosimo's part to pull this off. By now we have come quite a distance from Donato Acciaiuoli's petition to Riccardo del Bene, who at least had been one of those actually charged with distributing the tax burden.

A letter written on November 30, 1441, to Cosimo's son, Piero, by Giacomino Tebalducci (*MAP* XVII, 24), introduces one further level of remove into the chain of tax-related favor seeking. It is not the letter's recipient who is to provide assistance, but the recipient's father:

> Noble sir and honorable friend, In this present life all of my hope remains solely in you. Thanks be very much to God who has clearly shown me, by means of you, that I must get out of the terrible shadow I have been living under on account of my insupportable taxes, and get my burden reduced to a more just level. For your information, we . . . remain debtors of this commune for *catasti* and *ventine* and *settime* 590 florins or more in total, and we have but seven small farms remaining to us. Therefore, humbly I pray of you, make known to your venerable father not only our need, but also [indicate to him] that he could not help any man who would so much desire to see the satisfaction of all those matters that pertain to your advantage and your honor (*l'utile e l'onore vostro*) as Giacomino does . . . Our affair could not be more insignificant in comparison to his great power.

Again we see that the *catasto*'s effects persisted a decade or more after its inception. And again, a writer provides multiple justifications for receiving assistance: his past burdens have been unjust, he has a great need, he desires that the Medici enjoy profit and honor. Furthermore, the assertion, "In this present life all of my hope is in you alone," recalls Federigo Sassetti's claim: "I have no other recourse but to you." Nevertheless, one may detect here yet another increment in the hyperbole of patronage-seeking communication: in none of our earlier letters is the "power" (*potere*) of the patron so explicitly recognized.

In the late 1440s, tax exactions surged again, particularly in 1446 and 1448. A variety of letters in the correspondence of Bartolomeo Cederni (see F. W. Kent 1991) deal with this new yet familiar climate, including a letter from Cederni's friend, Bernardo di Zanobi di ser Zello, in February 1447, to Pagolo di Zanobi da Ghiaccetto (*Conv. Soppr.* 78, 314: 264). Once more, even as past tax procedures were repeatedly consigned to the dusty bookshelf of

Florentine fiscal policy, they lived on in the memories and the discursive practices of Florentine citizens for many years, and they provided a warrant to justify assistance in terms of past injustices:

> Honorable brother, As you know much better than I, the *graziosa* [an unpopular tax implemented in 1442 and thought to have encouraged fraudulent declarations] put me on the bottom, and this burden that they are arranging is likely to undo me, because debts are not deductible, and I will have a tax burden that is not justly mine. And also when they did the first *catasto* I had a debt bigger than was registered to me, so that I had credits I had to sell or give away to those who needed them, paying out a good part of my assets. And with this one, I made a high estimate, since my debt and the personal deductions I have would cancel everything, but still this estimate imperils me, and having obligated all of my income to my creditors, it is necessary for me to act subtly if I want to keep my family alive.

This letter, rather than being purely a plea for help, functions more like a venting of frustration to a friend or associate, driven less by fear than by annoyance. Thus later in the letter Bernardo writes, in reference to the possibility of becoming *allo specchio*, "Use your ingenuity and contrive that I not have to deal with this nuisance" (*noia*). Further, Bernardo asks da Ghiaccetto to confer with the powerful patron Neri di Gino Capponi to initiate the process of having his tax share reduced, and yet he also writes toward the end of the letter, "I am not writing to Neri [directly] so as not to give him any annoyance" (*tedio*). Despite the fact that the jails were full of people who had not paid their taxes around 1446 (Conti 1984, 209, citing the chronicler Giovanni Cavalcanti), the language used here suggests that some of the bite was draining out of the *specchio* list as an instrument of state coercion.[12]

Some of the time-honored, pork-barrel machinations for dealing with tax relief as well as tax impositions are evident in this letter of November 23, 1447, written by Bono di Giovanni Boni to Bartolomeo Cederni (*Conv. Soppr.* 78, 314: 334):

> This is to advise you that your *sgravatore* (tax relief official) is Iacopo di Niccolò di Giorgio Betti Berlinghieri, and as soon as he was drawn I spoke to him of your need. I am also the tax relief person in my neighborhood, and I said to your *sgravatore* that if he was wanting any relief distributed in my neighborhood he should ask for it, and that I

was respectfully wanting relief for you[?], and he promised it to me. This morning at dawn I went to him, and he promised to do it. . . . Again I spoke to Mariotto Bartolini, who is his brother-in-law, that he remind him of it. I will do what I can. If I don't succeed, it will not be for not having reminded him of your need.

In the early 1450s, the tax burden again reached epidemic proportions. The tone of the following letter sent to Piero di Cosimo de' Medici by Francesco di Bivigliano Alberti dated March 5, 1451 (*MAP* XVI, 88) provides some insight into this period, although the taxes to which he refers go some ways back in time:

> For your information, when I was in Lombardy, a big assessment of the *ventina* and *novina* was levied against me by my neighborhood . . . which I had then to pay either in full or with *grazie*. To get myself out of such troubles (*tante noie*), I rented out a farm that gave me sufficient means to live on. And then I had to come here and request help from relatives and friends for several years, in such a way that everyone now regrets dealing with me. And in our house it has been many years since we lit the torches and the oil lamps. And (if I were) speaking to you in person, you would see that, by helping me, you would do toward me that which would make of me your servant. And don't ever forget it.

Alberti refers to taxes as *noie*, just as Bernardo di Zanobi di ser Zello did. But he paints a bleak picture of the effects of excessive taxation on his well-being. Having done so, he can hardly avoid making an open-ended offer of himself as Piero's "servant," and even driving home the point emphatically in the final sentence.

Finally, we have a letter of April 15, 1479, written during another year of heightened taxation. This one was written to Lorenzo the Magnificent by an eponymous descendant of Giovanni Morelli, the early-fifteenth-century diarist whose advice to his children included explicit directions for hiding wealth and lamenting excessive tax burdens (*MAP* XXXVII, 219). Once again, tax matters and eligibility for office are completely interwoven, very much as they were in Lionardo di Antonio de' Nobili's letter of 1439. Morelli even uses the same imagery of oblivion as Nobili did to describe his plight:

> Upon my departure from there, I requested by your grace that it be pleasing to you to lend me such favor, that this time around I were

eligible to be drawn for *gonfalonier* of justice, for the reasons I have many times said to you and which I know are well-known to you. And especially because in my house for so long there has not been any office-holder, so that it is fair to say we suffer oblivion (*essere nel dimenticatoio*). And once again, it is on account of the taxes running back [in time]—that which affects me is about nine hundred florins, and I recognize this to be our undoing. And although I am of a firm will and opinion in wanting to make every effort, and in order that I have the pleasure of comforting my brothers, that I had done my utmost for them, once again I pray of you that you concede to me this favor (*gratia*), by means of which I will repute myself to be like one resurrected from the dead (*un rilevato di terra*), and I will put this on the list of other obligations I owe to your Magnificence.

Here we find similarities with earlier letters, but also noteworthy differences. Whereas Nobili referred to Cosimo, only five years his junior, as a brother and addressed him familiarly, Morelli here uses formal language with Lorenzo, even though they are the same age. More importantly, whereas Nobili indulged in the traditional griping about taxation and cajolery to enlist the support of a patron, this is mostly absent from Morelli's letter. Furthermore, consistent with trends I reported in chapter 4, Morelli uses especially powerful language to convey the extent of his indebtedness to Lorenzo. This language is part and parcel of the project by which persons subject to state fiscal predations sought relief by means of interpersonal favor seeking, placing front and center their desire to serve the commune as participating citizens.

Conclusion: The Counterpoint of Society and State in Florence

A handful of documents do not a conclusive argument make. Nevertheless, they do reveal a pattern of behavior and of discourse whereby Florentines turned to their powerful fellow citizens for assistance whenever they were heavily burdened with taxes. This game of deference and demands, in which Florentines made explicit or implicit offers of return favors or personal loyalty to would-be *padroni*, was already in place before 1400, but it became especially urgent in the 1420s and 1430s, precisely around the time of the introduction of the *catasto*, which is widely recognized as the fifteenth-century's most innovative and forward-looking piece of tax-related legislation. Rather than evaporating, the culture of patronage remained, while the legacy of the *catasto* lived on in later tax-related correspondence. Florentines regularly commented on and devised tactics for coping with the various demands of the state in their private letters, tactics that often involved appeals to others.

Undoubtedly there were changes in the texture of this institution over time. For one, citizens switched from proactive strategies for avoiding high tax assessments to reactive strategies for paying off crushing tax burdens. Ironically, the *catasto* was meant to eliminate favoritism in the *distribution* of the tax burden, but it could not eliminate favoritism in the *repayment* of individual assessments. In examining letters over time, we can see a shift in the direction of more expressions of deference toward recipients and relatively fewer expressions of desert, at least when letters were addressed to one of the Medici. Finally, decisions regarding the distribution of taxes increasingly were made informally by persons other than those officially assigned by lot to handle the task. Virtually whenever the tax burden increased and/or methods for assigning shares of that burden were altered, individual Florentines responded with critical commentary on state policy and sycophantic letters to private citizens who could help them.

Consistently across many decades, though, the challenges the state faced with respect to tax collection, and the difficulties citizens faced with respect to tax payments, were intimately tied to office-holding, both at the level of official communal policy and within the confines of personal correspondence. As I have noted, Florentines' relationship to the state was both adversarial and participatory, and this duality had significant consequences for macro-political developments.[13] The city-state did not falter merely because of an excessive devotion to capital accumulation over coercive capacity (Tilly 1992). Most of the Italian city-states waged many wars, both on behalf of commercial enterprise and in pursuit of military security, with substantial resources at their disposal, for considerable lengths of time, at significant levels of financial sacrifice. More importantly, rather than shirking their responsibilities, a relatively small number of Florentine citizens who were *simultaneously* merchants and politicians (as well as fathers, ambassadors, neighbors, and so on) repeatedly carried a disproportionately large share of the office holding *and* fiscal burden of the city. Political savvy was not lacking, but it was attached to the *role* of "citizen" rather than to a distinct *group* in society.

Nor did it falter because of an unstable state pact between commercial patricians and the martial nobility (Spruyt 1994). Yes, the city fell prey to frequent and debilitating factionalism (Brucker 1962; D. Kent 1978), and the elite compromises forged in the face of such factionalism constrained political and economic policy options (Lachmann 2000; Emigh 2003; Tarrow 2004). But factions typically were constructed across class boundaries, rather than within them (Padgett and Ansell 1993; F. W. Kent 2002). More importantly, members of the Florentine ruling class had a greater diversity of interests and identities than a simple rendering of the map of class interests would lead us to believe. The multiple and cross-cutting nature of these identities may only be understood by examining *interpersonal* interaction. Such interaction could certainly be contentious (Rubinstein 1997; Tarrow 2004), but it was also frequently cooperative. The problem was that such cooperation across group and status boundaries also hampered the emergence of an autonomous state.

In short, problems with the emergence of a strong Florentine state brewed up from a shifting array of interactions among individuals constituted not by simple group identities but by multiple affiliations and roles, any number of which could be activated to achieve personal objectives. Among these identities were the roles of father and neighbor, for example, which suggested private interests at some odds with the state, and that of office holder, which suggested some congruence between the interests of the individual and the interests of the state. Only by studying interactions can we see how and when these identities were invoked, and with what consequences for the development of the state. This is because state institutions and rules of thumb for interpersonal interaction developed side by side.

To conclude, administrative change in Florence was accomplished within the constraints of a contest, not between state actors and civil society, but between citizens in their role as custodians of the state and the same citizens in their role as subjects to the state. Certainly the modest separation of the state from the citizenry allowed the onerous tax burden to be accepted as legitimate to a remarkable degree, recurrent grumblings of the populace aside. And yet the embeddedness of the state in its private citizenry affected the extent to which the state could develop in an autonomous manner. Administrative developments in the fiscal state — in fact, a succession of alternately modern and traditional strategies for accumulating resources necessary for the protection and growth of the territorial state — constantly and repeatedly created and reinforced personalistic, honor-driven relations. These relations ultimately jeopardized the state's strength and autonomy in a way very different from that suggested by a shorthand class analysis. However much Florentine state makers desired reform, they found it impossible or inconceivable to establish a fiscal regime that would decouple taxation from political participation. In fact, expansion of the privilege of political participation was repeatedly used, especially by the Medici, to quell potential unrest (D. Kent 1987; Najemy 1982, 1991). Accordingly, Florentine leaders countenanced and even encouraged widespread personalistic patronage. Just as incipient state building in the form of the *catasto* was a largely unintended consequence of Florentine collective fiscal decision making under crisis, so too the strengthening of informal, politically active networks that undercut state autonomy was an unintended consequence of the state-building process itself.

8

"Servants and Slaves in Everything and for Everything"

Renaissance Networking and the Emergent Modern Self?

In the Middle Ages . . . man was conscious of himself only as a member of a race, people, party, family, or corporation — only through some general category. It is in Italy that this veil dissolved first; there arose an *objective* treatment and consideration of the state and of all the things of this world, and at the same time the *subjective* side asserted itself with corresponding emphasis. Man became a spiritual *individual*, and recognized himself as such. . . . Not one of [the Italians] was afraid of singularity, of being and seeming unlike his neighbors.

Jacob Burckhardt

I am advised from Rome by Messer Niccolò my son and apostolic clerk, that Your Magnificence saw him cheerfully and with great humanity while visiting him and his brother Francesco, and himself alone many times, and made to them a promise upon your return to Florence to get us repatriated, from which I have had the greatest pleasure, thanking you as much as possible and praying to you; we hear of this news warmly. We have decided to have no other mediator but you to contrive this for us than Your Magnificence, so as not to have to render a favor nor remain obligated to anyone but you alone. And you may judge how gratifying it is to us, that it will seem to us like being pulled from the Inferno and placed in Paradise, and you may always dispose of me and my sons as much as your most faithful friends, servants, and slaves in everything and for everything (*quanto di vostri fedeli amici, servitori e schiavi in omnibus et per omnia*). You know of our innocence, and the long penance suffered for others' sins. Therefore, so as not to bore you further, I will not go on any longer about this matter. Recommending us, from the heart, to Your Magnificence as humbly as we can (*quanto più humilmente possiamo*).

Maso degli Albizzi to Lorenzo di Piero de' Medici, November 18, 1471

I began this book by arguing that networking is an activity both strategic for and constitutive of persons. Successful networking—the successful construction (or demolition) and maintenance of social networks—involves cultural work. Building networks grows out of the partly institutionalized, partly improvisational, combination of commonly available cultural frames, grammatical components, and rhetorical devices in social interaction. By means of such interaction, persons improve their life prospects, building a portfolio of ties (social capital) to influential others. Furthermore, they typically simultaneously assume social identities thereby that define who they are. *Both* resources and identities flow to actors through the practical cultural tools they use in interaction.

A key problem to solve in such interaction, in an environment where there may be many contenders for favored positions, is how to present a credible portrait of one's capabilities, one's previous accumulated ties and skills, and, critically, one's *self*—some representation of one's fundamental character and the primary values behind one's actions—such that one is perceived as *worthy* of becoming connected. Chapters 5 and 6 dealt with this problem in detail. Undoubtedly one is strategic in this activity, and yet all may be lost if one comes off as inauthentic. But beyond self-presentation in general, "talk of the self" in particular is a crucial, specific practice for anchoring and justifying our actions, a tactic that seems to convey authenticity. Certainly it seems so in contemporary American culture (for example, Bellah et al. 1985; Swidler 2001). And, as seen in the first quotation at the outset of this chapter, Jacob Burckhardt (1960) believed it to have been so in Renaissance Italy—crucially, for the first time in modernity.

Such "talk" may be especially important in situations in which we have to do some sort of repair work to our relationships or to our reputations (Garfinkel 1967). However, in the second quotation at the beginning of this chapter, Maso degli Albizzi undertakes such repair work in a way that seems very much at odds with Burckhardt's view of the Renaissance self (for a photograph of the letter, see figure 8). How do we reconcile Burckhardt's claim that "not one of [the Italians] was afraid of singularity, of being and seeming unlike his neighbors" with Albizzi's desire to be considered among Lorenzo's "most faithful friends, servants, and slaves in everything and for everything?" To make a claim to friendship in this way typically meant a claim to being treated or considered *like others*. Further, to claim the role of servant or slave was to adopt a role defined fundamentally in relation to others. Undoubtedly Maso distances himself here from members of an

Fig. 8. Maso degli Albizzi to Lorenzo de' Medici, November 18, 1471 (A.S.F., *MAP* XXVII, 517r). Used by permission of the Ministero per i Beni e le Attività Culturali, Italy.

important corporate group—his own patrilineage—by asserting the innocence of himself and his sons. Yet he likens Lorenzo's patronage to a well-known narrative of salvation, and in presenting himself as humbly as possible, he speaks "from the heart." Where is the triumphant, self-asserting individual in this particular outward representation of an inner self?

It is tempting to suppose that "talk of the self" corresponds to some "real" self actually present in us. The classic, modernist, and largely ahistorical symbolic interactionist view of interaction has provided subtle confirmation of this supposition. Through interaction, a person constructs a self that is, in the first instance, a *multiple* one, based on the multitude of different interactional settings in which he or she operates. In the second instance appears an internalized and ultimately *generalized* reflection of the expectations of others. Finally, in the third instance, there emerges a *free* subject, capable of contemplating itself and acting at least somewhat autonomously with respect to the institutions of society (Mead 1934).

A critical implication of Goffman's work, however, is that the core "self" publicly represented as such—the author of a book, the actor who plays various roles on stage—is also just a representation—perhaps deeper but not more ontologically real than the various voices or roles one adopts (Goffman 1974, chap. 8). Even a person examining himself in a mirror is playing a role for himself. Agency is not situated in a directorial ego, nor does agency necessarily create such a self. Here the self is multiple but never truly autonomous, in keeping with the idea that no self is actually independently *constructed*; all selves are interactively or *interdependently* constructed. To the extent a directing and coordinating self appears to exist, it is but another representation.

While we may say all selves are, as a matter of fact, interactively constructed, particular *representations* of the self may or may not acknowledge that fact. The *style* and content of such representations differs across situations, across multiple social networks, across institutions, across cultures, and, critically, across time. It is fair to say, therefore, that in interaction one must present and represent a *culturally relevant and recognizable* "authentic" self. For us, authenticity is crafted within a culture that valorizes the individual and individual autonomy (Durkheim 1984, 122; also see Pitkin 1984, chap. 1), even if this idea may be gradually eroding (Gergen 1991). As Mühlhäusler and Harré (1990, 5, 88) comment, even if the transcendental ego is "not an empirically presented entity, but a shadow cast on the mind by the grammatical forms used in the practices of self-reporting, avowing, etc.," some "sense of self," though different in different cultures, "is not to be denied." What may begin as a merely expository metaphor for, or narrative about, ourselves tends to become effectively constitutive.

Continuing with this notion of the representation of the self, we may distinguish between *outward* representations of the self to others, and inward representations, and even *conceptions*, of the self—conceptions that carry moral weight in terms, for example, of how much we feel we ought to depend on others, or how much we feel we ought to be free from their influence. We make representations of ourselves to others, but also crucially, to ourselves. Thus we may speak of multiple selves—not merely in the sense of chameleon-like multiple representations of oneself to others, but also in the sense of multiple ways of conceiving the self and what it is up to in different settings, and in the sense of distinguishing between how the person *represents* his or her self outwardly, and how he or she *conceives* of himself or herself inwardly.

These distinctions set up the core questions tackled in this chapter. What kind of selves were constructed in early Renaissance Florence, and how did Florentines represent their selves to each other and to themselves? What were the specific implications of the ecology of Florence's multiple and overlapping social networks, its political properties, and its cultural codes for representations of the self and conceptions of the self? Could the practice of representing a private self or core motivations behind public performances generate a new perception of the autonomy of one's selfhood, of one's particular individual being, even if predicated on obtaining validation through others?[1] How much craft and deception lies in the representation of oneself as, say, a "slave"? Since we can hardly know if a change in the public presentation of the private self betokens a change in the content of the self's private perception of itself, perhaps we should instead ask: Is there a discernible "shift in moral vocabulary" (J. Martin 1997) about the self in Renaissance Florentine interaction? And what kind of evidence might allow us to know if such changes in outward practices bespoke changes of inward orientation?

As I noted above, these questions are especially germane with respect to Florence, for we continue to grapple with Burckhardt's claim that the Italian Renaissance was the crucible for the emergence of one of the dearest institutions (or cultural constructs) of modernity: the "individual" (Connell 2002). Personal singularity, so he argued, became an object of aspiration; virtuosity and unique style in many diverse fields defined a well-lived life.[2] The term "Renaissance man" persists today to identify those individuals who combine their many gifts into a unique package — *uomini universali*, as their contemporaries called them.

For present purposes, I understand the label "individual" to signify something like what Charles Taylor (1989) means in his study of the modern Western self, or modern identity, under the tripartite formulation that includes: 1) the development of inwardness; 2) the affirmation of ordinary life; and eventually, 3) the appeal to nature as a source of moral authority and to personal inner nature as the basis for individual fulfillment. It is noteworthy that Taylor himself does not discuss the Italian Renaissance as a formative moment in the development of this self. Moreover, Florentine scholarship today, in particular the rich research on social history as opposed to high culture, has largely repudiated Burckhardt's thesis (Connell 2002).[3] At least, many historians agree that Florentines did not overly crave self-definition separate from the social networks and categorical groupings that lent them their identity and sense of belonging. Leon Battista Alberti, supposedly an exemplary Renaissance man, propounded his view of diligence (*diligenza*) as a critical "self-making" virtue in the face of *fortuna*, ironically, in the course of a text written to ingratiate himself with fellow Alberti family members (Kuehn 1991; Grafton 2000, chap. 1; Boschetto 2000).[4]

While Burckhardt's claim lives on today more as a foil to current scholarship than as truth, the distinctness of the modern Western self and its historical emergence remain topics of immense interest in many disciplines, including philosophy (MacIntyre 1981; Taylor 1989), social and cognitive psychology (de Vos 1985; Markus and Kitayama 1991; Baumeister 1987; Gergen 1991; Bruner 1986, 1996), history (N. Davis 1986; Biagioli 1993; Burke 1997; Porter 1997; J. Martin 1997; Becker 2002a, 2002b; Seigel 2005), cultural anthropology (Shweder and Bourne 1984; Dumont 1985; Carrithers 1985; Yang 1994), art history (Baxandall 1972; Boschloo 1998), linguistics (Mühlhäusler and Harré 1990; Harré 1998; Harré and Moghaddam 2003), sociology (Silver 1989, 1990; Luhmann 1986), and literary criticism (Greenblatt 1980; Montrose 1996). They are also essential topics in archaeologies of early modern European state formation and sovereignty (Elias 1978; Foucault 1977). Rather than some essential self becoming freed in the Renaissance from its medieval fetters, modern subjectivity—incorporating both the sense of subjective consciousness and the sense of subjection—is a construct, a product of specific historical and institutional forces (Meyer 1986). But distinctions between modern and premodern selves are blurry at best. The timing of the change is protracted and jerky rather than quick and clean, with different contexts, settings, and institutions providing more or less fertile soil and greater or lesser impetus. My brief review of historians' claims about the nature of privacy and subjectivity in Renaissance Florentine art, lifestyles, and material culture in this chapter will indicate as much: the evidence for the meaning of the self and the timing of its evolution is inconclusive.

Nevertheless, it is hard to banish the thought that, in a variety of respects, there really *is* something different about the Renaissance subject's practice and conception of the self, compared to earlier times. There is something distinctly recognizable to modern eyes about so much of the evidence found in the documents and material culture of Florentine social and political life. I believe that early Renaissance Florentines exhibited, probably for the first time since antiquity, a flexible, context-specific form of "interdependent self" (Bachnik and Quinn 1994; Wetzel 1994; Markus and Kitayama 1991).[5]

In part this change was rooted in social structural changes that occurred in the late 1300s, combined with the sudden availability of new (or long misplaced) cultural forms in the early 1400s. Florentine society was transformed from a collection of corporate bodies (above all, guilds in the mid-1300s), wherein individuals' primary public identities were fairly fixed, into a consensual regime run by a multiply networked elite whose identities and sense of personal worthiness were fairly fluidly defined (Najemy 1982; Padgett and Ansell 1993; Padgett and McLean 2006). In the aftermath of the Ciompi rebellion of 1378 and foreign threats, the elite expanded the pool of eligibles for office while simultaneously centralizing the procedure for approving and placing the chosen candidates—a strategy of simultaneously "widening access while tightening control" (Rubinstein 1997; McLean 2004). Over the decades, more and more individuals were nominated for office, but the names of those actually *selected* and thus deemed worthy came predominantly from an increasingly selective subset of the population.

Ostensibly each individual now entered the electoral arena as "an isolated and 'equal' participant," with offices "distributed according to criteria of personal and individual worth" (Najemy 1982, 299, 308). And whereas individual political opinion was stifled in the early 1300s, individuals' expressions of opinion (as indicated in the *Consulte e Pratiche* records of the late 1300s and early 1400s) and their distinctive leadership styles came to be critical inputs a century later (Becker 2002b, 276; Brucker 1962). But consensual politics meant accepting the elite as an embodiment of the commune—both moral exemplars and a group of worthies whose favor ordinary individuals were compelled to court. Consequently, whereas the fourteenth-century guild form of organization had largely discouraged the emergence of clientelism (Brucker 1962; Lansing 1991), the consensual politics of the early 1400s ignited it. Clientelism facilitated the emergence and diffusion of a new repertoire of words and deeds that both "comprised" the self and rendered it intelligible to itself. It seemed to warrant some kind of public exploration of the self: a construction of one's motives, character, and adaptive capabilities that together constitute an integral part of the way modern selfhood is practiced and even conceived. At the very least, the change fostered greater subtlety, nuance, and self-consciousness in the construction of an interdependent self; but perhaps there are trace elements of an adjudicating, prudential self there as well. In the balance of this chapter I will present documentary evidence to help us assess the matter.

Assessing the Emergence of the Modern Self in Europe

As Marcel Mauss (1985) classically formulated the issue, the notion of self for "primitive" peoples is bound up with fitting into slots within a differentiated role structure. In certain societies, like the Kwakiutl (Mauss 1985, 5) or the Balinese (Gergen 1991, 9), each individual receives a new name with each new stage of life, suggesting that individuals are identified with and by the roles they take up in these progressive stages. This conception changes with the Romans, who began to use *persona* as a legal term signifying the right to obtain property (Mauss 1985, 14), in addition to the obligation to perform duties associated with membership in a concrete social or political group (Carrithers 1985, 250). With the Stoics, this notion was dramatically transformed into the sense of what one desires to be according to the strength of one's will. As Dumont (1985) argues, Stoicism in part emphasized one's harmonious relationship with one's environment through the enactment of legitimate roles, but it also stressed one's individual conscience and striving after a kind of moral purity. Christians appropriated this Stoic development of inwardness and reinterpreted it in terms of one's relationship with God. Still, this inwardness is not coterminous with the modern conception of the self. Whereas Augustine, for example, clearly urges the Christian to turn inward, this is not a turn toward psychological, individualistic self-actualization but toward God, who inhabits the soul (Taylor 1989, 134; Dumont 1985, 96). For this reason Augustine's *Confessions* cannot be said to have initiated the genre of autobiographical writing as we know it today. Rather he urged the individual to find self-actualization only through humbling or "emptying" the self (Philippians 2:8). This initiated a deep vein of concern with inwardness and individual confession (Baumeister 1987, 32) in the Middle Ages and beyond, but not exactly a modern self.

Cohn (1992) has detected a change from the 1100s through 1425 in the commemoration of death in the Italian peninsula, whereby testators increasingly used wills to constrain their beneficiaries on the future use of their bequests and endowments and increasingly devoted resources to plaques, celebrations, and works of art that would sustain them in the minds of future generations. Both developments could be seen as prima facie evidence for a more individuated approach to death. And yet, as Cohn (1992, 286) points out, these innovative strategies occurred most commonly in cities where patrilineal descent and patrilineal control of property were strongest. Increasingly, ancestors and ancestry unofficially but indelibly constrained individuals' choices of burial and remembrance; the flip side was that individuals increasingly chose to uphold and advertise group identities through their choices. Ironically, a more individualized approach to death and its remembrance was evident in northwestern Europe in the 1400s rather than in Florence, the cradle of Burckhardtian individualism (Cohn 2002).

Portraiture in painting was revived in the middle of the fourteenth century, although it took some time to catch on (Braunstein 1988, 556). The first self-portraits are of painters merely on the margins of narrative religious art. Only gradually does the artist move closer to the center of the art, appear in contemporary dress, and/or direct his gaze outward (Boschloo 1998). Autonomous self-portraiture did not exist prior to 1500, and even then one of its early variant forms was the self-portrait as part of a group portrait—for example, among family members. Furthermore, Burke (1997, 26) reports that particular portraits were used to depict multiple different people! Thus there was an abiding emphasis on stylization and a lingering lack of concern for what we would consider accuracy.

During the fourteenth and fifteenth centuries, images of men at work began to be portrayed in painting, suggesting the valorization of ordinary life and this-worldly activity in all its multiplicity, which Taylor (1989) regards as central to the modern self. Donatello's bust of Niccolò da Uzzano and Ghirlandaio's portraits of members of the Tornabuoni family, for example, seem to offer clear glimpses into the personalities of their subjects. Yet at the same time, more devout, formalistic artists such as Fra Angelico continued to work.

After 1300 the modern notion of privacy seemed to develop with increasing strength (Duby 1988a; Chittolini 1996; Henderson 2002). Changes in the layout of the Florentine house lend some credence to the idea that a private self was emerging. Whereas the feudal household afforded little opportunity for solitude, now different parts of the house were designed for different purposes: some for entertaining guests, some for the nuclear family, some for the couple only. Many men had bedrooms and studies apart from their wives (de la Roncière 1988, 217). Locks became more abundantly used to privatize both physical spaces and texts (Duby 1988b, 511). Yet it is notoriously difficult to know what went on behind locked doors and in people's minds.

Witt (2000) has argued convincingly that the novelty of humanism first emerged through grammar and poetry, not rhetoric and public forms of prose, which retained more continuity with medieval practices. Humanism undoubtedly was a crucial factor in the development of a new conception of the self. Nevertheless, developments in three non-poetical literatures—the chronicle, the autobiographical confession, and the domestic memoir—provide more useful evidence concerning how and when a new conception of self emerged. The mid-twelfth-century writer Acerbo Morena used stock characters in his histories, but at least he understood the need to expand the palette of characters to accommodate the complexity of communal history (Becker 2002b). Later twelfth-century accounts begin to depart from strict conformity to rhetorical doctrine (Becker 2002b, 272). Still, various surviving accounts of the funeral of Louis the Bavarian in 1347 (Braunstein 1988, 559) provide quite discrepant details of Louis's physical features, even as they converge in stressing his elegance. It appears, therefore, that the king is described chiefly in terms of the chroniclers' idea of what a king *should* look like, rather than in terms of his actual features.

The chronicle form that flourished during the thirteenth and fourteenth centuries necessarily began with the author introducing him- or herself, as if he or she were located in a precise social context from which to comment on events authoritatively (Regnier-Bohler 1988, 378). But although a "self" got introduced into the telling of history, there was still little sense that the author's story might be merely an interpretation of the facts. Certainly with the fourteenth-century chronicles of Donato Velluti and Marchionne Stefani, there is considerable attention to human history largely divorced from religious or purely stylistic concerns. Velluti's characters are in no way stock ones, and he quotes the everyday speech of his protagonists (Becker 2002b, 268). Nevertheless, the mixing of stock representations with "unique" ones continued for a long time. Burke (1997, 23) claims that biographies of great men into the sixteenth century often followed a pattern, suggesting that they were in some way stylized rather than true to nature. Likewise, although the humanists' letters are laden with self-portraits, Burke claims that these portraits (and as I have argued, also the letters in which they appear) follow many literary conventions, such that it is hard to assess what degree of modern verisimilitude they achieve.

Undoubtedly one of the most remarkable Renaissance literary developments was the flourishing of the *ricordanza* (memoir) form (Klapisch-Zuber 1985b, 1990), which legitimized newfound social mobility while resonating with a new appreciation of the importance of memory (Ciappelli and Rubin

2000; D. Kent 2002). These documents helped to carve out "a gulf between the cultivated civic persona and the deepest recesses of interiority" (Becker 2002a, 256). Morelli's *ricordanza* descriptions of his brothers and sisters, for example, seem true to life rather than formulaic. But often *ricordanze* buttressed group rather than individual goals. They often were written in a relational framework to a vividly imagined familial reader, as in the *ricordanza* of Foligno di Giovanni di Conte de' Medici in the mid-1370s (*MAP* CLII, 2). According to Burke (1997, 27), diaries were often written less for self-expression than as preparations for confession. And we need look no further than Morelli to find abundant evidence that the persons of the late Middle Ages and early Renaissance lived in a world populated with spirits, a world of magic that entailed belief in the permeability of the soul and the salvation not so much of individuals but of a community of souls through the priest's sacrament of communion (see N. Davis 1986).

One literary figure is particularly central to the idea that a new sense of selfhood arose early in the Renaissance. That figure is Petrarch. His *Letter to Posterity* (Enenkel 1998) reads a bit like a personal statement for professional promotion. He also provided a layered depiction of himself in his *Secretum*, written in the mid-1300s, including attention to the needs of the earthly body, candid analyses of his own melancholy and anxiety, comments on the art of ingratiation, and admonitions to acquire knowledge of oneself. The very form of the text—a dialogue between Petrarch and St. Augustine—allowed Petrarch-the-author to distance himself from Petrarch-the-character; indeed, he observed and chastised himself through the voice of Augustine. Despite its layers, however, the text remains explicitly Augustinian in form and content. By contrast, Angelo Poliziano remarked late in the fifteenth century, "Someone says to me, 'You don't express yourself like Cicero.' 'What of it? I am not Cicero. I express myself'" (quoted in J. Martin 1997, 1339). This remarkable assertion clearly indicates a valorization of the self on its own terms in a way completely different from Petrarch. But further plumbing of the depths of the self and legitimation of the self as a moral standard seem not to have come about until the early sixteenth century, with most of the scholarly literature focused on literary authors such as Erasmus, Luther, Montaigne, More, and Calvin (J. Martin 1997, 1321), rather than on documentary evidence provided by less celebrated historical actors. However, if we want to understand the emergence of a new conception of self, I believe we ought to try to look for it among ordinary selves, and not only in the writings of philosophical luminaries.

Documentary Evidence of the Florentine Self-in-Interaction

In the rest of this chapter, I present three types of evidence from patronage letters that directly bear on an assessment of the quotidian Quattrocento Florentine conception of self. The first of these is hyperbolic expressions of connectedness that provide evidence of a self thoroughly interdependently represented, and apparently interdependently conceived. The second type hinges on the use of a set of keywords we would tend to associate with constructions of an interior self: sincerity, honesty, integrity, prudence, truth, and so on. Finally, the third type consists of letters written to the Medici in the aftermath of exile, when writers had an especially ripe opportunity either to throw themselves on the mercy of the Medici, or to "come clean" about their past opposition. The evidence presented will demonstrate the existence of a thoroughly contextual interdependent self, with only occasional hints of a more independent self and the cultural equipment that would come to be used to express such a self in the sixteenth century.

Ordinary and Extraordinary Hyperbole

As I have made clear in this book, there is overwhelming evidence of representations of the other-relatedness of the self in the rhetoric of Florentine patronage letters. We see this recurrently in letter *formulae*, as in this highly typical sign-off in a letter of March 1, 1431, from Niccolò di Lorenzo Soderini to Averardo de' Medici (*MAP* II, 311): "I say no more so as not to bore you, except that I am yours in every endeavor, and to you I recommend myself." But a more extensive example of the same kind of expression—in this case a letter from Agnolo di Diliano Panciatichi to Iacopo di Francesco del Bene on April 28, 1390 (*Carte del Bene* 49, 6)—adds depth and emphasis to the construction of the dependence of one's identity on another:

> I consider myself obligated to yours and to you, for I would consider myself singularly grateful to your elders and to you, that I might be able to serve you honorably. Therefore seeing your letter, I am responding and thus also saying to your friend, that in this and all other matters which were pleasing to you, I have been and am ready to do everything that were possible and in this especially to exert myself. When I can do something that were desirable to you, do not spare me, because I consider myself entirely yours.

A letter from April 30, 1437, offers yet a deeper and more elaborate construction of dependence, and hence a richer construction of the interdependent self. A certain Mariotto di Marco wrote to Agnolo di Palla Strozzi (*C.S. III*, 130: 159) to express—seemingly very sincerely—his indebtedness to Agnolo: "[I marvel at] the perfectly good and faithful love that you have always borne me—one knows it is not on account of my works, nor from any worthy feature which resides in me, but only on account of your own lovely humanity, with which you are so well endowed." Few people, he continues, could have his degree of loyalty to Agnolo, to the point of being his "servant."

But perhaps we may be suspicious of the oft-used expression "servant." This may be simply a trope, not necessarily an authentic depiction of Mariotto's sense of self. A more telling letter comes more than two years later, on October 20, 1439 (*C.S. III*, 128: 94). In a manner similar to that employed in his earlier letter, Mariotto equates his own happiness with that of Agnolo: "It would have been a great consolation to me to see your return. I see with the greatest honor that you are reconfirmed as lieutenant and governor general, which things are of the greatest honor and renown, so that I am very much contented with this, that you are still looked upon with such great respect." But Mariotto concludes the letter by writing:

> And do not be surprised that in my sign-off I adopted such presumption as to ennoble myself a little (*usai prosunzione in rinobilarmi un poco*), in the desire to begin a family name by calling myself "dalla Palla." For a little while it has come to me to do that which has not been my usual custom, to sign my name in this way, and you know, I want to hold onto it, despite the fact that I have seen, and see, all the thousands of knaves each wanting to make a lineage, those who do not add one florin of taxes. . . . For your most humble servant, Mariotto di Marco dalla Palla, Florence

The remarkable thing here has to do with Mariotto's strategic, and yet simultaneously constitutive, choice of surname. As he himself indicates, a lineage was a highly valued commodity in Renaissance Florence. It gave one a patina of respectability, a way of establishing one's position in relation to communal politics and in relation to the commune's history. It was, in a sense, a primary boundary marker between insider and outsider in Florentine society.[6]

It is all the more surprising then that Mariotto *dalla Palla* chooses his relationship with Agnolo *di Palla* as the substance of his primary public and personal identity, rather than a distinctive experience, a distinctive ancestor, a distinctive legacy, or a distinctive home region. Instead his self-concept derives from his association with Agnolo, a fact that seems consistent with the cognitive and motivational framework of the interdependent self. In a society that granted respect to those with a distinguished lineage—where a surname was a token of merit—Mariotto chooses a token that can hardly signify personal autonomy, or connection by blood to an illustrious ancestor (as with the Serristori and Ginori in the earlier fifteenth century). Yet it remains a choice. This is a key way in which the Quattrocento Florentine self conceived its value interdependently, while scheming "independently" to realize its connections to others.

Of course, this is simply one episode, but it is consistent with language in other letters that identifies clients as *creature* (for example, *MAP* V, 13; XII, 155; XVI, 11; *Conv. Soppr.* 78, 324: 269). A particularly noteworthy example of this latter usage is a letter of one Sandro di Bardo to Averardo de' Medici (*MAP* II, 382) of November 23, 1430, wherein he writes, "I have need of running to you for help and advice in my needs, hoping from you to be counseled like your dependent (*creatura*), for it is my belief that I have been, and always will be, and you can always dispose of me as your own." Although such language was later adopted by courtiers, it was a highly serious step politically and in terms of personal identity to label oneself so strictly in terms of another. Similarly extreme are such expressions of dependence as offered to Lorenzo the Magnificent in a letter of June 10, 1472, by a certain Alessandro (*MAP* XXV, 168), who not only referred to himself as "your slave and servant," but also placed himself in Lorenzo's hands: "like a dead man, that you do with me what you will." Finally, recall the letter from Maso degli Albizzi to Lorenzo the Magnificent printed at the beginning of this chapter. Maso likens Lorenzo's favor to an unexpected salvation, while promising, "You may always dispose of me and my sons as much as your most faithful friends, servants, and slaves in everything and for everything." The Albizzi had been the arch-enemies of the Medici in the 1430s: hence the reference here, almost forty years later, to the distant sin of another, namely Maso's own father (although he lived apart from his father in 1427). On the one hand, this letter rhetorically ruptures the contemporary Albizzi's tie to their damaging familial past by asserting their own "innocence." On the other hand, it constructs the image of a self-in-relation in the extreme. With the language of "servants," "slaves," and "progeny," Florentine patronage seekers were claiming identities that were relational by definition.

Surely Florentine dispensers of favor would take assurances of loyalty such as this with a grain of salt. Treachery, flattery, and exaggeration exist in all times and places. Yet it also seems to have been the case that in making efforts to evaluate the loyalties of individuals, they used consistency of assurances and behaviors as an indicator of trustworthiness. Alternatively, as in the following excerpt from a letter of Giannòzzo degli Strozzi to his kinsman Agnolo di Palla Strozzi on August 22, 1467 (*C.S.* III, 150: 33a), they relied on third party judgments concerning others' motives, justifying the worthiness of requests in terms of the supplicant's consistency in expressing devotion to the prospective patron or friend:

> Honorable elder, This only to pass along a letter your Mariotto Davanzati, *podestà* of Montecatìno, sends you—who in his speech and gesture (*in bocca e in corpo*) appears not to have anyone but Agnolo di Messer Palla, and in his talk shows himself to be obligated to no one alive as much as he is to you, and he says he lives for you! And having seen how satisfied he has been that you have served and helped him, take heart to do what you can for him in his every affair; and so in his letter here he tells you that which he wishes. I know I do not have to encourage you to do this, nor recommend it to you, because I know and recognize your attitude toward your friends.

If by the later fifteenth century the Florentines were well aware of the hiatus between words and private thoughts, they nonetheless seem to have found the relational conception of the self sufficiently plausible to accept extreme assertions of personal loyalty as strategic *within* the framework of *amicizia*, not strategic in the sense of instrumentally violating the norms of *amicizia*. At the same time, it is worth considering these two ideas. First, as the rhetoric of connectedness and dependence becomes more inflated— as it comes to be asserted through more crafted efforts—the actor *doing* this crafting paradoxically *achieves* a certain kind of autonomy while denying that autonomy outwardly. A person may retain a greater amount of pride and self-respect when subjection is a choice rather than an inevitability (N. Davis 1986; Beauvoir 1949, chap.13). If flattery is a strategic choice, then someone—not just some physical someone, but some cognitive someone—must be making that choice. Second, clients' efforts at asserting their relational identities sometimes involved *denial* of relational constraints on

the patron himself. Cappone di Bartolomeo Capponi wrote to Lorenzo de'
Medici on August 22, 1472 (*MAP* XXVIII, 446), saying, "Insofar as I can,
I will with good intentions obey your will." And Monte di Buonaventura
wrote to Lorenzo on November 26 of that year to say, "Your letter I desire
so that whoever will lend me favor in your name could produce some sign
that this was indeed the will of Your Magnificence" (*MAP* XXVIII, 703).
In such instances a certain amount of stress was placed on the patron's "will"
(*volontà*). Thus the patron was rhetorically and somewhat fantastically constructed as a twofold paragon in this culture of patronage: a person who
exercises his own will to get what he wants (a perfectly independent self);
and yet a person so readily attuned to the needs of others that he needs no
encouragement to help them (a perfectly interdependent self).

Verbal Equipment of the Self: Sincerity, Prudence, and Honesty

It seems that hyperbole was used almost exclusively to enact social and political roles with strongly relational identities. So far I have provided little
direct evidence of the emergence of a more autonomously construed self.
However, there is another, more indirect way to assess whether a modern
self was emerging. We may look for the use of particular concepts and ideas
that later became crucial *equipment* for representing and constructing an independent self. Here I follow John Martin (1997) in believing subtle changes
in vocabulary provide traces in practices and ideas of elusive changes deeper
within. He writes (1997, 1322), "There was something significantly new
about the way in which the men and women of the Renaissance began to
conceptualize the relation between what they saw as the interior self on the
one hand and the expressions of one's thoughts, feelings, or beliefs on the
other." Through new styles and practices, new understandings of the self
arose in piecemeal fashion—not unlike the way the humanists' imitation of
ancient models brought about a change in their concepts and consciousness
as well (Witt 2000). In particular, Martin has detected an evolution of the
meaning of *prudence* toward the ideas of self-fashioning and self-masking,
and the gradual emergence of *sincerity* as a virtue. Together, these characteristics called upon a new kind of self, capable of either revealing itself to, or
concealing itself from, the outside world. In short, with the representation
and practice of sincerity and prudence comes about a self arbitrating between revelation and concealment.

Fifteenth-century Florentine patronage letters provide precious little
evidence of these particular changes, but a few examples are quite tell-

ing. While prudence is frequently invoked in recommendation letters, it often carries the connotation of wisdom (as in *MAP* XI, 169, where it is paired with *sollecitudine*) rather than circumspection. Only occasionally does a more political connotation of prudence as circumspection and political savoir-faire appear, at least in the first half of the century.[7] However, a letter of January 22, 1473, from Giovanni Tornabuoni to Lorenzo (*MAP* XXIX, 13), exhibits precisely the new sense of prudence of which Martin writes. Tornabuoni offers his evaluation of a certain Messer Santi, commenting, "He has made such proof of himself (*pruova di sè*) that it warrants that I should recommend him to you, and not in the vulgar sense (*non vulgaramente*). You are most prudent, and an excellent discerner (*optimo cognoscitore*) of the devisings (*ingegni*) of men, but I pray of you strictly that you regard him as recommended to you." Here prudence clearly means discernment, and specifically discernment concerning the degree of correlation between others' outward actions and their inward dispositions. Equally strikingly, Tornabuoni here comments on the recommendation letter genre, trying to distinguish his support from that offered in more run-of-the-mill letters.

It is perhaps not surprising that this connotation of prudence first appears in my data in a letter from one of Lorenzo's intimates. The notion of sincerity similarly first appears in letters written by other intimate friends. Martin (1997) suggests that the notion of sincerity was only gradually emerging in the later fifteenth century and the early sixteenth, replacing the more medieval notion of *concordia* that signaled an agreement between one's heart and one's words and/or a harmonious relationship among persons (or regimes) in the company of God. "Sincerity," by contrast, signified a verbal commitment to expressing one's own self and one's authentic "inward affections." That is what seems to be signaled in the following excerpt from a recommendation letter written to Lorenzo de' Medici by Francesco della Stufa on April 30, 1472 (*MAP* XXVIII, 29):

> Knowing that I am so intimate (*tanto affezionato*) with your household, they have prayed that I should wish to write to you in their favor about how very affectionate they are toward you, and that I should recommend them to you. First knowing their goodwill to be sincere and true (*sincera e vera*), it has seemed to me I ought to accede to their just petition and request.

In the opening sentence of a letter of August 10, 1472, quoted above in chapter 4, Niccolò di Giovanni di Ser Nigi (*MAP* XXVIII, 385) also seems to use the term in its modern sense: "My Lorenzo, if my writing seems to be full of presumption, consider it to be driven by a sincere love (*sincero amore*) and charity that presses me toward you." In the first example, della Stufa is offering a judgment about others' inward feelings. In the second example, Niccolò is trying to strengthen the claim he makes about his own feelings. Both letters are about selves crafted in relation to others; and the second in particular perhaps retains traces of the notion of *concordia*. Nevertheless, sincerity is a new term for talking about whether representations of inward feelings are believable.

A somewhat similar term that was used very occasionally in the first half of the fifteenth century is *semplicità*, which connotes simplicity but also directness, and which therefore is linked to the idea of authenticity. For example, one finds it in an anonymous letter to Cosimo de' Medici in 1434 (*MAP* XI, 39), in which the writer speaks of a friendship in the following terms: "with such sincerity (*semplicità*) on your part and my part as if we were monks." It was also used by Palla di Nofri Strozzi in a recommendation letter written to his kinsman Simone di Filippo Strozzi on February 8, 1422 (*C.S.* III, 132: 33) in reference to a certain Piero—possibly a cleric. He writes, "I hear he is moved by sincerity (*semplicità*), although in this case as you will learn, he has not behaved with prudence." Certainly this is very early to observe the tension between prudence and sincerity that Martin (1997) documents only for the late fifteenth century and the early sixteenth.

A contemporary Italian-English dictionary translates "sincerity" as *sincerità*, but also as *onestà*. As I noted at the beginning of chapter 3, however, *onestà* is a complex and subtle word, carrying connotations of honor as well as honesty and sincerity. Indeed, in the letters I have gathered, *onesto* virtually always means "honorable," or honest in the sense of fair and/or morally upright.[8] Consequently it is often idiomatically paired with *giusto* (just) or *ragionevole* (reasonable), and it is typically predicated of "matters" (*cose*) or requests rather than persons or personalities. "Honesty" is simply not widely regarded as a virtue or mark of authenticity in this period.

Verbal Equipment of the Self: Nature, Words and Deeds, and Proof

A few other expressions besides sincerity and prudence seem to provide more substantial glimpses of a new conception of self in formation. Najemy (1993, 141ff.) has pointed out how the notion of a durable "nature" or habitual set of practices arises in the correspondence between Machiavelli and

Francesco Vettori in the second decade of the 1500s, signifying the fairly hard-wired modus operandi of any given political actor. To the extent a writer invokes the idea of *natura*, he may well be alluding to a kind of core identity, or core set of dispositions, that in effect constitute a distinctive self. The use of the word *natura* is not common in patronage letters, but it does appear occasionally throughout the fifteenth century. Early on, it seems to express the idea of good-naturedness or goodwill as a virtue.[9] But a letter of February 11, 1474, from Filippo de Valsagne (*MAP* XXIX, 76), suggests a subtle shift: "It would not be possible that I should change my nature and the condition that has characterized my whole life. A poor person cannot have been more ready nor more attentive. . . . With perfect and good faith no one will ever surpass me." Here Filippo suggests that his nature is to be ready to do others' bidding, but he also alludes more explicitly than is seen in earlier letters to the idea of a nature as an unchangeable fact of one's character. The same meaning is seen in a letter of May 13, 1471, of Recco Capponi (*MAP* XXIII, 341), who claims he must do what is right and proceed deliberately concerning a favor for a certain Duti Masi: "For doing otherwise has never been my nature" (*altramente non fu mai mia natura*).

As I have noted many times before, undoubtedly Florentines could not be certain that they would be served well by others; trust was an abiding problem. But it is possible that the techniques by which trust was sought changed over time. A key element here is the power of words alone to convince others of one's good intentions. This did seem to change noticeably, at least on average, over time. In the 1420s and 1430s, "words" (*parole*) appear to be regarded either as adequate to discern intentions, or as unnecessary to confirm previously discerned intentions. Thus for example, Bartolo Corsi recommended a certain Ser Gherardino to Averardo de' Medici in 1427, saying, "He will demonstrate in words that he is your good friend" (*MAP* II, 76). In the same year Bartolomeo di Tommaso Sertini wrote to Filippo di Lionardo Strozzi (*C.S.* III, 145: 2): "Because you know for a long time there has been between us a love as between brothers, it appears to me unnecessary to use those words one would perhaps use with others" (*perche tu sai egli piu tempo che trannoi fu amore quanto tra fratelli mi pare con teco non dovere essere quelle parole usi forse tra altri*). In 1430, Giovanni Bartolini wrote to Matteo Strozzi to express his need "with few words" (*con poche parole*) (*C.S.* III, 112: 32b). Also in 1430, Tommaso Corbinelli asked of Averardo on his behalf, "That it please him to say a few words to Giovanni di Antonio or any others as you see fit" (*MAP* II, 284). In an official communication in 1429,

Rinaldo degli Albizzi wrote the *Dieci* expressing his desire that his reports of what was happening in the field would be trusted: "in such a form that with words and not with conjectures we will be able to judge" (*in tale forma che con parole e non per conietture abbiamo a judicare* (Guasti 1873, #1184). And in a letter from 1439, Giovanni Cappelli wrote to Agnolo di Palla Strozzi, recommending a certain "noble and worthy" doctor who "with few words [shows himself to be] a lover of his own honor and that of his superior" (*C.S.* III, 128: 130). In each of these cases, words are taken to be revelatory of inner intentions, with few words often being preferred to many.

The value of words in expressing loyalty did not disappear entirely.[10] But even as explicit trust in the power of words continued to be expressed into the late 1430s and on into the 1450s, changes were also afoot. In 1438, Alberto Alberti wrote a letter to Cosimo de' Medici following up on an earlier request, saying, "I am certain I used many more words than were necessary, but I was carried away with affection" (*MAP* XI, 194). In 1437, Talianus Furlanus wrote a letter to Cosimo de' Medici in which he offered himself in the following terms: "with the intention of acting with results in everything pleasing to you, much more than could be said with words" (*MAP* XI, 138). The adequacy and/or authenticity of words began to be questioned. The problem with words alone was strikingly called into question in a letter written in October 1434 by Matteo Panciatichi to the Medici in the aftermath of the exile they suffered the year before (*MAP* XIII, 70). "I hope to find myself there soon, and not with words but with actions you will see if I have not always been a friend to you" (*non con parole ma con effetti vedrete se suto mi sono sempre amico*). Further, some people's words mattered more than others. Niccolò di Giovanni Carducci wrote to Averardo de' Medici on August 24, 1431 (*MAP* IV, 79), on a matter of military business, asking him to write a letter that would advise the officials involved in the matter: "for they will believe that which they hear from you and not my words."

By the 1470s, the concern for deeds in addition to words had become stronger. Alessandro di ser Antonio Pucci wrote to Lorenzo de' Medici to claim that "in deeds and words" (*in fatti e in parole*) he had shown himself to be a dedicated employee of the Medici bank (*MAP* XXIX, 1). And on July 8, 1472, Giovanni Tornabuoni wrote to Lorenzo recommending to him a group of brothers who had been exiled from Arezzo in 1431. Of one of them, he says, "I have tried out (*provato*) in our bank and in our affairs, and I have found and still find him to be completely faithful and loving [toward us], and never from his mouth have I heard him say anything less than good and respectful." He goes on to say, "Never have they spoken ill of our magnificent Signorìa, and toward us in the bank they have always served with great loyalty and diligence." Words *and* deeds mattered jointly.[11] Along similar lines, in a letter of July 25, 1472, Matteo Buonaguisi asked Lorenzo to "spend some words" on his behalf, that his name might be included in the upcoming scrutiny. But he implicitly recognized that words were not enough to demonstrate his own loyalty and that deeds would suffice more: "You will find me more faithful than many others to you and to your affairs, and even if I [my actions] were not sufficient to give a sign of this, I would desire to be chosen for the scrutiny as many others are, to allow me to find myself in such places where I could please you and your friends."

Linked to this subtle change is an expressed willingness to offer proof (*pruova*) of one's loyalty, as in a letter of July 10, 1472 (*MAP* XXVIII, 286) written to Lorenzo de' Medici, in which Filippo de' Medici wrote concerning a recent beneficiary of Medici assistance: "You will find him desirous of offering every proof" of his gratitude. Giovanni Tornabuoni's "non-vulgar" recommendation of Messer Santi, quoted above, offers another example. Similarly, on July 22, 1472, a certain Ghonfiotto wrote to Lorenzo on behalf of a certain Baldo (*MAP* XXVIII, 321): "I recommend him to you because he has done work (*a fatto opera*) of a sort and with such spirit, and once again he would take care to provide proofs of himself (*pruova di sè*), so you may place him among your other faithful servants." In a letter of January 9, 1471 (*MAP* XXIII, 311), Marco di Salvadore del Caccia asked Lorenzo for help in the midst of his own financial problems, promising that his six sons "will prove themselves to be the most faithful of servants," which Lorenzo could "bet on as a most certain thing" (*vi fareno pruova di fedellisimi servidori e questo mettete per cosa certissima*). Finally, on August 22, 1471, Vanni de' Medici wrote to Lorenzo (*MAP* XXV, 107) in his own favor, saying, "I recommend myself to you, advising you that there is no man in Florence of whom you could speak with more abandon than I, proving it in many ways" (*non è uomo a ffirenze di chi voi possiate parlare al abandonata più che di me, pruovandolo in molti modi*).[12]

Perhaps these invocations of proof were not so different from the past.[13] Nevertheless, they do suggest an awareness of the inadequacy of words for divining intentions. This certainly would become a hallmark of early sixteenth-century European culture (Silver 1990, J. Martin 1997).

Repair Work in Letters

Flattery is a style in which the self is overtly represented as deeply relational; meanwhile, a strategic, scheming independent self is being nurtured
indirectly or even surreptitiously. Flattery therefore seems to us to be a self-
conscious, strategic activity. What happens, though, with a sudden change
in the *circumstances* or *flow* of interaction? One idea is that in those changing
times people may have to get more inventive in their talk about themselves
(Swidler 2001). However, one might argue that in those circumstances
people then have little time to innovate and may feel a good deal of aver-
sion to the risk of trying out new accounts of themselves. Breakdowns in
communication or relationships will probably first compel people to fall
back on readily available scripts to construct post hoc accounts of who they
are, what they did, and what they want in the future. More rarely will we
find someone offering a truly innovative account of themselves in the midst
of crisis.

Thus, if we look at letters written to the Medici by their factional opponents in the wake of the Medici restoration in September 1434, we may
gain an interesting insight into which presentations of the self, motives,
and emotions were available and valorized. Were the opponents of the
Medici candid about their past actions, justifying themselves in terms of
self-interest and interpreting politics in realist terms? We treat candor as
a sign of reliability; might not the Florentines have done so also? Alternatively, did they attempt to reinterpret past events with an eye toward re-
habilitating themselves by reasserting their relation to the Medici, despite
seemingly overwhelming evidence to the contrary? More often, it seems,
the latter course was taken.

The best evidence for a forthright construal of an independent self in
such letters is an anonymous letter written to Cosimo employing the familiar *tu* on September 26, 1434 (*MAP* XI, 39). The author claims, rather im-
plausibly (Kent 1978, 340f.), that he did nothing to harm the Medici until
the priors themselves began to distrust them. He begins his letter rather
nonchalantly by saying that he has not previously responded to Cosimo's
letters for a lack of news, but now seeing Cosimo's extensive grievances,
especially concerning himself, he has decided to write these few lines with
the explicit aim of cutting short Cosimo's complaints and setting straight
the excuses offered by the *reggimento*. With this remark, he sets the stage for
candor. He continues with this tone: "I do not maintain that I should ask

for pardon, so do not threaten me that you will not pardon me. And I say to you I have confessed many times and also communicated this: that I do not ask for pardon." Thus the author makes some effort at self-justification without, however, going so far as to claim that his actions were defensible pragmatically or on the basis of self-interest.

The author's forthright talk suddenly gives way to a discussion of his and Cosimo's friendship, which on the face of it might suggest a turn to the representation of an interdependent self. However, the language used to represent this relationship is intriguing: it is rather traditional in likening their friendship to a relationship between monks, but it is also perhaps modern in characterizing it, on both Cosimo's part and his own, in terms of *semplicità*.[14] Furthermore (although it is hard to be certain because of damage to the letter), the writer seems to say he cannot imagine a friendship more characterized by honest conversation (*onesta conversazione*). Such talk foreshadows a later time period in which informal settings perhaps allowed for a fuller exploration of the self on its own terms.

In an odd letter of October 26, 1434 (*MAP* XIII, 70), Matteo Panciatichi disingenuously apologizes for not coming to visit the Medici, claiming that his legs will not respond to his will (*le gambe non rispondono all'animo*). Here we have the construction of an innocuous discrepancy between inward will and outward action. But this discrepancy finds a parallel in the end of the letter, wherein Panciatichi writes, "Not with words but with actions will you see if I have not always been a friend to you." As I noted earlier, this formulation is putatively modern in posing the possibility that words deceive, while actions provide a truer measure of the self.

But other letters from anti-Mediceans afford less evidence of a new construction of self. A letter written to Lorenzo de' Medici by Tinoro Guasconi on October 12, 1434 (*MAP* XX, 49) reveals an author determined to cast his identity in terms of his relationship with his alter:

> Dearest honored brother, I have not written to you recently for there has not occurred any occasion. Now hearing of the return of Cosimo and you and others of yours and your complete reinstatement, from which you must have such consolation that I do not know what could have happened whereby I could be happier. Thanks be to God for providing for your health and restitution! There occurs to me a certain doubt and suspicion which I have brought to Cosimo's attention in my letters, and I prayed to him, and so as not to make you weary, I

described [these things] to him. . . . I have kept to him and to you at this point because many times I have had great aid from you in any matter that affected me. I want to pray to you that you be attentive to my affairs; and seeing if against me anyone wanted to attempt any harm, to come to my aid as much as it were profitable to you. So that in God you may have me as recommended to you, and whatever were necessary for my escape you and Cosimo would contrive for me. You know my way of life, the way it has always been, that I have never been given to [political] passions, and the places in which I have situated myself I have well demonstrated. And so I would not lie that I have been treated evilly, but my hope is in God and then in Cosimo and in you; by God, may I be recommended to you. . . . . It would be very dear to me to have some response from you.

Many of the sentiments expressed in this letter were palpably false, for the Guasconi were one of the more heavily punished families when it came time to assess blame for the Medici ouster, and Tinoro's own opinions had been hostile in the 1433 *Consulte e Pratiche* discussion (D. Kent 1978, 319). The opening assertions concerning his joy at the return of the Medici were surely a lie; note therefore how strange is Tinoro's claim toward the end that he would not lie about his political position or about conspiracies that he thought were being plotted against him, probably by Medici stalwarts. Yet the letter ends with a supplicant's plea for mercy, reiterating the framing of himself as friend and beneficiary of the Medici in the past—and in fact likening the assistance of the Medici to the assistance of God. This letter therefore demonstrates considerable ability to engage in deceptive writing; but we cannot look simply for deception to judge the self. Rather we are looking for the *means* of deception and the *means* of expressing sincerity, the public presentations of private self. Here Guasconi chooses to depict himself in terms of his role relationship with the Medici, rather than charting out a course that, as it turned out, could have been no more a failure than the strategy he actually adopted. He and other members of his family were exiled.

Two letters from Baldovinetto di Alesso Baldovinetti, one written on January 26, 1435, and the other on October 9, 1435 (*MAP* XI, 621; and XII, 132), are, like Guasconi's letter, rather pathetic, though in a slightly different way. Baldovinetto was not himself one of the exiles, but two of his kinsmen were. He begins dramatically: "Magnificent and respected one, dignified vanguard of justice in Florence, It was to me a great pleasure when I heard of your return, and the greatest benefit, of which I your most humble servant am the beneficiary, that you worthily reign in your position of rank." He apologizes for not coming in person and then goes on to narrate his specific needs: namely, that he has been stationed at Silano for sixteen months without receiving more than ten florins of his pay, and without any income for the last two pay periods. As a result his family is nearly starving to death; and whereas in the past he might have called on his own kin to assist him, now he and they have abandoned each other. His kinsmen are in exile, and Baldovinetto seems equally intent on distancing himself from them. He is "*scalzo*" (barefoot, impoverished), "having neither bread nor any pledge of support." This has led him, he writes, "To leave my family at Silano in the greatest poverty which it shames me to speak of—though not for fault of mine as much as for wanting to be loyal and upright toward my city." Thus Baldovinetto reveals his internal sense of shame while still giving priority rhetorically to communal attachment as his chief motivation. He is excessively obsequious, repeatedly invoking Cosimo's famous mercy and apologizing for having presented Cosimo with this annoyance (*noia*). Finally, he twice refers to himself as Cosimo's "least servant." We find here, then, the representation of a multiply connected self.

This pathetic plea evidently had no effect, as Baldovinetto despondently remarks at the beginning of his second extant letter: "From you I have gleaned no intention to hear me. I believe the cause of this were my not having provided you an adequate demonstration of [my needs]." Now he pleads for an opportunity to see Cosimo in person, advising him that he has a matter of great importance to discuss with him: "You will know about the matter I will tell you, how much it means"; and "immediately as I will have it, I will carry myself there to your house, and I will inform you fully of things." It seems likely that Baldovinetto hoped to regain favor by providing information about the Medici's enemies abroad, and his excitement about this possibility is conveyed in his assertion, "It has been pleasing to God to have intervened in these affairs of mine, and so I will show myself again to be the most faithful servant of yours and of your regime there, not being content to see my homeland subordinated." Although it seems he had no previous connection to the Medici *consorti*, Baldovinetto now tries to frame himself as "a faithful friend" of Cosimo—suggesting a willingness and a capacity to adopt a more political orientation—and as a lover, not simply of his city (*commune*), but of his homeland (*patria*), especially his homeland under Cosimo's able direction. There is no hint of pride or autonomy here: only a desperate effort to define himself in terms of Cosimo and a willingness to betray other associates—perhaps even family members—to accomplish that goal.

Oddo di Vieri Altoviti also found it necessary to redraw boundaries of attachment in writing to Cosimo on January 5, 1435 (*MAP* XI, 33). Having dispatched his nephew Vieri to Cosimo with a request, he finds it necessary to report, "Vieri always ran with me and not with the rest of my brothers." Among these were Sandro and Antonio di Vieri, both of whom exiled in 1434 for their anti-Medicean activities. One could hardly think that Cosimo would be particularly anxious to help without this preemptive description of Vieri's loyalties. But it is important for the present inquiry that Oddo does not write, "Vieri is his own man and thinks for himself." Such a description would give us much more confidence in the idea that repertoires of accountings of the independent self were as available or legitimate in Florence in the 1430s as were efforts to link individuals to meaningful others.

A final example from the immediate aftermath of the return of the Medici is a letter of Bartolomeo di Verano Peruzzi to Cosimo written on October 12, 1434 (*MAP* XIII, 45; see D. Kent 1978, 341). Peruzzi claims he had unsuccessfully tried to visit Cosimo and Lorenzo a few days earlier once he had—quite belatedly—heard the news of their difficulties:

> And you may be certain that in my heart I was pained by every adversity of yours, and faithful to your [friends], for I have always wanted the best for you, and likewise for the memory of your good father. And thus as I was discontented by the above mentioned events, as I can confirm with your friends, especially Bernardo Carnesecchi, with whom I many times spoke of these matters, now I am very much comforted and happy in every good fortune of yours, and if in the course of this matter against you it can be shown I have performed any bad act or demonstration, be certain that it was not done secretly with ill will. Other deeds have been attributed to me[?], but every such demonstration that I have outwardly appeared to make has been forced by one who was more powerful than I; and out of my fear of him. There are many things that, were it pleasing to God and to you to reveal, I may most abundantly demonstrate and declare to you. And thus I pray of your kindness that it be pleasing to you not to be-

lieve so much that is said of me, but rather be content to wish to use me as you would any other of your friends, and to be content that I return to the life I led before, and to place me among the number of your friends, for you will find me free and faithful (*libero e fidele*).

This letter is remarkable first of all for the extent to which it adopts the language of patronage discussed throughout this book. For example, Cosimo "may be certain" of Bartolomeo's feelings. Bartolomeo prays of Cosimo that he will not believe evil rumors, but instead consider him among the number of his friends, a phrase redolent of partisanship. He explicitly names one of the strong Medici supporters, Bernardo Carnesecchi, as witness to his past dispositions, even if he consistently excludes himself from the Medici inner circle by using the pronoun *vostro*. He implies that as a test of his loyalty, he is willing to betray others, probably including his own staunchly anti-Medicean kinsmen. Thus Bartolomeo writes with less appeasement and more candor than we have seen in most of the examples so far, even going so far as to adopt fairly contractual language. In an unusual move, he even refers to himself as "free." He does not explicitly mention earlier letters he wrote to the Medici, although doing so would have strengthened his claim to a relationship with them.[15] Even though he sloughs off responsibility for his own actions by claiming they were coerced, he approaches Cosimo and Lorenzo in terms of what he might offer them in the future, proceeding at least minimally from the political reality of the situation. This language did not spare Bartolomeo exile, but I am not presently concerned so much with the efficacy of language as with the *tactics* of self-protection.

Exile was not an event; it was a prolonged condition. Indeed, the theme of exile was an important one in Italy from Dante on (Starn 1982; Brown 2002). But anecdotal evidence suggests that while the strategic flattery in patronage letters was heightened when exile or return from exile was at stake, the characterization of the self in such cases was one of interdependence and relationship rather than independence. For example, consider a letter of Giandonato di Antonio Barbadoro, a member of a long-exiled Florentine family, written to Lorenzo the Magnificent from Bologna on September 22, 1466 (*MAP* XX, 234). Some fifty Florentines were exiled that year in the aftermath of the Pitti conspiracy, but a number of earlier exiles were granted clemency at the same time (Brown 2002, 346), with members of the Barbadoro family apparently among them. Giandonato begins with the kind of *captatio benevolentiae* often found in patronage letters, before proceeding to his request, which is to return to his homeland from exile. Not only is the homeland (*la patria*) a cardinal image of corporate identity; Giandonato further justifies his request for return on the basis of his blood connection to the Medici, another cardinal basis of relatedness.

> Respected sir and honored elder, The joy I have had, Lorenzo mine, from the victory you have gained against your adversaries, one could not express with a hundred languages. I pray of God that He will give you enjoyment for a long time, and maintain you for a long time in a happy and peaceful state. The offers you made to me from your humanity when you were here have encouraged me. Now is the time to request of you a favor, and to pray you that you might wish to be intercessor with the Magnificent Piero your father, that he be content to do to us such a favor that we may return all together with your other relatives and friends to inhabit our homeland. I have become certain, that having been always the most faithful relatives and servants of your house, as your father knows, and also as we are reminding him in a letter, I hope most certainly that you will offer to us this singular favor, reminding you that the good you will do to me, you will do to the flesh and blood of your own house (*casa*). . . . And I pray of you that with works you will make proofs of your words.

Giandonato concludes by acknowledging the possible discrepancy between words and actions, inviting Lorenzo and Piero to act with integrity by following through on their promise. Thereby it participates in the patronage system's fantasy that political leaders have the autonomy to make self-interested decisions. But for the most part, appeals to relatedness inform the rhetoric here, notably conjuring an image of the Medicean state as a network of kin.

About six weeks later, Alessandro de' Bardi wrote to Lorenzo from Rome (*MAP* XX, 243) asking for similar clemency on behalf of a relative:

> Magnificent and honored like an elder brother, The affection and love that you have always demonstrated toward me gives me confidence in you. And in this case there is a relative of mine named Andrea di Francesco de' Bardi, who in '58[16] remained confined like many others on account of the father's actions, and knowing that this *balìa* has restored many . . . I would desire that he were not [left] in a worse position than the rest.

Alessandro continues:

> Both here [in Rome] and there he has been more a citizen than a
> thousand that are in Florence, for which reason I pray of you strictly
> that it be pleasing to you to contrive with Piero your father and with
> your other friends, that if others are restored as I hear, that he be
> among the number of these. . . . To me you will do a singular favor
> and similarly to our family, such that I will be most obligated to you.
> And if for a first request I adopt too much presumption, I beg pardon.
> I recommend myself to you, and I pray of you that you recommend
> me to Piero and to Mona Contessina.

This letter adopts several conventional means of requesting a favor: the invocation of long-standing "love"; the formula "I pray of you strictly that
it be pleasing to you to contrive" (*io vi priego strettamente vi piacque a operare*);
and the expression of open-ended obligation in return for a specific favor.
In addition, he recommends himself to specific members of the Medici
family, and he humbles himself at the end, preemptively blaming himself if
he has spoken with "too much presumption." Both of these latter elements
were increasingly common practices as the century progressed. It is interesting, however, that Alessandro justifies clemency for Andrea on the basis
of his citizenship—not his loyalty (*fede*) nor his love (*amore*) for the Medici.
Perhaps these virtues are implicitly what Alessandro means to highlight;
perhaps he also alludes to the high status of the Bardi compared to the new
men of the Medicean era. But it is equally possible he means to highlight
the importance of independence and candor, as well as patriotism, in a virtuous citizenry. In this way he foreshadows Machiavelli's praise for republicanism in the *Discourses* and *The Art of War*, which make forthrightness a
civic virtue. Not private cabals, but reasonable public accusations and strong
stands by steadfast persons "who honor and reward excellence" and who
"esteem private less than public good" make for a vigorous regime. "Where
the mass of the people is sound, disturbances and tumult do no serious
harm" (Machiavelli 1950, 166 [*Discourses* I: 17])—an apt assertion to heed
in the aftermath of the Pitti conspiracy. Republics are more able to adapt
to the winds of Fortuna, "for the diversity of the genius of her citizens en-
ables the republic better to accommodate herself to the changes of the times
than can be done by a prince" (Machiavelli 1950, 442 [*Discourses* III: 9]).

Thus a republic must be comprised of at least somewhat independent
selves. At the same time, however, citizenship is an identity forged as a kind

of collective project, a shared public freedom wherein participation with others is integral to individual worth. This fact lends citizenship an equally deeply interdependent quality. In Pitkin's (1984, 22) words, "If personal autonomy is construed as either sovereign solitude or cynical distrust, it becomes incompatible with the mutuality of citizenship and thus undermines community autonomy." This formulation captures nicely the paradoxes of the political self in Florence in the fifteenth century, which was transitional between a somewhat purer medieval form and a modern one.

Conclusion

The hope of finding crystal clarity in the expression of an independently construed self à la Montaigne in Florentine patronage letters remains unfulfilled. This is to be expected, since patronage interaction is a peculiar setting in which convincing one's alter of one's desire for relationship is paramount. Nevertheless this chapter has documented the emergence of certain practices and certain phrases by means of which Florentines signaled, increasingly over time, that they understood that private selves lay behind public presentations. Their everyday acknowledgment of this reality suggests traces of an emergent autonomous self, although rather less grandiose and less fully mature at birth than the one imagined by Burckhardt. A deeper and broader investigation of extant documentary evidence, rather than literary evidence, would provide subtler traces still of changes in those patterns of cognition and social interaction that eventuated in the modern self.

Ultimately, the model of the contextually pliable, interdependent self better characterizes the fifteenth-century Florentine psyche than the Burckhardtian independent self, although the quest for connections and relationships did entail crafty agency on the part of many individuals. A final letter in this chapter speaks directly to the primacy of the interdependent self while also recognizing that through relationships individuals erected valorizing identities for themselves. On February 10, 1474, a certain Piero di Battista wrote to Lorenzo de' Medici (*MAP* XXIX, 70):

> This [letter] only to advise you how I have been served with being drawn by the commission previously left to Francesco the goldsmith, for which I do not know how to begin to offer infinite thanks to Your Magnificence, because, before, in the community I have been

most obligated to you, and now in particular I have to repay an infinite debt to Your Magnificence, and especially the humane friendship (*familiarità*) I have received in your household, and further seeing how lovingly you have exerted yourself for me in my need with your most ornate speech (*ornatissimo parlare*) . . . I do not know how one could resist it! . . . And I am most certain that you have not done this for any merit on my part, nor anything I could do for you, but solely it has come from your magnanimity and courtesy, and verily I do not believe that in the Emperor Octavian could one ever find a similarly gracious, caring, humane, pleasant, and courteous [act], such that one could not adequately say on paper how much I remain obligated to you, nor thank you as much as I ought for how you have served me for the better. Having a firm hope in your prudence, you will undoubtedly understand my spirit, which I did not know how to explain by means of this brief letter. And therefore, I pray of you as much as I know and am able that it be a pleasure to you to consider me among the number of your lowly faithful servants. . . . So much am I obligated to you, for if you only knew the reputation/authority (*riputassione*) it has given me, and how much because of your love I am regarded with astonishment — this I hold as a singular treasure and pray of God that he preserve me in your favor, to which always I humbly recommend myself.

By now you, dear reader, may have become accustomed to the ritualized prostrations of many Florentine letter writers and their flowery expressions of thanks, obligation, indebtedness, love, and faithfulness toward their would-be patrons. "Words fail me," they say — although each inevitably used words to express his gratitude. Only the words of a special person, like Lorenzo, made things happen, or called reality into being. By contrast, all Piero di Battista could hold onto is the reputation and recognition he had achieved by virtue of his connection to Lorenzo. Nevertheless, so he claims, apparently with some modicum of sincerity, Lorenzo has made him. Lorenzo *is* his reputation.

Conclusion

Culture and the Network

My respected and honored elder, I have not written to you for the past while not having had any need (*non essere suto di bisogno*). Now hearing that there the scrutiny is proceeding, and having the most singular faith (*singularissima fede*) in you, confidently (*con sicurtà*) I offer you these few verses (*questi pochi versi*) praying of you (*pregandovi*) as much as I know and am able (*quanto so e posso*), and also considering the fine recollection of Cosimo and thence your father Piero, to whom our family (*la casa nostra*) was always recommended, thus I pray that your kindness (*vostra benignità*) will do the same [as they did], placing at our feet such benefits as much as we have always received from your family, and I especially as much as possible (*quanto posso*) recommend myself to you (*mi raccomando a voi*) with two of my sons, offering myself to be always ready (*sempre aparechiato*) to satisfy your desire as your good and faithful servant (*come buono e fedele servidore*), as I have been, and am, and will be and always want to be, yours.

Niccolò di Lorenzo di Ceffo Masini Ceffi to Lorenzo de' Medici,
November 29, 1471

In this letter, Niccolò Masini Ceffi repeats a whole host of standard compositional techniques for writing letters to powerful others in order to pursue opportunities for upward mobility. The salutation is a common one. To begin by explaining that one has not written sooner was a stock beginning. To express confidence about one's request was a typical form of the brinkmanship so common in patronage letters. To refer to one's letter, or the letter of recommendation one was requesting, as "these few verses" (*questi pochi versi*) was commonplace. To claim one was making a request as much as one knew and was able was perhaps beyond commonplace. To refer to the patron's "kindness" (*benignità*) was a frequent technique of ingratiation. To recommend oneself was perhaps *the* core objective of all this writing. To claim to be ready to do the patron's bidding was a regular feature of letters, but more so in the first half of the fifteenth century. To refer to oneself as a "good and faithful servant" was to draw on an extremely common biblical image that saturated Florentine popular culture. To end a letter cadentially with a three- or fourfold repetition of the same idea or phrase had roots in the medieval tradition of the *cursus*. Read this letter out of its historical context and one sees hyperbole. Read it in context and one sees institutionalization approaching ritualization.

Flash forward now several hundred years to contemporary America to an article that appeared in the *New York Times* of May 22, 2005 while I was writing this conclusion.[1] "In me you will discover a reliable, detail-oriented and extremely hard-working associate, one who will serve as a model to encourage other staff members to demonstrate a high standard of professionalism." So wrote four completely unconnected applicants in their cover letters for a position as a receptionist in an office in Manhattan. Except they didn't exactly write it. The phrase was lifted verbatim by each of them from the Microsoft Office Web site's template gallery.

So what really has changed in the world, if anything? Reliance on form, and even formulae, remains an essential element of social interaction. If these people were writing a term paper, we would call it plagiarism, but we do not sanction people in this case for imitating acceptable forms. The article makes clear that none were eliminated from consideration on account of it. More likely we would sanction them for flouting such forms. Nevertheless, as the article also makes clear, we believe—perhaps we need to believe—that an individualized document is a more compelling one, and that it can effect a change in the feelings or actions of the one to whom it is addressed. The Florentines came down more on the side of form and less on the side of originality, but even in this fairly formulaic interactional domain they worked to paint credible portraits of themselves for others. Did the Florentines "mean it" when they wrote what they did? I think they did, and I think we do, even when we copy others' words and make them seem to be our own.

When a Florentine wrote a letter such as Masini wrote, he was undoubtedly aiming to achieve some concrete improvement in the circumstances of his life. This was not easily accomplished, as the competition for a patron's favor was typically quite heated. Sometimes he was also aiming to assure a flow of benefits to his posterity, as Masini was here in trying to obtain office-holding eligibility for his sons. This raised the stakes even higher. Salaries came with such offices, as well as a good deal of social prestige. But in so writing, our typical Florentine was also rhetorically committing himself to an identity with strong behavioral consequences. He was committing himself to goals that made Florentines worthy in the eyes of their compatriots. He was committing himself to an identity-defining relationship with another. Thus he was both looking for a benefit and *remaking himself and the others to whom he was connected*. These two facets of networking are analytically distinguishable but practically interwoven.

"Networking" is a strategic technique for accumulating social capital, but it is not only that. Networks convey identities, but we also err when we succumb to the convenience of treating social network positions as simply determinative of identities. That would be to shortchange agency and make it more difficult (though perhaps not impossible) to explain system dynamics.

Networks are, ironically, more about flux than stasis. To keep them going takes cajolery, reassurances, and other sorts of artful symbolic effort. New entrants contribute to shifts in patterns beyond the control of most or all participants. Relationships with others to whom one is connected must be repeatedly managed, deepened, or contained as circumstances change. Positions must be improved or the people in them languish. Thinking of networks this way suggests their dependence on a lot of creative, strategic, cultural work. But the irony on the other side is that strategy may be more mimetic and recombinant than virtuosic. Again consider the letter of Masini. To the untrained eye, it may appear sycophantic or otherwise artificial to the point of implausibility. To the Florentine eye, it is eminently recognizable. The reader knows what Masini wants and why he wants it. It is very helpful if the rhetoric is slightly exaggerated in some places — one must be more persuasive than others competing for the same scarce prize — but strategic effort is rarely cut out of entirely new cloth. So, although networks depend on cultural work to keep them going, that cultural work often resembles standard operating procedures more than virtuosic display. That is why Swidler's (1986, 2001) image of culture as a toolkit remains so compelling. It is just that the art of the network seems more urgently strategic than talk about love (Swidler 2001), while also being more loosely determined by structural positions than Bourdieu's (1990a) model would suggest.

My chief theoretical objective in this work, then, has been to articulate a sociology of culture that keeps both strategic and constitutive aspects in focus. Networking has seemed like a particularly apt venue to study to accomplish this goal, one that inherently treats culture as taking place interactionally. Fifteenth-century Florence was an historical venue par excellence of networking activity.

Precisely because networking as cultural practice is interactional, and because it involves the crafting of new identities, the self is implicated in it. In fact, presentation of self seems to be one of its most critical elements. One must appear to be culturally competent, but also superior to others in order to be perceived as worthy of favor. One's identity cannot usually be simply asserted. It must be crafted in a plausible way that conveys competency and, better still, authenticity within the terms of the culture in which it operates.

How do writers present themselves in order to build careers and gain trust? First, in large measure they follow *formulae*. In Florence many young men evidently learned standardized stylistic techniques and a finite set of tropes, images, and stock phrases with which they not only crafted public presentations of their wants and needs, but also simply managed to sustain interpersonal interaction. In short, they learned the forms for networking.

But what did these formal practices signify, concretely? The answer is not obvious. What Florentines desired and what they valued changed over time. They might call it honor, but honor was actually an accretion of multiple different meanings: family loyalty, virtuous conduct, circumspection, political participation, scrupulous conduct of business, learnedness, civic philanthropy. Or they might call it friendship, but friendship was also a mix of different desiderata.

Interactional forms and collective representations were the raw materials for participation in valued social networks. But we can never simply assume that the raw materials will be clearly expressed in a representative way in actual episodes of interaction. In particular, "high cultural" representations may be scarce in everyday interaction—as is, for example, the language of *virtù* in Florence. We also have more culture than we use, and we lean on some tools far more than others. If we want to discern cultural patterns, and if we want to distinguish an exceptional cultural product from an ordinary one, then we must examine and classify a large number of cases. If we want to know *what* culture gets used and *how*, we must examine concrete everyday practices, preferably through both quantitative and qualitative lenses. The frequency of particular gestures will ebb and flow over time, across different types of interactions, and between different types of subjects—the way, for example, that office-seeking patronage letters, as an entire corpus of patterned discourse, slid fairly imperceptibly from one dominant framing (honor) to another (servanthood) over a period of fifty years. What one discovers is unlikely to be entirely surprising, but one may find more adaptation to new constraints than is visible to the naked eye. Alternatively, one may discern somewhat less dramatic change in everyday institutions than regime-based periodizations of history would lead us to expect.

For particular interactions to be efficacious, they cannot be merely formulaic. To forge ties to others, to improve our network position, we must paint non-formulaic pictures of ourselves. This means writing *strategically*, but doing so in the service of constructing relations that will be *constitutive* of identities. We must say what we are not as well as who or what we are. We must distinguish ourselves from others. We often must communicate that we expect to be assisted by others. We invoke stock forms, such as the academic recommendation letter, in order to demonstrate that that is not quite what we are doing in this instance. These kinds of discursive strategies—speaking for others, communicating an expectation of assistance, manipulating pronouns to draw social boundaries, re-keying the frame, breaking standard forms, stitching together multiple frames, and so on—are what allow some deeper and more distinct self to be presented to others.

Many of these strategies were used throughout the fifteenth century in Florence. Nevertheless, there were also subtle shifts over time in the verbal equipment of interpersonal interaction, and of self-presentation in particular. These new terms suggest not only new forms of self-presentation, but a new kind of *self to be presented*, a hesitatingly emergent *conception* of self as an autonomous, discreet, and elusive agent. A notion of sincerity begins to emerge that resembles our own. There was a growing awareness of the inadequacy of words to discern intentions, and a desire for proofs of inner dispositions. And there were the beginnings of talk about personal wonts and preferences as ingrained natural phenomena. The manifestation of these changes, while sporadic and fragmentary, has profound historical and theoretical implications.

The main long-term historical implication is easy to identify: these changes betoken the slow creep toward a self that is more like our own. The modern self was not there yet, but seeds of its growth were being planted. The main theoretical implication is perhaps yet more profound and thought provoking. From our standpoint, we read these letters and may well think, "These Florentines were awfully sycophantic and strategic!" But in retrospect, we can see better that concern about the masking of the self was much *less* present in early Quattrocento Florence than it became later. In everyday discourse, early Quattrocento Florentines spoke *less* frequently about the need for deeds to confirm the sincerity of words than would their sons and grandsons. Patronage interaction—networking—therefore was not so much a game played by already constituted, strategically adept, and cunningly disposed players. Rather it was a game that *made and remade* the players participating in it. It was a game that made the Florentines into something like us, having been something *unlike* us previously.[2] I have taken a *case* that seems rather foreign to us and tried to convince you in the first place that you are looking in the mirror, and that Florentine strategic interaction in some sense is an exemplary illustration of our social life—a well-chosen case in the sociology of (contemporary) culture. Perhaps it remains instead inescapably foreign, as foreign as the sortition-based participatory governance the Florentines practiced—a world we misapprehend through the lens of our own self-consciousness. Then again, our self-consciousness may lead us astray in understanding the circumstances of our own constitution as well.

Notes

1. Networking as a Social Process

The epigraph to this chapter is from Archivio di Stato di Firenze, *Mediceo Avanti il Principato* II, 292. Henceforth references to this collection will be abbreviated as *MAP*. The translations of all letters throughout this book are my own unless otherwise indicated.

1. For example, the class schedule in the spring 2003 Rutgers College Recreational Services brochure includes courses titled "The Conversation Connection" and "Conversation for Networking," in addition to courses on yoga, ballroom dancing, kickboxing, swimming, and the rest of the usual topics. Furthermore, the academy itself functions as a complex set of partially overlapping social networks, with these networks having a significant impact on individuals' prospects of mobility (for example, see Burris 2004).

2. Recent historiography sees the period as exhibiting more continuity with the Middle Ages, more discontinuity with modernity, more flux in institutional forms, and more internal inconsistency and heterogeneity in politics, economics, social life, and conceptions of the self than were imagined previously.

3. For example, Giannozzo Alberti, a character in Leon Battista Alberti's *I libri della famiglia*, comments:

> Do you know what a friend of mine does? . . . He has a technique for dealing with irresponsible people who come with their importunate demands under color of friendship, kinship and old acquaintance. The greetings of such a fellow he returns with an infinite number of greetings. If he smiles, my friend returns a warmer smile. If he praises him, my friend praises him still more than he has been praised. . . . To all his words and his whining, my friend lends a willing ear, but when he comes to the story of his needs, my friend immediately invents some of his own to tell, and as the man comes to the point of actually asking him, in conclusion, for a loan or at least to stand surety for one—suddenly he is deaf. He misunderstands and gives a reply to something else, and quickly changes the subject. (Alberti 1969, 239)

4. For treatments of this notion of exempla, see Hayden White 1978; Bakhtin 1981; Cicourel 1973, 28; Holland and Skinner 1987, 87; Tannen, ed. 1993. Observing

patterns of practical action also links to the new institutionalism's view of institutions as "loosely coupled arrays of standardized elements" (Dimaggio and Powell 1991, 14).

5. Rhetoricians writing in the sixteenth century conceived of rhetorical figures as a kind of trespassing, a tool for making persuasive connections that breached boundaries between objects, between persons, and between truth and opinion. See Rebhorn 1995, 115, 241.

6. For example, Mische and White (1998, 701) note somewhat simplistically that "in earlier historical periods, switches between idioms or dialects were ceremonial and lockstep." Swidler (2001, 74) distinguishes our voluntarist market society from other, implicitly earlier types. I am arguing that late fourteenth- and fifteenth-century Florence *was* a voluntarist market society in her sense of the term.

7. For some recent attempts to explore this terrain, see Ansell 1997; Carley 1993; Emirbayer 1997; Emirbayer and Mische 1998; Mohr and Duquenne 1997.

8. A long tradition in organizational analysis links rule following to uncertainty reduction. See, for example, March and Simon 1958; Dimaggio and Powell 1991, 19ff.

9. The theme of trust has received considerable attention in the last few years (for example, Gambetta 1988; Braithwaite and Levi 1998; Cook 2001; Hardin 2002; Ostrom and Walker 2003).

10. The oscillation sometimes occurs within the work of particular authors, as well as between contending scholars' viewpoints. I borrow this imagery of oscillation from Mark Granovetter's (1985) critique of Oliver Williamson's version of transaction cost economics. Granovetter sees Williamson, like Hobbes, as shifting abruptly from an undersocialized view of intensely opportunistic economic actors in a would-be state of nature to an oversocialized view of them as compliant subordinates in a hierarchically structured firm. Indeed both assumptions exist simultaneously (Granovetter 1985, 488). Pierre Bourdieu (1990a, 46) adopts similar language in his critique of rational choice theory: that it oscillates between viewing choice as radically unconstrained on the one hand, and as mechanically and systematically determined and predictable on the other. Mustafa Emirbayer (1997, 284) points out that both rational actor and norm-based accounts of action treat individuals as "self-propelling, self-subsistent entities," thus failing to give primacy to the relationality of social life.

11. For a good but now dated review, see Portes 1998. For critical reviews, see Baron, Field, and Schuller 2000; and McLean, Schultz, and Steger 2002. For compendia of empirical studies of social capital, see van Deth et al. 1999; Dasgupta and Serageldin 2000; Dekker and Uslaner 2001; Lin, Cook, and Burt 2001; Saegert, Thompson, and Warren 2001; Badescu and Uslaner 2003; and Body-Gendrot and Gittell 2003.

12. Rarely do theorists of social capital acknowledge that Marx understood eco-

nomic capital as deeply relational as well, collectively produced, with a status and legitimacy that shapes the terms of joint action. See Postone 1996, 75ff.

13. Coleman sees "control" as something like gaining the upper hand, or bringing one's own agenda to fruition. Contrast this with Harrison White's notion of control in *Identity and Control* (1992), where it means in the first place something more like getting a grip on a situation, the conquest of uncertainty, or seeing flux transformed into routine. White's conception resembles Wittgenstein's (1958) treatment of learning as a "Now I can go on" phenomenon, rather than a self-conscious bid for dominance. Small wonder White's (1990) hostility toward Coleman's book, given this radically different notion of control.

14. Podolny and Baron (1997) identify "mentorship" as a type of social relation that is hard to classify in terms of whether flows of resources or constructions of identity are more important. Of course mentorship and patronage are quite similar.

15. I would especially concur with Jackman and Miller's criticism of the simplicity of Putnam's formulation of political culture. I will discuss further the notion of political culture later in this chapter.

16. Political networks in Florence were constructed out of a variety of other social networks, such as kinship, neighborhood, or business relationships (Brucker 1962, 1977; D. Kent 1978; Padgett and Ansell 1993). The eruption of factional strife in Florence was always a matter of acute concern to the city fathers. As Brucker notes (1962, 129), "In the *Consulte e Pratiche* records of July 1351 is the first notice [of] a theme that appears with monotonous regularity in later protocols: *unitas civium*. 'All citizens should be led back to unity,' intoned Ser Domenico da Certaldo, and his sentiments were echoed by his colleagues, none of whom publicly favored the pastime of quarreling with neighbors—a pastime in which nearly all of them engaged."

17. Consider a letter of the famous merchant of Prato, Francesco di Marco Datini, dated August 4, 1392, concerning an old partner who had abandoned him:

> I am advised by many letters that Basciano is not there. You will have spoken with him about these blessed accounts that, by his shortcomings, are not settled, and truly it is a great wrong; this is not the friendship (*amicizia*) and brotherhood (*fratelanza*) that I had with him, and he has not done well in clamming up with me (*pigliare gozzo*), and I don't know why. . . . And I must observe that when he made accounts with me in Avignon, . . . we had such a great relationship, so that one could go so far as to say that if I owed him 1,000 florins, I would approach him and say to him how I considered him more than a brother (*più che fratello*), and I still do. (Frangioni 1994, appendix, letter 8)

18. Contrast this with Bourdieu's claims about the "stylistic unity" of all of the choices a person makes in the most varied areas of practice (1990a, 13).

19. For a similar illustration, see D. Davis (2004).

20. This notion of "form" is important. A Florentine version of the relevance of form is found in the work of the sixteenth-century moralist Guazzo, who argued that those who do not act formally are simply outside society (Trexler 1980, 106). The Florentines lived in a world where there was a right way of doing everything, including soliciting the help of God and the saints through the mediation of sacred relics, and soliciting the help of more powerful men through a similar rhetoric of reverence and supplication. "From form springs the sensation of honor, which is then fed back, 'through a certain reflection,' to the original subject" (Trexler 1980, 107). For a different statement about the relevance of form to meaning, see Berezin (1994). Elias (1978) provides the classic sociological statement of the evolution of various etiquettes in early modern Europe.

21. Trexler (1980, 92ff.) offers a native Florentine double meaning of frame: gilded frames for works of art both helped to establish the value of the work and identified its owners. Thus framing simultaneously created worth and predicated it of the person(s) behind the thing, defining "text" and context.

22. See for example, Schegloff (1980) on action projections, Hewitt and Stokes (1975) on the use of disclaimers in interaction, and Tannen (1985) on explicit claims of how sender and recipient are alike.

23. William Reddy (1997, 155) notes the same tension in nineteenth-century French discourse. "Honor had a rhetoric as well as a set of practices . . . this rhetoric involved a careful balancing of a vocabulary of merit and a vocabulary of deference and gift giving. The two are often sandwiched close together in the stock phrases of bureaucratic prose, but they contained an underlying tension."

24. After Snow's work, the topic of framing in social movement theory drifted toward the idea of leaders' manipulation of followers, getting them to participate in accordance with already fixed and inherently persuasive visions of the organization's purpose. For criticisms, see McAdam 1996; Benford 1997; Steinberg 1998, 1999; Goodwin and Jasper 1999. This drift was not in the original spirit of Snow's work.

25. On Machiavelli's use of pronouns, see Connell (2005).

26. For examples in particular letters, see Archivio di Stato di Firenze, Carte Strozziane III, 112: 33, 112: 126, 113: 111. Henceforth all references to this collection of letters will be abbreviated as *C.S.* III.

27. I make no claim that my way is the only way to study political culture. Zaret (1989, 1996), for example, provides rich historical analyses of the emergence of new forms of political communication that contribute to the vibrancy and direction of political culture. Brubaker (1992) and Dobbin (1994) provide rich comparative historical analyses of abiding institutional practices that recurrently and durably shaped national political cultures.

28. See the concluding discussion of the problem of cultural logics in Swidler (2001) for a lucid treatment of this issue.

2. Rhetoric and Design

1. In a strikingly parallel way, Rebhorn (1995) discusses the body of Renaissance texts and treatises on rhetoric as a discourse.

2. Unofficial favor-seeking correspondence partook in some partial way of the rhetoric of official diplomatic correspondence. Similarly, daily written correspondence — for example, among branches of a given economic concern such as the Datini empire of the late fourteenth century (Frangioni 1994) — periodically rose in intensity to adopt some of the standard devices used in favor-seeking writing.

3. Another point of comparison between rhetoric and art is the similarity between what *facilità* meant in painting, and what it might have meant in interpersonal relations: that is, a combination of natural talent and skills acquired through exercise highly esteemed in the Renaissance. Alberti (a theorist of both painting and interpersonal relations) calls it diligence conjoined with quickness (*diligenza congiunta con prestezza*). Both rhetoric and art require skill and competence in a kind of canon of formulaic gestures, though each also demands inventive expression.

4. Indeed, F. W. Kent (2002) documents at length the co-presence of severe class-based disdain and cross-class bonds of friendship and sociability. Undoubtedly some cross-class connections were of the "bread and circuses" variety (Trexler 1980, chap. 11), but others were clearly heartfelt and substantial, leading one to wonder what bases such ties had beyond simple characterizations of class positions or neighborhood proximity.

5. Florentine historians are familiar with Giovanni Morelli's advice to his descendants to search for a marriage partner first within the *gonfalone* and then within the quarter before looking farther (Branca 1986, 195), in order to have a second father as close at hand as possible. Paolo Da Certaldo offered similar if less precise advice to his mid-Trecento readers: "Keep in mind always to stay, while you can, in your own territory . . . and thus get yourself married among the citizens of that place, and not with foreigners, because that's where you have to live and die" (Branca 1986, 46, #242; translation mine). Debate continues as to how obsolete this advice became as the Quattrocento progressed, with the city's elite increasingly integrated into a single marriage market spanning neighborhoods and quarters (Cohn 1980; Molho 1994) and knit together by means of banking partnerships that increasingly spanned neighborhood boundaries, even as they exploited neighborhood identities in the construction of clienteles (Padgett and McLean 2002).

6. Adovardo degli Alberti remarks on the model of Alcibiades who, "as they say, could imitate the chameleon, an animal which according to reports is able to vary its color to suit its environment. With melancholy men we will be rather austere, with liberal men magnanimous. In general, as Cicero said to his brother, let us suit our expression, countenance, words, and gestures to men's desires" (Alberti 1969, 311). This is a recurrent theme, and one popular even before the humanists' reappropriation of Cicero in the 1400s.

7. A greater sense of the rhythm of Alberti's text is understood from the original:

> E ben sai, in *tanta* diversità d'ingegni, in *tanta* dissimilitudine d'oppinioni, in
> *tanta* incertitudine di volontà, in *tanta* perversità di costumi, in *tanta* ambi-
> guità, varietà, oscurità di sentenze, in *tanta* copia di *fraudolenti, fallaci, perfidi,*
> *temerarii, audaci e rapaci* uomini, in *tanta* instabilità di tutte le cose, che mai si
> credesse colla sola simplicità e bontà potersi agiugnere amicizia, o pur cono-
> scenze alcune non dannose e alfine tediose? Conviensi contro all fraude, fal-
> lacie e perfidia essere *preveduto, desto, cauto* . . . (emphasis added)

8. Giannozzo's prefatory flattery of Piero is of interest here:

> All of us, and especially I myself, would certainly be happy (*grato*) if you
> would here and now take this burden (*fatica*) on yourself, Piero . . . [and] set
> forth all your thoughts and ideas to make the rest of us learn, as these days we
> are all eagerly trying to do, how to make ourselves well loved. We would, by
> this means, do our family much good and obtain for it as much support and
> favor (*favore*) as possible. It will be most useful, certainly, and most relevant
> to our discussion to hear all that you did (*ogni tuo gesto*; literally "your every
> gesture") and to learn to imitate both your prudence and your zeal (*diligenza*).
> (1969, 252)

Grato, fatica, favore, and *diligenza* are all critical words in patronage letters.

9. The narration of this favor, however — the intercession of Piero's dogs to ward
off a bear threatening the king during a hunting episode (after Piero had just "come
upon him") — sounds so classical that one wonders if some aesthetic dimension is not
also creeping into the construction of this friend-making event. Compare Jerrold
Seigel's (1968, 33) remark that "sometimes the facts of Petrarch's biography are difficult to determine, so closely does his own account of them follow some passage in
Cicero."

10. The theme of such gift giving is quite pervasive. From the letters I have
studied, it appears that gift giving was customarily handled modestly. The following
letter from Alexo di Matteo Galluzzi, notary, to Giovanni di Cosimo de' Medici on
June 18, 1442 (*MAP* V, 461) depicts as much: "My honored elder, On the eleventh
of this month I sent you twelve watermelons, and today I am sending more to you
via Domenico di Piero Beccuti. I trust they will be good. Nothing more; I am at
your convenience." Consider also this excerpt from *MAP* XVI, 135: "I am sending
you a pair of pheasants and a hare. I recognize that these are small things to Your
Honor, but I know that in your humanity you have received them as though they
were something great. And nothing else occurs to me to say at present except that I
forever recommend myself to you." Simpler still is this note to Giovanni, although

it indirectly indexes the value of the gift: "I am sending you ten bottles of my Trebbiano Montughino. Those of this year seem to me particularly fine. I recommend myself to you" (*MAP* XVI, 199).

Responses to gifts were typically more elaborate, especially when addressed to an individual of superior status. The following letter from Andrea Nardi to Giovanni de' Medici on September 17, 1441 (*MAP* V, 427) is a response to a gift proffered: "Dearest brother, Larione di Chonte wrote to me saying how graciously out of courtesy you sent him a goshawk which he was to send to me in turn, and so he has done; for this I thank you, and I remain only too (*troppo*) obligated."

Gift giving could be embedded in other forms of ingratiation as well. For example, we have the exaggeratedly flattering letter that Batista Lanfredini wrote to Forese Sacchetti in 1426: "I consider you, and I have faith in you as in, my own father (*mio padre carnale*) and my singular elder, and I pray that you want to have in me a son and faithful servant. I have nothing else to offer but myself and whatever I can do." Nonetheless he proceeded: "I am sending to you via the present bearer a basket of one thousand oranges. I hope you will wish to have them" (*Conv. Soppr.* 78, 325: 479).

11. Godparentage was a widely used institution for connecting oneself to others of the same rank as well as those of superior and inferior social ranks; it was at least as potentially instrumental as *amicizia* in general (Klapisch-Zuber 1985a). As for entertaining friends and neighbors, also see da Certaldo, #141: "To get together sometimes each year with your neighbors and friends to eat is certainly good. According to your ability, invite them and do them honor, and they will do the same to you, and thus will increase the love between you and them" (Branca 1986, 31; my translation).

12. Witt's (2000) book, *"In the Footsteps of the Ancients,"* provides a masterful synthetic statement concerning the diverse strands, various sources, and historical development of Italian humanism. What I offer here can barely scratch the surface of the vast and erudite literature of which it is an exemplar.

13. It would be more accurate to say that the distinction between writing and face-to-face communication is a *marked* distinction: when authors note it, they are constructing their obligations, and/or their social distance from patrons, in a particular way. For example, Bartolomeo Ridolfi writes to Averardo de' Medici (*MAP* III, 126) saying "dearer it would have been to me to have been able to see you and speak to you in person" (*a bocca*). Another indication of the difference between written and oral communication is given by a letter from Luigi Guicciardini to Agnolo di Palla Strozzi on June 3, 1437. Luigi writes that "it would be difficult to be able to thank you enough . . . for your courteous writing and the generous things you have done for me, so I will limit my response here to one part [of our affairs], reserving for myself the task of expressing my duty to you [more extensively] in person (*a bocca*)."

14. Nevertheless, some French *dictatores* of the late twelfth century permitted bending the truth somewhat to deceive the audience (Shepard 1999, 14–16), recognizing that the narration had to be somewhat stylized.

15. There were some negative views of such boundary crossing, however. Giovanni del Vergilio (fl. 1319) thought rhetoric was basically a dignified art, except for "the small part of it called letter-writing that calls forth rustics . . . and adorns the dishonorable with honors" (quoted in Rebhorn 1995, 31).

16. W. Glynn Williams's prefatory note on Cicero's letters of recommendation (Cicero 1926, 4) suggests that Cicero followed a formula for composition very similar in thrust and detail to that of Quattrocento letters.

17. Cosimo de' Medici, one of the greatest patrons of the new humanism, some of whose letters composed in Latin have survived, probably scarcely knew how to write in Latin at all. Most of his surviving letters feature, in James Hankins's words, a "racy Italian," while his Latin letters are not in his own hand (1992, 70, 74). He must have read Latin, but almost anyone familiar with communal statutes would have had this ability.

18. Commercial correspondence infrequently invokes fictive kinship and generally refrains from rhetorical brinkmanship and superlative expressions of open-ended reciprocity as discussed below. Nevertheless, these tactics do appear there periodically, suggesting that these letter-writing strategies were part of the social interaction toolkit of Florentines simultaneously active in the marketplace and in the world of politics.

19. Dale Kent (1978, 83–104) has succinctly begun the description of some of these concrete practices, beginning with their formal properties. However, Kent does not discuss the source of the practices found in correspondence, she does not make any explicit attempt to identify these characteristics as social interaction tactics, and she does not sufficiently emphasize that patronage correspondence constituted a corpus of patterned discourse, the properties and content of which can be analyzed quantitatively as well as qualitatively. These are all points I wish to stress here.

20. In business correspondence, the timing of deliveries of goods, the dating of bills of exchange, and the delays rampant in premodern international commerce made such careful recording of the dates of received instructions essential. This no doubt carried over into other kinds of less long-distance, more politically oriented correspondence.

21. There are also many instances when writers indicate in fairly stock terms that they have not yet received a letter they were expecting. For example, a letter from Giovanni di Amerigo to Francesco di Iacopo del Bene of November 19, 1378 (*Carte del Bene* 49, 126) notes, "I marvel very much (*Io mi maraviglio assai*) that, since I got here I have not had any letter from you, and I wrote to you via Messer Baldassare and from him I have not had any response." There is a kind of disingenuousness in these letters, as supplicants could not fail to understand that favors were scarce goods, and

not having had a response was not likely caused by a failure of the courier service but more likely by the would-be patron's decision not to be of service.

22. Compare certain other letters in this regard: Giovanni Guicciardini wrote in an upbraiding tone to Averardo that he was disappointed that Averardo had not paid sufficient attention to "the honor or the profit of your friends" (*MAP* II, 50); and Vanni de' Medici wrote to Averardo in 1427 asking that he might "beg" for a position for him with the marquis of Ferrara or the marquis of Modena, so that Vanni might "bring a great deal of honor and profit" to the family (*MAP* II, 78).

3. The Socially Contested Concept of Honor

The sources for the three epigraphs to this chapter are, respectively, Branca 1986, 552; *MAP* II, 349; and Alberti 1969, 149.

1. Moreover, friends frequently acknowledge each other's *onori* in writing. For example, Palla di Nofri Strozzi begins a letter to Simone di Filippo di Messer Lionardo Strozzi on September 17, 1416 (*C.S.* III, 132: 32) with "I heard that your name was drawn for the position of *podestà* [an official charged with maintaining public security] of Pieve di Santo Stefano. The arrival of each of your appointments (*ogni tuo honore*) gladdens me as much as my own." Almost exactly the same language is used by Giovanni di Cocco Donati in a letter to Averardo de' Medici of June 27, 1431 (*MAP* III, 144): "I heard that you are the commissioner there with the Captain. I am extremely pleased by this and by every honor of yours (*ogni tua honoranza*), which I esteem more greatly than my own."

2. Indeed, *onestà* is probably better translated as honesty, truthfulness, or personal integrity than honor. Yet there are good reasons for seeing honor and *onestà* as closely associated concepts (Stewart 1994). A brief recommendation letter from Orlando di Guccio de' Medici to Averardo, on behalf of his "most faithful friend," a certain Gualterano di Corbizzo da Modigliane (July 19, 1431; *MAP* III, 283), concludes with the following: "I pray and beg of you that it be pleasing to you to act in his service however he indicates, for it is an honorable affair" (*cosa onesta*). More tellingly, a letter from Palla di Nofri Strozzi to Simone di Filippo Strozzi of August 11, 1421 (*C.S.* III, 132: 50) uses the word *onestà* in precisely the place and sense where others use *onore*: "I am writing to you praying that you operate to the extent honor demands (*quanto l'onestà richiedesse*) that Galeotto _____ were elected *podestà* of this place. . . . May it not be bothersome to you to arrange the consent of Raffacane, who is one of the electors. And recommend [Galeotto] to him, and contrive some action in this matter as much as you see possible, while retaining honor (*quanto vedi con onestà potere farne operatione*). He is a man of such *virtù* that I do not doubt that he would honor (*honorare*) those who were to elect him, and who were to perform any favor for him."

3. As Georges Duby (1980) writes in the foreword to the English translation of

his book *The Three Orders: Feudal Society Imagined*, "This is a book about the political and cultural uses of a social idea." For other efforts at elucidating cultures of honor, see Neuschel (1989) on Renaissance France, Reddy (1997) on nineteenth-century France, and Ikegami (1995) on nineteenth-century Japan.

4. A further irony is that Alberti himself uses this formula in his prologue wherein he seeks favor from his Alberti audience:

> Never while I have ability and strength, neither for effort nor sweat nor even myself will I excuse myself from doing everything to contribute to the health and profit of the Alberti family; and all this willingly, with a happy spirit, with the greatest diligence, when I see my work looked upon with thanks by you. And so I pray of you, young Albertis, continue to do as you do now; strive for the good, increase the honor, spread the fame of our house, and listen to what our Alberti ancestors, the most studious, learned and civilized men, judged what was necessary to the family and how to bring it about. Read me and love me. (my translation)

5. The term *brigata* also appears with some frequency in Quattrocento correspondence. It sometimes means a military company or platoon in some wartime correspondence, or a family entourage, male and female, in the later fifteenth century; but it sometimes signifies a group of friends or clients surrounding the recipient of patronage letters. Trexler claims that the *brigata* had a ritual significance in the fifteenth century, its purpose being to demonstrate the extent of family honor through distinctly chivalric games (1980, 225ff.). The lists of the members of certain *brigate* also imply an underlying political purpose.

6. Cavallar, Degenring, and Kirshner (1994, 41) remark that "Florence stands alone in the late Middle Ages with its government that surveyed, registered, and thereby regulated the adoption of coats of arms by its magnate families."

7. As Weinstein points out concerning sixteenth-century Tuscany, both nobles and would-be nobles subscribed to this particular code of honor (2000, 149). The hegemonic visions of honor come to infect non-ruling groups as well, sometimes to a greater extent than their original proponents. Subordinate actors often do more of the work of enforcing the boundary separating them from inferiors than do elites (Bourdieu 1984; Lamont and Fournier 1992).

8. Giannozzo arrives in Book 3 from the Palazzo della Signorìa where he had gone "to serve the honor and advantage of a friend of mine" (my translation of *per servire all'onore e utile d'uno mio amico*; see Alberti 1969, 156). Here again we have the stock pairing of *onore* and *utile*. Alberti explicitly identifies the aim of Book 3 as a description of the proper *pater familias* (154).

9. Lansing argues (1991, 223) that Dante accepts ancestry in a patriotic and civic-minded family as a good indicator of nobility, since he uses this argument in his own defense and for his own glorification in the *Paradiso*.

10. Nevertheless, Bartolus asserted elsewhere that when a person commits treason, his heraldic arms "must be destroyed wherever they are depicted in his honor" (quoted in Cavallar, Degenring, and Kirshner 1994, 55). Legal judgment here forms the solid basis for aligning outward markers of honor with demonstrated behavior.

11. This stands in stark contrast to Dante, who claimed that according to the common manner of speech, "the word 'nobility' means the perfection of the nature proper to each thing" (1990, 4.xvi.4).

12. The drift away from Dante on this score is rather surprising in light of Salutati's text, *De seculo et religione*, as well as his deepening Christian religiosity (Kohl and Witt 1978, 86; Witt 1983 and 2000). It is plausible that his own views on the active life and on noble privilege evolved as his own position within the Florentine power elite solidified.

13. We know that Lapo was many times elected to the Signorìa, that he worked extensively for the Parte Guelfa, helping them out of "the gravest dangers" (Castiglionchio 1753, xli), and that he was many times a participant on key ambassadorial missions with other distinguished Florentines. He also had his house burned down by the *popolo* during the Ciompi uprising in 1378, a strong indication of his patrician, Guelfist sensibilities.

14. The topic of developments in the Florentine economy is far too vast to be summarized here. For English-language treatments of some of these developments, see Goldthwaite 1968, 1985, 1987; Padgett 2001; and Padgett and McLean 2002, 2006.

15. To be Guelf essentially meant being socially bourgeois, politically conservative, and, especially, pro-papacy. In Florence in particular, it signified attachment to the republican regime begun in the late 13th century.

16. Branca notes that this passage resembles a passage from Franco Sacchetti's work, as if da Certaldo were citing some stock list of life's joys. Included in this list is the joy of attaining knighthood, a perspective that seems to fit very nicely with da Castiglionchio's viewpoint, and later with Pitti's, but which jives poorly with da Certaldo's otherwise stolid sensibilities.

17. "The wise know God and contrive to do well and help themselves: and God wants that you help yourself and with effort strive for perfection" (*i savi hanno vantaggio, che conoscono Idio e aoperano bene e aiutansi meglio: e Dio vuole che tu t'aiuti e colla tua fatica venga a perfezione*). The words *aoperare* and *fatica* are common in patronage letters and bespeak a certain ethic of self-reliance.

18. The problem with the *equites* was precisely that the modern, Weberian distinction between individual and office was effaced: they retained status and preferred treatment even while they were not performing their specific function.

19. This in no way precludes the fact that participation in the Guelf party had become a somewhat nefarious mark of status and a codeword for political reactionism.

Consequently, at the philosophical level, Bruni offers a strongly civic conception of honor, even as the discourse and justifications that he gives were easily exploitable to signal commitment to a conservative and partisan agenda. The primacy of the Guelf party is the subtext of Bruni's civic philosophy. In the *Laudatio*, he also likens the Guelf party to a *paterfamilias* (Griffiths, Hankins, and Thompson 1987, 120).

20. But does it have the same meaning of virtue? In his discussion of the *vir virtutis*, Quentin Skinner (1978, 94ff.) documents how virtue after Petrarch but especially in Alberti comes to mean something like diligence, or talent and ability, in the face of cruel, impersonal fortune, rather than purity, as was implied in the Dantean version. The change is crucial; now honor is something actively to be striven after on a personal level, a mark of human achievement instead of a gift bestowed by God. Thus, in keeping with the praise of the *vita activa*, and in keeping with the new proto-Machiavellian sense of virtue, a new sense—even a new content—of honor/nobility arises involving personal agency and independence.

21. The argument is reminiscent of Bourdieu's argument that ideologies are "doubly determined" by the interests of the dominant class and the interests of the intellectual class that produce them (1991, 169).

4. What Gets Said When

1. In some cases, however, it appears that the transition to new vocabulary took place in the early Medicean period. Among the multitude of letters written to Lorenzo the Magnificent, I focused on a sample from the early 1470s. Later letters would almost certainly be more deferential than the ones I use in this book.

2. For example, those addressed to less powerful persons, such as Bartolomeo Cederni (F. W. Kent 1991), do differ somewhat in character.

3. For the sake of clarity and concision, the table displays findings for only a very small number of the keywords for which I searched. The figures in each cell of the table are arrived at by dividing all occurrences of a keyword by the total number of letters in which it could appear. Thus multiple occurrences in any given letter drive up the average frequency for letters of that type. I recognize that any given patronage letter often has multiple purposes, but it was necessary to pick one that seemed primary for purposes of parsing the data.

4. The words co-occur in about six dozen of the letters in my dataset.

5. For example, Bishop Donato de' Medici of Pistoia wrote to Lorenzo on December 17, 1471, on behalf of a certain Ser Antonio di Iacopo di Giorgio (*MAP* XXVII, 572) to say that "we are certain that he will do honor to you and to us."

6. Naturally there are exceptions. See *MAP* III, 13, another part of which is quoted in this chapter. Carlo Bonaiuti asks Averardo de' Medici that, given "his immense virtues," he exercise his "clearest intellect" and expend effort to have Carlo reappointed to his present position. Also see, for example, *MAP* XI, 169; XI, 194; XVI, 42; XXVIII, 674.

7. I will show more fully in the next chapter how *amicizia* and *servigio* function more as alternatives than complements in letters about office seeking in particular. References to *amici* or *amicizia* appear in 327 of my letters, while references to service or servants appear in 358. References to both together appear in 122 letters. This joint use occurs especially in recommendations, requests for release from prison, and ecclesiastical benefice letters.

8. See, for instance, *MAP* II, 325; V, 568; XXV, 228; XXVIII, 193, 385, 440; and *C.S.* III, 132: 98.

9. Edler (1934) indicates that the word *fede* came into commercial usage as a term for a kind of receipt, but seemingly only in the mid-sixteenth century. By contrast, the words *obrigo* or *obligo*, meaning something like "a written obligation to pay," had entered commercial parlance before 1400, alongside the term *promessa*.

10. Note that the word *volentieri* (willingly) is also used more often than average in assurance letters, also suggesting this positive framing of commitment.

11. For other examples of the *aiuto et favore* pairing, see *MAP* XXVIII, 215, 651, 652, 653; XXIX, 5.

12. See also the full texts of *C.S.* III, 128: 94 and *MAP* XXIX, 70, both discussed in a slightly different context in chapter 8.

13. However, McLean (1996, 269ff.) shows that differences in ways of writing to the Medici as opposed to other families such as the Strozzi or the Sacchetti were actually not substantial prior to 1434.

14. Although I label the periods using individual and/or family names, the periods gather together letters written to a variety of alters.

15. See, for example, *MAP* XXIII, 519; XXV, 168, 181; XXVII, 517; XXVIII, 27, 167, 223, 246, 273, 321, 355, 629, 643, 688; XXIX, 76, 98.

16. For examples, see *MAP* XXIII, 519; XXVIII, 26, 305, 321. For use of the expression "our state" (*stato nostro*), see *MAP* V, 179; XI, 132, 269. For an example of the expression "your state" (*vostro stato*) seemingly meant in a political sense during the Cosimo period, see *MAP* XII, 69. Also see Connell (2005) for a perceptive discussion of Machiavelli's use of definite articles and personal pronouns.

17. However, historians should also take note of the surge in frequency of some of these inflationary terms in letters written to Cosimo in the immediate aftermath of his return to Florence in 1434.

18. A set of rules governing acceptance of communal offices, among which was the proscription of debtors and of recent incumbents.

19. Other examples can be found in *MAP* XXVIII, 703, 709, 712; XXIX, 9; XXXI 169, 318.

20. However, see the letter of May 26, 1473, from Giovanni del Caccia to Lorenzo de' Medici (*MAP* XXIII, 531). In the letter, Giovanni expressed his hope that he would be able to carry out the responsibilities of his job as *podestà* of Montepulciano "by means of the grace of God and your worthy self" (*mediante la grazia di dio e lla vostra degna persona*).

21. Boscoli, incidentally, had married the daughter of Orlando di Guccio de' Medici in 1455, who seems to have been Lorenzo's sixth cousin once removed.

22. A great deal of this information, pertaining to tens of thousands of Florentines, has been collected into a database by John Padgett of the University of Chicago. I am most grateful to him for my ongoing use of this database. It, in turn, is based on the invaluable data-gathering efforts of many generations of scholars, including distinguished scholars of recent decades such as David Herlihy, Christiane Klapisch-Zuber, Lauro Martines, Richard Goldthwaite, Dale Kent, F. W. Kent, Anthony Molho, and Samuel Kline Cohn, and scholars of past centuries such as Luigi Passerini and Pompeo Litta. Gene Brucker (1962), Dale Kent (1978), and most recently Alison Lewin (2002) have made great use of the records of communal political deliberations (*Consulte e Pratiche*).

23. In Florence, a key measure of status was how early any member of one's family had obtained an office in the priorate. Thus comparative status can be measured by subtracting the writer's family's year of first entry from the recipient's family's year of first entry. Year of birth is available for many individuals in Padgett's dataset, making it possible to assess the relative ages of sender and recipient at the time of composition. Florentine families tended to live in the same neighborhoods for generations, as evident in communal records. On the basis of Padgett's dataset, it was possible to calculate the number of direct marriage ties between sender's and recipient's families, and the path distance between the two families in the marriage market, in the period running from approximately thirty years prior to the letter to two years after it. This was deemed an appropriate sampling window because most marriages contracted in this time would still be active or in the midst of being contracted at the time of letter composition. I myself gathered data on creditor-debtor relations between sender's and recipient's families from the *catasto* of 1427. Because that source is unparalleled for later decades, this kind of tie was coded only for letters written in the 1424–30 period.

24. The predicted effects of path distance are confounded by the intimacy of letters written between a handful of individuals—the Cederni/Boni correspondence and the Bucelli/Sacchetti correspondence in particular. They were either quite distant from each other in the marriage market, or data on their marriage networks is incomplete.

5. The Dynamics of Office Seeking

The epigraph to this chapter is from *MAP* XXVIII, 393.

1. However, when similar patterns appear across many samples, we can feel more confident that the algorithm is finding something real about the world, even without a statistic of significance.

2. Of course, the fact these contrasting terms co-occur there pulls them toward each other in figure 3, despite their conceptual distinctness.

3. A variety of keyword lists was used to generate a variety of MDS images. This list was settled on for figures 3 and 4 because it incorporates all keywords occurring more than ten times in this sample (except *pregare*, which occurs so frequently that including it distorts the relative positioning of the other keywords), while retaining a high degree of legibility. Across these many iterations, the east-west split in the placement of letters remains quite stable. The distinction between northern and southern peripheries is more volatile.

4. Take note, therefore, that while the east-west orientation of figures 3 and 4 is the same, their north-south orientations are inverted. The spatial orientation of MDS plots is largely arbitrary. What matters is the placement of points in relation to each other.

5. A letter written to Lorenzo by Antonio Ferrucci (*MAP* XXIII, 207) quoted in chapter 4 is similar. There Ferrucci attributes his boldness in asking for a favor to the love Lorenzo has already shown him. Only thus could he make his request "intimately" or "informally" (*dimesticamente*).

6. Neri Cambi sent a somewhat similar letter to Lorenzo on February 1, 1473 (*MAP* XXIX, 33):

> I will not consider myself too presumptuous, taking heart from your Magnificence (*pigliando sicurtà in tua magnificenzia*), to ask you about certain matters that concern me, and especially about one that belongs principally to you—and your friends, one of whom I consider myself to be, albeit of little worth—to decide. For it happens that this election of *signori* includes *gonfaloniere di giustizia* in Santa Maria Novella. I would desire that you bestow upon me this favor (*grazia*), that I were seen for *gonfaloniere*. . . . Obtaining this benefit would be the greatest that our family could receive from you. It would be an obligation forever for us and for those who descend from us, although we are already obligated to you in the extreme, to the extent of our power. For God's sake, may it please you to bestow on me this benefit, so that I not seem to be forgotten by you.

7. The opposite tendency appears more often in the early Laurenzian period. That is, rather than expressing confidence in being served, writers pose requests and then back off of commitment to them. For example, consider letters 58 and 62, both in the core of figure 3. Matteo Morelli (*MAP* XXIII, 236; April 9, 1469) requested that his nephew be honored with an office or eligibility for office, but he concluded by saying "I remain most content with whatever you will judge to do." And similarly, Daniello Canigiani (*MAP* XXIII, 398; November 29, 1471) asked Lorenzo that he bestow on him the pleasure of seeing one or more of his sons succeed in the scrutiny, but he concluded by saying "Nevertheless, I have always been happy with every decision of yours." In such cases, writers back away from their request and rhetorically maintain the discretion of the patron. One could even say that the word "nevertheless" (*non di meno*) here stitches together two aspects of the patron-client

relation: an assertive one, and a deferential one (Harrison White 1995; Mische and White 1998).

8. Whereas Ormanno repeatedly asserts his obsession with his own honor, his father Rinaldo guarded his honor through silences. In his correspondence with the *Dieci* (a committee to which was delegated the responsibility of directing the Lucca war), Rinaldo repeatedly refused their framing of his actions in terms of personal responsibility and the jeopardization of his honor, claiming that he was acting in a way conducive to protecting *their* honor, but only his own well-being. When the *Dieci* claimed to have defended his honor from vicious rumors in the city, Rinaldo implicitly denied that his honor could ever have been at issue. In discourse with those outside his own family, Rinaldo does not even countenance a framing of his honor as a point of contention. Silence can be just as significant as speech, a fact MDS may not handle very well.

9. Similarly, in his third letter Ormanno reiterates the need for his allies and supporters to get talking about his appointment, as though talk in itself could bring about a more favorable decision-making climate. In this way, too, he contextualizes his request in terms of the favorable disposition expressed toward it by relevant outside actors (Gumperz 1992).

10. At the end of the fourth letter, Ormanno recommends Messer Batista Durazino of Genova to Averardo, calling him "our friend" (*nostro amico*), but he goes on to clarify his meaning by saying, "He has always been a friend of the Florentines," underscoring that he uses the notion of friendship here in a military context, and "our" in reference to the commune.

11. Here see letters to Averardo from Mariotto di Francesco Segni (*MAP* II, 196), Michelozzo di Bartolomeo Michelozzi (*MAP* II, 201), and Segni together with Riccardo di Niccolò Fagni (*MAP* II, 221). Fagni writes,

> At your request, and on account of his capacity (*virtù*), we arranged that Ormanno would be elected *padrone* of the galley . . . and having heard this day the Dieci has committed to your office the fact of arming the ship and picking the leader and everything, may we remind you most urgently of your honor and ours, which is that Ormanno command it, and that your office provide everything he needs; for it being otherwise, it would mean a loss of honor for Ormanno and us, and it being ours, so too would it be yours.

Thus Fagni engages in the same play of drawing group boundaries using the concept of honor as did Ormanno earlier, suggesting the group implications of challenges to individual honor. Fagni concludes by reminding Averardo, "We are certain, on account of his *virtù* and his good soul, he will serve the commune most well. And if you were not also certain of this, you would not have spoken as urgently as you did."

12. I have mentioned "tone" several times in this chapter. A letter from Mari-

otto Segni to Averardo de' Medici of February 10, 1430 (*MAP* II, 196) enacts such a change of tone dramatically. The first paragraph is a formulaic endorsement of Ormanno; the second is an enthusiastic recommendation of Segni's neighbor, Iacopo di Tommaso Frescobaldi. Segni concludes the first paragraph by saying "I am certain I need not recommend Ormanno to you." But rather than following that up with a strong ritual endorsement such as "Nevertheless I recommend him to you as much as I know and am able," Mariotto writes merely "I remind myself that he be recommended to you." Mariotto withholds confident endorsement of Ormanno, perhaps pending clarification of Averardo's own commitment to him. By contrast, his endorsement of Frescobaldi is noticeably more enthusiastic and strewn with superlatives. Frescobaldi is a man one can trust abundantly (*larghissimamente*) to keep his eyes closed (and probably his mouth shut), a man "apt for any matter," a man whom Segni prays "most strictly" (*strettissimamente*) be given a position. To remove him from the position would be a disservice to the commune and "singularly displeasing to me" (*a me in singularità ne sarebbe fatto dispiacere*). The contrast creates a kind of categorical boundary between Ormanno and Frescobaldi, and it presents a direct juxtaposition of the frames of duty/honor/patronage and friendship/partisanship that animate and separate the rhetorics of the Albizzi and Tedaldi letters.

13. Averardo received a letter from Bartolomeo di Verano Peruzzi on February 23 recommending Papi in strikingly similar terms (*MAP* II, 240): "My honored elder, Even though I am certain that concerning the affairs of Papi Tedaldi you would do as for a son, nonetheless I recommend him to you as much as I am able: that he have the *galeotta* that Mariano had, and that you have regard for his advantage and honor."

6. Friends of Friends

The epigraph to this chapter is from *MAP* XXV, 233.

1. As Rubinstein (1997) notes, the *accoppiatori* were a special group of officials responsible for distributing the names of political eligibles into different bags from which names were drawn by lot for different offices. One wanted to have one's name put in the *gonfaloniere di giustizia* bag most of all; hence Guicciardini's request here. Rubinstein further notes (1997, 220–21) that the *accoppiatori* were called in on August 23 for one day only to provide additional names for the *gonfaloniere di giustizia* bag.

2. The term is even more polyvalent than I suggest here. For example, Lewin (2003, 32) notes that towns subject to Florentine hegemony in the late fourteenth century sought to be *raccomandati* of or by their more powerful neighbor. Thus the idea of *raccomandazione* could apply to collective entities as well as individuals.

3. For example, Mazzei composed a letter for Datini to send to Niccolò da Uzzano, one of the tax officials, in which Datini apologized copiously for requesting a tax break, expressing his hesitation at incurring shame from having bestowed this nuisance on Niccolò. He went on, asserting his love for Niccolò, and petitioning for

treatment commensurate with what is fair for the least citizen. He signed the letter, "your servant." For writing to Domenico Giugni, his *padrone*, Datini was to use the exact same opening material, but add reference at the end to their friendship, stressing their common position, and likening Giugni to his old deceased helper Guido del Palagio. For writing to Aghinolfo Popoleschi, again the same opening was to be used, this time adding, "I cannot, however, believe of the sage men who lead the commune, that they would wish to do anything other than what is most reasonable to my peers." A letter to Nofri di Andrea del Palagio would follow the da Uzzano form *verbatim*, while a letter to Andrea di Messer Ugo della Stufa would address the recipient directly by name and refer to their special relationship. Finally, a letter to the politically minded Francesco Federighi would explicitly ask him to consider speaking of Datini's tax situation with his *amico*, Vanni Rucellai, on the tax examination board. All of this micro-framing and rhetorical manipulation demonstrates clearly that Mazzei would have been an outstanding practitioner of the customized mail merge. But it also highlights how much letters on the same topic to different authors might share a common lexical framework while change framing around the edges.

4. Furthermore, recommendations are designed to connect people remote in space from each other while imposing less commitment between them than other types of letters. Thus it may be that underlying social positions are more loosely connected to writing strategies than is true in other situations.

5. Even with a sample of over two hundred recommendation letters, it is hard to generate sufficient subsamples of different triadic types to link the types convincingly with patterns of other social relations and positions. Besides, distinctions between triadic types are gray in actual execution. Further, there is the problem that the number of possible triad types expands exponentially as the number of possible framings of connectedness—family, friendship, servanthood, objective need, and so forth—increases.

6. See also my discussion of another letter of Cosimo's—*C.S.* III, 120: 138—in chapter 4.

7. *Parentado* refers to many kinds of kin relations, but it is used mostly to talk about marriage-based relations.

8. The rhetoric of father-son was also available for drawing an inclusive boundary around writer, recipient, and recommendee. Both the Albizzi and Tedaldi sets of letters in chapter 5 use it. In his letter to Averardo de' Medici of February 17, 1430 (*MAP* II, 218), Rinaldo degli Albizzi asked him to treat Ormanno in a familial manner: "like the son I know that you consider him to be" (*come di figliolo ch'io so che tu te lo riputi*). Bartolomeo Tedaldi also framed Papi Tedaldi as if Averardo thought of him as a son in *MAP* II, 253: "of him you make no other account than as a son" (*di lui non fai altro conto che di figliolo*). Also see, for example, a letter of January 28, 1430 (*MAP* II, 160), written to Averardo by Benedetto Strozzi on behalf of a certain Panfilio di

Messer Antonio da Lanfianesi. There Benedetto asks that Averardo treat Panfilio as he would treat his own son, Giuliano, and he expresses hope in Averardo "as a son has hope in his father."

9. Ostensibly the letter has two recipients, but most of the time dall'Antella writes as if he were addressing only one.

10. The repeated mention of justice to some extent adds an element of objectivity to what otherwise is usually a personalistically rooted relationship.

11. I should note, however, that the way Francesco completes the letter does not extend the *affezione* framing to his own relationship with the non-Florentines: "Knowing first their goodwill to be sincere and true (*sincera e vera*), it has seemed to me I ought to accede to their just petition and request." He hardly expresses much positive commitment to them with this phrasing.

12. For another such keying of a letter in contrast to run-of-the-mill variants, see the letter of January 22, 1473, from Giovanni Tornabuoni to Lorenzo de' Medici (*MAP* XXIX, 13). I cite and briefly discuss this letter in chapter 8. A letter of Salvi di ser Piero di ser Tommaso written to Cosimo and Lorenzo de' Medici on September 15, 1434 (*MAP* XIII, 32) is similar. Salvi writes on behalf of a certain Maso of Fiesole and marks his recommendation as a voluntary one: "I am certain it was not necessary to give you the bother of reading this, as you have always been, and will do, for Maso as much as one must for a dear friend, but on account of my *parentado* with him and my affection, I wanted to write to you about it."

13. The claim of intimacy appears sometimes to have a kind of superlative or even oath-taking quality, as when, in a letter of January 21, 1430, Stefano di Francesco di ser Segna asked Averardo de' Medici to include him and his family "in the number of" his "intimate friends, even if" they "were to suffer harm on account of it" (*MAP* II, 147). Similarly, Giovannozzo di Franceso Pitti wrote to Averardo in a letter of November 13, 1430: "I return to you as to the most intimate friend I consider myself to have, like unto a father" (*MAP* II, 380). However, the word *intimo* seems to have practically disappeared from patronage vocabulary after the 1430s.

14. See also a letter of September 19, 1436, from Aperthon Alberti to Agnolo di Palla Strozzi (*C.S.* III, 130: 129), in which Alberti calls Bartolomeo di Ceccolino da Todi both his "dearest friend" and his "intimate friend"; but then, however, Alberti writes, "It seems to me I am obliged to recommend him to you."

15. Other letters of Filippo (for example, *MAP* XXVIII, 645; XXIX, 94) are similar in style and tone.

16. Recall that honor and advantage, while seemingly veering in opposite directions, are tropically paired together in Florentine patronage correspondence, following upon a Ciceronian precedent.

17. Del Bene was an important patron in the early 1400s. For examples of favor-seeking letters addressed to him, see *Carte del Bene* 49, numbers 274, 288, 289, 291, 294, 308, and 323. A certain "Averardo" is mentioned in a letter written to Iacopo

di Francesco del Bene on July 7, 1393 (*Carte del Bene* 49, 30). Also, Vieri de' Medici wrote a letter to Iacopo on May 22, 1393 (*Carte del Bene* 49, 24), addressing him there as "Dearest friend" (*Amico carissimo*).

18. The use of *vostri* (your) here in connection with Averardo's friends seems strange. Throughout the letter Andrea has used the informal pronouns *tu, tuo, te,* and *teco.* Why not *tuoi* here? He seems to be using *vostri* not formally, but in a plural sense: not the friends of Averardo as an individual, but the friends of Averardo *and his other friends.* He thereby invokes a collectivity—whether family or patronage group—of which Averardo is a member.

7. The Stalled Transformation of the State

The epigraph to this chapter is from ASF, *Carte del Bene* 49, 289.

1. A confusion of analytically modern and traditional elements characterized Florentine political and economic institutions in a variety of respects. There was a bona fide "politico-juridical transformation" of the state (Fubini 1994); meanwhile, the distinction between public and private remained chronically blurred (Chittolini 1996). Respect for constitutional tradition was juxtaposed with an increasingly self-interested orientation among communal leaders (D. Kent 1987; Rubinstein 1997). Different parts of the *contado* simultaneously manifested "forward-looking" and "backward-looking" forms of landholding (Emigh 1998). Investments in agriculture were not inconsistent with capitalist underdevelopment (Emigh 2003). Innovative business organizational forms such as the holding company (de Roover 1966) and modern business practices such as current accounts and double-entry bookkeeping (Melis 1991; Dini 2001) emerged alongside traditional conceptions of obligations to partners and fellow businessmen (Goldthwaite 1985, 1987) and a patronage-like market structure (Padgett 2001; McLean and Padgett 2004). And a smattering of locally negotiated contracts with subject cities persisted in the midst of the consolidation of the regional state (Fasano Guarini 1996; Cohn 1999; Connell and Zorzi 2000; Epstein 2000a, 2000b; Petralia 2000).

2. This fact was widely recognized. Citizens reported the value of their shares of the *Monte* using officially sanctioned discount rates in their 1427 tax returns. Often they went the state one further, contracting prices for the exchange of *Monte* shares that reflected greater depreciation than the pegged rate (see for example, *Catasto* 68: 144; 75: 146).

3. A letter of April 26, 1431, from Ser Niccolò Tinucci to Averardo de' Medici (*MAP* III, 121, but labeled number 122 in the published inventory), gives a sense of what the *specchio* list meant to contemporaries. He wrote, "Although I do not expect to be *allo specchio* for a variety of reasons, and also because the notary of the priors of our quarter indicates as much, that I am eligible to be drawn, all the same I am sending you there Piero this artillery soldier who comes to remind you. And in the event

anything must be paid, I told him to come to you and you will give [the money] to him; so that if it were the case for any reason that I were *allo specchio*, which I don't believe I will be, I pray you that you will endeavor to pay that which is necessary, and write a note recording what you are lending, and I by the first mail will pay it back." Tinucci twice denies that he is really in danger of being placed *allo specchio*. He tries to adopt a businesslike tone on the topic, but his anxiety is betrayed by his repetitions, and his precautionary tactic of contacting Averardo.

4. Unpaid *prestanzoni* from the mid-1420s show up abundantly in the *catasto* records of 1427. Among a group of 401 affluent and politically important house-holds, 18 percent carried some kind of *prestanzoni* debt into 1427. The strategy of seeking *grazie* to pay fractions of the total tax due was quite common. Businessmen used their companies to pay personal taxes (e.g., *Catasto* 60: 252; 65: 46, 143, 471; 68: 91; 76: 169), and some companies appear to have paid *prestanze* on behalf of their em-ployees (*Catasto* 69: 107; 74: 15; 78: 68) or out of customers' accounts (*Catasto* 79: 85). There are also explicit cases of individuals assuming others' tax assessments in return for specified or unspecified interest (for example, *Catasto* 78: 97).

5. For a list of citizens in such speculation, see McLean 2005. This futures market is an intriguing indication of the sophistication the Florentines achieved in the area of financial instruments.

6. It was common for the commune to initiate a tax rebate effort almost im-mediately after any new tax was collected. On the one hand, Conti suggests that the Medici made a habit of reducing the number of officials responsible for the assign-ment and collection of taxes after 1434, probably allowing the Medici greater con-trol of these *impositori* and facilitating a more circumscribed practice of favoritism. On the other hand, the number of *sgravatori*—officials charged with distributing tax rebates or relief—was considerably greater, as in the days of the Albizzi regime, un-doubtedly so that many more citizens experienced more directly and personally the supposed largesse of the Medici regime.

7. Figure 7 also suggests that the most significant antidote to Florentine fiscal ruin would have been diplomacy: keeping out of wars, such as during the 1454–78 period, did more to stabilize the regime's finances than any innovative administra-tive actions could have.

8. Herlihy (1991: fig. 8—mistakenly referred to as fig. 9 in his discussion of it) documents that the number of citizens *allo specchio* because of tax delinquency rose and fell more or less in lockstep with the fluctuating demands of the state, except in two respects: 1) in general they lag slightly behind the years of heaviest taxes, as if citizens could keep up with heavy assessments for some period of time before running short; and 2) a great number of citizens were found to be in arrears in the mid-to-late 1440s, even though the tax burden at that time was relatively light.

9. Besides the *licenzia*, various other written instruments such as the *bollettino*, the *sicurtà*, and the *salvacondotto* were sought by those in tax arrears (or facing other kinds

of obligations) in order to secure a certain period of exemption from prosecution or incarceration, to liquidate their assets, and to settle their debts (Conti 1984, 307). For an example of the *salvacondotto*, see *MAP* XII, 132, a letter from Baldovinetto di Alesso Baldovinetti to Cosimo de' Medici in Florence, October 9, 1435. Baldovinetti calls himself Cosimo's "least servant," and he claims to have been "most loyal" to Cosimo in the hopes of obtaining a *salvacondotto* while his tax petition is pending. An example of the request for a *bollettino* is Antonio Baldesi's letter to Forese Sacchetti of November 12, 1418 (*Conv. Soppr.* 78, 324: 171), in which he begs Forese, on behalf of Agnolo di Francesco da Pulciano, "that, retaining your honor always, it might be pleasing to you to concede a *bollettino* to Agnolo so that by means of this the said Agnolo is able to come there safely" (*conservando sempre onore piaccia concedergli uno bollettino sichè mediante quello il detto Agnolo possa venire costà sicuramente*), in order that he might pay off his creditors bit by bit.

10. See *C.S.* III, 132: 161, 186, and 196, all from late 1425. In the first, Piero di Carlo writes to Matteo di Simone that a certain Ser Filippo had been charged with paying Piero's *prestanzoni*; but in the event this had not been done, he asked Matteo to take care of it: "Do not forget this, because I would not like to end up in the company of magnates, nor *allo specchio*." Biagio Strozzi wrote concerning his own tax problems, recommending himself to Matteo: "I am completely certain that you will act in this matter as if it were your own affair." Nanni Strozzi's brief note to Matteo comes from the other side of the request ritual: "Your diligence concerning my affairs is that which merits the affection I have for you. I thank you for the money that you provided that I should have."

11. Cantucci, above, referred to the *vergogna e danno* he faced; Orlandini refers to *danno e vergogna*.

12. A letter from Piero di Giorgio Serragli to Bartolomeo Cederni dated January 26, 1449 (*Conv. Soppr.* 78, 314: 435) has similar elements. Piero prays of Bartolomeo that it please him to ask Soldo di Antonio del Soldato to help keep him off the *specchio* list, so that he not receive the damage (*danno*) associated with such an occurrence.

13. I discuss recent theoretical literature touching on the history of the Italian city-states at greater length in McLean 2005.

8. Servants and Slaves

The first epigraph to this chapter is from Burkhardt (1960, 121f.). The source of the second epigraph is *MAP* XXVII, 517.

1. Compare what Shotter (1993, 169, 183) has to say about the emergence of intimacy—a set of special, nonargumentative speech genres seemingly unique to particular interactions but actually formed historically as a shared resource within a whole cultural tradition: "Indeed, if it is the case that all of our personal modes of

being are constructed in, and emerge out of, the general self-other dimension of interaction within which they are embedded, how in history might these special enclaves of privacy, in which people orientate towards each other, *not* in terms of their social positions, have been constructed?"

2. Leonardo Bruni's early fifteenth-century encomia and Vespasiano da Bisticci's late fifteenth-century biographical sketches of great men exemplify this development. Bakhtin (1981, 143ff.) links the origins of self-consciousness to these genres, which gave normative content to individual lives. However, these developments do not provide sufficient evidence of the emergence and diffusion of the modern self.

3. Arguably Burckhardt meant that during the Renaissance individual character became a common, socially recognizable and sanctioned phenomenon—in his words, a "psychological fact"(1960, 122). Undoubtedly the rise of humanism in various forms and arenas offers prima facie substantiation of the Burckhardtian thesis, but the evidence warrants detailed examination.

4. The tension between Machiavelli's dedication of *The Prince* and the substance of his argument concerning self-reliance is more palpable than the tension here, but it is of the same sort. We assume Machiavelli is speaking ironically in the first instance. However, Pitkin (1984, 7, 80, 105) identifies a pervasive tension in Machiavelli's work between autonomy in the sense of personal independence and autonomy in the sense of the interdependence of virtuous republican citizens together facing a hostile world.

5. The literature contrasting independent and interdependent self-construals is vast. The interdependent self is one defined in relation to others. Such a relation may be defined in relation to a type of other, or in relation to particular others. It may be stable, perduring across situations, or fluid, changing as others enter an interaction setting. For example, as Bachnik (1994, 158) reports, in Japan intimacy may be enacted with non-intimates when others present are even more remote from ego. The Japanese "I" is identified not only necessarily with reference to others, but also is indexically defined within ever changing relationships with others. Even within the space of one interaction, individuals may toggle back and forth between formal (*soto*) and informal or colloquial (*uchi*) modes of address (Sukle 1994). Linguistic resources for indexing individual responsibility for action are weak (Mühlhäusler and Harré 1990, 93). Finally, some experimental evidence (for example, Matsumoto 1999) is persuasive that such public constructions of self are not just outward styles, but also privately held constitutive construals.

6. For a compelling depiction of fifteenth-century Florentine *mentalités* and practices through the lens of "outside" versus "inside," see Brown (2002).

7. See, for example, a letter from Simone Canigiani to Cosimo de' Medici of June 13, 1439 (*MAP* XI, 269). Canigiani writes on behalf of "the prudent man, Giovanni di Giusto." Wrote Canigiani of Giovanni, the bearer of the letter, "[He] will narrate to you the various things that concern the state of our commune and the conserva-

tion of this country. Therefore may it be pleasing to you to give him your complete trust as much as you would to me personally."

8. See, for example, *MAP* II, 160; III, 283; IV, 117; XI, 28, 39, 150, 210, and 287; *C.S.* III, 112: 65, 120: 138, and 150: 70b; and *Conv. Soppr.* 78 324: 146.

9. See, for example, *MAP* II, 40 for *buona natura.* See *MAP* XI, 217 and especially *MAP* V, 748 of August 12, 1459, for *la natura e buona usanza tua.*

10. See, for example, a letter of Filippo di Lionardo Bartoli to Lorenzo de' Medici of August 22, 1472 (*MAP* XXV, 198), in which he reminds Lorenzo of the words of loyalty another member of the Bartoli family had spoken before.

11. See also letters from two non-Florentines in *MAP* XXVIII, 217 and 229.

12. See *MAP* XXIII, 397; XXV, 120; XXVIII, 705 for further examples.

13. For examples from the 1420s and 1430s, see *MAP* II, 104; III, 151; and V, 642. In the last of these, after speaking of his sense of obligation to the Medici, Matteo di Niccolò Cerretani promised Cosimo de' Medici, "When for my part I can do something pleasing to you, I will provide proof of it."

14. See my brief discussion of *semplicità* above, and see J. Martin (1997, 1334).

15. See the letters between Bartolomeo di Verano Peruzzi and Averardo de' Medici in 1430 and 1431 (*MAP* I, 62; II, 240, 266; IV, 102; V, 147). In the first of these, Bartolomeo addresses Averardo as "Honored elder, like a brother," and he claims that in all respects he has confidence in Averardo. In the next, he wrote in support of the Medicean Papi Tedaldi, and in the third he recommended to Averardo's attention a certain Niccolaio, who has suffered "too many injustices," urging him to attend to the matter, saying, "as much as I can." Furthermore, Bartolomeo's business partner in 1427 was Giovanni di Domenico Giugni, a staunch Medicean.

16. Nearly eighty citizens were exiled in 1458 (Brown 2002, 346).

Conclusion: Culture and the Network

The epigraph to this chapter is from *MAP* XXV, 117.

1. David Koeppel, "Want Your Letter to Stand Out? Here's a Tip: Write It Yourself," *New York Times*, May 22, 2005, sec. 10, p. 1.

2. Whether or not this happened anywhere other than Florence, or how much, I cannot say. The extent to which the same changes appeared in other spheres of life in Florence besides the political I hesitate to judge. And the degree to which these practices simply stuck once the structural and cultural conditions that gave rise to them waned is a question that requires much more research.

Bibliography

Archival Sources from the Archivio di Stato, Firenze

Conventi Soppressi, 78 [*Conv. Soppr.*]
Carte del Bene, 49
Carte Strozziane, 3rd series [*C.S.* III]
Catasto, 1427 [*Catasto*]
Mediceo Avanti il Principato [*MAP*]

Published Sources

Abbott, Andrew. 1992. "From Causes to Events: Notes on Narrative Positivism." *Sociological Methods and Research* 20 (4): 428–55.

———. 1995. "Sequence Analysis: New Methods for Old Ideas." *Annual Review of Sociology* 21: 93–113.

Adams, Julia. 1994. "The Familial State: Elite Family Practices and State-Making in the Early Modern Netherlands." *Theory and Society* 23 (4): 505–39.

Aguilera, Michael B., and Douglas S. Massey. 2003. "Social Capital and the Wages of Mexican Migrants: New Hypotheses and Tests." *Social Forces* 82 (2): 671–701.

Alberti, Leon Battista. 1969 [~1430]. *The Family in Renaissance Florence. [I Libri della famiglia.]* Translated by Renee Neu Watkins. Columbia: University of South Carolina Press.

Alexander, Jeffrey C. 1990. "Analytic Debates: Understanding the Relative Autonomy of Culture." In *Culture and Society: Contemporary Debates*, edited by Jeffrey C. Alexander and Steven Seidman, 1–27. Cambridge: Cambridge University Press.

Alexander, Jeffrey C., and Philip Smith. 1993. "The Discourse of American Civil Society: A New Proposal for Cultural Studies." *Theory and Society* 22: 151–207.

Almond, Gabriel A., and Sidney Verba. 1963. *The Civic Culture: Political Attitudes and Democracy in Five Nations.* Princeton, N.J.: Princeton University Press.

———, eds. 1980. *The Civic Culture Revisited.* Boston: Little, Brown and Company.

Anderson, Carolyn J., Stanley Wasserman, and Bradley Crouch. 1999. "A p* Primer: Logit Models for Social Networks." *Social Networks* 21: 37–66

Anheier, Helmut K., Jürgen Gerhards, and Frank P. Romo. 1995. "Form of Capital and Social Structure in Cultural Fields: Examining Bourdieu's Social Topography." *American Journal of Sociology* 100 (4): 859–903.

Ansell, Christopher K. 1997. "Symbolic Networks: The Realignment of the French Working Class, 1887–1894." *American Journal of Sociology* 103 (2): 359–90.

Arditi, Jorge. 1998. *A Genealogy of Manners: Transformations of Social Relations in France and England from the Fourteenth to the Eighteenth Century.* Chicago: University of Chicago Press.

Auyero, Javier. 2001. *Poor People's Politics: Peronist Survival Networks and the Legacy of Evita.* Durham and London: Duke University Press.

Bachnik, Jane M. 1994. "Indexing Self and Society in Japanese Family Organization." In *Situated Meaning: Inside and Outside in Japanese Self, Society and Language,* edited by Jane M. Bachnik and Charles Quinn, 143–66. Princeton, N.J.: Princeton University Press.

Bachnik, Jane M., and Charles Quinn, eds. 1994. *Situated Meaning: Inside and Outside in Japanese Self, Society and Language.* Princeton, N.J.: Princeton University Press.

Badescu, Gabriel, and Eric M. Uslaner, eds. 2003. *Social Capital and Transition to Democracy.* London: Routledge.

Baker, Wayne E. 1984. "The Social Structure of a National Securities Market." *American Journal of Sociology* 89 (4): 775–811.

Bakhtin, M. M. 1981. *The Dialogic Imagination: Four Essays.* Edited by Michael Holquist. Translated by Caryl Emerson and Michael Holquist. Austin: University of Texas Press.

Barabási, Albert-László. 2002. *Linked: The New Science of Networks.* Cambridge, Mass.: Perseus Publishing.

Baron, Hans. 1966. *The Crisis of the Early Italian Renaissance.* Princeton, N.J.: Princeton University Press.

Baron, Stephen, John Field, and Tom Schuller, eds. 2000. *Social Capital: Critical Perspectives.* Oxford: Oxford University Press.

Bashi, Vilna Francine. 2007. *Survival of the Knitted: Immigrant Social Networks in a Stratified World.* Stanford: Stanford University Press.

Baumeister, Roy F. 1987. "How the Self Became a Problem: A Psychological Review of Historical Research." *Journal of Personality and Social Psychology* 52: 163–76.

Baxandall, Michael. 1972. *Painting and Experience in Fifteenth-Century Italy.* Oxford: Oxford University Press.

Bearman, Peter S. 1993. *Relations into Rhetorics: Local Elite Social Structure in Norfolk, England, 1540–1640.* New Brunswick, N.J.: Rutgers University Press.

Beauvoir, Simone de. 1949. *The Second Sex.* Translated and edited by H. M. Parshley. New York: Vintage.

Bec, Christian. 1967. *Les marchands ecrivains: Affaires et humanisme a Florence 1375–1434.* Paris: Mouton and Co.

Becker, Marvin B. 2002a. "An Essay on the Quest for Identity in the Early Italian

Renaissance." In *Florentine Essays: Selected Writings*, collected by James Banker and Carol Lansing, 239–57. Ann Arbor: University of Michigan Press.

———. 2002b. "Individualism in the Early Italian Renaissance: Burden and Blessing." In *Florentine Essays: Selected Writings*, collected by James Banker and Carol Lansing, 258–84. Ann Arbor: University of Michigan Press.

Bell, Rudolph M. 1999. *How to Do It*. Chicago: University of Chicago Press.

Bellah, Robert N., Richard Madsen, William M. Sullivan, Ann Swidler, and Steven M. Tipton. 1985. *Habits of the Heart: Individualism and Commitment in American Life*. New York: Harper and Row.

Benford, Robert. 1997. "An Insider's Critique of the Social Movement Framing Perspective." *Sociological Inquiry* 67 (4): 409–30.

Berezin, Mabel. 1994. "Cultural Form and Political Meaning: State-Subsidized Theater, Ideology, and the Language of Style in Fascist Italy." *American Journal of Sociology* 99 (5): 1237–86.

———. 1997. "Politics and Culture: A Less Fissured Terrain." *Annual Review of Sociology* 23: 361–83.

Biagioli, Mario. 1993. *Galileo, Courtier: The Practice of Science in the Culture of Absolutism*. Chicago: University of Chicago Press.

Bian, Yanjie. 1997. "Bringing Strong Ties Back In: Indirect Ties, Network Bridges, and Job Searches in China." *American Sociological Review* 62 (3): 366–85.

Blau, Peter. 1964. *Exchange and Power in Social Life*. New Brunswick, N.J.: Transaction.

Body-Gendrot, Sophie, and Marilyn Gittell, eds. 2003. *Social Capital and Social Citizenship*. Lanham, Md.: Lexington Books.

Boschetto, Luca. 2000. *Leon Battista Alberti e Firenze: Biografia, Storia, Letteratura*. Firenze: Olschki.

———. 2003. "Incrociare le fonti: Archivi e letteratura. Rileggendo la lettera di Leon Battista Alberti a Giovanni di Cosimo de' Medici, 10 aprile [1456?]." *Medioevo e Rinascimento* 17 n.s. 14: 243–64.

Boschloo, Anton W. A. 1998. "Perceptions of the Status of Painting: The Self-Portrait in the Art of the Italian Renaissance." In *Modelling the Individual: Biography and Portrait in the Renaissance*, edited by Karl Enenkel, Betsy de Jong-Crane, and Peter Liebregts, 51–73. Amsterdam: Rodopi.

Bourdieu, Pierre. 1977. *Outline of a Theory of Practice*. Translated by Richard Nice. Cambridge: Cambridge University Press.

———. 1984. *Distinction: A Social Critique of the Judgment of Taste*. Translated by Richard Nice. Cambridge, Mass.: Harvard University Press.

———. 1985. "Social Space and the Genesis of 'Classes.'" *Theory and Society* 14: 723–44.

———. 1986. "The Forms of Capital." In *Handbook of Theory and Research for the Sociology of Education*, edited by J. G. Richardson, 241–58. New York: Greenwood Press.

————. 1990a. *The Logic of Practice.* Translated by Richard Nice. Stanford, Calif.: Stanford University Press.

————. 1990b. *In Other Words: Essays Towards a Reflexive Sociology.* Translated by Matthew Adamson. Cambridge: Polity Press.

————. 1991. *Language and Symbolic Power.* Edited and introduced by John B. Thompson. Translated by Gino Raymond and Matthew Adamson. Cambridge, Mass.: Harvard University Press.

————. 1998. *Practical Reason: On the Theory of Action.* Stanford, Calif.: Stanford University Press.

————. 2000. *Pascalian Meditations.* Cambridge: Polity Press.

Bourdieu, Pierre, and Loic Wacquandt. 1992. *An Invitation to Reflexive Sociology.* Chicago: University of Chicago Press.

Braithwaite, Valerie, and Margaret Levi, eds. 1998. *Trust and Governance.* New York: Russell Sage Foundation.

Branca, Vittore, ed. 1986. *Mercanti scrittori: Ricordi nella Firenze tra Medioevo e Rinascimento [Paolo da Certaldo, Giovanni Morelli, Bonaccorso Pitti e Domenico Lenzi, Donato Velluti, Goro Dati, Francesco Datini, Lapo Niccolini, e Bernardo Machiavelli].* Milano: Rusconi.

Braunstein, Philippe. 1988. "Toward Intimacy: The Fourteenth and Fifteenth Centuries." In *A History of Private Life,* vol. 2, *Revelations of the Medieval World,* edited by Georges Duby, translated by Arthur Goldhammer, 535–630. Cambridge, Mass.: Harvard University Press, Belknap Press.

Brehm, John, and Wendy Rahn. 1997. "Individual-Level Evidence for the Causes and Consequences of Social Capital." *American Journal of Political Science* 41 (3): 999–1023.

Breiger, Ronald L. 1974. "The Duality of Persons and Groups." *Social Forces* 53 (2): 181–90.

Brown, Alison. 2002. "Insiders and Outsiders: The Changing Boundaries of Exile." In *Society and Individual in Renaissance Florence,* edited by William J. Connell, 337–83. Berkeley: University of California Press.

Brown, Penelope, and Stephen C. Levinson. 1987. *Politeness: Some Universals in Language Usage.* Cambridge: Cambridge University Press.

Brubaker, Rogers. 1992. *Citizenship and Nationhood in France and Germany.* Cambridge, Mass.: Harvard University Press.

Brucker, Gene A. 1962. *Florentine Politics and Society, 1343–1378.* Princeton, N.J.: Princeton University Press.

————. 1983. *Renaissance Florence.* Berkeley: University of California Press. [Originally published in 1969 by John Wiley and Sons, Inc.]

Bruner, Jerome. 1986. *Actual Minds, Possible Worlds.* New York: Plenum Press.

————. 1996. *The Culture of Education.* Cambridge, Mass.: Harvard University Press.

Burckhardt, Jacob. 1960. *The Civilization of the Renaissance in Italy.* Edited and introduced by Irene Gordon. New York: New American Library, Mentor Books.

Burke, Peter. 1987. *Historical Anthropology of Early Modern Italy: Essays on Perception and Communication*. Cambridge: Cambridge University Press.

————. 1997. "Representations of the Self from Petrarch to Descartes." In *Rewriting the Self: Histories from the Renaissance to the Present*, edited by Roy Porter, 17–28. London: Routledge.

Burris, Val. 2004. "The Academic Caste System: Prestige Hierarchies in PhD Exchange Networks." *American Sociological Review* 69 (2): 239–64.

Burt, Ronald S. 1992. *Structural Holes: The Social Structure of Competition*. Cambridge, Mass.: Harvard University Press.

————. 1997. "The Contingent Value of Social Capital." *Administrative Science Quarterly* 42 (2): 339–65.

————. 2001. "Bandwidth and Echo: Trust, Information, and Gossip in Social Networks." In *Networks and Markets*, edited by James Rauch and Alessandra Casella, 30–74. New York: Russell Sage Foundation.

Calhoun, Craig, Edward LiPuma, and Moishe Postone, eds. 1993. *Bourdieu: Critical Perspectives*. Chicago: University of Chicago Press.

Carley, Kathleen. 1993. "Coding Choices for Textual Analysis: A Comparison of Content Analysis and Map Analysis." *Sociological Methodology* 23: 75–126.

Carrington, Peter J., John Scott, and Stanley Wasserman. 2005. *Models and Methods in Social Network Analysis*. New York: Cambridge University Press.

Carrithers, Michael. 1985. "An Alternative Social History of the Self." In *The Category of the Person*, edited by Michael Carrithers, Steven Collins, and Steven Lukes, 234–56. New York: Cambridge University Press.

Castiglionchio, Lapo da. 1753. *Epistola o sia Ragionamento di Messer Lapo da Castiglionchio, celebre giureconsulto del secolo XIV*. Bologna: Girolamo Corciolani ed Eredi Colli.

Castiglione, Baldassare. 1959. *The Book of the Courtier*. Translated by Charles Singleton. Garden City, N.Y.: Anchor Books.

Cavallar, Oswaldo, Susanne Degenring, and Julius Kirshner. 1994. *A Grammar of Signs: Bartolo da Sassoferrato's Tract on Insignia and Coats of Arms*. Studies in Comparative Legal History. Berkeley: University of California, Robbins Collection Publication.

Chittolini, Giorgio. 1996. "The 'Private,' the 'Public,' the State." In *The Origins of the State in Italy, 1300–1600*, edited by Julius Kirshner, 34–61. Chicago: University of Chicago Press.

Ciappelli, Giovanni, and Patricia Lee Rubin, eds. 2000. *Art, Memory, and Family in Renaissance Florence*. New York: Cambridge University Press.

Cicero. 1926. *The Letters to His Friends*. Vol. 3. Translated by W. Glynn Williams. London: William Heinemann Ltd.

Cicourel, Aaron V. 1973. *Cognitive Psychology: Language and Meaning in Social Interaction*. New York: Free Press.

Cohn, Samuel Kline, Jr. 1980. *The Laboring Classes in Renaissance Florence.* New York: Academic Press.

———. 1992. *The Cult of Remembrance and the Black Death: Six Renaissance Cities in Central Italy.* Baltimore: Johns Hopkins University Press.

———. 1994. "La storia secondo Robert Putnam." *Polis* 8: 315–24.

———. 1999. *Creating the Florentine State: Peasants and Rebellion, 1348–1434.* Cambridge: Cambridge University Press.

———. 2002. *The Black Death Transformed: Disease and Culture in Early Renaissance Europe.* New York: Oxford University Press.

Coleman, James S. 1990. *Foundations of Social Theory.* Cambridge, Mass.: Harvard University Press, Belknap Press.

Collins, Randall. 1981. "On the Microfoundations of Macrosociology." *American Journal of Sociology* 86 (5): 984–1014.

Connell, William J. 1990. "Libri di famiglia." *Italian Culture* 8: 279–92.

———. 1994. "Changing Patterns of Medicean Patronage: The Florentine Dominion During the Fifteenth Century." In *Lorenzo il Magnifico e il suo mondo*, a cura di Gian Carlo Garfagnini, 87–107. Firenze: Olschki.

———. 2005. "A Note about the Text and Translation." In *The Prince*, by Niccolò Machiavelli. Translated by William J. Connell, ix–xiv. Boston and New York: Bedford St. Martin's.

———, ed. 2002. *Society and Individual in Renaissance Florence.* Berkeley: University of California Press.

Connell, William J., and Andrea Zorzi. 2000. *Florentine Tuscany: Structures and Practices of Power.* Cambridge: Cambridge University Press.

Conti, Elio. 1984. *L'imposta diretta a Firenze nel Quattrocento (1427–1494).* Roma: Istituto storico italiano per il medio evo, Palazzo Borromini.

Cook, Karen S. 2001. *Trust in Society.* New York: Russell Sage Foundation.

Dante [Alighieri, Dante]. 1990. *Dante's Il Convivio (The Banquet).* Translated by Richard H. Lansing. Garland Library of Medieval Literature 65, series B. New York: Garland Publishing.

Dasgupta, Partha, and Ismail Serageldin. 2000. *Social Capital: A Multifaceted Perspective.* Washington, D.C.: World Bank.

Davis, Deborah S. 2004. "Talking about Property in the New Chinese Domestic Property Regime." In *The Sociology of the Economy*, edited by Frank Dobbin, 288–307. New York: Russell Sage.

Davis, Gerald F. 1991. "Agents without Principles? The Spread of the Poison Pill Through the Intercorporate Network." *Administrative Science Quarterly* 36 (4): 583–613.

Davis, Natalie Zemon. 1986. "Boundaries and the Sense of Self in Sixteenth-Century France." In *Reconstructing Individualism: Autonomy, Individuality, and the Self in Western Thought*, edited by Thomas C. Heller, Morton Sosna, and David E. Wellbery, 53–63. Stanford, Calif.: Stanford University Press.

Dekker, Paul, and Eric M. Uslaner, eds. 2001. *Social Capital and Participation in Everyday Life*. London: Routledge

De la Roncière, Charles. 1988. "Tuscan Notables on the Eve of the Renaissance." In *A History of Private Life*, vol. 2, *Revelations of the Medieval World*, edited by Georges Duby, translated by Arthur Goldhammer, 157–309. Cambridge, Mass.: Harvard University Press, Belknap Press.

De Roover, Raymond. 1966. *The Rise and Decline of the Medici Bank, 1397–1494*. New York: W. W. Norton.

De Vos, George. 1985. "Dimensions of the Self in Japanese Culture." In *Culture and Self*, edited by A. Marsella, G. De Vos, and F. L. K. Hsu, 149–84. London: Tavistock.

Dimaggio, Paul J., and Walter W. Powell. 1991. "Introduction." In *The New Institutionalism in Organizational Analysis*, edited by Walter W. Powell and Paul J. Dimaggio, 1–38. Chicago: University of Chicago Press.

Dini, Bruno. 2001. "Le forme e le tecniche del prestito nel tardo Medioevo." In his *Manifattura, commercio e banca nella Firenze medievale*. Firenze: Nardini Editore.

Dobbin, Frank. 1994. *Forging Industrial Policy: The United States, Britain, and France in the Railway Age*. New York: Cambridge University Press.

Donati, Claudio. 1988. *L'idea di nobiltà in Italia, secoli XIV–XVIII*. Roma: Editori Laterza.

Douglas, Mary. 1982. "Cultural Bias." In *In the Active Voice*, 183–254. London: Routledge and Kegan Paul.

———. 1986. *How Institutions Think*. Syracuse, N.Y.: Syracuse University Press.

Duby, Georges. 1980. *The Three Orders: Feudal Society Imagined*. Chicago: University of Chicago Press.

———. 1988a. "Introduction: Private Power, Public Power." In *A History of Private Life*, vol. 2, *Revelations of the Medieval World*, edited by Georges Duby, translated by Arthur Goldhammer, 3–31. Cambridge, Mass.: Harvard University Press, Belknap Press.

———. 1988b. "Solitude: Eleventh to Thirteenth Century." In *A History of Private Life*, vol. 2, *Revelations of the Medieval World*, edited by Georges Duby, translated by Arthur Goldhammer, 509–33. Cambridge, Mass.: Harvard University Press, Belknap Press.

Dumont, Louis. 1985. "A Modified View of Our Origins: The Christian Beginnings of Modern Individualism." In *The Category of the Person*, edited by Michael Carrithers, Steven Collins, and Steven Lukes, 93–122. New York: Cambridge University Press.

Duranti, Alessandro, and Charles Goodwin, eds. 1992. *Rethinking Context: Language as an Interactive Phenomenon*. Cambridge: Cambridge University Press.

Durkheim, Emile. 1984 [1893]. *The Division of Labor in Society*. Introduction by Lewis A. Coser. Translated by W. D. Halls. New York: Free Press.

Eckstein, Nicholas A. 1995. *The District of the Green Dragon: Neighbourhood Life and Social Change in Renaissance Florence*. Firenze: Olschki.

Edin, Kathryn, and Laura Lein. 1997. "Work, Welfare, and Single Mothers' Economic Survival Strategies." *American Sociological Review* 62 (2): 253–66.

Edler, Florence. 1934. *Glossary of Medieval Terms of Business: Italian Series 1200–1600*. Cambridge, Mass.: Medieval Academy of America.

Eisenstadt, S. N., and L. Roniger. 1980. "Patron-Client Relations as a Model of Structuring Social Exchange." *Comparative Studies in Society and History* 22 (1): 42–77.

———. 1984. *Patrons, Clients and Friends: Interpersonal Relations and the Structure of Trust in Society*. Cambridge: Cambridge University Press.

Elias, Norbert. 1978 [1939]. *The Civilizing Process*. Translated by Edmund Jephcott. Oxford: Basil Blackwell.

Eliasoph, Nina. 1998. *Avoiding Politics: How Americans Produce Apathy in Everyday Life*. New York: Cambridge University Press.

Eliasoph, Nina, and Paul Lichterman. 2003. "Culture in Interaction." *American Journal of Sociology* 108 (4): 735–94.

Elster, Jon. 1989. *Nuts and Bolts for the Social Sciences*. New York: Cambridge University Press.

Emigh, Rebecca Jean. 1998. "The Mystery of the Missing Middle-Tenants: The 'Negative' Case of Fixed-Term Leasing and Agricultural Investment in Fifteenth-Century Tuscany." *Theory and Society* 27: 351–75.

———. 2003. "Economic Interests and Sectoral Relations: The Undevelopment of Capitalism in Fifteenth-Century Tuscany." *American Journal of Sociology* 108 (5): 1075–1113.

Emirbayer, Mustafa. 1997. "Manifesto for a Relational Sociology." *American Journal of Sociology* 103 (2): 281–317.

Emirbayer, Mustafa, and Jeff Goodwin. 1994. "Network Analysis, Culture and the Problem of Agency." *American Journal of Sociology* 99 (6): 1411–54.

Emirbayer, Mustafa, and Ann Mische. 1998. "What Is Agency?" *American Journal of Sociology* 103 (4): 962–1023.

Enenkel, Karl. 1998. "A Critical Edition of Petrarch's *Epistola Posteritati* with an English Translation." In *Modelling the Individual: Biography and Portrait in the Renaissance*, edited by Karl Enenkel, Betsy de Jong-Crane, and Peter Liebregts, 243–81. Amsterdam: Rodopi.

Epstein, S. R. 2000a. *Freedom and Growth: The Rise of States and Markets in Europe, 1300–1750*. London: Routledge.

———. 2000b. "Market Structures." In *Florentine Tuscany: Structures and Practices of Power*, edited by William J. Connell and Andrea Zorzi, 90–121. Cambridge: Cambridge University Press.

Erickson, Bonnie. 1996. "Culture, Class, and Connections." *American Journal of Sociology* 102 (2): 217–51.

Fabbri, Lorenzo. 1991. *Alleanza matrimoniale e patriziato nella Firenze del '400: Studio sulla famiglia Strozzi*. Firenze: Olschki.

Fantazzi, Charles. 1991. "The *Epistulae ad Exercitationem Accomodatae* of Gasparino Barzizza." In *Acta Conventus Neo-Latini Torontonensis: Proceedings of the Seventh International Congress of Neo-Latin Studies*, edited by Alexander Dalzell, Charles Fantazzi, and Richard J. Schoeck, 139–46. Medieval and Renaissance Texts and Studies 86. Binghamton, N.Y.: Center for Medieval and Early Renaissance Studies: State University of New York, Binghamton.

Fasano Guarini, Elena. 1996. "Center and Periphery." In *The Origins of the State in Italy, 1300–1600*, edited by Julius Kirshner, 74–96. Chicago: University of Chicago Press.

Faulhaber, Charles B. 1978. "The 'Summa dictaminis' of Guido Faba." In *Medieval Eloquence: Studies in the Theory and Practice of Medieval Rhetoric*, edited by James J. Murphy, 85–111. Berkeley: University of California Press.

Faulkner, Robert. 1983. *Music on Demand: Composers and Careers in the Hollywood Film Industry*. New Brunswick, N.J.: Transaction.

Fernandez, Roberto M., Emilio J. Castilla, and Paul Moore. 2000. "Social Capital at Work: Networks and Employment at a Phone Center." *American Journal of Sociology* 105 (5): 1288–1356.

Foucault, Michel. 1977. "Two Lectures." In *Power/Knowledge: Selected Interviews and Other Writings, 1972–1977*, 78–108, edited by Colin Gordon. New York: Pantheon Books.

Frangioni, Luciana. 1994. *Milano fine Trecento: Il carteggio Milanese dell'Archivio Datini di Prato*. 2 vols. Florence: Opus libri.

Frank, Kenneth A., and Jeffrey Y. Yasumoto. 1998. "Linking Action to Social Structure within a System: Social Capital within and between Subgroups." *American Journal of Sociology* 104 (3): 642–86.

Fubini, Riccardo. 1994. *Italia Quattrocentesca: Politica e diplomazia nell'età di Lorenzo il Magnifico*. Milano: Franco Angeli.

Gambetta, Diego, ed. 1988. *Trust: Making and Breaking Cooperative Relations*. New York: Basil Blackwell.

Garfinkel, Harold. 1967. *Studies in Ethnomethodology*. Englewood Cliffs, N.J.: Prentice-Hall, Inc.

Geertz, Clifford. 1973. *The Interpretation of Cultures*. New York: Basic Books.

Gergen, Kenneth J. 1991. *The Saturated Self: Dilemmas of Identity in Contemporary Life*. New York: Basic Books.

Gibson, David R. 2000. "Seizing the Moment: The Problem of Conversational Agency." *Sociological Theory* 18 (3): 369–82.

Gibson, James L. 2001. "Social Networks, Civil Society, and the Prospects for Consolidating Russia's Democratic Transition." *American Journal of Political Science* 45 (1): 51–68.

Gladwell, Malcolm. 2000. *The Tipping Point: How Little Things Can Make a Big Differ-ence.* Boston: Little, Brown and Company.

Goffman, Erving. 1967. *Interaction Ritual: Essays on Face-to-Face Behavior.* New York: Pantheon Books.

———. 1969. *Strategic Interaction.* Philadelphia: University of Pennsylvania Press.

———. 1974. *Frame Analysis: An Essay on the Organization of Experience.* New York: Harper Colophon Books.

———. 1981. *Forms of Talk.* Philadelphia: University of Pennsylvania Press.

———. 1983. "Presidential Address: The Interaction Order." *American Sociological Review* 48 (1): 1–17.

Goldthwaite, Richard A. 1968. *Private Wealth in Renaissance Florence: A Study of Four Families.* Princeton, N.J.: Princeton University Press.

———. 1985. "Local Banking in Renaissance Florence." *Journal of European Economic History* 14 (1): 5–55.

———. 1987. "The Medici Bank and the World of Florentine Capitalism." *Past and Present* 114: 3–31.

Goodwin, Jeff, and James M. Jasper. 1999. "Caught in a Winding, Snarling Vine: The Structural Bias of Political Process Theory." *Sociological Forum* 14 (1): 27–54.

Gould, Roger V. 1995. *Insurgent Identities: Class, Community, and Protest in Paris from 1848 to the Commune.* Chicago: University of Chicago Press.

———. 2003. "Why Do Networks Matter? Rationalist and Structuralist Interpre-tations." In *Social Movements and Networks: Relational Approaches to Collective Action,* edited by Mario Diani and Doug McAdam, 233–57. New York: Oxford University Press.

Gould, Roger V., and Roberto M. Fernandez. 1989. "Structures of Mediation: A Formal Approach to Brokerage in Transaction Networks." *Sociological Methodology* 19: 89–126.

Grafton, Anthony. 2000. *Leon Battista Alberti: Master Builder of the Italian Renaissance.* New York: Hill and Wang.

Granovetter, Mark S. 1973. "The Strength of Weak Ties." *American Journal of Sociology* 78 (6): 1360–80.

Granovetter, Mark. 1985. "Economic Action and Social Structure: The Problem of Embeddedness." *American Journal of Sociology* 91: 481–510.

Greenblatt, Stephen J. 1980. *Renaissance Self-Fashioning: From More to Shakespeare.* Chicago: University of Chicago Press.

Greenstone, J. David. 1993. *The Lincoln Persuasion: Remaking American Liberalism.* Princeton, N.J.: Princeton University Press.

Greif, Avner. 1989. "Reputations and Coalitions in Medieval Trade: Evidence on the Maghribi Traders." *Journal of Economic History* 49 (4): 857–82.

———. 1994. "Cultural Beliefs and the Organization of Society: A Historical and Theoretical Reflection on Collectivist and Individualist Societies." *The Journal of Political Economy* 102 (5): 912–50.

Grendler, Paul F. 1989. *Schooling in Renaissance Italy*. Baltimore: Johns Hopkins University Press.

Griffin, Larry J. 1993. "Narrative, Event-Structure Analysis, and Causal Interpretation in Historical Sociology." *American Journal of Sociology* 98: 1094–1133.

Griffiths, Gordon, James Hankins, and David Thompson, trans. 1987. *The Humanism of Leonardo Bruni: Selected Texts*. Medieval and Renaissance Texts and Studies 46. The Renaissance Society of America Renaissance Text Series, 10. Binghamton, N.Y. Center for Medieval and Early Renaissance Studies: State University of New York: Binghamton.

Guasti, Cesare, ed. 1873. *Commissioni di Rinaldo degli Albizzi*. Vol. 3. Firenze: M. Cellini and Co.

Gumperz, John J. 1992. "Contextualization and Understanding." In *Rethinking Context: Language as an Interactive Phenomenon*, edited by Alessandro Duranti and Charles Goodwin, 229–52. Cambridge: Cambridge University Press.

Hankins, James. 1992. "Cosimo de' Medici as a Patron of Humanistic Literature." In *Cosimo 'il Vecchio' de' Medici, 1389–1464: Essays in Commemoration of the 600th Anniversary of Cosimo de' Medici's Birth*, edited by Francis Ames-Lewis, 69–94. Oxford: Clarendon Press.

Hanks, William. 1992. "The Indexical Ground of Deictic Reference." In *Rethinking Context: Language as an Interactive Phenomenon*, edited by Alessandro Duranti and Charles Goodwin, 43–76. Cambridge: Cambridge University Press.

Hardin, Russell. 2002. *Trust and Trustworthiness*. New York: Russell Sage Foundation.

Harré, Rom. 1998. *The Singular Self: An Introduction to the Psychology of Personhood*. Thousand Oaks, Calif.: Sage.

Harré, Rom, and Fathali M. Moghaddam, eds. 2003. *The Self and Others: Positioning Individuals and Groups in Personal, Political, and Cultural Contexts*. Westport, Conn.: Praeger.

Hedstrom, Peter, and Richard Swedberg, eds. 1998. *Social Mechanisms: An Analytical Approach to Social Theory*. New York: Cambridge University Press.

Henderson, Judith Rice. 2002. "Humanist Letter Writing: Private Conversation or Public Forum?" In *Self-Presentation and Social Identification: The Rhetoric and Pragmatics of Letter-Writing in Early Modern Times*, edited by Toon van Houdt, Jan Papy, Gilbert Tournoy, and Constant Matheeussen, 17–38. Leuven: Leuven University Press.

Herlihy, David. 1991. "The Rulers of Florence, 1282–1530." In *City States in Classical Antiquity and Medieval Italy*, edited by Anthony Molho, Kurt Raaflaub, and Julia Emlen, 197–221. Ann Arbor: University of Michigan Press.

Herlihy, David, and Christiane Klapisch-Zuber. 1985. *Tuscans and Their Families: A Study of the Florentine Catasto of 1427*. New Haven, Conn.: Yale University Press.

Hewitt, John P., and Randall Stokes. 1975. "Disclaimers." *American Sociological Review* 40 (1): 1–11.

Holland, Dorothy, and Debra Skinner. 1987. "Prestige and Intimacy: The Cultural

Models Behind Americans' Talk about Gender Types." In *Cultural Models in Language and Thought*, edited by Dorothy Holland and Naomi Quinn, 78–111. Cambridge: Cambridge University Press.

Holland, Paul W., and Samuel Leinhardt. 1970. "A Method for Detecting Structure in Sociometric Data." *American Journal of Sociology* 76 (3): 492–513.

Hood, William. 1990. "Fra Angelico at San Marco: Art and the Liturgy of Cloistered Life." In *Christianity and the Renaissance: Image and Religious Imagination in the Quattrocento*, edited by Timothy Verdon and John Henderson, 108–31. Syracuse, N.Y.: Syracuse University Press.

Ikegami, Eiko. 1995. *The Taming of the Samurai: Honorific Individualism and the Making of Modern Japan*. Cambridge, Mass.: Harvard University Press.

———. 2003. "Bringing Culture into Macro Structural Analysis in Historical Sociology." Paper presented at the meetings of the American Sociological Association August 16–19, Atlanta.

Inglehart, Ronald. 1988. "The Renaissance of Political Culture." *American Political Science Review* 82 (4): 1203–30.

———. 1990. *Culture Change in Advanced Industrial Society*. Princeton, N.J.: Princeton University Press.

———. 1997. *Modernization and Postmodernization: Cultural, Economic, and Political Change in 43 Societies*. Princeton, N.J.: Princeton University Press.

Jackman, Robert W., and Ross A. Miller. 1996. "The Poverty of Political Culture." *American Journal of Political Science* 40 (3): 697–716.

Jepperson, Ronald L. 1991. "Institutions, Institutional Effects, and Institutionalism." In *The New Institutionalism in Organizational Analysis*, edited by Walter W. Powell and Paul J. Dimaggio, 143–63. Chicago: University of Chicago Press.

Kadushin, Charles. 1995. "Friendship among the French Financial Elite." *American Sociological Review* 60 (2): 202–21.

Kane, Anne. 1991. "Cultural Analysis in Historical Sociology: The Analytic and Concrete Forms of the Autonomy of Culture." *Sociological Theory* 9: 53–69.

Kent, Dale. 1978. *The Rise of the Medici: Faction in Florence, 1426–1434*. Oxford: Oxford University Press.

———. 1987. "The Dynamic of Power in Cosimo de' Medici's Florence." In *Patronage, Art and Society in Renaissance Italy*, edited by F. W. Kent and Patricia Simons, 63–77. Canberra: Humanities Research Centre.

———. 1992. "The Buonomini di San Martino: Charity for 'the Glory of God, the Honour of the City, and the Commemoration of Myself.'" In *Cosimo 'il Vecchio' de' Medici, 1389–1464: Essays in Commemoration of the 600th Anniversary of Cosimo de' Medici's Birth*, edited by Francis Ames-Lewis, 49–67. Oxford: Clarendon Press.

———. 2000. *Cosimo de' Medici and the Florentine Renaissance: The Patron's Oeuvre*. New Haven, Conn.: Yale University Press.

———. 2002. "Michele del Giogante's House of Memory." In *Society and Individual in Renaissance Florence*, edited by William J. Connell, 110–36. Berkeley: University of California Press.

Kent, D. V., and F. W. Kent. 1981. "A Self Disciplining Pact Made by the Peruzzi Family of Florence (June 1433)." *Renaissance Quarterly* 34 (3): 337–55.

Kent, F. W. 1977. *Household and Lineage in Renaissance Florence: The Family Life of the Capponi, Ginori and Rucellai*. Princeton, N.J.: Princeton University Press.

———. 1991. *Bartolommeo Cederni and His Friends: Letters to an Obscure Florentine*. Introductory essay by F. W. Kent and texts edited by Gino Corti with F. W. Kent. Florence: Olschki.

———. 1992. "Patron-Client Networks in Renaissance Florence and the Emergence of Lorenzo as 'Maestro della Bottega.'" In *Lorenzo de' Medici: New Perspectives*, edited by Bernard Toscani, 279–313. New York: Peter Lang.

———. 2002. "'Be Rather Loved than Feared': Class Relations in Quattrocento Florence." In *Society and Individual in Renaissance Florence*, edited by William J. Connell, 13–50. Berkeley: University of California Press.

Kent, F. W., and Dale Kent. 1982. *Neighbours and Neighbourhood in Renaissance Florence: The District of the Red Lion in the Fifteenth Century*. Locust Valley, NY: J. J. Augustin.

Kent, F. W., and Patricia Simons, eds. 1987. *Patronage, Art and Society in Renaissance Italy*. Oxford: Clarendon Press.

Kirshner, Julius. 1977. "Pursuing Honor While Avoiding Sin: The *Monte delle doti* of Florence." *Studi Senesi* 89: 175–258.

———. 2002. "Li Emergenti Bisogni Matrimoniali in Renaissance Florence." In *Society and Individual in Renaissance Florence*, edited by William J. Connell, 79–109. Berkeley: University of California Press.

Kirshner, Julius, and Anthony Molho. 1978. "The Dowry Fund and the Marriage Market in Early Quattrocento Florence." *Journal of Modern History* 50 (3): 403–38.

Klapisch-Zuber, Christiane. 1985a. "Compèrage et clientelisme à Florence (1360–1520)." *Ricerche Storiche* 15 (1): 61–77.

———. 1985b. *Women, Family and Ritual in Renaissance Italy*. Translated by Lydia Cochrane. Chicago: University of Chicago Press.

———. 1990. *La maison et le nom: Strategies et rituels dans l'Italie de la Renaissance*. Paris: Editions de l'Ecole des Hautes Etudes en Sciences Sociales.

———. 2000. *L'ombre des ancêtres : Essai sur l'imaginaire médiéval de la parenté*. Paris: Fayard.

Kohl, Benjamin G., and Ronald G. Witt. 1978. *The Earthly Republic: Italian Humanists on Government and Society*. Philadelphia: University of Pennsylvania Press.

Kreps, David. 1990. "Corporate Culture and Economic Theory." In *Perspectives on Positive Political Economy*, edited by J. Alt and K. Shepsle, 90–143. Cambridge: Cambridge University Press.

Kristeller, Paul Oskar. 1983. "Rhetoric in Medieval and Renaissance Culture." In *Re-*

naissance Eloquence: Studies in the Theory and Practice of Renaissance Rhetoric, edited by
James J. Murphy, 1–19. Berkeley: University of California Press.

Kuehn, Thomas. 1982. *Emancipation in Late Medieval Florence*. New Brunswick, N.J.:
Rutgers University Press.

———. 1991. *Law, Family and Women: Toward a Legal Anthropology of Renaissance Italy*.
Chicago: University of Chicago Press.

Lachmann, Richard. 2000. *Capitalists in Spite of Themselves: Elite Conflict and Economic
Transitions in Early Modern Europe*. New York: Oxford University Press.

Laitin, David D. 1986. *Hegemony and Culture: Politics and Religious Change among the
Yoruba*. Chicago: University of Chicago Press.

———. 1991. "The National Uprisings in the Soviet Union." *World Politics* 44 (1):
139–77.

Laitin, David D., and Aaron Wildavsky. 1988. "Political Culture and Political Preferences." *American Political Science Review* 82 (2): 589–96.

Lamont, Michèle. 1992. *Money, Morals, and Manners: The Culture of the French and the
American Upper Middle Class*. Chicago: University of Chicago Press.

Lamont, Michèle, and Marcel Fournier, eds. 1992. *Cultivating Differences: Symbolic
Boundaries and the Making of Inequality*. Chicago: University of Chicago Press.

Lamont, Michèle, Jason Kaufman, and Michael Moody. 2000. "The Best of the
Brightest: Definitions of the Ideal Self among Prize-Winning Students." *Sociological Forum* 15 (2): 187–224.

Lansing, Carol. 1991. *The Florentine Magnates: Lineage and Faction in a Medieval Commune*. Princeton, N.J.: Princeton University Press.

Lee, Sunwha, and Mary C. Brinton. 1996. "Elite Education and Social Capital: The
Case of South Korea." *Sociology of Education* 69 (3): 177–92.

Levi, Margaret. 1988. *Of Rule and Revenue*. Berkeley: University of California Press.

———. 1996. "Social and Unsocial Capital." *Politics and Society* 24: 45–55.

Lewin, Alison Williams. 2003. *Negotiating Survival: Florence and the Great Schism, 1378–
1417*. Teaneck, N.J.: Fairleigh Dickinson University Press.

Lin, Nan. 2001. *Social Capital: A Theory of Social Structure and Action*. New York: Cambridge University Press.

Lin, Nan, Karen Cook, and Ronald S. Burt, eds. 2001. *Social Capital: Theory and Research*. New York: Aldine de Gruyter.

Lin, Nan, Walter M. Ensel, and John C. Vaughan. 1981. "Social Resources and
Strength of Ties: Structural Factors in Occupational Status Attainment." *American Sociological Review* 46 (4): 393–405.

Lin, Nan, Yang-chih Fu, and Ray-May Hsung. 2001. "The Position Generator: Measurement Techniques for Investigations of Social Capital." In *Social Capital: Theory
and Research*, edited by Nan Lin, Karen Cook, and Ronald S. Burt, 57–84. New
York: Aldine de Gruyter.

Luhmann, Niklas. 1986. "The Individuality of the Individual: Historical Meanings and Contemporary Problems." In *Reconstructing Individualism: Autonomy, Individuality, and the Self in Western Thought*, edited by Thomas C. Heller, Morton Sosna, and David E. Wellbery, 313–25. Stanford, Calif.: Stanford University Press.

Machiavelli, Niccolò. 1950. *The Prince and The Discourses*. Introduced by Max Lerner. New York: Random House, Modern Library.

MacIntyre, Alisdair. 1981. *After Virtue: A Study in Moral Theory*. South Bend, Ind.: University of Notre Dame Press.

Malone, Martin J. 1997. *Worlds of Talk: The Presentation of Self in Everyday Conversation*. Cambridge: Blackwell.

March, James G., and Herbert A. Simon. 1958. *Organizations*. New York: Wiley.

Markus, Hazel Rose, and Shinobu Kitayama. 1991. "Culture and the Self: Implications for Cognition, Emotion, and Motivation." *Psychological Review* 98 (2): 224–53.

Marsh, David. 1980. *The Quattrocento Dialogue: Classical Tradition and Humanist Innovation*. Cambridge, Mass.: Harvard University Press.

Martin, John. 1997. "Inventing Sincerity, Refashioning Prudence: The Discovery of the Individual in Renaissance Europe." *American Historical Review* 102 (5): 1309–42.

Martin, John Levi. 2003. "What Is Field Theory?" *American Journal of Sociology* 109 (1): 1–49.

Martines, Lauro. 1963. *The Social World of the Florentine Humanists*. Princeton, N.J.: Princeton University Press.

———. 1968. *Lawyers and Statecraft in Renaissance Florence*. Princeton, N.J.: Princeton University Press.

Matsumoto, David. 1999. "Culture and Self: An Empirical Assessment of Markus and Kitayama's Theory of Independent and Interdependent Self-Construals." *Asian Journal of Social Psychology* 2 :289–310.

Mauss, Marcel. 1985. "A Category of the Human Mind: The Notion of Person; the Notion of Self." Translated by W. D. Halls. In *The Category of the Person*, edited by Michael Carrithers, Steven Collins, and Steven Lukes, 1–25. New York: Cambridge University Press.

Maynard, Douglas W. 1991. "Interaction and Asymmetry in Clinical Discourse." *American Journal of Sociology* 97 (2): 448–95.

Mazzei, Lapo. 1880. *Lettere di un notaio a un merchante del secolo XIV, con altre lettere e documenti*. A cura di Cesare Guasti. Two volumes. Firenze: M. Cellini.

McAdam, Doug. 1996. "The Framing Function of Movement Tactics: Strategic Dramaturgy in the American Civil Rights Movement." In *Comparative Perspectives on Social Movements: Political Opportunities, Mobilizing Structures and Cultural Framings*, edited by Doug McAdam, John D. McCarthy, and Mayer Zald, 1–20. Cambridge: Cambridge University Press.

———. 2003. "Beyond Structural Analysis: Toward a More Dynamic Understanding of Social Movements." In *Social Movements and Networks: Relational Approaches to Collective Action*, edited by Mario Diani and Doug McAdam, 281–98. Oxford: Oxford University Press.

McLean, Paul D. 1996. "Patronage and Political Culture: Frames, Networks, and Strategies of Self-Presentation in Renaissance Florence." Ph.D. diss., University of Chicago.

———. 1998. "A Frame Analysis of Favor Seeking in the Renaissance: Agency, Networks, and Political Culture." *American Journal of Sociology* 104 (1): 51–91.

———. 2004. "Widening Access While Tightening Control: Office-Holding, Marriages and Elite Consolidation in Early Modern Poland." *Theory and Society* 33: 167–212.

———. 2005. "Patronage, Citizenship, and the Stalled Emergence of the Modern State in Renaissance Florence." *Comparative Studies in Society and History* 47 (3): 638–64.

McLean, Paul D., and John F. Padgett. 1997. "Was Florence a Perfectly Competitive Market? Transactional Evidence from the Renaissance." *Theory and Society* 26: 209–44.

———. 2004. "Obligation, Risk and Opportunity in the Renaissance Economy: Beyond Social Embeddedness to Network Co-Constitution." In *The Sociology of the Economy*, edited by Frank Dobbin, 220–54. New York: Russell Sage Foundation.

McLean, Scott L., David A. Schultz, and Manfred B. Steger, eds. 2002. *Social Capital: Critical Perspectives on Community and "Bowling Alone."* New York: New York University Press.

Mead, George Herbert. 1934. *Mind, Self, and Society from the Standpoint of a Social Behaviorist.* Edited by Charles W. Morris. Chicago: University of Chicago Press.

Mecatti, Giuseppe Maria. 1754. *Storia genealogica della nobiltà e cittadinanza di Firenze.* Napoli: Presso Giovanni di Simone.

Melis, Federigo. 1991. *L'azienda nel medioevo.* Firenze: Le Monnier.

Meyer, John W. 1986. "Myths of Socialization and of Personality." In *Reconstructing Individualism: Autonomy, Individuality, and the Self in Western Thought*, edited by Thomas C. Heller, Morton Sosna, and David E. Wellbery, 208–21. Stanford, Calif.: Stanford University Press.

Mische, Ann. 2003. "Cross-talk in Movements: Reconceiving the Culture-Network Link." In *Social Movements and Networks: Relational Approaches to Collective Action*, edited by Mario Diani and Doug McAdam, 258–80. Oxford: Oxford University Press.

Mische, Ann, and Philippa Pattison. 2000. "Composing a Civic Arena: Publics, Projects, and Social Settings. *Poetics* 27: 163–94.

Mische, Ann and Harrison White. 1998. "Between Conversation and Situation: Public Switching Dynamics across Network Domains." *Social Research* 65 (3): 695–724.

Mohr, John W., and Vincent Duquenne. 1997. "The Duality of Culture and Practice: Poverty Relief in New York City, 1888–1917." *Theory and Society* 26: 305–56.

Molho, Anthony. 1971. *Florentine Public Finances in the Early Renaissance, 1400–1433*. Cambridge, Mass.: Harvard University Press.

———. 1979. "Cosimo de' Medici: Pater Patriae or Padrino?" *Stanford Italian Review* 1: 5–33.

———. 1987. "L'amministrazione del debito pubblico a Firenze nel quindicesimo secolo." In *I ceti dirigenti nella Toscana del Quattrocento*, by the Comitati di studi sulla storia dei ceti dirigenti in Toscana, Atti del V e VI Convegno, 191–208. Firenze: Francesco Papafava Editore.

———. 1994. *Marriage Alliance in Late Medieval Florence*. Cambridge, Mass.: Harvard University Press.

———. 1996. "The State and Public Finance: A Hypothesis Based on the History of Late Medieval Florence." In *The Origins of the State in Italy, 1300–1600*, edited by Julius Kirshner, 97–135. Chicago: University of Chicago Press.

Monfasani, John. 1988. "Humanism and Rhetoric." In *Renaissance Humanism: Foundations, Forms, and Legacy*, vol. 3, *Humanism and the Disciplines*, edited by Albert Rabil Jr., 171–235. Philadelphia: University of Pennsylvania Press.

Montrose, Louis Adrian. 1996. *The Purpose of Playing: Shakespeare and the Cultural Politics of the Elizabethan Theatre*. Chicago: University of Chicago Press.

Mühlhäusler, Peter, and Rom Harré. 1990. *Pronouns and People: The Linguistic Construction of Social and Personal Identity*. Oxford: Basil Blackwell.

Murphy, James J. 1971. "Introduction." In *Three Medieval Rhetorical Arts*. Berkeley: University of California Press.

———. 1974. *Rhetoric in the Middle Ages: A History of Rhetorical Theory from St. Augustine to the Renaissance*. Berkeley: University of California Press.

———, ed. 1983. *Renaissance Eloquence: Studies in the Theory and Practice of Renaissance Rhetoric*. Berkeley: University of California Press.

Najemy, John M. 1982. *Corporatism and Consensus in Florentine Electoral Politics, 1280–1400*. Chapel Hill: University of North Carolina Press.

———. 1991. "The Dialogue of Power in Florentine Politics." In *City States in Classical Antiquity and Medieval Italy*, edited by Anthony Molho, Kurt Raaflaub, and Julia Emlen, 269–88. Ann Arbor: University of Michigan Press.

———. 1993. *Between Friends: Discourses of Power and Desire in the Machiavelli-Vettori Letters of 1513–1515*. Princeton, N.J.: Princeton University Press.

———. 2002. "Giannozzo and His Elders: Alberti's Critique of Renaissance Patriarchy." In *Society and Individual in Renaissance Florence*, edited by William J. Connell, 51–78. Berkeley: University of California Press.

Neuschel, Kristen B. 1989. *Word of Honor: Interpreting Noble Culture in Sixteenth Century France*. Ithaca, N.Y.: Cornell University Press.

Oakes, James. 1990. *Slavery and Freedom: An Interpretation of the Old South*. New York: Knopf.

O'Barr, William M. 1982. *Linguistic Evidence: Language, Power, and Strategy in the Court-room*. New York: Academic Press.

Ostrom, Elinor, and James Walker. 2003. *Trust and Reciprocity: Interdisciplinary Lessons from Experimental Research*. New York: Russell Sage Foundation.

Padgett, John F. 2001. "Organizational Genesis, Identity, and Control: The Transformation of Banking in Renaissance Florence." In *Networks and Markets*, edited by James E. Rauch and Alessandra Casella, 211–57. New York: Russell Sage Foundation.

Padgett, John F. and Christopher K. Ansell. 1993. "Robust Action and the Rise of the Medici, 1400–1434." *American Journal of Sociology* 98 (6): 1259–1319.

Padgett, John F., and Paul D. McLean. 2002. "Economic and Social Exchange in Renaissance Florence." Santa Fe Institute working paper 02–07–032.

———. 2006. "Elite Transformation and Organizational Invention in Renaissance Florence." *American Journal of Sociology* 111 (5): 1463–1568.

Passerini, Luigi. 1869. *Gli Alberti di Firenze: Genealogia, storia e documenti*. 2 vols. Firenze: M. Cellini.

Pattison, Philippa, and Garry Robins. 2002. "Neighborhood-Based Models for Social Networks." *Sociological Methodology* 32: 301–37.

Paxton, Pamela. 1999. "Is Social Capital Declining in the United States? A Multiple Indicator Assessment." *American Journal of Sociology* 105 (1): 88–127.

———. 2002. "Social Capital and Democracy: An Interdependent Relationship." *American Sociological Review* 67 (2): 254–77.

Petralia, Giuseppe. 2000. "Fiscality, Politics, and Dominion in Florentine Tuscany at the End of the Middle Ages." In *Florentine Tuscany: Structures and Practices of Power*, edited by William J. Connell and Andrea Zorzi, 65–89. Cambridge: Cambridge University Press.

Pitkin, Hanna Fenichel. 1984. *Fortune Is a Woman: Gender and Politics in the Thought of Niccolò Machiavelli*. Berkeley: University of California Press.

Pocock, J. G. A. 1975. *The Machiavellian Moment*. Princeton, N.J.: Princeton University Press.

Podolny, Joel M., and James N. Baron. 1997. "Resources and Relationships: Social Networks and Mobility in the Workplace." *American Sociological Review* 62 (5): 673–93.

Polletta, Francesca. 2002. *Freedom Is an Endless Meeting: Democracy in American Social Movements*. Chicago: University of Chicago Press.

Porter, Roy, ed. 1997. *Rewriting the Self: Histories from the Renaissance to the Present*. London: Routledge.

Portes, Alejandro. 1998. "Social Capital: Its Origins and Applications in Modern Sociology." *Annual Review of Sociology* 24: 1–24.

Portes, Alejandro, and Julia Sensenbrenner. 1993. "Embeddedness and Immigration: Notes on the Social Determinants of Economic Action." *American Journal of Sociology* 98 (6): 1320–50.

Postone, Moishe. 1996. *Time, Labor, and Social Domination: A Reinterpretation of Marx's Critical Theory*. Cambridge: Cambridge University Press.

Powell, Walter W., and Paul J. Dimaggio, eds. 1991. *The New Institutionalism in Organizational Analysis*. Chicago: University of Chicago Press.

Putnam, Robert D. 1993. *Making Democracy Work: Civic Traditions in Modern Italy*. Princeton, N.J.: Princeton University Press.

————. 2000. *Bowling Alone: The Collapse and Revival of American Community*. New York: Simon and Schuster.

Rabil, Albert, Jr., ed. 1991. *Knowledge, Goodness, and Power: The Debate over Nobility among Quattrocento Italian Humanists*. Medieval and Renaissance Texts and Studies 88. Binghamton, N.Y.: Center for Medieval and Early Renaissance Studies: State University of New York, Binghamton.

Rebhorn, Wayne A. 1995. *The Emperor of Men's Minds: Literature and the Renaissance Discourse of Rhetoric*. Ithaca, N.Y.: Cornell University Press.

Reddy, William M. 1997. *The Invisible Code: Honor and Sentiment in Postrevolutionary France, 1814–1848*. Berkeley: University of California Press.

Regnier-Bohler, Danielle. 1988. "Exploring Literature." In *A History of Private Life*, vol. 2, *Revelations of the Medieval World*, edited by Georges Duby, translated by Arthur Goldhammer, 313–93. Cambridge, Mass.: Harvard University Press, Belknap Press.

Rubinstein, Nicolai. 1997. *The Government of Florence under the Medici (1434 to 1494)*. 2nd ed. Oxford: Clarendon Press.

Sacks, Harvey. 1992. *Lectures on Conversation*. 2 vols. Edited by Gail Jefferson. Cambridge, Mass.: Blackwell.

Saegert, Susan, J. Phillip Thompson, and Mark R. Warren, eds. 2001. *Social Capital and Poor Communities*. New York: Russell Sage Foundation.

Sarat, Austin D., and William L. F. Felstiner. 1995. *Divorce Lawyers and Their Clients: Power and Meaning in the Legal Process*. New York: Oxford University Press.

Schegloff, Emmanuel. 1980. "Preliminaries to Preliminaries: Can I Ask You a Question?" *Sociological Inquiry* 50: 104–52.

Schiffrin, Deborah. 1987. *Discourse Markers*. New York: Cambridge University Press.

————. 1993. "'Speaking for Another' in Sociolinguistic Interviews: Alignments, Identities, and Frames." In *Framing in Discourse*, edited by Deborah Tannen, 231–55. New York: Oxford University Press.

Scott, James C. 1985. *Weapons of the Weak*. New Haven, Conn.: Yale University Press.

Scott, John. 2000. *Social Network Analysis: A Handbook*. 2nd ed. Thousands Oaks, Calif.: Sage.

Seigel, Jerrold E. 1968. *Rhetoric and Philosophy in Renaissance Humanism: The Union of Eloquence and Wisdom, Petrarch to Valla*. Princeton, N.J.: Princeton University Press.

————. 2005. *The Idea of the Self: Thought and Experience in Western Europe since the Seventeenth Century*. New York: Cambridge University Press.

Shepard, Laurie. 1999. *Courting Power: Persuasion and Politics in the Early Thirteenth Century*. New York: Garland Publishing.

Shotter, John. 1993. *Cultural Politics of Everyday Life: Social Constructionism, Rhetoric and Knowing of the Third Kind*. Toronto: University of Toronto Press.

Shweder, R. A., and E. J. Bourne. 1984. "Does the Concept of the Person Vary Cross-Culturally?" In *Culture Theory: Essays on Mind, Self, and Emotion*, edited by R. A. Shweder and R. A. LeVine, 158–99. Cambridge: Cambridge University Press.

Silver, Allan. 1989. "Friendship and Trust as Moral Ideals: An Historical Approach." *Archives européennes de sociologie* 30: 274–97.

————. 1990. "Friendship in Commercial Society: Eighteenth-Century Social Theory and Modern Sociology." *American Journal of Sociology* 95 (6): 1474–1504.

Simmel, Georg. 1950. *The Sociology of Georg Simmel*. Translated and edited by Kurt H. Wolff. New York: Free Press.

————. 1955. "The Web of Group Affiliations." In *Conflict and the Web of Group Affiliations*. Translated by Reinhard Bendix. New York: Free Press.

Skinner, Quentin. 1978. *The Foundations of Modern Political Thought*. Vol. 1, *The Renaissance*. Cambridge: Cambridge University Press.

Snow, David A., and Robert D. Benford. 1988. "Ideology, Frame Resonance, and Participant Mobilization." *International Social Movement Research* 1: 197–217.

————. 1992. "Master Frames and Cycles of Protest." In *Frontiers of Social Movement Theory*, edited by Aldon D. Morris and Carol McClung Mueller, 133–55. New Haven, Conn.: Yale University Press.

Snow, David, E. Burke Rochford Jr., Steven K. Worden, and Robert D. Benford. 1986. "Frame Alignment Processes, Micromobilization and Movement Participation." *American Sociological Review* 51: 464–81.

Somers, Margaret R. 1995. "What's Political or Cultural about Political Culture and the Public Sphere? Toward an Historical Sociology of Concept Formation." *Sociological Theory* 13 (2): 113–44.

Spruyt, Hendrik. 1994. *The Sovereign State and Its Competitors*. Princeton, N.J.: Princeton University Press.

Starn, Randolph. 1982. *Contrary Commonwealth: The Theme of Exile in Medieval and Renaissance Italy*. Berkeley: University of California Press.

Steinberg, Marc W. 1998. "Tilting the Frame: Considerations on Collective Action from a Discursive Turn." *Theory and Society* 27 (6): 845–72.

————. 1999. "The Talk and Back Talk of Collective Action: A Dialogic Analysis of Repertoires of Discourse among Nineteenth-Century English Cotton Spinners." *American Journal of Sociology* 105 (3): 736–80.

Steinmetz, George. 1992. "Reflections on the Role of Social Narratives in Working Class Formation: Narratives and Social Sciences." *Social Science History* 16 (3): 489–516.

Stewart, Frank Henderson. 1994. *Honor*. Chicago: University of Chicago Press.

Stokes, Susan C. 1995. *Cultures in Conflict: Social Movements and the State in Peru*. Berkeley: University of California Press.

Sukle, Robert J. 1994. "*Uchi/soto*: Choices in Directive Speech Acts in Japanese." In *Situated Meaning: Inside and Outside in Japanese Self, Society and Language*, edited by Jane M. Bachnik and Charles Quinn, 113–42. Princeton, N.J.: Princeton University Press.

Swartz, David. 1997. *Culture and Power: The Sociology of Pierre Bourdieu*. Chicago: University of Chicago Press.

Swidler, Ann. 1986. "Culture in Action: Symbols and Strategies." *American Sociological Review* 51: 273–86.

———. 2001. *Talk of Love*. Chicago: University of Chicago Press.

Szreter, Simon. 2002. "The State of Social Capital Theory: Bringing Back in Power, Politics, and History." *Theory and Society* 31: 573–621.

Tannen, Deborah. 1985. "Relative Focus on Involvement in Oral and Written Discourse." In *Literacy, Language, and Learning: The Nature and Consequences of Reading and Writing*, edited by David R. Olson, Nancy Torrance, and Angela Hildyard, 124–47. New York: Cambridge University Press.

———, ed. 1993. *Framing in Discourse*. New York: Oxford University Press.

Tarrow, Sidney. 1996. "Making Social Science Work Across Space and Time: A Critical Reflection on Robert Putnam's *Making Democracy Work*." *American Political Science Review* 90 (2): 389–97.

———. 2004. "From Comparative Historical Analysis to 'Local Theory': The Italian City-State Route to the Modern State." *Theory and Society* 33 (3–4): 443–71.

Taylor, Charles. 1989. *Sources of the Self*. Cambridge, Mass.: Harvard University Press.

Thompson, Michael, Richard Ellis, and Aaron Wildavsky. 1990. *Cultural Theory*. Boulder, Colo.: Westview Press.

Tilly, Charles. 1992. *Coercion, Capital and European States, 990–1992*. Cambridge, Mass.: Blackwell.

———, ed. 1975. *The Formation of National States in Western Europe*. Princeton, N.J.: Princeton University Press.

Trexler, Richard C. 1980. *Public Life in Renaissance Florence*. New York: Academic Press.

Van Deth, Jan, Marco Maraffi, Kenneth Newton, and Paul F. Whiteley. 1999. *Social Capital and European Democracy*. London: Routledge.

Villani, Giovanni. 1935 [~1348]. *Cronica*. In *Cronisti del Trecento*, a cura di Roberto Palmarocchi. Milano e Roma: Rizzoli.

Walsh, Katherine Cramer. 2004. *Talking about Politics: Informal Groups and Social Identity in American Life*. Chicago: University of Chicago Press.

Wasserman, Stanley, and Katherine Faust. 1994. *Social Network Analysis: Methods and Applications*. Cambridge: Cambridge University Press.

Wasserman, S. and Phillipa Pattison. 1996. "Logit Models and Logistic Regression for Social Networks: I. An Introduction to Markov Graphs and p*." *Psychometrika* 61: 401–25.

Watts, Duncan J. 1999. *Small Worlds: The Dynamics of Networks between Order and Randomness.* Princeton, N.J.: Princeton University Press.

———. 2003. *Six Degrees: The Science of a Connected Age.* New York: W. W. Norton.

Weinstein, Donald. 2000. *The Captain's Concubine: Love, Honor, and Violence in Renaissance Tuscany.* Baltimore: Johns Hopkins University Press.

Weinstein, Eugene A., and Paul Deutschberger. 1963. "Some Dimensions of Altercasting." *Sociometry* 26: 454–66.

Weissman, Ronald F. E. 1982. *Ritual Brotherhood in Renaissance Florence.* New York: Academic Press.

———. 1989. "The Importance of Being Ambiguous: Social Relations, Individualism, and Identity in Renaissance Florence." In *Urban Life in the Renaissance*, edited by Susan Zimmerman and Ronald F. E. Weissman, 269–80. Newark: University of Delaware Press.

Wetzel, Patricia J. 1994. "A Movable Self: The Linguistic Indexing of *Uchi* and *Soto.*" In *Situated Meaning: Inside and Outside in Japanese Self, Society and Language*, edited by Jane M. Bachnik and Charles Quinn, 73–87. Princeton, N.J.: Princeton University Press.

White, Harrison C. 1990. "Control to Deny Chance, but Thereby Muffling Identity [Review of Coleman's *Foundations of Social Theory*]." *Contemporary Sociology* 19 (6): 783–88.

———. 1992. *Identity and Control: A Structural Theory of Social Action.* Princeton, N.J.: Princeton University Press.

———. 1995. "Network Switchings and Bayesian Forks: Reconstructing the Social and Behavioral Sciences." *Social Research* 62: 1035–63.

———. 2002. *Markets from Networks: Socioeconomic Models of Production.* Princeton, N.J.: Princeton University Press.

White, Harrison C., Scott A. Boorman, and Ronald L. Breiger. 1976. "Social Structure from Multiple Networks I: Blockmodels of Roles and Positions." *American Journal of Sociology* 81 (4): 730–80.

White, Hayden. 1978. *Tropics of Discourse: Essays in Cultural Criticism.* Baltimore: Johns Hopkins University Press.

Wildavsky, Aaron. 1987. "Choosing Preferences by Constructing Institutions: A Cultural Theory of Preference Formation." *American Political Science Review* 81 (1): 3–21.

———. 1991. "Resolved, That Individualism and Egalitarianism Be Made Compatible in America: Political-Cultural Roots of Exceptionalism." In *Is America Different? A New Look at American Exceptionalism*, edited by Byron E. Shafer, 116–37. Oxford: Clarendon Press.

Williamson, Oliver. 1981. "Economics of Organization: The Transaction Cost Approach." *American Journal of Sociology* 87: 548–77.

———. 1986. "What Is Transaction Cost Economics?" In *Economic Organization: Firms, Markets and Policy Control*. New York: New York University Press.

Witt, Ronald G. 1976. *Coluccio Salutati and His Public Letters*. Genève: Librairie Droz.

———. 1983. *Hercules at the Crossroads: The Life, Works and Thought of Coluccio Salutati*. Durham, N.C.: Duke University Press.

———. 1988. "Medieval Italian Culture and the Origins of Humanism as a Stylistic Ideal." In *Renaissance Humanism: Foundations, Forms, and Legacy*, vol. 1, *Humanism in Italy*. Philadelphia: University of Pennsylvania Press.

———. 2000. *"In the Footsteps of the Ancients": The Origins of Humanism from Lovato to Bruni*. Leiden: Brill.

Wittgenstein, Ludwig. 1958. *Philosophical Investigations*. Translated by G. E. M. Anscombe. New York: Macmillan Publishing Co., Inc.

Woolcock, Michael. 1998. "Social Capital and Economic Development: Toward a Theoretical Synthesis and Policy Framework." *Theory and Society* 27 (2): 151–208.

Yang, Mayfair Mei-Hui. 1994. *Gifts, Favors and Banquets: The Art of Social Relationships in China*. Ithaca, N.Y.: Cornell University Press.

Zaret, David. 1989. "Religion and the Rise of Liberal-Democratic Ideology in 17th-Century England." *American Sociological Review* 54 (2): 163–79.

———. 1996. "Petitions and the 'Invention' of Public Opinion in the English Revolution." *American Journal of Sociology* 101 (6): 1497–1555.

Index

Paul D. McLean is an associate professor of sociology at Rutgers University.